Also by John Brady:

THE CRAFT OF INTERVIEWING

THE CRAFT OF THE SCREENWRITER

Interviews with Six Celebrated Screenwriters

by
JOHN BRADY

A TOUCHSTONE BOOK
Published by Simon and Schuster
NEW YORK

First Touchstone Edition, 1982

Published by Simon and Schuster
A Division of Gulf & Western Corporation
Simon & Schuster Building
Rockefeller Center
1230 Avenue of the Americas
New York, New York 10020

TOUCHSTONE and colophon are registered trademarks
of Simon & Schuster

Designed by Stanley S. Drate

Manufactured in the United States of America

1 2 3 4 5 6 7 8 9 10
1 2 3 4 5 6 7 8 9 10 Pbk.

Library of Congress Cataloging in Publication Data

Brady, John Joseph, date.
   The craft of the screenwriter.

   Includes index.
   1. Screen writers—United States—Interviews.
I. Title.
PN1996.B72   812'.54'09   81-8894
                                     AACR2

ISBN 0-671-25229-1
ISBN 0-671-25230-5 Pbk.

For My Father

Frank J. Brady

September 17, 1918–April 19, 1952

ACKNOWLEDGMENTS

My thanks to Philip Spitzer and to Diane Cleaver for help in shaping this book at the outset; to Allen Rivkin and the Writers Guild of America, West; to Val Almendarez of the National Film Information Service at the Academy of Motion Picture Arts and Sciences in Beverly Hills; to Jeanne T. Newlin, curator of the Harvard Theatre Collection, and to Anne K. Ames of the Houghton Library at Harvard University; to Anne G. Schlosser of the American Film Institute in Beverly Hills, and to Debbie Davidson of the American Film Institute in Washington, D.C.; to Gay Talese for encouragement and a postcard; to Susan Bolotin for editorial patience and steering; to Diana Valentine for transcribing and typing with diligence and care into the wee hours; to Jim Ritz for letting me hang out while doing interviews in Hollywood; to Lilia F. Brady for hanging in there with me on this one all the way; to Catherine Shaw and Jim Daly for careful loving work between the lines; and to Nan Talese of Simon and Schuster— the editor and secret star of this production.

—J.B.

CONTENTS

CONTENTS

INTRODUCTION

Screenwriters used to be Hollywood's doormat. Producer Jack Warner once called them "schmucks with Underwoods." Director Joseph Mankiewicz said, "The screenwriter is the highest-paid secretary in the world." Even legendary producer and studio head Irving Thalberg, a visionary by most Hollywood standards, once wondered aloud, "What's all this business of being a writer? It's just putting one word after another."

Today the screenwriter has come of age; in fact, the era of the screenwriter as superstar is at hand. "I suspect it's probably more difficult to be a great screenwriter than it is to be a great novelist or a great playwright," says Norman Mailer. Adds producer Robert Evans, responsible for *Rosemary's Baby*, *Love Story*, *The Godfather*, *Chinatown*, and more: "I think the writer is the biggest star of any movie. If I have a good script, I can get any actor I want in the film."

The road from doormat to something approaching dominance on a project has been long and winding. A brief history of screenwriting in Hollywood helps explain the reversal of roles—and is a useful prologue for the interviews that follow.

In the beginning was *not* the word. When Americans first gazed at moving pictures on a screen in the 1890s, who needed words? The early years of moviemaking are populated with cameramen, editors, directors—it was a world of technicians. But no writers. Not until sound came to movies in the late 1920s did studios recognize a need for someone more literate than a title-card scribbler or a "scenarist," often an ex-vaudevillian whose job it was to come up with funny situations that the technicians could then handle.

Writers came to Hollywood in the thirties from Broadway, from the worlds of books and by-lines, and at one time or another during the decade some of the best-known writers in the world pounded out scripts for the screen: F. Scott Fitzgerald, William Faulkner, Dorothy Parker, Nathanael West, Robert Sherwood, Ben Hecht, Charles MacArthur, Clifford Odets, Christopher Isherwood, Bertolt Brecht, Thomas Mann. According to S. J. Perelman, who wrote scripts for the Marx Brothers, it was work that "contributes little to one's prose style." It was work that contributed nicely to one's bank account. In 1932, William Faulkner earned $3,000 in salary and $3,000 for film rights to a story—more than he had ever earned in his life. When Scott Fitzgerald began writing for MGM in 1937, he was deep in debt. Within six months he was earning $1,250 a week, and within eighteen months he had paid back over $40,000 he owed. Nathanael West, whose first two books earned but $780 in royalties, earned $400 a week in Hollywood during the Depression. "Thank God for the movies," he reflected in 1939.

Of course, there were trade-offs. Hollywood in the thirties was assembly-line writing—a closed shop in which studio executives had a stranglehold on their studio's creative talent. A producer would often have a script written and rewritten by different writers, or have several writers working on the same script—each without knowledge of the others—and he would choose the one he liked best for filming. Writers worked in the worst offices at the studio and under time-clock conditions. At Paramount they were categorized and wrote two to four scripts a year, depending on their A, B or C status. Each writer worked from nine to six and to noon on Saturday—handing in eleven pages every Thursday, or else. At Warners the writers who didn't perform were fired at Christmas. A veteran screenwriter told columnist Jim Bishop how the studio had Al Jolson, dressed as Santa, bring in a truckload of Christmas baskets as the writers peered fearfully through their venetian blinds. If Jolson knocked on a writer's door and roared, "Merry Christmas! Ho, ho, ho!," the writer was finished. Those who did not get a farewell gift got the opportunity to write for another year.

The emphasis was on quantity. Moguls like Harry Cohn at Columbia, Louis B. Mayer at MGM and Jack Warner at Warner Bros. cranked out some five hundred pictures a year, most of them geared to a starry-eyed and unsophisticated audience. In such circumstances, an individual screenwriter's commitment to quality hardly mattered. Julius and Philip Epstein, for instance, wrote *Four Wives*, a sequel to the 1938 John Garfield hit *Four Daughters*. In the original, Garfield played a composer who committed suicide, and in the sequel Jeffrey Lynn was to finish Garfield's concerto. "Everybody expected us to write the concerto as a success," Julius Epstein recalled recently in the Los Angeles *Times*. "We argued that Garfield was a failure in life and would be a failure in death. The concerto should fail. Warners liked the way we turned the cliché around. Then Max Steiner says, 'This picture has a flop concerto? And the credits will read Music by Max Steiner?' Suddenly we were back in our office, typing, *The audience leaps to its feet, yelling 'Bravo!'* That tells you the status of the writer."

Producers kept the production lines going through the forties, and screenwriter employment peaked just after World War II when some 560 writers were under contract in Hollywood, including 175 at MGM alone. But life in a script factory was not easy. The contract writer was handed an idea that the studio had purchased on the recommendation of its story department—a book, play, magazine story or occasionally something to be written expressly for the screen. The writer had to come up with a synopsis of the idea for a producer to review. Typically this ran from five to ten pages, but some producers were deemed so important and so busy that the writer had to tighten it to a page or even a paragraph. "One important producer is known to hire actors to act out the story for him while he cogitates on more important matters," reported Lewis Herman in a 1951 text called *A Practical Manual of Screen Playwriting*. If the producer liked what he read (or saw enacted while cogitating), a story conference followed.

The story conference was attended by the producer, the writer and the studio's supervising producer. If a director had been chosen for the project, he might sit in, too. Location, budgets, stars and the story were thrashed out—after which the writer returned to his typewriter with his superiors' ideas. It was now his job to write a fifty-page "treatment" of the idea, and to write it in the present tense as a short story. If the treatment was acceptable, another story conference followed. Here story, dialogue and action were explored—always to the producer's satisfaction. Then the writer came up with a finished treatment that went not only to the supervising producer, but also to the story department and to other heads at the studio and their assistants, all of whom had the right to make suggestions for improvement.

"The shreds of the treatment are then returned to the writer for coordination," reported Lewis Herman. "He, of course, is told that he may reject or accept the suggestions as he sees fit. But if he is experienced, he rejects only minor changes and suggestions and accepts most of those made by his salary-superiors, the exact number of acceptances being in direct proportion to the importance of his critics in the studio hierarchy, and to the writer's desire to retain his job and to get further assignments."

The revised treatment was sent around for further approval, and eventually the writer might begin work on a shooting script. Then: more conferences, more changes, more writing and rewriting—until a "final" script was arrived at, agreed upon, and sent to Mimeo. But that was not necessarily the end of the saga. The script might be shelved, another writer assigned to the same idea—and all went back to square one. Or another writer might be called in for a "polish." He might be followed by another writer to improve the dialogue . . . then another and another. Finally, the producer made his choice from the half-dozen final scripts in front of him. With screenwriters often working in pairs, as many as ten could be in the battle for credits once the script was off to production. Bob Thomas, veteran Hollywood correspondent for the Associated Press, once composed, with tongue only slightly in cheek, a sample list of film credits that could ensue:

Screenplay by Rod N. Reel and Corona Smith
Adaptation by Claude Hopper and David Drudge
Additional Dialogue by Patrick Participle
Original Story by Leo De Lyon
Based on a Novel by Leo F. Semicolons

There was often much confusion as to who did what—a greedy director could step in and claim part or all of the writing credit, and who could argue? Even the revered Jean Renoir, who could barely speak English, took writing credit for *The Southerner*, a script written by William Faulkner. So obscure was the screenwriter's lot that the Writers Guild undertook to create a directory giving credit where it was long overdue. "Those of us who write for the screen are all too aware of the epithets that have been hurled against us," observed Leonard Spigelgass, who edited *Who Wrote the Movie, and What Else Did He Write?* (1960) for the Guild. "Over the years we have been called hacks, high-priced secretaries, creatures of the director or producer, pulp writers, craftsmen, sell-outs, cop-outs, mechanical robots. Indeed, we have been excluded from the writing elite: the dramatist, the essayist, the poet, the novelist, the journalist. No Pulitzer Prizes for us, no Nobels, no mention of our names even, through the years, in some reviews of the pictures we wrote." It was an age in which the writer was downtrodden, the producer was king. The producer chose the story, the stars, the director, the cameraman, the editor and the writers, of course—all under contract. If a writer did not want to work on a certain project, he was placed on suspension without salary.

Somehow a few writers were able to gain a measure of equity and creative control over their work. John Huston, for instance, came to Hollywood in the thirties on the strength of some stories he had published in *The American Mercury* magazine. Once he became established as a screenwriter at Warners, he had a clause put in his contract that required the studio to give him a chance to direct—which he requested when he and Allen Rivkin finished the screenplay for *The Maltese Falcon* (1941). Preston Sturges also made the leap from writer to director. Meantime, stars began to rebel against the studio contract system. Many took a more active role in script selection, searching for roles they found appealing. When Katharine Hepburn announced to Louis B. Mayer that she was interested in a script by Ring Lardner, Jr., and Michael Kanin called *Woman of the Year* (1942), the screenwriters received $100,000. "When the stars began to look for scripts, they created the spot market for screenwriters," recalls Allen Rivkin, whose 175 screenwriting credits date back to 1931. "Screenwriters took the gamble and left studio jobs to free-lance. The risk was great, but so were the rewards. By the late forties, writers began to make more money than they ever imagined was possible."

When the Supreme Court ruled in 1950 that studios owning chains of movie theaters were in restraint of trade, the old monopoly days were over. Television became another threat to the industry, and suddenly the age of the mogul was over too. Writers now worked on project contracts, not yearly ones. This is not to say that screenwriters were equal to the forces that they still had to work under. There were still temperamental stars, intimidating directors and off-camera influences that could maul a writer's work. "It still happens that the director will rewrite the script after a long conference with his wife," observed Billy Wilder, a writer turned director. And there remained some brooding moguls who chose to demonstrate how wholesome and innocent they were before Congress in the witch-hunting fifties by instituting the infamous blacklist whereby writers even suspected of "red" leanings found themselves out of work in an industry they had helped make the source of America's favorite entertainment. Nonetheless, screenwriters endured—and ultimately prevailed.

Most of the "Hollywood Ten," and the scores of other writers deprived of the chance to work in the movies from 1947 to 1960, went underground. They used someone as a "front" to get an assignment, wrote screenplays for cut-rate fees, then used pseudonyms for screen credits. Dalton Trumbo, the highest-paid screenwriter in Hollywood when he was blacklisted in 1947, won the Academy Award as "Robert Rich" for best original story for 1956 with *The Brave One*. When *The Bridge on the River Kwai* (1957) won the Academy Award for best screenplay from another medium, the Oscar went to Pierre Boulle, the French author of the novel (who could barely speak English), though it was commonly known that Michael Wilson and Carl Foreman—both blacklisted—had written the script. The blacklist was eventually broken, ending all the years of exploitation and fear, when Trumbo was given credit for both *Spartacus* and *Exodus* in 1960, but by then a new notion had arrived in town to push the screenwriter around: the *auteur* theory.

First proposed in 1954 by then-film-critic François Truffaut in *Cahiers du Cinema*, the theory evaluated films according to the *politique des auteurs*—the policy of authors. Truffaut maintained that the dominant creative personality behind a movie was the director, and only directors who produced work with a personal style were considered artists. The theory took hold in French filmmaking, led by those directors who were labeled "The New Wave" of the late fifties: Claude Chabrol, Georges Franju, Jean-Luc Godard, Louis Malle, Alain Resnais, Jacques Rivette, Eric Rohmer, Roger Vadim and of course Truffaut himself. Insofar as American filmmaking was concerned, Truffaut felt that "cinema cannot be an art so long as it is the result of the work of a group," though certainly some directors could elevate themselves from the pack. His admiration for Alfred Hitchcock was long-standing, and there were also other American directors who somehow managed to put their personal imprint on movies made under the stifling Hollywood studio system. Truffaut singled out little-known director Samuel Fuller (*I Shot Jesse James, Merrill's Marauders,* etc.), for instance—a tiny star in a crowded sky, indeed. American critic Andrew Sarris, in a two-part essay published in *Film Culture* in 1962, found other American director *auteurs* as well (notably Charles Chaplin, D. W. Griffith, Howard Hawks and John Ford), and the battle was underway in this country. The *auteur* school of criticism led to sharp disagreement among leading American movie critics and to abuses within the ranks of advocates—most often a blind allegiance to a favorite director, no matter what the quality of a particular film. As *New Yorker* critic Pauline Kael pointed out, it was an approach that could lead to the celebration of routine movies that had a father figure in their director. Nor was it generally a workable theory in the United States, for while European directors might often be the authors of their film works, American movies were still made under vastly different conditions requiring constant collaboration. Shaky though it was, the *auteur* theory had a three-way effect in Hollywood.

One, it showed how little some of the *auteur* critics knew of the collaborative American moviemaking process. As scholar-critic Richard Corliss observed in his "Notes on a Screenwriter's Theory, 1973" introduction to his book *Talking Pictures,* "First the specialized journals, then the mass-market magazines, then *The New York Times, Cue* and *TV Guide* began crediting directors not only with authorship but with ownership: 'Arthur Hiller's *Love Story.*' By the time the trend had reached Hollywood, it had become something of a joke. Thus *Play It*

Again, Sam—starring Woody Allen, screenplay by Woody Allen, from a play by Woody Allen—is heralded in the screen credits as 'A Herbert Ross Film.' "

Two, it began a period of director adulation by the attendant movie press that probably peaked in 1970 with the publication of *The Film Director as Superstar*, by Joseph Gelmis. Indeed, in Hollywood chronicles the 1960–80 period might aptly be called The Age of the Director—a narrow-minded view of film history that even had Andrew Sarris backpedaling by 1974. "I certainly never meant *auteur*ism to be a running advertisement for the Screen Directors Guild," he said in a preface to Corliss' book, "and I was very careful to point out that the *auteur* theory, such as it was, was more the first step than the last stop in the rediscovery and revaluation of the American cinema. . . . Even I, arch *auteur*ist that I am alleged to be, consider Erich Segal both author and *auteur* of *Love Story*, and Woody Allen both author and *auteur* of *Play It Again, Sam*."

Three, the theory polarized the screenwriter and the director in Hollywood, bringing writers closer together than ever before and making them cognizant of their own rights to claims of *auteur, auteur.*

Gore Vidal first confronted the *auteur* theory at the Cannes Film Festival in 1964. Speaking later to students at the American Film Institute, Vidal recalled how he had written the play *The Best Man*, had written the screenplay for the movie, yet "there was a banner with the title in French and 'Un film de Franklin Schaffner.' Well I hit the ceiling. This was my play, my movie. I had helped put the thing together—we had hired Frank. 'Un film de Franklin Schaffner.' " Six years later at the same festival critic Derek Prouse sent a review back to America raving about *M*A*S*H* and mentioning everyone and everything in the review *but* the screenplay by Ring Lardner, Jr. When Lardner was acknowledged for his work at a Writers Guild banquet in 1971, he accepted the praise—but not the system that had so misled the gullible press—saying: "It would be amiss, I think, for me to accept this honor without one sentence about the director, Bob Altman. Never, or rarely, in my experience has so much imagination, resourcefulness and creative invention been expended—in a series of press interviews!"

"The screenwriter knows that there is nothing more ludicrous than a director without a screenplay he can *auteur*, like a Don Juan without a penis," said writer-director Carl Foreman in his 1972 essay "Confessions of a Frustrated Screenwriter." "At the same time, the screenwriter knows that without a director he has no audience and, even worse sometimes, no money for the rent. So he accepts the fact that when the film is released it will be A Sam Z. Schwartz Production and A Film by Roderick Robinson, or whoever." Thus, to take the money was also to take it on the chin as a writer in Hollywood. And the money could be considerable. "Hollywood overpays for silence," William Goldman told an interviewer for *New Times*. "If you argue too hard you have too much to lose." And Hollywood was still the only game in town if you wanted to work on movies. For the writer this frequently meant working on the company's terms in a business that thrives on intense pressure, too little time and too much compromise—all overseen by a director. "There's basically an adversary relationship between writers and directors," adds Goldman. "Personally, I don't like directors; I think they're jealous, petty and frustrated. They'd like to be writers, only they can't do it."

And what are a director's qualifications for doing rewrites on a script? Well, he's . . . the director. Irwin Shaw once worked with a director who changed every line the novelist wrote. "I am well known as a writer," Shaw told the man. "I am being paid an inordinate amount of money for my script. You, on the other hand, have never written anything on your own. Do you really think what you write is better than what I write?" "No," said the director. "But I like what *I* write better."

Today things are different. While the beginning screenwriter is surely vulnerable, and the veteran is hardly king on the set as producers and stars of old might have been, the screenwriter in general is more powerful than ever before. "Screenwriting is the toughest craft, and when you write well, when you can create a good story, people with good characters that truly relate to each other, that evoke tears or laughter that is human and durable, then you can write your own ticket," Mel Brooks told students at the American Film Institute in Los Angeles recently. That ticket is increasingly a one-way trip to creative control of one's own project. "The best way to become the director is to become the author," added Brooks. "Anybody can direct. There are only eleven good writers. In all of Hollywood."

Today the successful screenwriter is on a monetary par with directors, producers and all but a handful of actors. In the past there have been writers who became directors to control their own work, but such progressions were rare. Today, if a writer is successful, screenwriting is the pathway to power. John Milius, for example, realized while in film school that if he could make himself expensive enough as a screenwriter, he would have the leverage necessary to become a director of his own projects. He now directs and considers himself a "film novelist." Gloria Katz and husband Willard Huyck also wanted to direct when they graduated from film schools, so they concentrated on screenwriting. When their script for *American Graffiti* clicked, they moved into directing and producing. Paul Schrader likewise speaks of his "game plan" to become a director—by first becoming a powerful screenwriter. "I learned a few more things about it as I went along, but essentially it's a plan that has worked," he reflects after directing three films that he also wrote.

Schrader is but one of an upsurge of young filmmakers who came on strong in Hollywood in the late seventies. Dubbed "the film brats" because of their audaciousness and their refusal to come up through the old writing ranks on back lots and B-movies, they are winning battles that are the outcome of a long fight for writer recognition on the job. Maureen Orth reported on this phenomenon for *New York* magazine in 1978. There is a "new young power" on the rise in Hollywood, she discovered. "Creative people have never been more powerful. While stars are still high up in the pecking order, the scripts may now be as important." In the two months preceding Orth's article, four young screenwriters had signed to direct new scripts they had written—"something Hollywood veterans cannot remember ever happening before." As part of the purchase price for their scripts, Nicholas Meyer (*The Seven-Per-Cent Solution*), Matthew Robbins (*MacArthur*), John Byrum (*Harry and Walter Go to New York*) and Willard Huyck (*American Graffiti*) had included themselves as directors. Here the script was clearly the most "bankable" element in the project—so much so that the backers were willing to take a chance with a new director. And why not? Writers have known for decades how pedestrian most directorial duties truly are.

Stirling Silliphant, veteran Oscar-winning screenwriter for *In the Heat of the Night,* calls the director "just another hand on the crew. One of the bosses. Just another foreman. No more." And often considerably less. In *Fade-In,* a short-lived publication sponsored by the Writers Guild of America, West, Silliphant sounded a clarion call for writers and put directors in their place: "Let's flat-out admit that for most directors the act of making a film is neither a science nor an art. It is, in cold fact, an unforgiving routine of administration and traffic control. It calls more for patience, stamina and a pair of sturdy legs than it does for inspiration and creativity." Silliphant, a writer-producer on many of his projects, observed that actors and actresses often looked to the writer, not the director, for guidance—and who was better qualified? "Since so few directors are either willing, capable or trained to work with actors, since their judgment of what is and is not a truly realized performance is clouded by other considerations and pressures— the quality of the sound, the framing of the shot, the focus, the mechanics—why not separate the responsibility for performance—give some of it to the writer?" After all, actors are "searching for ways into the character created not by the director, but by the writer. They are hunting for choices, for index tabs out of their own personal files. Which drawer to open? What memory to evoke?"

Actors realize this, too. "You know, in baseball the knowledgeable people say that seventy-five percent of winning is pitching," says actor Gene Wilder, who shares writing duties on his films. "You say, well, what are you talking about? Look at Reggie Jackson, look at the second baseman, look at the fielding, look at all those things. That's true, they're all crucial, but it's the pitching. And just like pitching, in a movie the script is seventy-five percent." Actors, like enlightened directors, prefer to have a writer on the set to make sure the lines are all just so. When Larry Gelbart was involved with another writing project and could not be on the set of *Rough Cut* in London, Burt Reynolds summarized the problem and the value of a screenwriter's guidance: "Once you start a movie and you've got different locations and some actors prove to be better than others, you do need to make changes. That's our problem. Larry isn't here, and working without a writer around is like working in a circus without a net."

A partial list of writers who have become directors or "hyphenates" (writer-director, writer-producer) and powerful decision makers in their own creative endeavors in recent years includes the following: Colin Higgins, Joan Tewkesbury, Mel Brooks, Charles Eastman, Robert Benton, Abraham Polonsky, Walter Hill, Terrence Malick, Jay Presson Allen, Michael Crichton, Bryan Forbes, John Milius, Paul Schrader, Robert Towne, Woody Allen, George Lucas, Paul Mazursky, Steve Shagan, Walter Bernstein, Marshall Brickman, Richard Brooks, Blake Edwards, Ernest Lehman, Paddy Chayefsky, Neil Simon and Francis Coppola. Perhaps the toughest-minded screenwriter star today is Joseph Wambaugh, the novelist who was so disenchanted with movie versions of his early novels that he decided to take his work into his own hands. When his script for *The Choirboys* was rewritten and turned into what he called "an ugly thing about policemen as fascists," Wambaugh sued Universal, saying the studio had not kept its word. His suit, based upon a verbal contract that no changes would be made in his script, was settled when the studio took his name off the project and gave Wambaugh $1 million for his residual interests in the film—which bombed.

"In order to get my work up on the screen the way I wrote it, I have to do it myself," explained the writer. Wambaugh started his own production company, and his films to date (*The Onion Field* and *The Black Marble*) have been critical successes, but not popular ones. "A lot of people are anxious for me to fall on my ass," he told a reporter between films. "Most of them are power-crazed producers, directors, studio executives and hotshot lawyers who hate the idea of a little guy, an independent, beating them at their own ball game. I have nothing but contempt for these people. They waste money, particularly by paying themselves exorbitant salaries and bonuses, and they often ruin a great story by hoking it up for the screen. That's what happened when director Robert Aldrich got his hands on *The Choirboys*. I had written a book about the emotional roller coaster of being a cop, and Aldrich turned it into a dreadful, slimy, vile movie."

In the old days, when a writer sold a script, he sold it outright. He no longer had control over it, and the final product—if it reached the screen—might bear little resemblance to the original story. The only recourse the writer had was to petition the Writers Guild to have his name removed from the credits. Increasingly, though, there is a new toughness in the business of screenwriting, and, while Wambaugh's approach may be extreme, his attitude is not at all uncommon. More writers are controlling their projects from the script through the production stages, and more of what they write is actually making it to the screen. Stirling Silliphant, for instance, not only talks with the actors on a project: "I never leave them alone. If they have any lingering questions about the character I've created for them, *I* —not the director—want to clear it up for them. I want them to go on the set knowing what their choice is within any scene— what they're going for—what is the given circumstance of that scene—what they are hoping to break through *toward*—what can be *unsaid*—what dialogue we can *cut*—what can we *play* —what can we suggest to the ultimate theater viewer?

"Any director who feels threatened by the writer engaging in this kind of interplay should, in my fervent opinion, be condemned to write his own screenplays throughout the remainder of his career," adds the writer. "I would earnestly suggest that all screenwriters insist in their contracts that they not only be invited on the set but are *expected* to be there for the edification of the actors and actresses, who will finally have somebody to turn to. If this creates conflict between the director and the writer, good. A better film can emerge from the clash. On Broadway, in any dispute between the writer and the director, let's remember it's the director who gets bounced. With more and more original scripts being bought by the studios, it is to be hoped the creators of those scripts will start to get as hardheaded about '*mis*direction' as New York playwrights are."

Some writers want nothing to do with directing, of course; but even then it is possible to remain the most dominating force on a film. Such is the power of the writing of Neil Simon and Paddy Chayefsky, for instance, that they are clearly the most powerful figures in their movies. "The directors of these movies are basically in the service of the screenwriter," acknowledges writer-director Peter Bogdanovich, "and their personalities, if they have any to express, are kept firmly in check."

Why is the screenwriter, historically the low man on the totem pole, suddenly writing and riding so high? Three reasons.

One, many of the talented newcomers to movies are coming from film school backgrounds, and from classrooms and workshops where there is esteem for the importance of the screenwriter in the moviemaking process. Among the "film brats" coming from the campuses at UCLA or USC, for example, are George Lucas, Francis Coppola, Paul Schrader, Colin Higgins, Nancy Dowd, Gloria Katz, Willard Huyck and David Ward. Ward's second script was *The Sting*, from which he has made an estimated $2 million to date.

Two, the cost of making movies has risen dramatically in the last decade; and as costs have gone up, so too has esteem for the forger of scripts. Today the emphasis is not only on scripts; it is on great ones. Few B-movies are being made, and the average per-film cost is close to $10 million, plus an additional $6 million per picture for marketing and advertising. Add to this the reluctance of proven actors and actresses to commit to a project "until I see the script," and the whole blockbuster mentality comes to focus even more sharply on the screenwriter's role. Moviemakers know, too, that big names and big budgets do not necessarily make big money for the backers. The last decade is filled with costly flops, made more on the basis of their stars than on their story lines: *Lucky Lady* (starring Gene Hackman, Liza Minnelli, Burt Reynolds), *Buffalo Bill and the Indians* (Paul Newman), *The Hindenburg* (George C. Scott, Anne Bancroft), *The Missouri Breaks* (Marlon Brando, Jack Nicholson), *Brubaker* (Robert Redford), *Bronco Billy* (Clint Eastwood), *Urban Cowboy* (John Travolta), and more. "Good scripts are hard to find," says producer Tony Bill, "and they are the key to any movie."

Three, as the studio system has faded, so too has the power of the studio executive—who used to buy a property or idea for a movie, then hire a writer to do the screenplay to order. Today studios are increasingly financing and distributing agencies, and the new "mogul" is more an accountant than a creative decision maker. The writer is more likely to come up with an idea and create an original screenplay, then have his agent look for a producer to do the movie. "We are the pigs," George Lucas told Michael Pye and Lynda Myles, authors of *The Movie Brats,* a book on "how the film generation took over Hollywood." The writer-director explains: "We are the ones who sniff out the truffles. You can put us on a leash, keep us under control. But we are the guys who dig out the gold. The man in the executive tower cannot do that. The studios are corporations now, and the men who run them are bureaucrats. . . . They go to parties and they hire people who know people. But the power lies with us—the ones who actually know how to make movies."

Thus, the screenwriter has come a long way in a half century on the job—from anonymity to contract slave shops to periods of bullying and blacklisting to a new age of personal creativity and professional clout. Screenwriting, too—long a despised and ignored form of writing—is at last on the verge of acceptance, applause and acclaim. For the screenwriter it is an age of more original screenplays, more money and more mention in the movie press. Barely ten years ago it was an altogether different world. "From the presses have come bloated volumes extolling the qualities and virtues of stars," lamented Hollis Alpert in the *Saturday Review* in 1970. "My own bookshelves can no longer contain the innumerable studies of directors, and I've started stacking them in the hall closet. But I've yet to come across any full-fledged biographical or critical treatment of a film writer. . . . The relationship of writer to film and, perhaps more important, of writer to director has never been sufficiently explored, one reason being that few people ever bother talking to writers."

I began talking to screenwriters shortly after the success and remarkable critical reception of *Chinatown.* It was the summer of 1974, and I was working at Warner Bros. Records in Hollywood at the time. The then-editor of *Writer's Digest* asked me to interview Robert Towne for that magazine's pages . . . and it was the beginning of a long conversation. Three years later I was still talking with Towne, I had long blown the deadline of the magazine (which I now found myself editing), and I was well underway with a book that called for long conversations with other celebrated screenwriters as well.

The Writers Guild of America, West, has a membership of some 5,300, of which approximately 800 are screenwriters. Employment in the field has always been highly competitive, and an average of only 250 screenwriters are working at any one time. Still, while crowded at the bottom, there is room at the top—and the great writers turn down projects regularly. Just as there are about a dozen actors who can command six-figure fees for their work, there are about a dozen screenwriters who can write for six figures as well—and six of those screenwriters are here.

I decided on six because that is all that the confines of a book-length effort would allow if the interviews were to have the depth and substance I wanted. And six celebrated screenwriters quickly became naturals for the book's lineup—for their work has been distinctive in style, achievement and recognition:

• *Paddy Chayefsky,* the pugnacious, poetic wordsmith, has often brought theater to the screen.

• *William Goldman,* a novelist at heart, works with an impatience and a measure of success that Scott Fitzgerald, Nathanael West and his other literary forebears could only have envied and admired.

• *Ernest Lehman,* a transitional giant, is one of the few writers to adapt his talents to film over three decades.

• *Paul Schrader,* one of the new breed, is the complete writer-filmmaker—whose scholarly background is tinged with a realistic view of what makes a movie commercially viable.

• *Neil Simon,* the writer with the most absolute clout on his screen projects, mingles celebrity with success, and Broadway with Hollywood—at a time when Broadway and Hollywood comedy writing have been considered barren zones.

• And *Robert Towne,* California-born and -bred, is a writer who gained his early reputation as "script doctor," finishing films others had started, and who now pursues his own art as a forger of strikingly original screenplays.

All the interviews were taped over a period of time ranging up to seven years. The tapes were transcribed, verified by the subjects and edited for clarity and coherence. In general, only conversational fat was trimmed from the interviews; nothing substantive was altered or touched up by the subjects. All the screenwriters were refreshingly candid—in a business often given to as much hype as your recorder can hold. I was generally given access to the writers' personal libraries and script files for my research as well, and to a remarkable amount of their most precious commodity: time.

That is the past; this is the prologue. Now let the screenwriters speak for themselves.

—JOHN BRADY

PADDY CHAYEFSKY

"Paddy Chayefsky is a square," observed Josh Logan in a recent memoir. Logan, who produced the play *Middle of the Night* and the movie version of *Paint Your Wagon* with Chayefsky, was quick to clarify: "When I say square, I'm talking about his physical appearance and effect. Paddy is built something like an office safe, one that fits under the counter and is impossible to move."

Paddy Chayefsky at fifty-eight has spent the better part of his writing life being impossible to move. When he forges a script, it often contains speeches that run for paragraphs and even for pages—"a virtual violation, a heresy of filmmaking," he concedes. "The first thing they said when they got the script of *The Hospital* was, 'We've got to cut the long speeches,'" he told a reporter for *The New York Times*. Chayefsky paused, then added very slowly: "We didn't cut one word."

Chayefsky's toughness goes back to the Bronx playing fields of the early forties, when he played semiprofessional football for the Kingsbridge Trojans. Though only 5 feet 6 inches and 183 pounds, he played "pocket guard." "In those days you played defense and offense," he recalls. "There was no platooning. I was the running guard who pulled out and led the interference." He went overseas as a machine gunner during World War II, stepped on a land mine in Germany, received the purple heart, and wrote the book and lyrics for a GI musical comedy while recovering in a London hospital. The show, *No T.O. for Love*, impressed Josh Logan, who happened to be in the audience for a performance. "When those diamond-bright lyrics came out from the cast—much funnier, much clearer, much more professional than anything

I had heard in a long time—'The Air Corps, the Air Corps, That cozy, easy chair corps'—I was so impressed that I made a trip backstage to meet the lyricist," recalls the producer. "The bulky office safe in suntans came trundling up with a chip on his shoulder and a square haircut and said, 'I wrote 'em—Paddy Chayefsky. P-A-D-D-Y.'

"I told him how much I liked them, expecting him to warm up a bit and become a very friendly person," recalls Logan. "Not at all. He knew they were great—he'd written them."

Chayefsky, whose given name is Sidney, has been called Paddy ever since an Army lieutenant was dubious when the Jewish writer asked to be excused from KP duty to attend Mass. After the war, he took up writing seriously, and in the fifties Paddy Chayefsky became the golden boy of TV's golden age—a time when there was original, live drama, and a greater willingness to experiment with talent and quality writing. Chayefsky wrote original plays for the "Philco-Goodyear Playhouse" and for the "NBC Playhouse." His best-known work, *Marty*, a 1953 NBC production, became the first television script to be made into a motion picture—and was a giant first step in Chayefsky's screenwriting career. The simple story of a butcher and his plain girl friend—Chayefsky said he wanted it to be "the most ordinary love story in the world"—led to the writer's first Academy Award. He won his second Oscar for *The Hospital* in 1971. In between he wrote screenplays for *The Bachelor Party, The Goddess, Middle of the Night, The Americanization of Emily* and *Paint Your Wagon*. He won his third Oscar in 1976 for *Network*, a satirical indictment of the TV industry's boardroom and bedroom wars for ratings. In the furor that followed, Chayefsky insisted he was absolutely serious about the demise of an industry where he had once been the golden boy. "It's the world that's gone nuts, not me," he said. "It's the world that's turned into a satire."

Chayefsky's latest movie, about which he would say little, is *Altered States,* a satire on the scientific community. In his novel, Chayefsky chronicles the adventures of a young scientist who, using drugs, moves backward through evolution, "first as a primate, then on to the ultimate matter of life." The author came up with the idea during a bull session with writer Herb Gardner and director Bob Fosse at the Russian Tea Room. "I hit on *Dr. Jekyll and Mr. Hyde,* and I knew I had something—an updated version of the classic with a philosophical twist," Chayefsky told Dan Weaver of the Literary Guild. "It's not an evil story. It's a love story—very positive." The author had a falling out with director Ken Russell on the project, however, and took his name off the film, using a pseudonym (Sidney Aaron) instead "because it's a requisite of the Writers Guild that somebody have the writer's credit." He refused to go into what had been a painful experience, reflecting, "To me the dirty laundry of movie productions is terribly uninteresting material."

Our conversations took place in the screenwriter's Seventh Avenue office, a converted efficiency apartment that includes a kitchenette used for filing cabinets, a small room for a secretary who comes in once a week, and a large corner room that looks more like a songwriter's office than a place for pounding out scripts. In one corner is a baby grand piano that Chayefsky said he was going to have tuned. "I used to play a great deal every day, but not in the last year or two. I play poorly." One wall is filled with bookshelves with titles ranging from Theodore Bernstein's *Reverse Dictionary* and *The Mis-Speller's Dictionary* to Robert Ardrey's *African Genesis* and *Powers of Mind,* by "Adam Smith." There is also a complete file of *National Geographics* from January 1965 to the present. "I don't know what I'd do without them," said Chayefsky. "I've traveled a great deal, but I just hate travel now. I'm so *bored* with it. In *Altered States,* though, you'll read about Mexico, India. I've never been to Mexico. I just go to that shelf and pick it all up."

In the opposite corner of the room there is an L-shaped desk with a large Olympia manual typewriter. The writer sat in a black chair at his desk, sipped a Sanka, and asked that no picture be used with the interview. "I want my privacy," he said. "I don't like to be recognized." In fact, as the sounds of the city drifted up from the streets to his eleventh-floor office, Paddy Chayefsky explained why he has allowed few interviewers to invade his privacy.

———

CHAYEFSKY: I don't, as a rule, do interviews.

BRADY: Why not?

CHAYEFSKY: I have never understood their function.

BRADY: I think people are interested in the creative process, and you are at the heart of it.

CHAYEFSKY: I'm not sure I understand the creative process. I've never given much attention to it. I understand how *I* work, but I don't really know what psychological things happen in the creative process, or why somebody creates. I have certain rules that I've learned over the long run. I even tried to teach them one semester. I'm not sure I got them across. I think everybody has to develop their own rules.

BRADY: Where did you try to teach them?

CHAYEFSKY: City College of New York, my old school.

BRADY: You had a professor there named Theodore Goodman, I believe.

CHAYEFSKY: Yes, my short-story teacher. I never understood what *he* talked about either. The one thing I do remember from the course—he was a great teacher, by the way—I remember him quoting Henry James, or perhaps it was William, saying, "We always learn to swim in the winter." Many years after I'd finished his course, I began to understand what he was talking about. I learned to swim too late, you see. I did learn to read in his course, if not to write. Our textbook was *Dubliners,* by James Joyce, so I got to be a big Joyce fan in those days. "The Dead," I think, is one of the finest stories written.

BRADY: It sounds as though your background, at least your education, was for the most part in fiction rather than drama.

CHAYEFSKY: There was no education in drama at all that I

knew of then. Was there a Yale Drama School in those days? There was a Dramatic Society at City College; it was extracurricular; there was no formal theater department. This was in the early forties.

BRADY: You graduated from high school in 1939 at sixteen, and you were rather precocious, weren't you?

CHAYEFSKY: I was offensively precocious. I was one of those kids in the front row with his hands up all the time.

BRADY: And it was Sidney *Q*. Chayefsky at the time?

CHAYEFSKY: The Q was a gag—a high school gag. It was Sidney NMI Chayefsky in the Army.

BRADY: In your high school yearbook you said your future occupation was to be a "Muckraker."

CHAYEFSKY: It's a good high school aspiration.

BRADY: Might it have had some bearing on the turn your career has taken? Did you have aspirations of becoming a journalist?

CHAYEFSKY: I was very impressed with Lincoln Steffens in high school, but I never got into journalism. It was a discipline I could never master. My mind doesn't work that way. I get impressions rather than facts. I always have to go back over and over again for the facts, so I research rather than pick up the information the way a journalist does. I never would have amounted to a competent muckraker anyway. I was editor of the high school magazine, and I was on the school newspaper; but I couldn't make either of them in college.

BRADY: Did you do any writing in college?

CHAYEFSKY: I was writing satirical little ditties and songs and things for classmates. I did a song about the Rapp-Coudert Committee, our local witch-hunting, Red-hunting committee in New York. Just for classmates. Nothing for pay.

BRADY: So you really didn't take yourself seriously as a writer then.

CHAYEFSKY: Oh, I always knew I wanted to be a writer, but it was too much work to be on the college newspaper. *The Campus,* our college paper, was a daily; you worked all day, all night. You were lucky to get a class in. And I was having a hard enough time getting passing grades at college, for all my facility and precocity. City College was filled with very precocious young fellows in the front row waving their hands.

At City College, to get in, you had to have an eighty-five average in high school, I think, at least the year I got in. I had an eighty-six something. But I'd become tired of being bright, you know. I used to put in a lot of time in the gym, playing ball a lot, being one of the fellows. No, I didn't pursue any kind of writing career, per se, in college. I took the writing courses. I took Professor Goodman's course. I took all the lit courses. But I majored in the social sciences.

BRADY: I read that your folks did some business in Yonkers. A dairy.

CHAYEFSKY: My father was president of Morrisania Milk Farms and Dellwood Dairies. Still very reputable firms.

BRADY: But they went broke in 1934.

CHAYEFSKY: They went bankrupt, as a matter of fact. But *he* didn't go bankrupt. He wound up paying off everything. We went broke, and he went into the construction business, building houses. Then he got back into the milk business again later as a workingman.

BRADY: I assume that your childhood years, in addition to being sensitive ones, are filled with things that are of use to you as a writer. I get the impression that your perceptions of the family and the love between father and mother is home-brewed.

CHAYEFSKY: We were a very close family. My two brothers and I are still very close. The sisters-in-law all get along famously. It's a very unusual situation.

BRADY: Is there something about your growing-up experience that motivated you later to capture at least some of it on paper?

CHAYEFSKY: I expect writers write about what they know. I wrote about the lower-middle-class life I came out of. Writing, in a lower-middle-class Jewish family, is a highly respected career, and I think that is one of the reasons I became a writer. It's the sort of thing that would certainly bring approval from your parents.

BRADY: It is respected among Jewish families?

CHAYEFSKY: It sure is. Not *song*writing. All my friends who were songwriters, like Julie Styne, Frank Loesser—their parents always wanted to know when they were going to get steady jobs even after they were celebrated. No, I mean *writing*. Journalism, drama, literature—any kind of writing. It was respectable—almost as good as being a poet. A poet was terrific among lower-middle-class Jews.

BRADY: That's even more surprising.

CHAYEFSKY: At least in my family. My mother was a particularly well-read lady. For an immigrant girl who came from the Ukraine, she had a very good schooling. There must have been some middle-class Jewish families that preferred their sons to be doctors and lawyers and who would have thought writing was something that you did on the side. But my family never thought that at all, ever.

BRADY: In *The Season,* Bill Goldman speaks of the high percentage of Jewish playwrights on Broadway, and Jewish writers are important to the film as well—Neil Simon, Bob Towne, Goldman, Ernie Lehman, yourself.

CHAYEFSKY: Well, it was one of the avenues for getting out of the ghetto. And writing, I imagine, became a highly respected career for Jews. There's also an endlessly long tradition of bookishness among Jews. A book, the Bible, is the core and probably the most sustaining thing, the most continuing factor in the history of the Jews, which is now three or four thousand years old. The Bible itself is well over two thousand. Bookishness, attention to books, learning, literature, that sort of thing, seems to be part of the genetic structure of Judaism. It was for a long time. It may be dissipating now as Jews become less and less Jewish per se. If you notice, there are a hell of a lot of black writers around now coming up in the theater. It's a way out of the ghetto.

BRADY: Were your parents able to share your successful years as a writer?

CHAYEFSKY: My mother did. My father was anxious about me. He told my brothers he was worried about my making it as a writer. But my mother was around to see me successful.

BRADY: You mentioned not doing interviews. Recent pictures of you are scarce, too.

CHAYEFSKY: I don't care to be recognized. I don't like public attention. I don't like to be photographed.

BRADY: You have a way of attracting it.

CHAYEFSKY: I know it's kind of silly—and I'm in a curious business to avoid it, too—but I do try to stay away from the camera; I try to be behind it. I have in all my contracts that I do not have to do any publicity whatsoever. And I do it only if the stars won't do it—those are the only sorts of public appearances I make at all. Fortunately, on *Network* we had terrific stars—Bill Holden and Peter Finch. I didn't have to do anything. Faye did a little bit, but not much. The new generation of stars doesn't want to do publicity; then they get annoyed when nobody recognizes them.

BRADY: There's a kind of toughness to you in person, and I think you have a reputation of being a pretty tough guy in addition to being able to write gracefully.

CHAYEFSKY: I dislike bullshit, especially my own. I don't know if I would describe that as toughness, but that's what it comes down to.

BRADY: That is a difficult quality to maintain in a business where there is often a lot of committeelike work. I'll quote from a study of your works by John Clum. He says, regarding *The Goddess* in 1958, that "Chayefsky's dual role as producer and writer led to a great many tempestuous scenes as the writer fought with everyone to preserve his concept of the film. One former colleague was once quoted as saying that, 'Paddy is an expert on everything. You'll find he has expertise in directing, selling, photography, promotion, sales, everything it takes other people 15 or 20 years to learn; a real octopus, that man. He has to have a hand in everything.' "

CHAYEFSKY: Yes, that's the way I was.

BRADY: No more?

CHAYEFSKY: I have a producer now. I don't know how to produce. I don't know the first damn thing about producing. In movies the producer is the most important man there is.

BRADY: You really think so?

CHAYEFSKY: Oh, absolutely!

BRADY: How so?

CHAYEFSKY: Well, he's the fellow who organizes the whole show. He gets the script put together, he hires the director, he hires the talent. He's the man who really stamps the show. So I have a partner who is the producer in fact. I mean, I share the stamp of the picture with Howard Gottfried.

Howard is a full-fledged partner. That is to say, he's a great showman; he knows story as well as anybody I know; he's a delight to work with; he's also an abrasive man; he has no interest in whether you like him or not, which is one of the reasons I like him so much. He's utterly honest. So I don't have to worry about that. For a long while—after *Goddess*—I stopped making my own pictures. I went back to it when I met Howard.

BRADY: You lost a bundle on *The Goddess?*

CHAYEFSKY: We lost every penny.

BRADY: Nothing trickles in eventually on a film like that?

CHAYEFSKY: Nothing the bookkeepers tell me about. You know about film bookkeeping.

BRADY: Yes. Exotic.

CHAYEFSKY: I'm sure they didn't lose quite as much as I did.

BRADY: Do you consider yourself a pretty good businessman now?

CHAYEFSKY: No. I only know what I want. I know enough about making movies now so that I know that what I want will not interfere with the profits of the other people. In that sense, I'm a good businessman. And I'm good in the sense that my positions are always nonnegotiable. That is to say, if you have an agent, you automatically are saying that your position is negotiable. I don't have an agent. My position is nonnegotiable. That's how much I want and what kind of controls I want. It is up to the other side to figure out how to make it palatable to themselves, because there is plenty of room left for everybody to make all the money they want. I never ask for a great deal of money. It sounds like a great deal of money, but start dividing it over four years, which is how long it takes me to make a film, and it's not very much money. But I don't negotiate. I just say, "Look, fellas, you can be clever and phrase it any way you want to—as long as it comes out right." Then my lawyer takes care of the rest. He sees that the language is executed so that we don't get screwed. And I always deliver. If I don't deliver, I give the money back. I never commit myself unless I think it can be done.

There are only a few of us who do this now. The only ones I know of who make their own pictures are Doc Simon, Mel Brooks, Woody Allen and myself. We are the production company. We take the responsibility of making the film. Perhaps Bob Towne. I don't know Towne's situation at Warners.

That's the only way to do films as a writer; otherwise, you're a hired hand. You can get fired. Nobody can fire me. Nobody can fire Doc Simon, nobody can fire Mel Brooks, nobody can fire Woody Allen. Since we do the firing. That's the only way I know that a writer can make his own film.

BRADY: You've had this capability for some time, haven't you? Most writers are just coming into this area of power today.

CHAYEFSKY: It was more workaday than contractual. For example, I was the associate producer on *Marty*. I was also the codirector on *Marty* because I was afraid they might fire the director I wanted, and I wanted to make sure I still had control if such a thing were to happen. Well, when the picture was finally finished and the director—Delbert Mann—had *not* been fired, I tried to get my name off it. The credit had been merely technical; I never did any directing. I had more trouble getting my name off that picture than getting it on it. I had asked for the director's credit only because contractually I had very little control. Whatever controls I did have I got by bargaining off my salary.

BRADY: You were paid thirteen thousand dollars plus five percent of the net.

CHAYEFSKY: Net profit *after* participation, after everybody else's participation.

BRADY: Did you ever make any meaningful money off that film, as great as it's been?

CHAYEFSKY: Over twenty years, I think perhaps a total of sixty thousand dollars. I never made much money on it. I don't know why people think I make a lot of money. I don't. I never did. Not even in the theater. And let's face it—there you work two or three years on a play, and then you may go off in a week. That's hardly worth the gamble. The young playwrights have a new attitude. They have no particular interest in Broadway. They'll go anywhere to do a play.

BRADY: I think that's healthy.

CHAYEFSKY: It sure is. When you're young, you can go anywhere. When you get on in years, it's a little uncomfortable to go anywhere to do a play. I mean, you really have to get involved with a lot of people who are not that skilled as actors and are not that terrific as directors and suddenly you feel all the lacks. You've got to be young to cope with that. I like the best and biggest talent I can get at all times.

BRADY: In something resembling anger, you took *The Latent Heterosexual* away from Broadway.

CHAYEFSKY: I tried. We did it in Dallas. We did it in Los Angeles. And I gave it to the San Francisco theater. We did it in London. The London production is the only one I enjoyed.

BRADY: Are you thinking of returning to Broadway?

CHAYEFSKY: If the next picture is a hit. I have to have some money underneath me to indulge myself in a play. It amounts to two years of work, then a year of gathering the production, and then you go on. You have no idea how long you'll run. There isn't much of an audience for a straight play that I know of.

BRADY: It sounds as though your lover's quarrel with Broadway is near an end.

CHAYEFSKY: No, it's just that I can afford it now. I've been unable to afford it for years. I had three hits on Broadway. That's to say, they paid off the backers: the definition of a hit. "Three hits," to quote a friend of mine, "is about as much as any man should reasonably expect in his lifetime." That's enough. My hits didn't make *that* kind of money. *Gideon, Middle of the Night, Tenth Man*. We made money. But we didn't make the kind of money where I could rest or I could spend another two years writing another play. I couldn't stay in the theater as a working writer and pay my bills, which were not very high. So I went to the movies. By the time I quit the theater I was fairly well entrenched in the movie business.

BRADY: You speak of two years to write a play?

CHAYEFSKY: At least.

BRADY: That's your normal pacing?

CHAYEFSKY: It takes me that long to write a movie.

BRADY: That sounds like a lot of work. Is it steady work, nine to five?

CHAYEFSKY: It averages out to about nine to five. Right now I have steady hours, but there are long periods where I don't sleep well and my hours become very erratic; but they average out to about a fifty- to sixty-hour workweek. Most writers will tell you that.

BRADY: Do you like writing?

CHAYEFSKY: Sure. What am I doing it for? I've gotten as much as I need to get as a writer in terms of approbation. I don't write for money, because if I had a lot of money, what would I do with it? I write because I like to write.

BRADY: But you're obviously in a position where you have to market yourself, too.

CHAYEFSKY: I'm afraid so. Money is all we talk about. The fact is, you can trust a writer who talks about money all the time. I'd be very careful of a writer who starts talking about his art. Highly suspect. I met a woman once, bitterly complaining: She had just met Picasso, and all he talked about was how much he charged per square inch of canvas. I said, "What did you expect him to talk to you about—his art?" To an artist, his art is his private business. Artists don't talk about art. Artists talk about work. If I have anything to say to young writers, it's stop thinking of writing as art. Think of it as work. If you're an artist, whatever you do is going to be art. If you're not an artist, at least you can do a good day's work. It's what you come in every morning to do. When the painter comes in, he looks at the canvas and he throws some paint up on it; he sees something that affects him, he gets an idea, and he goes to work. And he calls on another artist because he's stuck, or the writer calls in another writer because he's hung up. And they don't talk about The Art. They talk about "What's your problem?" What's the *work* problem? It's work. And if you're an artist, it'll come out art. Automatically. Art, if it is to be defined, is simply the product of an artist.

If you're an artist, certain sensibilities, certain perceptions produce an effect that gives some shred of meaning to an audience or a viewer or a reader. That's *you*—you as a person. There's nothing that will make you that, nothing that will teach you that. That's *you*. But the way you do it is a day's work. And frequently it is just plain physical work. It is saying, "Oh, Jeez, that's all wrong," and having to sit down and mechanically retype fourteen pages. And while retyping, you say, "No, that's wrong," and change something, then retype it again to get it right. It's hard physical work. You keep saying, "No, that's wrong, I can do it better." You have an original, fresh concept; you want to fulfill it as precisely and as completely as you can, and in the effort to achieve that, the constant self-demand is, in essence, what art is.

BRADY: You said earlier of Howard Gottfried that he "knows story." What do you mean by that?

CHAYEFSKY: You can talk story to him. He understands the problems of script, of writing. He has a good feel for what will play and what won't play. Story conferences with Howard are usually productive and not bullshit. When I really get stuck, I go to Herb Gardner—who wrote *A Thousand Clowns*. Herb is almost unbelievable with other guys' scripts. Herb is a painter and a sculptor as well as a writer. He is a real, honest-to-God, Bohemian artist. But you'll never hear him talk about anything but "I think you need more yellow up there." Or, "Your canvas is too big for the damn picture." It's work; it's never art. Art is for academics. Art is for scholars. Art is for audiences. Art is not for artists.

BRADY: You must have a certain amount of impatience with people who deal in heavy-handed film criticism—extracting symbols and such.

CHAYEFSKY: Never read it. I once got caught up in a *New York Times Magazine* piece about Fellini, who had hired an amateur actor and couldn't get the effect he wanted from him. Fellini kept telling the actor, "Back farther, back farther, now start. No, no that's wrong." Finally, Fellini backed the guy so far he fell off the scaffolding he had been standing on. The guy got up in a fury, did the scene, and Fellini said, "*Now* you have it!" I could have told Fellini he should have gotten himself a professional actor, who would have done it for him the first time 'round. Good actors can do that, you see; you don't have to get amateurs and beat them to death. I also don't believe for one minute that that incident actually happened, or that anybody would believe that story, let alone write it up as an instance of serious filmmaking. I don't know Fellini, but I can't believe anybody operates in so amateurish a manner as that. It's nonsense. You get a perfectly capable professional actor, he'll deliver what you want from him.

BRADY: Do you believe in any improvisation at all when the film is underway?

CHAYEFSKY: In rehearsal, I do. We always rehearse two, three weeks on my stuff. And the actors can improvise all they want to at that time.

BRADY: Do you rehearse the script chronologically?

CHAYEFSKY: Yes. We do the whole damn thing, mapping it out just like you do a stage play. We work exactly like you do in the theater. I need a director who comes out of the theater. We go through two, three weeks of rehearsal, scene by scene, working on each scene, directing the actors, me hovering in the background if they need me. Actors love it. Gives them a lot more confidence by the time they're in front of that camera. They know where they are. They know what they're trying to do. They know what they can do. And they can improvise all they want to during the first two-thirds of rehearsal. After that, we've got to nail it into place so it's down. That's what happens on my shows. I can't speak for anybody else's shows. I remember a show called *A Man and a Woman,* a Lelouch film. Obviously, a good deal of improvisation. It worked like a charm. Lelouch is terrific. But I've also seen a great many films, by directors I won't mention, in which improvisation is the core of the process, and such films are dreadful. It really depends, you know—on getting actors who are terrific improvisors. I don't know many. Most of them are very dull improvisors.

BRADY: How, exactly, is a script like *Network* pounded into place through this interplay between actor and director and yourself?

CHAYEFSKY: It's exactly like the theater. The thing is carefully written to start with. Then the director comes in on it. Conferences. Revisions are made with the director because it is nonsense for the director to go out on the floor, take over a film, if he is not happy with the script. Before Sidney Lumet went into rehearsal with *Network,* that script was just the way he wanted it, just the way I wanted it, and just the way Howard Gottfried, the producer, wanted it. We went into rehearsal, Sidney simply took over as the director, and if the actors had any ideas or suggestions, they were free to do whatever they wanted—then after a while we nailed it into place. There wasn't much changing. The actors were not unhappy with the script. Lumet's remarkable with actors. They all came out terrific . . . Bobby Duvall . . . they were all just terrific. Sidney loves actors. I love actors. Howard loves actors. You never saw such a comfortable bunch of actors. Actors feel it. They can tell.

BRADY: I heard Bill Holden speak of the difficulty of that long farewell scene with Faye Dunaway, in which he tells her that she's the product of television. That's a pretty tough piece of dialogue there.

CHAYEFSKY: The writing has a strange style. It's difficult to say it and make it sound real. Holden is a wonderful actor.

BRADY: Holden said that he wanted to change some lines there and he talked with you about it.

CHAYEFSKY: Sure. In the end he went back to the original lines. But you see a good actor—guys like Holden or Freddie March, people like that—what they really do, I think, is they go home, put the whole script in their own language so they can understand what was meant. Then they say, "Oh, *now* I understand what that guy wants." Then they come back to the original lines, but I think first they must make it their own before they can return to what's written. What Bill did was to make it his own language for a while. And then said, "Oh, wait a minute, it does sound better the other way." Because I had spent more time working on it. I write for actors. I expect them to enjoy the words, the lines. I want them to enjoy them. I'll do a lot to make them happy. I'll change a lot. I don't usually get asked much, though.

BRADY: I get the impression that you command a certain amount of respect that someone without the background you bring to a film is not likely to have.

CHAYEFSKY: It's not me personally. It's workaday. You're dealing with a lot of other talent; of course, you've got to let them have their rights, too.

BRADY: What does "workaday" mean?

CHAYEFSKY: You have no contract that gives you any control. Whatever authority you exercise is worked out in everyday relationships at rehearsals. At least, so it works with me. You and I know lots of writers who grab the money, run, couldn't care what happens. I do care. And there seems to be a growing bunch of writers who do care what happens to their writing, who put their name on it and don't want to be embarrassed by it. A film writer's work gets brutalized so much that sooner or later the writer either gives in to it or takes a stand and says, "From now on, I'll make the picture and I'll control it." By control I don't mean like a wounded mother tiger. It just means that in the end your ideas cannot be disposed of that easily. In moviemaking the actor has you over a barrel once you've started the picture, anyway. You shoot five, six weeks, and if the star doesn't like the director, he can have the director fired. Otherwise you're going to have to reshoot five, six weeks. Nobody can afford that anymore. Expenses and the cost of making the film are so phenomenal, once you're in five or six weeks, you're stuck.

BRADY: This would seem to be slightly at odds with what you said earlier about the producer being the most important person on a film.

CHAYEFSKY: The star's the most *powerful* person on the film; the producer is the most *important,* in putting the film together.

In the old big-studio days, the producers were the important people. They would pick their writer, and the writer would go off with the producer, and they'd work together and produce a script. They would turn it in to the front office, who would read it, approve it, and one day a director would walk into his office and there would be the script sitting on his desk with a note saying this is your next picture. The director would then call up the producer and say I'm your new director. The producer had probably asked for him. They get together—the writer, director, and producer—become a little group. But the producer was boss of everything in the big-studio days.

BRADY: Aren't you now in the position where you hire a producer?

CHAYEFSKY: No, he's my partner. The kind of producer you can get—"Listen, here's a couple of thousand dollars a week. You're the producer"—isn't worth the couple of thousand dollars a week. A real producer requires great experience, a lot of show business sense, a great deal of taste, great knowledge of what he's doing. He must also be a terrific businessman and know how much each keg of nails costs.

BRADY: All of this conversation on how a film is put together and where the power rests suggests that at some point in your career your writing was mauled. And you've learned to insulate yourself from that.

CHAYEFSKY: Yes. More than once.

BRADY: Was it your television writing that left you scarred?

CHAYEFSKY: No. Movies. And the theater. *The Latent Heterosexual* scarred me—the production in Dallas and Los Angeles scarred me for years. I couldn't get a director for the Russian play, *The Passion of Josef D.,* so I directed it myself, and that was a disaster. I have no temperament to be a director at all.

BRADY: Why couldn't you get a director for that?

CHAYEFSKY: I don't know. I tried a lot of people. At one point there was a chance Olivier would do it at the National Theater of England, but Kenneth Tynan turned it down. (He was at that time the head of the National Theater.) I have a hunch he turned it down for ideological reasons: It was a little too revisionist, I think. At any rate, I didn't get the production or the National Theater. Eventually, I directed the play myself, and it was a disaster. Horrible.

I thought I would imitate Tyrone Guthrie and that would do the trick, and it just doesn't. I have no ability to deal with other creative people, except to respect them. I could never get anybody to do what I wanted. I had a lot of terrific ideas. Now if I had had a good director—if I had had Bob Fosse or Jerry Robbins, either would have jumped at some of my ideas and gotten them done. They would throw out a lot of them, but they would take some of them. But, as the director, I couldn't get anything done. I'm not a good boss. I scare actors as a director, whereas I'm a benign influence with actors as a writer. The whole thing is that everybody on a production is really important—a significant person with contributions. And as soon as you learn that, as soon as you get really big talent in each capacity, then you don't have to be the presumptuous fellow I was on *The Goddess,* screaming at everybody, yelling at everybody, going into tantrums over and over again and carrying on very badly. You let the real talents exercise their province of activity, which they know how to do better. You don't have to be an expert in everything; you don't have to be knowledgeable in everything.

The writer's job is to take charge of the script, to take full responsibility for the script. Don't depend on anyone else to get it done for you. Don't count on the director covering holes for you; don't count on the actors covering for you. Get the script done yourself. Be constantly responsible for it throughout the show. That's what I mean by don't defend your script like a wounded tiger; but take the responsibility of producing the best script possible on your own shoulders. Don't wait for anybody to tell you about it. Come in the next morning and say, "I've made some cuts." Don't wait till somebody tells you. Or, "There's a bad spot in the script and it's not working." Figure out how to do it yourself. Maybe the director can help you with an idea, but you've got to do the writing yourself. If you take that responsibility for yourself, other people will give you respect. Once you've got a good script, you're on your way to a good movie. That's enough. A lot of the anxiety goes out of the production if the script is solid. On those occasions when I was mauled, it was because the scripts were imperfect, and I was not taking care of them myself.

BRADY: Because you were busy in other areas as well?

CHAYEFSKY: Because I was lazy, because I was unsure, because I was young, because I hoped other people would solve the problems for me and they didn't. You know when you write it when you're going to run into trouble. You know even as you glide over it, you say, "Uh-oh, this is going to cause trouble later." So the mauling produced not so much a desire to make my own films as the desire to make sure I knew the script was right. Once the script was right, I wanted to make sure nobody screwed it up. And the only way to do that is to make your own film.

BRADY: Has anyone ever actually changed, say, the ending or a key scene or anything meaningful that you've written?

CHAYEFSKY: I once wrote a story called *A Few Kind Words From Newark*. It was made into a picture called *As Young As You Feel* with Monty Woolley. The part was written for William Powell. Monty Woolley was wrong for that part. The story was made into a screenplay by another writer, and the director was an editor, his first job as a director. Thelma Ritter was signed for it, a tiny role, but by the time they got around to making the picture, Thelma had done *Letter to Three Wives,* or something that made her into a star—*Miracle on 34th Street,* I forget what —so they decided to enlarge her part. By the time that picture showed up on screen, it was completely deformed.

The second time it happened, I sold a television show called *Catered Affair* to the movies, outright. I didn't participate in the production. And that's the last time I ever sold one of my properties outright. Ever since then I've done them all by myself, never let them out of my hands.

BRADY: Those maulings occurred in the early fifties, but you'd been in Hollywood in the late forties, as I recall.

CHAYEFSKY: I was at the Actors' Lab.

BRADY: Junior writer, or something?

CHAYEFSKY: I was on the GI Bill of Rights. I was an actor, technically speaking. I had a bit part in *A Double Life* with Ronald Colman. It was just a way of covering my entree into the film industry, to get into the business. I wasn't much of an actor. I know Hollywood very well. I lived there, went to the Actors' Lab school, and I worked in the studios, in the days of the big studios. But I live in New York now. I go to Hollywood periodically, only when I have to.

BRADY: Is New York your living preference, or is it a working necessity?

CHAYEFSKY: I just don't know how not to live in New York. It's where I live. When you move, you've got to get new doctors and dentists and lawyers. It's more than I could possibly face up to.

BRADY: One movie credit often overlooked is *The Cincinnati Kid*. Weren't you on that film?

CHAYEFSKY: I quit. I couldn't lick it. Not only that, I couldn't get along with the director. I said to the producer, it's either me or him, and the producer said, "Goodbye."

BRADY: Were you first writer on it?

CHAYEFSKY: As a matter of fact, yeah, I think I was. I think Dick Jessup, the guy who wrote the book, might have written something. I'm not sure. Then they called in Terry Southern, I think, after me, and Norman Jewison took over the directing.

BRADY: Have you ever peeled off a scene or a couple of pages and found yourself saying, "This is bad"—but it works, others like it, it plays.

CHAYEFSKY: Yes, I've done that. It plays and I said, "Boy, are we getting away here!" Yeah, many times. There's no way of writing a perfect script. There are many spots in every script that any writer is only too grateful to cover up or get away with. As long as the basic thing is there, though, you know you're all right.

BRADY: Do you think your films will work ten years from now?

CHAYEFSKY: Sure, they'll hold up. Those are well-made movies, so they'll hold up well.

BRADY: I think of *Network,* for example, a movie about television here and now, and I wonder if ten years from now . . .

CHAYEFSKY: *Network* will hold up very well; *Network* is a good picture. A good picture always holds up. I looked at my old TV shows; they hold up. They're period pieces. They deal with a world that is almost gone. But they hold up as statements of their time.

BRADY: In 1954 when you turned *Marty* into a screenplay, you had certain clauses written into the contract, including the requirement that you be on stage for rehearsals of the movie. What motivated you to insist upon this at the time?

CHAYEFSKY: They didn't let writers on the set. It was just never done. Nobody wanted a writer around. But as I said, you never write a perfect script. There's a lot of improvement to be made.

BRADY: In this particular case, you were taking a television play, which ran fifty-three minutes or thereabouts—

CHAYEFSKY: Right, and making an hour-and-a-half movie out of it.

BRADY: —and expanding it. Was there any uncertainty in your mind about that expanded area?

CHAYEFSKY: It was very hard. We didn't expand it. We deepened it. There's no way of opening up that story any wider than it is. Essentially, it was a portrait, and a portrait can only be done in detail and depth. So instead of expanding it, we made it deeper. It was a nice little portrait.

BRADY: I see one motif in several of your films: the older or middle-aged man and the young woman, as found in *Middle of the Night, The Hospital* and *Network.*

CHAYEFSKY: I am a middle-aged guy, so I write about what I know, though I don't remember why I made the hero middle-aged in *Middle of the Night,* because I wasn't middle-aged at the time I wrote it. There must have been some sort of demand in the story for it. Generally speaking, in drama you create a set of incidents, and you develop characters to execute those incidents. The characters take shape in order to make the story true. Of course, nothing is ever that clear-cut in writing, but as a rule your character has to be capable of performing the incidents required by the story. I assume that's why the hero of *Middle of the Night* was made middle-aged.

BRADY: *The Latent Heterosexual* has satirical overtones that seem to have matured in your later work, notably *Hospital* and *Network*.

CHAYEFSKY: I don't know. I always thought of myself as writing satire. I thought *Marty* was a satire. In rehearsals of *Marty* for television, we all laughed like hell.

BRADY: You did?

CHAYEFSKY: It was character satire, satirizing lower-middle-class social values. But, of course, television has an audience of only two or three or four people at a time, and three and four people don't laugh; they cry a lot. Everybody came out crying. I was startled the first couple of times in television when I would call home and ask, "How'd you like it?" "Oh, God, we cried our eyes out." I didn't believe it. It amazed me. And then I realized that in television we were writing for criers, not for laughers.

I mention it only because I don't think I actively set out to be a satirist. I always thought I was. Even in college I wrote jingles, satirical sketches, things like that. I've got a somewhat weird perspective on things.

BRADY: How so?

CHAYEFSKY: Writers of comedy simply see things a little differently than most people and expose another aspect to the audience.

BRADY: What other moving targets do you see for satire?

CHAYEFSKY: I don't have an idea in my head right now.

BRADY: You once told William Goldman, "I came in on the end of the Great Broadway, and I belong to that generation that still thinks it does its best work for the theater. So I wrote plays and I do movies to make a living."

CHAYEFSKY: Now I write plays and I call them movies. They're still plays. I still write them in three-act structure. There are still a lot of set-piece scenes. I count on the director and a lot of other people to help it look more like a movie. But I also have a pretty good visual eye for movies . . . and I kind of know how to hide the seams now. At least I don't have the curtain dropping. In *Goddess* I actually put the legends *Act I, Act II, Act III* right up on the screen. I don't have intermissions anymore, but I still structure the story as if it were a play. The three-act structure is the form that I grew up in the theater with. You generally present a situation in Act I, and by the end of Act I the situation has evolved to a point where something is threatening the situation. In Act II you solve that problem, producing a more intense problem by the end of Act II. In Act III you solve that problem, either happily or unhappily, depending on whether you have a comedy or a tragedy or a drama: You work out a final solution accordingly. It sounds nice and pat, but it never really works that way. Nothing ever works that easily. But by now I kind of know—I can always get a feel: That's Act I . . . that belongs in Act III. You get a *feel* for it.

BRADY: Do these story fragments come at you from different directions?

CHAYEFSKY: They come out of a lot of talk with friends, or out of wandering around the streets, or sleeping . . . that's why it takes so long to write. You just have to let it go through you; you have to keep imagining. Then come bits and pieces, it gets here and there, and eventually it becomes a full thing.

BRADY: You say you write plays and call them movies. That seems a bit patronizing toward the business of making films.

CHAYEFSKY: Not at all. I would rather be doing movies than anything. All that statement represents is that my training is still that of a playwright. That's why I could never be a film director. I don't know much about mobility, in terms of film. I don't have that kind of sense. Go see Bob Fosse's *All That Jazz* or Lelouch's film *Cat and Mouse*. I sit there and marvel at the facility at which their minds dart around, just in terms of the technical mobility of the medium. I have no command of that at all. My stories move just like a play moves.

BRADY: Do you think of them as movies to be *listened* to?

CHAYEFSKY: I would be delighted to be able to cut the dialogue. I'm a very good cutter—but in the end they are talk pieces. When we go abroad we always have a lot of trouble because so many subtitles have to be put in. I tend to write a more literary type of screenplay than is proper for the medium.

BRADY: Allan Lewis, in *Contemporary Dramatists,* edited by James Vinson, says, "When he did not win full glory on Broadway, Chayefsky turned to Hollywood." Is that accurate?

CHAYEFSKY: He's got his facts all wrong. I was doing movies before I did Broadway. In 1954 I made my first movie with *Marty.* I didn't write plays until 1958. *Middle of the Night* was the first play I had on. In the course of doing my own research, I find that academics tend to get everything a little screwed up just to make their point. The fact is, I was writing for film in the 1940s. I sold *As Young As You Feel* at the end of 1948 or 1949. I went into television in 1953, and I sold *Marty* and did the screenplay of *Marty* in 1954. I must have done *Bachelor Party* a year or two later. Then I did a play, *Middle of the Night*—a big hit. Then I did the movie *The Goddess.* Then I did another play, *Tenth Man*—an enormous hit. So I had been doing movies long before I got to the theater.

You know, I never heard of Allan Lewis. Who is he?

BRADY: He wrote *The Contemporary Theater,* and the Vinson book is pretty standard reference for contemporary dramatists. Lewis says, too, that you turned to Broadway declaring that television was "not related to adult reality."

CHAYEFSKY: Oh, I know what he's talking about. I may have sometimes complained about the fact they wouldn't let you come to grips with certain things, yes. I had a lot of trouble in the TV show *Bachelor Party* having the girl say to her mother, "I'm pregnant." They didn't want me to use the word "pregnant." I mean, that kind of reality. But the real reason I left television was because by the time I came back from the filming of *Marty,* there was no television anthology left. It was all specials, spectaculars—and most of those were adaptations of plays. "Studio One" was still going, but it was starting to spread to one a month or something like that, and the pressures to do a television show were becoming so enormous that you might as well do them on

Broadway. The plain fact was that there was no television drama left.

BRADY: To stick with Mr. Lewis just a little bit further. He says that Paddy Chayefsky turned to Broadway, but "the television techniques pursued him," namely, "pat resolutions that are a bit too comfortable and reassuring."

CHAYEFSKY: I have no idea what that means. As a matter of fact, television techniques did pursue me, but that wasn't it. For example, could Mr. Lewis show me a play that doesn't have "pat resolutions"? How about *Hamlet?* How about *Romeo and Juliet?* How about *The Cherry Orchard?* I'm not quite sure what he means by that. When I did *Middle of the Night* on Broadway, I was, in fact, pursued by other television techniques. I never stopped to think there were eleven hundred people sitting in the audience. I remember telling Josh Logan, "That's not a laugh line; that's meant to be a chuckle." And Josh said, "But Paddy, eleven hundred chuckles make a loud noise." So I really had lost sight of what my audience was. In that sense, television technique pursued me. But this business with "pat answers," that's snobbism. All theater has pat answers.

How about *A Doll's House?* How about *Death of a Salesman?* They're all resolved. The whole point of the theater is, to paraphrase Arthur Miller, to bring one shred of meaning or insight into the otherwise meaningless life of the audience. The whole idea is there's a resolution, at least in the theater. It's more justifiable for a playwright to be pat than it is for a critic. We have, after all, to entertain an audience. Critics have no excuse for being pat. Critics don't have to entertain anybody.

BRADY: What's your attitude toward critics in general?

CHAYEFSKY: I never read them. I've never understood the mentality of a critic. Imagine, spending your life writing about somebody else's writing. I've never understood that.

BRADY: Well, I think that if people are going to pay fifteen or twenty-five dollars for a theater ticket, they do care, and people who have twenty to thirty films to choose from do want some guidance.

CHAYEFSKY: I'm not arguing whether they serve a function or not. I've just never understood why anybody would want to do it. I'm sure that that's their social function, to cull the wheat from the chaff for the benefit of their readers.

Walter Kerr is a fine writer. And damned perceptive. He's one of the few critics I've ever read and learned something from. He explained *Marat-Sade* to me a hell of a lot better than I understood it when I saw it myself.

BRADY: You've been quoted as saying you turned to the film because you were a "playwright who has no theater."

CHAYEFSKY: True. By the sixties anyway, there had been a very definite movement toward the director's theater, toward a kind of quasi-absurdist theater that I was simply uncomfortable in. I was completely out of fashion. So the theater sort of passed me by. I wrote in the old tradition.

BRADY: Then you moved back to films.

CHAYEFSKY: Yes.

BRADY: Well, in the foreword to your collection of television plays, you say that you cannot "calculate the debt I owe to television for the amount of sheer craft I have learned. I have achieved a discipline and a preciseness of thinking and even a certain notoriety upon which every writer feeds whether he admits it or not." Can you expand on the craft that you learned from TV writing?

CHAYEFSKY: Well, you learn by your mistakes. It's trial and error, really. You learn, for example, that if it's not right when you write it, it's never going to be solved by other people. The hole is going to show up. You learn to take the responsibility for the script. Nobody is going to write it for you but yourself.

You learn how to cut. Television is the greatest place to learn cutting because of the time limitations. They simply do not have time for indulgence; you've *got* to get the five minutes out. I think I cut as well as anybody in the whole world. Emlyn Williams used to be the best cutter in the world, I've been told. Somerset Maugham was a great cutter, I understand. Now I have Somerset Maugham's rules and I have Emlyn Williams' basic rule, and I have a whole bunch of my own rules.

BRADY: What are the rules?

CHAYEFSKY: Well, I'm not sure I'm quoting Somerset Maugham's rule absolutely correctly—you can get it from Garson Kanin; he told me the rule—but I think it is, "If it should occur to you to cut, do so." That's the first basic rule of cutting. If you're reading through and stop, something is wrong. Cut it. If something bothers you, then it's bad. Cut it. Somerset Maugham's rule is absolutely practical. It works. Josh Logan told me about Emlyn Williams' rule; he once saw Emlyn Williams cut forty minutes out of a play without cutting a cue—in other words, he cut within speeches. That's impossible, actually, to cut forty minutes without cutting a cue. But it's not a bad way to approach cutting. If you can cut inside the speech, you're really cutting most effectively.

BRADY: That's condensing.

CHAYEFSKY: It's purifying. It's refining. Making it precise. Precision is one of the basic elements of poetry. Economy, they used to call it. My own rules are very simple rules. First, cut out all the wisdom; then cut out all the adjectives. I've cut some of my favorite stuff. I have no compassion when it comes to cutting. No pity, no sympathy. Some of my dearest and most beloved bits of writing have gone with a very quick slash, slash, slash . . . these four pages out. Because something was heavy there. Cutting leads to economy, precision, and to a vastly improved script.

In TV you also learn to get along. You learn what it means to be with a lot of other high-strung nervous talent. You learn not to cry your heart out if you don't do well. You learn to go on because there's another show next week. You learn to say, "It's just another play, it's just another movie." We mustn't don the mantle of posterity every time we sit down to a typewriter. You learn to say, "Let the rest of the world worry about posterity. I'll just go on with what I want to do." You learn a lot of things.

BRADY: What about that "notoriety," though, as a fuel for the writer?

CHAYEFSKY: I think it's significant in his early years.

BRADY: Do you have to work at it? Is notoriety something that you are *conscious* of creating?

CHAYEFSKY: I think that when you're a kid you fantasize like hell about being a great writer, earning the plaudits of the world and the critical community and all of that. I don't really give much of a goddamn for approbation now, but I think wanting to be approved and acclaimed is basic when you're young. You've got to have reasons for going through the hell of writing. And until you get to learn to like it, one of the reasons is the need for acclaim, approbation, notoriety, celebrity.

BRADY: But initially you sought it as a basement on which to build a career?

CHAYEFSKY: You write to be published. You write to be a successful writer. Nobody writes calculatedly not to be. I have friends—fine writers—who have been writing for years who are not successful. More than anything else, they want to hit with just one book, just one.

BRADY: What effect does notoriety have on you? You were an Academy Award winner when you were barely thirty. You are *the* golden boy in every chapter written about television's golden age. Did it have any effect on your writing or on your temperament as a writer?

CHAYEFSKY: You learn to hate it. You learn to know it for the fraud it really is. The only real terrific satisfaction you get out of that is knowing that your colleagues think you're good: that's a wonderful feeling. However, if I were to advise my son, who is twenty-five, I would say that the most impure motives are useful for a writer—just to get your name in the columns is not an improper motivation for a writer, when you're a kid, when you're young. The need for fame and notoriety I think is part of the package that brings you into show business. That is not acceptable, though, once you start writing. Once you put the page in the typewriter or the notebook in front of you, and you start to write, then you have to write as well as you know how, whether it gets you fame or oblivion. I think you said earlier, for a fellow who doesn't like public attention, I'm in a pretty strange business. I mean, you get in this business to get attention, whether you like it or not.

BRADY: You can get it by trying to do without it, too. J. D. Salinger, for instance.

CHAYEFSKY: I try to keep my mouth shut and stay out of the media. I get attention by chance. It falls on me. I didn't ask Vanessa Redgrave to get up and make that stupid, vicious statement at the Academy Awards. I sat there praying somebody would say something. But I was not going to just sit there and let somebody make cracks about Jews without saying anything about it. Since nobody else said it, I said it. I would have been delighted not to have had to get into it. I sat around for two hours and nobody said anything. I did it for myself. But it seems to have been something a lot of people wanted said, and all of a sudden I had become visible again. I didn't try for it, believe me. And I've never seen so much mail in my life. I couldn't answer it. All of it disapproving of Redgrave.

BRADY: The year before when you asked Peter Finch's widow to come up on stage and accept his Oscar for *Network* . . .

CHAYEFSKY: It was Finchie's heritage; it was part of what he left his wife. It had nothing to do with me. Billy Friedkin seemed to think there was something sentimental in the gesture. "Billy," I said, "what the hell do you think the Academies are? This is *I am Mrs. Norman Main*. You can't throw away a moment like that." I never thought Peter Finch was going to win, by the way. They never give posthumous awards that I know of. Not even to Spencer Tracy, who was really one of the most beloved of actors.

BRADY: You are unique among writers in that your accomplishments are in all three areas of drama writing: television, the Broadway stage and movies. Is it a matter of flexing different muscles within you as a writer? Or is it skillfully marketing your talents as a dramatist? Or is it a sense of development—outgrowing one and moving on to another?

CHAYEFSKY: Damned if I know, John. I don't know how it works. I most prefer, and originally I come out of, the tradition in which a writer does his best work for the stage. I tried to transfer that tradition to the movies, but movies have become too expensive.

BRADY: There's such an emphasis on the monster hit.

CHAYEFSKY: They cost so much to make, you have to have a monster hit to pay it off. It's a joke. They're pricing themselves out of production. I mean, *Marty* cost four hundred thousand dollars something like twenty-five years ago. *Hospital,* done in 1971, two million dollars. *Network,* three and a half million dollars. A picture today automatically has a budget of five million under the line. Five million in just *costs,* not counting salaries. Special effects and other costs are unpredictable. The picture may go between ten and fifteen million dollars. It's becoming insane. For a picture to cost ten to fifteen million dollars means you've got to make between thirty and forty-five million dollars in rentals. Three pictures a year do that. They're making it so it's almost impossible to make a film.

BRADY: From what you said earlier, you get the best talent you can, and I assume it's often the highest-paid talent.

CHAYEFSKY: It frequently works that way; it's not necessarily the case.

BRADY: When you're writing a script, do you think in terms of who is going to direct the film?

CHAYEFSKY: I do, but I try not to. There are very few really terrific directors around. A handful. There are very few terrific anything around.

BRADY: Does a director working for your company have all the latitude that a director traditionally has?

CHAYEFSKY: Absolutely. With the single exception that the script is written by me. But I see to it that he is happy with the script before he goes on the floor.

BRADY: Does shepherding a screenplay into production cut into your writing time?

CHAYEFSKY: The production is all part of the screenplay. Casting, art directors, special effects—they're all part of the writer's job.

BRADY: Which part of screenwriting do you find the most fun, the most elevating?

CHAYEFSKY: I really don't know, but I expect it's probably finally getting that original concept. When you finally say, "Oh boy, what an idea for a picture." But there are many terrific moments along the way. Each scene has some. You come in tired, you sit down, you begin to boil up a little, and pretty soon things are moving—you have a lucky day and things click and all of a sudden synapses start picking up things you had forgotten and eight, nine and ten good pages come out, while previously it took three weeks before you had one paragraph come out. And you write something you say is terrific, to yourself. These kinds of satisfactions occur often; otherwise you couldn't keep at it. It's a year and a half, two years' work, a good original script.

When I had this terrific idea for a picture, *Altered States,* I wrote it up as a novel first. I'll never do that again—that's for sure.

BRADY: Was it done in tandem with your screenplay?

CHAYEFSKY: No, I did the screenplay after I wrote the novel. The screenplay was much better than the novel. I always write a prose treatment. I write about half the story in prose to keep order among all the elements of the plot so I don't get stuck when I do the screenplay. So somebody said, "You put hard covers on that, and they will call it a novel." But it has always been a treatment for a movie to me. I still haven't learned to call it a novel. I still refer to it as "the script." Unfortunately, by the time I'd written the damned thing and rewritten it for the publishers, and by the time it got into hardback, I was so bored with it I could barely bring myself even to look at the screenplay. I'll never go that route again. To keep doing the same thing over and over is very tiresome.

The novel did comfortably well, but I'm not a novelist, and I don't care much to be one. I consider writing novels déclassé. I think it's much classier to write screenplays and dramas than it is to write novels—after all, drama has been around since the Orphic rites; the novel has been around only since Cervantes or thereabouts. It's a much more demanding medium, drama. Far more demanding than novel writing. When I sat down to do the screenplay for *Altered States,* all the holes came out. You can get away with a lot in prose that you can't get away with at all in drama. I threw out seventy pages of screenplay because I tried to follow the book, and it didn't work. I started from scratch and went back and did a proper screenplay.

BRADY: What sort of writing habits do you maintain?

CHAYEFSKY: I stop off, get a container of Sanka, come upstairs. Ordinarily the cover is off the typewriter. I take those last eight or nine or ten pages, and I start rereading and cutting through it, changing it, and trying to build up the momentum from the day before. And then, with luck, you carry it home with you that night. And you just keep going, because by that time you'll have had your treatment, you'll have worked out your scenes, you'll know what you want; what you're trying now to do is to produce a variety of things, but one of those things is life. You're trying to produce and create a moment of life that people will believe. On top of that, you're trying to produce a certain theatricality. Beyond that, you're trying to make something entertaining. There are a lot of things you're trying to do. There's a lot of fun along the way, and there are many agonizing holes of depression. Real abysses of despair. But frankly, once you get your treatment down, it's a lot easier.

BRADY: You sit right there from nine to five?

CHAYEFSKY: I usually get in half-past nine, quarter to ten, and on a workday I work to one-thirty. Then as leisurely a lunch as I can manage, and, depending on how I feel, I bum around or go back to work or go over to the gym. If you can get in four good hours a day, you're in terrific shape.

BRADY: Do you ever have any stretches where you just can't write?

CHAYEFSKY: Sure. It's a form of despair and impotence, and the only way I know is to just grind at it and grind at it and get it done, even if you don't like it. When you read it later, you'll wonder, "What was it that bothered me?" Sometimes the despair can go on for a couple of years. That, of course, is disaster. It happened to me once. Just horrible.

BRADY: What years would those be?

CHAYEFSKY: After the Russian play.

BRADY: You're often praised for your "tape recorder dialogue." Do you ever dictate or use a tape recorder?

CHAYEFSKY: No. I write laboriously worked-out dialogue. There's no tape recording involved at all.

BRADY: Would you say, then, that dialogue is all a form of condensing?

CHAYEFSKY: I wouldn't say it's all that. I have a flair for it, but mostly what I do is I cut very well. I can think of several writers who can write finer dialogue than I do. This guy in England writes brilliant dialogue, Tom Stoppard. Raphael, the guy who wrote *Two for the Road* and had *The Glittering Prizes* on TV. A brilliant British playwright—Ayckbourn or something like that —does terrific dialogue. My dialogue is precise. And it's true. I think out the truth of what the people are saying and why they're saying it.

BRADY: Your dialogue is somewhat epigrammatic.

CHAYEFSKY: It's stylized. That's one of the reasons Bill Holden had trouble at first. Finch had no trouble, because he comes from a stylized theater. But Bill got it later. I remember in *The Americanization of Emily,* Jimmy Garner realized he was working mostly with phrasing rather than realism. I can write naturalistic dialogue. There's no problem. In TV I wrote a great deal of it. I have a good ear for language, for idiom. But recently it's very difficult dialogue I give actors; it's stylized and it's supposed to be real at the same time. Very tough for actors.

BRADY: How do lines come to you? Do you have the dialogue first and then build the scene around it? In *Hospital,* someone says to entrepreneur Dr. Welbeck, "You ought to be investigated by the Securities and Exchange Commission, not a board of doctors."

CHAYEFSKY: That's a gag, not real dialogue.

BRADY: Or another doctor, "forgotten to death in the Emergency Room."

CHAYEFSKY: Dialogue comes because I know what I want my characters to say. I envision the scene; I can imagine them up there on the screen; I try to imagine what they would be saying and how they would be saying it, and I keep it in character. And the dialogue comes out of that. I think that goes for every writer in the world. Then I rewrite it. Then I cut it. Then I refine it until I get the scene as precise as I can get it.

BRADY: Do you ever deal in stage directions for the director?

CHAYEFSKY: I write master scenes which include master shots and certain close-ups. I do not expect a director to go along with them. It is simply the way I would shoot it if I were doing the directing. Often as not the director will use them because there's nothing startling in what I'm suggesting. But the main thing is I write a master scene. And I write stage directions in, as I would on a stage play: *He crosses the room quickly, opens the window and leaps out.* I do not describe what setups the camera should be set up for in order to pick up that action. I sometimes write stage directions so the script will read well, so that when the director reads it, he will get a feeling for what I'm trying to get. But I rarely write specific shots in. Sometimes I write specific shots in because it is the only way I know to get the damn scene moving. If I wrote it all in stage directions, it would be interminable. So I'll say, *Reverse shot looking across Joe's shoulder onto Mary's face;* and in one line I've wiped away a ton of stage directions. Then I'll go on to the dialogue. But not for a moment do I expect the director to use a reverse there if he doesn't want to.

BRADY: I should think your television writing taught you to work with camera techniques in mind.

CHAYEFSKY: I never learned the camera. Live television, which I worked for, had, I think, four shots. You shot straight ahead; you shot from forty-five degrees this way, from forty-five degrees that way; and you shot close-ups. There was nothing to it. Don't forget, we did live shows in old radio studios where you couldn't put the camera up high and you couldn't move it far away. It was just four setups, and that was it. I have a pretty good idea of what I like to look at up there on the screen when I write, but I am perfectly willing to defer to people with better visual eyes. Directors, as a rule, have better visual concepts than I do.

BRADY: Even small roles in your films are memorable. I envision actors and actresses clamoring to get into a Chayefsky picture when word gets around.

CHAYEFSKY: You've got me; I have no idea. As I say, I have as little to do with casting as possible. I know when the actor is wrong; I don't know when he's right for the part.

BRADY: What do you mean by that?

CHAYEFSKY: I mean I'll say, "No, that actor is wrong." But I will rarely say, "That's the right actor. I want that actor." I don't think I've ever said that. I really don't know that much about acting. And I'm not sure that what the actor is showing me is what I should look for. I do know the wrong quality when I see it. If the director says, "I think he'll be terrific," I'll say, "As far as I see, he has the right quality. I'm sure he'll be good." Sometimes I know the actors, of course. "Oh," I'll say, "he can play anything." Most shows I've done are filled with actors I've never met before.

BRADY: You're generally working with strangers?

CHAYEFSKY: Professional strangers are not strangers long. It's very compressed atmosphere, making a film. You get to be very close friends very fast. I never met Peter Finch before *Network*. I'd met Bill Holden fifteen years earlier. Twice maybe. I'd met Faye once in my life and never met Bobby Duvall. I consider all of them good friends now.

BRADY: Do you ever work with a collaborator on a script?

CHAYEFSKY: Never in my life. I just don't think the same way other writers do. I never met a writer who felt the same as I do.

BRADY: On some of your adaptations, did you ever work with the original author on a property?

CHAYEFSKY: Tried to, but in the end I just went off on my own. For example, *Cincinnati Kid,* which I couldn't lick.

BRADY: As president of the company that produces your films, the only writer you have to deal with then is yourself?

CHAYEFSKY: Right. And my contracts say the script must be shot as written.

BRADY: Is there much unfinished business in your writing life? Do you often abandon a project after starting it?

CHAYEFSKY: Yes. Many times. I wrote one about the Dead Sea Scrolls called *The Habakkuk Conspiracy* that never got on. Then I wrote a show about a trade convention. You know, one of these gatherings where all the people meet in McCormick Hall in Chicago for three days of sales and trades. I was going to make a film out of it, but I couldn't. I put it away. It's still hanging around somewhere in a carton. My partner wants me to go back to it, but I still don't think I can lick it. *Network* was the result of an idea that I'd abandoned two or three years earlier.

BRADY: Why did you abandon it?

CHAYEFSKY: I couldn't lick it.

BRADY: What was the problem?

CHAYEFSKY: I don't remember. I just kept saying, "Goddamn it, Howard, I know there's a movie in television. Let's go do it again." We went back to it, and it worked the second time. Very often I don't get the idea executed the first time out.

BRADY: You have chastised television, observing, "There's a substantial thing called America with a very complicated, pluralistic society that is worth honest presentation. If I were in charge of a network, I would insist that one-third at least of prime time be used to depict that, whether people watch it or not, because some people will watch it."

CHAYEFSKY: Yes, that quote's true. I said that. I don't know where I said it, but I said it.

BRADY: You said it in *Time*. With that thought in mind, why aren't you writing for television today? Aren't you biting the hand that fed your talents pretty well?

CHAYEFSKY: No, I'm not biting anything. I look back at my year in television as one of the fondest memories I have. I was only in it for a year. I'm not writing for television for a lot of reasons. One is, I can't get any control in television. For example, NBC wanted to do *The War Against the Jews*. That's before they did *Holocaust*. I said the subject was simply too painful for me to write about. But if I had agreed to do it for television, I'd have had to make a soap opera of the whole thing. You'd have to get high emotional moments, regularly, because you have these damn ten-minute intervals all the time. You can never really accumulate the power; you have to capsulize a lot of emotion, and you have to overdramatize things. In fact, the word critics used on *Holocaust* was "trivialize," and in a sense that was an unfair criticism, even though accurate. Trivialization *is* television. What did they expect? But let's say that they had agreed not to have a commercial every ten minutes. Let's say I sat down and I wrote a nine- or ten- or twelve-hour show, which is what they wanted. That's five or six years of work. And in the end they're not going to let me do it. They're going to cut it any way they want to cut it. They're not going to give me the final control. I don't mean final cut. I mean they're not going to let the script go through. They want to make it their way because they have to sell it to mass advertisers. So there is no way I could really get into television. I tried a couple of years ago. I wrote a pilot for a series, a sitcom.

BRADY: What was it?

CHAYEFSKY: A show with Jimmy Coco: *Your Place or Mine?* NBC backed off on it. It was about the singles scene in New York. It was nice, kind of fun. I thought I might enjoy doing it. Boy, am I glad they turned me down. Imagine getting into *that* hysterical society again.

BRADY: I assume it would be something that you would sell and then move on.

CHAYEFSKY: No, no, I meant to write them all.

BRADY: You envisioned doing the twenty-six shows a year?

CHAYEFSKY: Twenty-two, I think. It looked like it would be kind of fun. I wrote the pilot in two weeks. I haven't done anything that fast in a long time.

BRADY: Television does have the ability to do the long, documentarylike program that's unique.

CHAYEFSKY: And, in a curious way, without drama: a parade of things that happen, that have no real drama to them. It's a curious medium. I don't know how to write it.

BRADY: You indicate with the writing of *Network* and in some personal comments that the television networks have been consumed by an unhealthy concern for ratings. But weren't there rating wars even in the fifties when you were writing for television?

CHAYEFSKY: Yes, but there's more money involved now. That's why there is no drama in television. It doesn't get good ratings. When we're talking about ratings, we're talking about dollars. That's all ratings mean. One rating point is millions and millions of dollars. It's just more profitable not to have dramas, so they don't have them. They have series. Series is not drama. Series is a bunch of people that the audience gets to be ingratiated by, and they tune in to see these people week in and week out, regardless of the quality of the drama.

BRADY: How golden was TV's golden age?

CHAYEFSKY: I was only there for a year, and it sure was golden in the sense of friends and stimulation in Bohemia. Nobody made any money. I worked for nine hundred dollars a script.

BRADY: Was that your top fee?

CHAYEFSKY: No, the top I got was three thousand. The last fee I ever got. For *Marty,* it was nine hundred. I wrote nine one-hour shows, I got seventeen thousand dollars in one year. That's the equivalent of three full-length plays, or four movies.

BRADY: I thought you did eleven shows.

CHAYEFSKY: Nine hour shows; two half-hour shows.

BRADY: What's your opinion of television for the beginning writer today?

CHAYEFSKY: Well, I know nothing at all about television writing anymore. There is none that I know of. There are TV Movies of the Week, but that's a special form that requires something written in ten-minute segments, which is very unusual kind of drama; I don't really know how to do that. I will say this: There's a lot of writing going on in television. There's a lot of drama— usually a series, which is not really writing. But it still remains a hell of a way to learn how to write. An enormous market for writers. But some inner integrity had better keep you from falling into that terrible trap of earning a very good living at television writing if you want to get to some real good writing. At the moment it doesn't look like you can do really good writing in television.

BRADY: Do the rating codes affect your screenwriting? Do you know what code you're aiming for from the first page, or does that sort of thinking come later?

CHAYEFSKY: Well, I couldn't conceivably write an X if I wanted to. R seems to be my style. That's, of course, because of the language. But if the thing isn't an R, then it'll be a GP. I don't need to use profanity.

BRADY: There's a pretty heavy amount of swearing in *Network*.

CHAYEFSKY: There was more than actually is true, but there's a lot of cussing in television circles.

BRADY: How did you find that out? It's rather unflattering vocabulary for a profession.

CHAYEFSKY: Walter Cronkite doesn't swear much. John Chancellor doesn't. Peter Finch didn't in my picture. The only thing he ever said was, "I ran out of bullshit." That's the only time he ever used a dirty word. Many of the executives swear like troopers. I overdid it; I wanted to cut some out, and I didn't, and I'm sorry I didn't.

BRADY: Was there any difficulty selling *Network* to TV in view of the thin skins there?

CHAYEFSKY: The point of *Network* is that the networks will do anything for a rating. Somebody at Metro thought we'd never be able to sell it to television. We said, "You're nuts. All it has to do is be a hit; they'll buy it like a shot." It's got four terrific names in it. It's a great TV thing, and it was bought by CBS almost immediately after it became a hit. But if you leave the editing of a film, the censoring of a film, up to the TV cutters and editors in their Standards and Practices Department, they'll cut vital scenes to get rid of one dirty word. Rather than leave it to them, we made our own sanitized sound track; it's not really sanitized, but we accommodated the conventions of television. We got rid of the dirty words. And we cut out the vague suggestion of nudity that was in the film, of which there was practically none. That doesn't mean that CBS won't chop it up to suit themselves anyway, but they'd be foolish to do so. If they have it for a couple of runs, they'd be crazy to destroy their second audience by making a mess out of the first.

BRADY: I have a quote from Lin Bolen—

CHAYEFSKY: I don't know her.

BRADY: —in *New York* magazine: "When I went to a screening," Lin Bolen told a reporter, "and Dunaway got up there and said, 'I'm tellin' you, this fuckin' show is gonna be a fuckin' hit,' I wanted to go under the seat. It wasn't me. I could have said some of those speeches, but it kind of makes me feel sad to think that someone perceived me that way."

CHAYEFSKY: I never perceived her in my life. I don't know who she is.

BRADY: Lin Bolen is the former head of daytime programming at NBC.

CHAYEFSKY: The reason Lin Bolen identifies with this picture is that Faye Dunaway wanted to meet a woman executive in television. So my partner, who comes from television—he probably knows Lin Bolen, I don't know—called Lin Bolen and said, "Would you mind if Faye Dunaway followed you around for a day?" I didn't know about that until about a week ago. But I have never met Lin Bolen; I still don't know who she is. The Faye Dunaway character is *me*. It wasn't modeled on anybody.

BRADY: According to Louise Farr in *New York* magazine, Lin Bolen "knew something was up well before the movie came out when Paddy Chayefsky was observed taking notes in the corridors of NBC."

CHAYEFSKY: That's true. I was up in NBC with John Chancellor, an old pal of mine. We were going through the newsroom, watching how they do it. That's all. I never met a Lin Bolen up there, though. I'm a little tired of hearing people tell me about Lin Bolen. I never heard of her.

BRADY: Was *Network* researched on the scene at different networks, or was it written for the most part from your own experience in the television wars?

CHAYEFSKY: I went to NBC because I'm closer to NBC and

the people there than at any other network. Peter Finch spent some time, I think, with John Chancellor. We also visited ABC and CBS. Walter Cronkite is a close personal friend of director Sidney Lumet's, and a friend of mine. Somebody took us around the executive offices at CBS.

BRADY: So you were doing on-the-spot research for texture, not for story line or character development?

CHAYEFSKY: No, not at all. I just wanted to know what the reality of it was. What is the normal day in the life of an anchorman, for example.

BRADY: Do you have any help when you do research? Do you do all of your own?

CHAYEFSKY: Yes. The more farcical the story, the more authentic I want the details.

BRADY: So everything in *Hospital* and *Network* is plausible.

CHAYEFSKY: Medical journals gave *Hospital* our best notices. And all of them said pretty much the same thing: *At last, what really happens in a hospital.* What it's really like to struggle in a hospital. They all agreed it is authentic. There isn't one inaccurate inch in that picture.

BRADY: The notion of someone getting in a hospital to take revenge on an institution is a bit remote, don't you think?

CHAYEFSKY: Whatever the case, the way the character killed them was authentic. Everything that happened in that picture happened in a hospital somewhere at sometime. Now, most people who go into a hospital to this day call me up and say, "Jesus, you weren't kidding! That's exactly the case!" *Network* wasn't even a satire. I wrote a realistic drama. The industry satirizes itself. As *TV Guide*'s George Slaughter said, *Network* was a documentary, not a satire.

BRADY: There is a "happy news" format, of course, but "the soothsayer" in *Network* seems remote, don't you think?

CHAYEFSKY: There will be soothsayers soon. Do you think what's happening over there at ABC News—the "happy" news —is much different from what I said was going to happen? Instead of turning it over to Programming, they're turning it over to Sports. What's the difference? It's all going to happen.

BRADY: Where did you get the idea for the scene in which the Faye Dunaway character goes to bed with Holden and talks about ratings. How does a scene like that come to you?

CHAYEFSKY: I don't know how it came to me. I had a lot of exposition to put in and that struck me as the funniest way to get it in. Also, it was necessary that the love story proceed. The love story is the core of the picture. It's a metaphorical love story: she represents television; he represents humanity; and it's the core story.

BRADY: Yet the first line of the script is "This story is about Howard Beale, who is the network news anchorman on UBS." And the closing line is "This was the story of Howard Beale, who was the network news anchorman on UBS." *Network* seems to me to be a profile of someone caught in the anguish of working for a network; the love affair comes across as secondary.

CHAYEFSKY: All the anguish and all the networks must be reduced to some kind of personality drama; you have to be represented by people. Television networks are represented in the script by the Faye Dunaway character. And we have to tell her personal story, her drama. The love story is the important story to me because the love story incorporates the metaphorical characters. They represent the important aspects of the theme. Sure, the story is also the story of Howard Beale, but that's on a lesser level, from a structural point of view anyway. In order to structure the piece, the love story is the thing I used to build the story of *Network*.

BRADY: Where did you get the idea for the scene in which Peter Finch has everyone roll their windows down and yell, "I'm as mad as hell and I'm not going to take this anymore!"

CHAYEFSKY: I just made it up. That's one of those things you count on from impetus. You're writing and writing and all of a sudden it starts to build and build and build, and then come those moments I told you about where things click and you get these images and ideas and everything works.

BRADY: In *Hospital,* too, George Scott goes to a window and shouts out of it, "I love you!" Is this something you're fond of —if you can't say it, shout it?

CHAYEFSKY: It never occurred to me. It's just that here's a guy who couldn't say, "I love you" to her; he had to say it to somebody, a crack of emotion in a rigidly controlled personality.

BRADY: In both *Hospital* and *Network,* you use a narrator. What determines that device?

CHAYEFSKY: Otherwise there would have been too much exposition to write. I don't like narrators, unless it's a matter of saving twenty minutes of film—if you can tell twenty minutes in five lines. I used a narrator in *Altered States,* too. I'm into very highly specialized areas here. The audience doesn't recognize things instantly; you have to tell them what it is.

BRADY: When you're writing a script, are you mindful of time? How long is a film allowed to be?

CHAYEFSKY: I just write it until it ends.

BRADY: You don't think of it in terms of a certain number of film minutes?

CHAYEFSKY: You kind of get a feel that this picture has to go around two hours, maybe two hours, five minutes. Something like that. You get a feel for it, but you don't worry about that in the script. Not in the first draft, no.

BRADY: The first draft is likely to be a long draft, I assume; then the cutting begins.

CHAYEFSKY: One hundred and seventy pages. By the time I send it in, it's one sixty. I'd rather overshoot than undershoot. Then we go through it carefully to cut out scenes that we know we are not going to shoot. Then we start pruning and cutting until we get it down into the tightest shape we can before shooting. That's usually around a hundred and forty pages. Trimming is mostly heads and tails of scenes, and things that we felt we needed for sequence, but are now recognizably unnecessary. I'd say the final cut—if there is such a thing as a final-cut script after editing, after shooting—would be around one hundred and twenty-five pages.

BRADY: Wolf Rilla, in his *The Writer and the Screen,* says that directors often have their own distinct style no matter who wrote the screenplay. "However, there are also screenwriters who are not their own directors and yet whose distinctive styles stand out in their films. Carl Foreman is one of these and Paddy Chayefsky another."

CHAYEFSKY: Doc Simon, Mel Brooks, Woody Allen. Of course, both Mel and Woody Allen are director-performers as well; but Doc has a very distinctive style that stands out no matter who directs them. A director with a very highly individualized style will still have that style come through, no matter who wrote the script. Sidney Lumet's style is very powerful. That's why we got Sidney, because we wanted his style. But Rilla is right, certain writers have a sufficiently strong style to withstand the impact of other contributors.

BRADY: He goes on to say, though, "It's perhaps significant that in both these cases"—that is, Foreman and yourself—"the writers are also usually the producers of their films."

CHAYEFSKY: That's true, too.

BRADY: Is it a little bit like being the boss's son?

CHAYEFSKY: No, it's like being the boss. You take the same responsibilities. I'm not, in fact, the producer. I'm the president of the company that made the film, and that's the boss. But you make the same decisions that any boss would make. It's not an empty title. You take the responsibility of bringing that picture in on budget.

BRADY: Bill Goldman maintains that it's misleading to compare a film to the novel on which it is based. Is it likewise unfair to compare a film to the play on which it is based?

CHAYEFSKY: True. They're all very distinct.

BRADY: As the adapter of several plays, can you make any comparisons of your own?

CHAYEFSKY: Comparisons of that sort are academic, and I'm not very good at that. A play is manifestly different from a screenplay. You've got a stage, a proscenium; you've got an audience sitting there that knows it's in a theater. They are willing to accept all kinds of conventions that go with the theater. It's a different discipline, almost a different genre. Film is a much more permissive—and in that sense, a much more difficult—medium. When I decide to make a play, I imagine a stage. When I decide to write a movie, I imagine a screen. You imagine what you want to see on the screen or on the stage, which creates different visual approaches. They're alike in that they are both dramas, but they are different disciplines.

BRADY: You seem as out of place on *Paint Your Wagon* as does Lee Marvin carrying a tune.

CHAYEFSKY: I sure was.

BRADY: What happened on that?

CHAYEFSKY: I was broke and they called me up and I said, "Yeah, I'll try it." I'd never written a western before. I tried it, and Lord knows I worked a long time on it, and I handed it in. I had some very good stuff in it. And then they rewrote everything. I don't think there were six pages of mine left in the whole picture. A couple of my ideas were left but barely recognizable. So I asked to have my name taken off. I was given a credit: "Adapted by." Whatever that means. I did not want the screenplay credit. It wasn't my screenplay.

BRADY: What was the thinking in asking you to do it? It was such an unusual casting, too.

CHAYEFSKY: I don't know. There are fellows who write westerns much better than I do and who write musical comedy much better than I do. It was not a good idea to get me—I never licked it, really. I do not include it in my list of credits.

BRADY: What do you look for in a novel that makes you say, "Yes, this can be a good screenplay"?

CHAYEFSKY: With any luck it might have a good last scene. That's about all. Some books are written to be filmed. My *Altered States* was conceived as a film from the beginning. Most books are slipshod, put together in a very makeshift manner, and you have to do a considerable amount of revision just to make the story sensible. Some writers have instincts for the film—Bill Goldman's books tend to make good and easy films. But generally speaking, you have to start pretty well from scratch with most books. Full of holes. Prose. You get away with murder in prose.

BRADY: What was your approach to *The Americanization of Emily* as adapter?

CHAYEFSKY: I made the whole thing up. For one thing, it was originally a serious drama. The book is very serious. I thought an admiral wandering around London saying that the most important thing to do in the war was to make a training film showing that Navy frogmen were the first people to hit the beaches of Normandy was nutty. That struck me as funny. I said to the producer, "You guys won't let me do it, but if you don't mind going for a comedy, this thing could be funny as hell." They said, "OK, we'll do it." I said, "You're not going to rewrite it on me or change it?" They said, "No," so I said, "Let's go," and I rewrote the entire book. I'll tell you what was good about the book. It was remarkably authentic. I did a considerable amount of research on that picture, too, but I needn't have had to, because the book itself, the details of D day particularly, was absolutely accurate. William Bradford Huie's a wonderful reporter. I couldn't catch him in one mistake in the reportage. And I read more books on the details of D day than you can imagine.

BRADY: Your screenplays are often heavily thematic—

CHAYEFSKY: They're always thematic.

BRADY: —and *The Americanization of Emily* was called "a spinning comedy that says more for basic pacifism than a fistful of intellectual tracts" in John Wakeman's *World Authors*.

CHAYEFSKY: Well, that's nice; I thought it did, too. I wasn't making a plea for pacifism; I was simply saying let's accept the fact that war is a part of the human character and find ways of avoiding it rather than saying it's an aberration in the human character. It's a genetic reality in man's character, man's nature. But if we deal with this as a reality rather than an aberration, we can maybe avoid wars.

BRADY: *Hospital,* too, was a dark comedy in which the incompetence of the hospital staff seems to represent the collapse of society.

CHAYEFSKY: It's a microcosm-of-society type of picture. The hospital represented a highly advanced, affluent, marvelously technological society that simply could not run itself.

BRADY: As a screenwriter, does theme merely emerge from the content, or is it something you are consciously aware of as you work along?

CHAYEFSKY: The best thing that can happen is for the theme to be nice and clear from the beginning. Doesn't always happen. You think you have a theme and you then start telling the story. Pretty soon the characters take over and the story takes over and you realize your theme isn't being executed by the story, so you start changing the theme. Now *Hospital* had a different ending originally. The ending was the familiar one of the sixties—everybody runs off to the hills. To hell with the hospital, and to hell with society—I'm going off to live the simple life in the mountains of Mexico with my girl. But I turned to my partner and said, "Well, Jesus, Howard, we're not running off, we're still here. We're telling a lie. Why are we saying run off when we're not running off?" When we realized that we were here, we examined our own motives and decided we were here because we were responsible middle-class people who didn't believe in running away. So I changed the theme and the ending to go with it.

BRADY: Had the original ending been shot?

CHAYEFSKY: No, this was in the writing stage.

BRADY: How do you arrive at the names of your characters?

CHAYEFSKY: Names are fun. In *Hospital* I used a lot of mystery writers. Had a nurse named Christie. A doctor is named Chandler. Sometimes I go to baseball box scores and pick out names. Sometimes I keep characters from one project to another—Arthur Landau, a lawyer, runs through a variety of things.

BRADY: Robert Towne says, "No matter how much you worked on a script, no matter how well you know the characters, if an actor is really good, he will know more about the character than you." Do you think that that's true?

CHAYEFSKY: If the actor is any good, he'll give body and fiber to the character. He's the one who presents it to the audience, so whatever he puts forth as the character is, in fact, the character. I expect technically that's true.

BRADY: Gore Vidal quotes an axiom used by someone he calls the Wise Hack at the Writers' Table in the MGM commissary "for the benefit of us alien integers from the world of Quality Lit, 'Shit has its own integrity.' " Then Vidal says, "It was plain to him (if not to the front office) that since we had come to Hollywood only to make money, our pictures would entirely lack the one basic homely ingredient that spells boffo worldwide grosses. The Wise Hack was not far from wrong. He knew that the sort of exuberant badness which so often achieves perfect popularity cannot be faked."

CHAYEFSKY: That's true. A good writer cannot write badly on purpose. In literature there are some who claim they have done it, like Arnold Bennett, who was supposed to have written trash for a living, and *The Old Wives' Tale* for glory. But the plain truth is a good writer cannot write badly. Shakespeare took a conventional story of his time about a ninth- or tenth-century Danish prince—a crude, one-generation Christianized, still-praying-to-tree-spirits type of prince—and he wrote his idea of Hamlet. Shakespeare probably set out to do a nice piece of commercial theater. But he couldn't help himself; in the end he wrote it the best he could, and he wrote it lousy in many areas because you can't take a crude story and make it into something elegant. He got into all kinds of trouble on that. It's just sheer genius that it plays as well as it does. No, I don't think a good writer can write badly. Yes, I think that many times a successful film is shit. There's no doubt about it. Lord knows they come up often enough. That doesn't preclude the fact that a good film can be successful. That's still possible. It's hard. But it can be done.

BRADY: Are you on a set much when a film is underway?

CHAYEFSKY: I'm on the set all day, every day. I'm at dailies every day. I'm in the editing room throughout. I'm in all the preproduction, and all the postproduction.

BRADY: Is it work that you enjoy?

CHAYEFSKY: I love editing. I hate sound mixing. I have no ear for it at all. But I'm there anyway, just in case.

BRADY: Bill Goldman said that the most exciting day in a screenwriter's life is his first day on the set, and the dullest day in the screenwriter's life is the second day on the set.

CHAYEFSKY: The first day is dull, too. It is impossible for anybody to enjoy watching the making of a movie in terms of interest. You enjoy the making of a movie in terms of friendship. And when those occasional moments come up where you have to pay attention, then it becomes creative. But it's mostly the lighting of sets, and how much can you enjoy watching somebody change bulbs in a lamp? It goes on for hours. But there's great camaraderie and a great deal of other work that goes on while all that lighting and construction are going on: conferences, discussions, things like that. It can be very interesting. I enjoy shooting films.

Truffaut said it in *Day for Night:* "You always start off saying, 'I'm going to make a great film.' Then when you finally get it down on paper, you say, 'This is going to make a damn good film.' But around the third week of shooting, all you want to do is get it over with. Just finish the damn thing."

BRADY: What is the work cycle? You spoke of four years on the job.

CHAYEFSKY: It's two years to do the script. There's a little bit longer that goes into negotiation. The real work in film is surrounded by an excess of appointments. The business of filmmaking is overdecorated with business. You're constantly involved in meetings, making deals, negotiating and lawyers. It goes on endlessly. That takes a good deal of time, too.

You'll find that most people, most writers, most any creative people in the film business will generally talk "deal" with you all the time rather than talk "film"; and I frankly don't like to talk either deal or film. Or they'll talk "industry." We call it "show business," and that it is: the business dominates so much of the time. In fact, in our interview, I'm sure, eighty percent has been about the business of film.

Then comes preproduction, the gathering of the film together, which is dependent on so many people's dates. Say we are after a particular special-effects man on our picture. If we can talk him into doing it, then we're pretty sure we can go for, say, an October shooting date. At which point we start trying to find the other production personnel and nailing them down to an October shooting date. And if you're using stars, then you may be in a lot of trouble because stars may not be available in October. Or we can have trouble finding a production manager for October. For some fluky reason, everybody in New York is hired. So you find yourself delaying months and months and months.

Finally, you shoot the picture—that takes three months, maybe; and you have three, four months of editing sound, music, all the work that goes into postproduction. You really do a full day's work on that, every day. And there's advertising and there's campaigns and there's distribution, and you find yourself screaming and yelling, carrying on because, frankly, the biggest talent in this business is not in the distributors' ranks. They have a great cunning *not* to make money. They work on a failure principle. They know how to deal with flops. But they really don't know what to do with hits. And they lose millions of dollars every year because they simply don't know how to distribute their own films.

By then you hope you've thought up another idea, because before you know it, it's another four years and the film is out.

BRADY: In an age of violence on the screen, you appear to be the thinking man's screenwriter. What is your attitude toward violence as an element of drama on the screen or in the screenplay?

CHAYEFSKY: There's no avoiding the fact that this is an age of violence, and if we are going to be dealing with truth, violence should be part of the movie world. I think, of course, that most screen violence is porno-violence, that is to say, the exploitation of violence: violence put on simply to attract an audience, not because it is a true depiction. I think I said earlier, there is a great deal of this society that is not violent and that never seems to be much portrayed. If you were to watch American television long enough, you would swear that the whole country was a bunch of pimps and prostitutes and gangsters and policemen in boots. In point of fact, as violent a country as we are, it is still a minority condition. There are many more problems besides violence.

BRADY: Do you see any violence being used in a Chayefsky screenplay?

CHAYEFSKY: If necessary.

BRADY: Is there any one screenplay that has given you the most satisfaction as both script and film? Is there any ranking or grouping?

CHAYEFSKY: I don't know if writers' opinions in these matters really count. There are some screenplays you like just because you licked them. I would say *Network* was a screenplay in which I licked a lot of problems I couldn't lick technically in *Hospital,* where I tried to do a variety of genres all within one overall framework—and I didn't pull it off. The film was deformed, as a matter of fact. In *Hospital* I had a detective story, a love story, a drama, a satire; I had all kind of genres all bouncing in the air at one time. I had the same thing in *Network,* and it came out a unified piece. In *Hospital* it didn't. You get a great deal of satisfaction in technical achievements that never show, as far as the audience is concerned. Just private satisfactions. So writers are really not very good judges of what is most satisfying. I was delighted with *Bachelor Party,* a script that I thought was deficient, mainly because I enjoyed working on the set so much. We did a lot on the set. That's the only reason. I never licked *Bachelor Party.*

BRADY: Why was *Hospital* deformed, in your judgment?

CHAYEFSKY: Well, the high point of the picture comes in the middle. The high point should come at the end. The set-piece scene between George C. Scott and Diana Rigg is the highest moment of the picture, and the structure should have placed that deep in the third act. You should always be able to top your second act. It was a deformed structure.

BRADY: You say a "set piece." Do you mean where he was about to commit suicide?

CHAYEFSKY: Yes. That was a set piece because it's like a theatrical scene. A scene to be played in a theater.

BRADY: Why didn't you move it back?

CHAYEFSKY: I couldn't. I couldn't figure out how to solve it. I consider very few scripts that I wrote sufficiently fulfilled. *Tenth Man* was one; *Network* was another.

I make movies, and that often means that I'm not entirely pleased with the script. It's the film that counts rather than the script.

BRADY: You've been pretty gentle and gracious in describing your relationship with directors in general.

CHAYEFSKY: I have never had trouble with a director—but one. Everybody is allowed one disagreement with a director.

BRADY: In 1974 when you received the Laurel Award from the Writers Guild of America, you took a shot at the *auteur* theory.

CHAYEFSKY: The *auteur* thing is all humbug, pure humbug, rubbish. It's a joke. Sure, there's an occasional director who really is a splendid filmmaker and he conceives his own films. Orson Welles was one. Bob Fosse, Stanley Kubrick, Bob Altman and, in Europe, Bergman is the greatest. There aren't many in Europe either. There are only four or five. But I'm also an *auteur*. So is Doc Simon, so is Mel Brooks, so is Woody Allen. That whole *auteur* thing is just some typical French humbug that came around. The French take their humbug seriously. Humbug is part of their national character.

BRADY: You've pooh-poohed the *auteur* theory, but in your remarks on receiving the Laurel Award, you suggest that there *is* an *auteur,* but it's the writer.

CHAYEFSKY: No, I didn't say that at all.

BRADY: Let me quote: "The movies may be a visual art, but they are still drama, and if there is an *auteur* concept involved, it is as often as not the writer who is the *auteur.*"

CHAYEFSKY: As often as not.

BRADY: "Even if you're the fifth writer called in to polish a script, it's your script when it gets into your hands, your image, your concept, your name goes down as the author."

CHAYEFSKY: Yeah, as often as not. I didn't say the author is always the *auteur.* Frequently the writer is called in to write somebody else's idea. What I'm saying to my fellow writers is, start taking the responsibility of the picture on your own shoulders and become an *auteur*—that is, the primary author of the picture.

BRADY: Do you see the screenwriter in a more powerful role

now? In a *New York* magazine article on the "new young power in Hollywood," Maureen Orth says that as a condition of sale many screenwriters are being signed to direct scripts that they've written.

CHAYEFSKY: I don't want to direct. It's not my style. I don't do that sort of thing. A lot of the fellows do. Paul Schrader is a director now. A very talented young writer, Joel Oliansky—he wrote a terrific piece of work for television called *The Law,* with Judd Hirsch—he's given up writing altogether last I heard and wants to be a director now because his generation has been director-oriented. But I think the director-*auteur* thing, the so-called subjective film, the expression of the director, has done extraordinary harm to the motion picture industry. I think we're reduced to fifty and less films a year now.

BRADY: What shifts have you observed in the lot of the screen-writer over the years?

CHAYEFSKY: I don't really know. I pay attention only to myself, and my shifts have not been all that much. As long as I can remember, I insisted on maintaining at least a playwright's control. Only briefly did I work as a hired screenwriter: *The Americanization of Emily, Paint Your Wagon, Cincinnati Kid.*

BRADY: You once commented, "I suppose my primary concern is the preservation of humanity in an increasingly dehumanized world."

CHAYEFSKY: Somebody pointed that out to me once, and I said, "Yeah, I guess so." I really don't look at my work from that kind of a Parnassian viewpoint, or an academic viewpoint, or a scholarly viewpoint, or even a critical viewpoint. I don't pay attention to fashion, trends; I never read notices; I never read critical studies. I think it's all rubbish. I just write.

BRADY: You maintain that your satire is not surreal. You told *Time* magazine, "I still write realistic stuff. It's the world that's gone nuts, not me."

CHAYEFSKY: That's a bit glib, but there's some truth in it. It's getting awfully hard to satirize these days.

BRADY: What writers do you read with admiration?

CHAYEFSKY: I don't read terribly much fiction nowadays. John

Gardner. I used to like Saul Bellow. I don't read much fiction now. Usually I read nonfiction, if I read anything, or I go back and reread old fiction. I finally got around to reading Proust. I tried all my life to read Proust. This time I finally got into it and did it. He's wonderful. They really don't write like they used to. They wrote better in those days. Turgenev. He's sensational. You know what was a disappointment? Joyce. *Ulysses*. I was really disappointed. Not only was it obscure, it was too topical. I mean, you really had to know Dublin in 1904 to know what the hell he was talking about.

BRADY: If you were a scrambling young writer today, what would you do to break into films?

CHAYEFSKY: I'd write movies. Believe me, if you can think of a good script, they'll grab it. There are not many good scripts around. Most of them are junk.

BRADY: Do you give counsel to young screenwriters?

CHAYEFSKY: The only counseling you can give a young writer is, if he has talent, let him know that he has it. That's all. You can't teach him; you can only encourage him.

BRADY: I assume that most of your ideas come from within yourself, but do people ever come to you with ideas—producers?

CHAYEFSKY: Sure they do. I don't want them. I never listen to them. And I don't look at unsolicited material. That's just sensible. Otherwise you get sued all the time.

BRADY: What do you do to get away from it all?

CHAYEFSKY: I go to the gym regularly. I'm not sure what it is I get away from. Sometimes New York itself can be terribly oppressive—in the winter, and when it gets rainy. You just have to wait it out. Otherwise, I'm not sure what it is I would want to get away from. At the gym, it's exercise, jogging, camaraderie. Sitting around with the fellas; lot of writers up there. Joe Heller, Joe Stein, Israel Horowitz. It's a literary community that lives close to the West Side Y. I have a lot of good friends up there. I like sports. Saturdays and Sundays I'll sit around on the terrace with a pal of mine and watch the games.

BRADY: And ultimately, how would you like to be remembered?

CHAYEFSKY: A writer is what he writes, and I would like to be remembered as a good writer. I would like the stuff I write to be done and read for many generations. I just hope the world lasts that long.

Author's Note:

My conversations with Paddy Chayefsky ended some three months before his death on August 1, 1981, at the age of 58. This was his longest and, I believe, his last interview.

—J.B.

WILLIAM GOLDMAN

Someone once called William Goldman "Hollywood's most sought-after screenwriter," and it is an observation that makes the forty-nine-year-old New Yorker bristle. He is a forthright, somewhat impatient man—someone who has never been late for an appointment, who grows irritable when precious time is being wasted, and who keeps a few thousand miles between his Manhattan home and the hype and hoopla that are Hollywood. "That kind of thing panics me," he says. "Always does. That's all bullshit. That's like saying, 'How do you feel being the hottest star in Hollywood this week?' I mean, saying that somebody is Hollywood's Most Sought-After *Anything* is basically bullshit. There are a lot of screenwriters who at this point in their careers are hot. I would think that if you had a chance to have me or Mel Brooks, a lot of people would rather have Mel Brooks, and rightly so; or Neil Simon, or Bob Towne, or Paddy Chayefsky, or whomever. It's basically a bullshit statement. Hype."

William Goldman has been fighting off the hype ever since *Variety* announced that he received $400,000 for the screenplay *Butch Cassidy and the Sundance Kid* in November 1967—a deal that left screenwriters and their agents mightily encouraged, and one that left Hollywood executives slightly aghast at the new role screenwriters would be forging in their budgets. "Breaking the $400,000 barrier in the realm of original screenplays has been a long time in coming," observed *Variety*. Indeed, six-figure deals for screenwriters previous to Goldman were but a handful. William Rose received a reported $200,000 for *Guess Who's Coming to Dinner* (1967), but the breakdown exemplified a typical deal for a top screenwriter of the day: $50,000 for developing the story in hopes it would be purchased; then $150,000 for the script, and some participation in the net profits—net usually meaning "nyet" as far as the writer was concerned in the hands of Hollywood's rapacious cost-accounting systems.

What made the *Butch Cassidy* deal significant, therefore, in addition to the generous purchase price, was that Goldman received $400,000 plus a share in profits *strictly as a writer of a complete screenplay*, and his preproduction work was to be minimal. Thus, Goldman had diminished a writer's fears that (1) his story, if purchased, might never be filmed; and (2) even if purchased, he might not be hired to do the screenplay. Goldman, whose screenwriting began with the 1966 film *Harper*, won an Academy Award for *Butch Cassidy* for 1969, and quickly moved forward with a series of other successful projects: *The Hot Rock, The Great Waldo Pepper, Marathon Man,*

All the President's Men (for which he received a second Oscar), *A Bridge Too Far* and *Magic*.

Despite his remarkable success as a screenwriter, William Goldman is not happy in the profession. He considers himself a novelist who just happens to turn out screenplays between books, many of which are bestsellers (*Boys and Girls Together, Marathon Man, Magic, Tinsel*, etc.). Between his novels and his screenplays, the output is both prodigious and, for Goldman, hateful. "I have a peculiar habit in terms of reading what I have written," he explains. "I never look at it. I don't like my writing. It's the best I can do, but it's not something that fills me with awe and splendor."

William Goldman is tall, angular, with a lean, athletic body that occasionally suffers from pain in the lower portion of the back. With his craggy good looks and his swooping mustache, the writer could be a silver-haired stand-in for the Sundance Kid Out West. Instead, he works at a small metal desk over a small gray Olympia typewriter in an unfurnished two-room apartment he rents as an office in New York City's East Eighties. "They call it a penthouse," says Goldman, who generally works here five days a week. "Actually, it's the top floor of an ugly twenty-two-story building." The author has been working in that building for thirteen years. Once, after his daughter Susanna was born, he and his wife Ilene tried to leave New York. "We decided to leave the city and give our children a healthy upbringing in the country with clean air. We rented a house in Princeton, moved in 1966 to live there forever, hated it after a year and a half, and came back to Manhattan.

"There's something about New York City that is abrasive, which I find helpful," reflects the screenwriter. "I don't know how people write in L.A. It's so pleasant there. It's just me, I guess." The sun tried to peer through the venetian blinds on three dusty windows in Goldman's office as I tried to find my note card with the opening question on clout and who has what.

BRADY: What sort of clout does a screenwriter have?

GOLDMAN: The clout you have depends entirely on how *useful* you are to people as the picture moves through the various stages. *A Bridge Too Far,* for instance, was a wonderful experience. I am still very close to the people involved. I was writing on it weeks after production started. There is a little introduction which we had always known we were going to put in because the movie audience is very young—they don't know what World War II was, or who Hitler was, or any of that. And so we had always planned to put in a ninety-second intro with stunning documentary World War II newsreel footage to kind of frame the movie. I wrote the thing, and Richard Attenborough came over, and Liv Ullmann did the narration—so, in other words, I remained very much involved in that film. But that involvement varies enormously from film to film, and it doesn't make a screenwriter the production's star.

A "superstar," for instance, in Hollywoodese is someone who is bankable, someone who is, as they say, An Element. And screenwriters aren't. Now, when I say screenwriters I mean people like myself, not people like Paddy Chayefsky, who is a screenwriter-producer, or Mel Brooks, who is a screenwriter-director, or Woody Allen, also a writer-director. In other words, there are no screenwriters *on their own* with enough clout to muscle a movie through. If a screenwriter wants to do a movie, no one is going to say, "OK, let's go ahead," whereas they would obviously say, "Let's go" if Francis Ford Coppola or George Roy Hill or Bob Redford or Clint Eastwood wanted to do it. In other words, they would do *anything* for those people, I would think. Bob Towne or Bill Goldman or whoever you want to consider who is *basically a screenwriter* hasn't that kind of superstar clout.

BRADY: Does the amount of involvement have to do with the amount of participation in the profit?

GOLDMAN: No. Profit percentage is meaningless.

BRADY: What if someone is getting a percentage of the gross?

GOLDMAN: No screenwriter that I know of gets a percentage of the gross. Maybe Neil Simon does. I doubt it. A percentage of the gross is meaningful. A percentage of the net profits is like the horizon that recedes as you get closer and closer. So when you say does the amount of work you do on a picture have to do with a percentage of the profit, the answer is no.

BRADY: The price of the screenwriter, though, has gone up—especially since the sale of *Butch Cassidy and the Sundance Kid*. Suddenly screenplays had monetary labels attached to them. That seems to be part of the press-release information now.

GOLDMAN: Yes, it's awful. One of the things about money that's so hateful is that nobody believes that that's not why one writes. Automatically, because I'm on a hot streak now, people say, "Oh, did you write your novel or the screenplay of it first?" Well, the idea that I would do a novelization of a screenplay is heinous to me because at heart I am a novelist. If anybody knew anything at all about screenplay writing they would know that in *Marathon Man* there's only one scene in the novel that translates well to film and that's Szell in the diamond district. That's an exterior scene. All the rest of the book is interior and was extremely difficult to try and make play in terms of a movie.

Ideas come to you in very different ways. Some people occasionally will ask, "Why didn't you do *Butch Cassidy* as a novel?" Because it came to me as a movie. The feel of it was a movie. Movies do some things wonderfully well that novels don't do. There's a marvelous narrative thing that movies have: they do size and scope. They aren't really very good at interpreting. I don't think they are much on complexity. But movies are marvelous in terms of a story's size and sweep that you can hardly do in a novel unless you are Tolstoy, but most of us aren't Tolstoy. So they are *entirely* different forms. The only similarity is that very often they both use dialogue. Otherwise, the way that one handles a scene in a movie and the way one handles a scene in a book have nothing to do with each other.

BRADY: Could you give me an example of that?

GOLDMAN: Yes. Rule of thumb: You always attack a movie scene as *late* as you possibly can. You always come into the scene at the *last* possible moment, which is why when you see a scene in a movie where a person is a teacher, for instance, the scene always begins with the teacher saying, "Well, class . . ." and the bell rings. And then you get into another scene because it's very dull watching a man talk to people in a room. This interview, if you had a camera on it, would have put people to sleep already—whereas in a book you could have a scene. There's a teaching scene in the book *Marathon Man* that must run three, four, five, seven pages where Babe goes to class. Well, that scene in the movie is very short. You truncate it somehow, as much as you can. In a book you might start with some dialogue, and then describe the room, and start with some more dialogue, and then describe your clothing, and more dialogue. The camera gets that in an *instant. Boom,* and you're on. Get on, get on. The camera is relentless. Makes you keep running.

The average screenplay, as you know, is very short. Rule of thumb: a page a minute. The ideal length for a screenplay is a hundred and thirty to a hundred and thirty-five pages because that lets everybody be creative when they get it. That means that the producer will be able to say, "Well, we must cut fifteen pages out of this." No matter what you give them, ultimately you end up with a hundred and fifteen pages, because that is how long the movie is. But if you gave somebody a first draft of a hundred and fifteen pages, they would say, "What's this, television?" So you have to give them a little extra to work with.

BRADY: Do you find yourself thinking that way?

GOLDMAN: No, but that's the way it works. For example, we knew *A Bridge Too Far* was going to be a long movie. It's such an enormous film, and there's so much narrative—we were going for two hours and forty-five minutes in the beginning. We ended up I think at two fifty-one. But we were always going for two forty-five. So my first draft was a hundred and seventy-five pages. Had I gotten to page one hundred of the first draft and felt I was only about one-third of the way through the material, I would have known I was in terrible trouble. There's no point in giving someone a two-hundred-and-fifty or three-hundred-page first draft of a film, because you have to lose one hundred pages, and *you* had better do the losing rather than let other people do it. So ultimately you develop a kind of intuition—or at least I have, I think. You want to come in with approximately what you know the needs are. I mean I'm basically a gun for hire. Someone hires me, and I do the best I can for as long as they want me. And then I'm gone.

The only—quote—"fun" in movie writing for me is the first draft. That's the only time it's really yours. And I work hard on my first drafts. I would like my first draft to be ideally as good as I can make it, because then the contingencies of the business come along. I mean, in truth, no one has ever heard me use the word "good" about any of my screenplays. I would never attribute that kind of quality—"good," "true" or "beautiful"—to a screenplay. A screenplay is a piece of carpentry; and except in the case of Ingmar Bergman, it's not an art, it's a craft. And you want to be as good as you can at your craft, and you want to give them what they need within the limits of your talents—and the only reason I am "hot" now has nothing to do with the quality of the films that I have been involved with. It has to do with two things: Some of the films have been successful, but, more important, *they have been made*. Again, there's a difference between films and the book business.

When you write a book, for the most part the writer makes his money when people buy the book. If you write a book that sells a trillion copies, you get royalties on each copy sold; and if you write a book that nobody buys, you get that much less. In the movie business basically you get paid off principal photography, that day when the director first rolls a camera with the first unit. Until that day, it's all development. And so one of the reasons why there are so many bad movies is that people get paid not on the success of the movie but on the *existence* of it. So a producer may say, "They're going to steal from me anyway in terms of profits, but what I want is that the film gets made." And in my case the films that I have written for the most part have been made. So someone will hire me, not because of any quality inherent in my screenplays, but because there's a good chance so far (knock wood) that the screenplay will become a film. Better that it should be a successful film, but the *crucial* thing is that it should be a film at all.

Another thing I would say is that nobody sets out to make a terrible film. It's too hard. It takes too long. Movies are these great gasping whales. They take *years* between finding the initial property and opening in your friendly neighborhood movie house. It's so hard, and it's so much of everybody's life, that for the most part those of us involved for any length of time want the movie to be good. If I spend six months of my life writing on a project, it's a certain percentage of my years here on this earth. And I would like the film to be something that I would not be embarrassed about. Sometimes it turns out that way, but I have been very lucky in my film career.

So far I have only done films that I have wanted to do—because in my head I am a novelist. I came to screenwriting in a strange way. I was a novelist for ten years before I was a screenwriter, and I live in New York and I don't know people in the picture business, and I am not involved in Hollywood, and all of that. I stay here and try to lead as ordinary a life as I can. I am not by the pool making deals. And that's very important. The first film that I did was *Harper*. And the second film was *Butch Cassidy*. Now I was involved in a couple of films before that, but not *really*. And *Harper* happened because it was basically my idea to do a book by Ross Macdonald as a movie. No one came to me and said, "Would you adapt *A Moving Target?*" So in a sense from the beginning I have initiated a lot of what I have been involved in, and I have only done films that I very much wanted to do. I have been very, very lucky that way.

BRADY: What gave you the idea to do a Ross Macdonald film?

GOLDMAN: I have always been a Ross Macdonald fan. A producer who had just seen a film by Richard Brooks called *The Professionals,* with Burt Lancaster, came to me and said, "I want to make a movie. I want to do a really ballsy film." And I said, "Read some Ross Macdonald." He called me a few days later and said, "Gee, I really like him." I said, "OK, I will read them all again. I'll find one and you option it." And he said, "Fine." And since I wrote my novels on spec—I'd never had a contract or advance on a novel in my life until *Marathon Man*— I did the same on this screenplay.

I worked on *Butch Cassidy* for eight years on spec before I wrote it. When the movie came out, the real title in everybody's mind was *Butch Cassidy and the Sundance Kid $400,000*. That's why, when the movie opened in New York, it got killed. We didn't get one good notice in New York City—there was a lot of anti-Hollywood sentiment. And we were hardly a bunch of Hollywood types on that film. There was myself, then living on Seventy-fifth, and George Roy Hill, who was living on Seventy-eighth, and Paul Newman, who had an apartment in the Fifties and a house in Connecticut. But we were all Hollywood types in there, you know, because of the numbers on the movie. People are so incredibly stupid that they assumed a studio would give me four hundred thousand dollars to go out and do a screenplay about two people no one had ever heard of. Obviously the reason why Fox paid four hundred was that other people were bidding three fifty. And it was an original screenplay that I worked on for eight years, then wrote. And Evarts Ziegler sold it—quite brilliantly, by which I mean Zig said, "It was a very good deal." I said "What do you mean?" And he said, "The next morning everybody was still speaking to me." Very often agents have that problem. Decent agents don't like to kill somebody, because there is a continuity in the business.

One of the things always looming is that I have a reputation as a money writer and—this sounds very bullshitty—I've *never* written for money. By which, I don't mean that I am artistic and pure. What I mean is, money has *happened*. It's gone along with what I've written—especially in film. And I like to think one of the reasons for that is I've wanted to do what I've done. I have gotten very few compliments that I treasure in my life, but one of them is from Stanley Donen, a wonderful director who is now out of repute (but who will be hot again because the wheel keeps spinning Out There). He said, "You're very tough." And I said, "Why?" And he said, "Because you cost a lot, and you have to want to do it." I think that's true, and I treasure that, because I *do* have to want to do it. I think that's true basically of almost everybody I know in the picture business that's above the water level on the iceberg. We're all clinging to the iceberg, and the water level is rising constantly.

A lot of people say things like, "Do you think Robert Redford was worth two million dollars for *A Bridge Too Far?*" Well, the answer is yes. Because *A Bridge Too Far* was already in profit before its release—in great part because we were able to get Redford's name on the picture; but also because, although it may be obscene to think of somebody getting two million dollars for four weeks of acting, in today's marketplace that's where you open with Bob Redford. Bob hasn't had a movie that hasn't done business in nine years. Whatever picture Clint Eastwood does, he's going to get his deal regardless. So you can assume that he only works on those projects that he likes. You can't *buy* Clint Eastwood. There's not enough money. He makes too much. He has too much.

BRADY: Money is the given.

GOLDMAN: For certain people in the business, yes.

BRADY: Can you recall those earliest days in which you began to see yourself as a screenwriter?

GOLDMAN: I was writing a novel called *Boys and Girls Together.* In the middle of it I stopped to do some Broadway work. And I stopped for almost a year. When I went back to *Boys and Girls Together,* I was stuck. I had half of it done—it was a very long book—but I was blocked. I read the paper one day, and the Boston Strangler was very much in the news. There was a very little article, in the *Daily News,* I think, telling of a new theory —that maybe there were *two* people who were stranglers. I've never had this experience before, and I never expect to again, but in the length of time it took me to walk the two blocks to my office, a novel fell into my brain based on that idea: What if there were two stranglers? And what if one got jealous of the other?

I sat down and in a *frenzy* wrote down the plot. I wanted to do the strangler book fast—and get back to *Boys and Girls*—so I wrote it with lots and lots and lots of chapters, because each time I had a new chapter—even if it was only one line long—I would have a fresh new page that I could number so it would run longer.

I ended up with a book that was fifty chapters long and probably a hundred and fifty pages.

Somehow Cliff Robertson got ahold of it before it was published, called me up on the phone, came and saw me. He said he'd read my *screen treatment,* and I did not say, "That was really a book." He had this marvelous short story called "Flowers for Algernon," by Daniel Keyes, and he said, "Would you try to make a movie out of it?" I said I would try.

BRADY: On spec?

GOLDMAN: No, I don't think so. There's a minimum you have to get in order to do a screen treatment. And then I panicked. I said to my wife, "What am I going to do? I've never written a screenplay." I zoomed down to a store (now closed) called Bookmasters, open twenty-four hours a day—on Seventh Avenue between Forty-second and Forty-third—looking frantically for a book on screenwriting. They had one that I looked at and realized I could never write in that form because it was full of all those awful capital letters and numbers and . . . it was an unreadable form. So I made up, in desperation, my own form. I decided to use "cut to" like I use "he said" in books. I use it for rhythm, to control the reader's eye. While I was writing this screenplay for Robertson, I got a call from an English producer saying there was a film that Robertson was going to do, which eventually got called *Masquerade;* Rex Harrison was to play the lead, but he had dropped out. Robertson was now going to do it, and they needed someone to Americanize the English dialogue. Robertson insisted on me—which was really weird because he had never read anything I'd written for film. He had not seen the screenplay yet for "Flowers for Algernon." So I went to London, and doctored *Masquerade.* Then, shortly after finishing that, I gave Robertson the screenplay for "Flowers for Algernon," and he immediately fired me. He hired Stirling Silliphant, who wrote him the screenplay *Charly* without a comma of mine in it—and it won Robertson the Oscar. So he was not dumb to fire me. But that's how I got into screenwriting. By now, I had gotten unblocked—the strangler novel went on to become the movie *No Way to Treat a Lady*—and I completed *Boys and Girls Together,* which was optioned for a movie by Elliott Kastner—then we had the conversation about him wanting to do a ballsy picture after he'd seen *The Professionals,* and I said he should read Ross Macdonald. So that kind of brings us up to *Harper.*

BRADY: Looking back on that first screenplay for Cliff Robertson, what did you do wrong?

GOLDMAN: I don't know. It was so strange. When I heard I was off the picture, I remember calling him up and *demanding* to know what I had done wrong. He just thought it stunk. He was probably right. It was a *very* good move on his part, considering what happened with the movie.

BRADY: In adapting Macdonald's book, why did they change protagonist Lew Archer to someone named Harper?

GOLDMAN: Well, I'm not privy. What I think happened was . . . they wanted to use the name Lew Archer, but they didn't want to buy the rights to the character. And I think what Macdonald's agent was saying is you can buy the book, but you can't use the character's name. It was a legal thing, because the character appeared in other books. So they put the name *Harper* on it because Paul Newman had made a couple of H movies—*Hud, The Hustler*—and it's not a bad title. He harps as well as he is an archer. It's a reasonable thing.

BRADY: One small sidetrack. You used the pseudonym Harry Longbaugh, which is the Sundance Kid's real name, on *No Way to Treat a Lady.* Is there some sort of Freudian identification going on here?

GOLDMAN: I loved the name Harry Longbaugh. We're talking about 1964, which is when *No Way to Treat a Lady* came out. I didn't sell *Butch* until 1967, but I'd been working on it off and on, researching it since the late fifties—and I loved the name Harry Longbaugh. I thought it was a fabulous name. My editor, Hiram Haydn, and others had high hopes for *Boys and Girls Together* critically—ho, ho, ho. So when I gave *No Way to Treat a Lady* to Hiram, he had no interest in a mystery, and he said, "I don't want to be the editor of this. Would you take it somewhere else and would you use a pseudonym? Because I think it would damage you if you used William Goldman." I went to various places, and eventually Gold Medal took it as an original paperback, and I used the pseudonym of Harry Longbaugh, which was a name I always loved.

BRADY: *Butch Cassidy,* then, was with you as an idea for eight or nine years. When you actually got down to the writing, did it come fast?

GOLDMAN: Yes. I tend to write everything fast.

BRADY: How fast?

GOLDMAN: *Very.* I tend to research my screenplays a lot, and then I write them very, very quickly. The reason that I am fast, if I know what I am doing, is that the scene is kind of *there.* And when I am stuck it can take me a long time; but in the case of *Butch,* I'd researched it for so long, I wrote the first draft very, very quickly—in less than a month.

BRADY: Do you have any research assistance?

GOLDMAN: No. When I am doing an adaptation, I read the source book. If I am not kicked by the source book, I can't do it; I have to *like* it. And after I have read it, and have said yes, and I am hired to do the job—what I do is I reread the book several times. The first time, I mark in color the things I think are useful. The next time I read it, I use a different color pen and mark things that I still think are useful; the fourth time, I use a different color pen . . . and then when I am very full with the material, I'll look at those things I marked *every* time, and I will think, "That must be good. I must try to use that." I throw away things that are only marked from *one* reading's color.

But that's not what I mean by a lot of the research. The Battle of Arnhem, although it's not famous in America, is probably, after Dunkirk, the single most famous action in World War II for the British. And almost everybody involved that survived wrote about the Battle of Arnhem; so in addition to reading *A Bridge Too Far* at least a half-dozen times, for instance, and interviewing a few people, I must have read twenty other books dealing with the Battle of Arnhem. That's what I mean by a lot of research. And for *All the President's Men* I read all the shit on Watergate.

BRADY: And there's a lot of shit to read about Watergate.

GOLDMAN: Well, there was a great, great deal. That's what I mean. Most people think that screenwriting is only dialogue, and that we're those people who write those dreadful lines that all those nice, wonderful actors have to say. And the reality is that the single most important thing contributed by the screenwriter is the structure. It's a terrible thing for a writer to admit, but in terms of screenwriting, dialogue really doesn't matter as much as in plays and books—because you have the camera. The camera gives you the actor's eyes. If you have a speech or a couple of lines that an actor feels awkward saying, and he can feel more comfortable changing your dialogue, and you get his emotion that way, then by all means that must be done, because what really works in a film is the actor's emotion. Movies are a group endeavor. We live in a world where people think the director is this giant genius "having dreams," as Robert Altman would say: "I woke up with a dream, and there it was." But basically there are seven people who are essential to a film, and if the film's going to be really any good, all seven have to be at their best.

BRADY: Who would the seven be?

GOLDMAN: In no particular order, certainly the director, certainly the producer, certainly the players, certainly the cinematographer, certainly the production designer, certainly the editor, and certainly the writer. Now sometimes the composer is essential, absolutely essential. But that varies from film to film. Sometimes the special-effects man is absolutely essential. The most important single thing in *Jaws,* for instance, was the shark, and the most important single thing I think in *The Exorcist* was Dick Smith's makeup on the girl. If you hadn't had that fabulous makeup, the reality that picture had for that vast audience would have gone out the window. Really dazzling makeup is hard to do.

Same is true of the cinematographer. The director doesn't look through the camera except to see if the shot is showing. Are the corners correct? Is it framed properly? Is that what they want to see? But the lighting—in other words, *how it looks on film*—is the province of the cameraman. One of the reasons cameramen have much better lives than writers is because nobody says to a cameraman, "I'll fix the lighting," because nobody knows how to do it. But *everybody* knows words.

Really dazzling production design is hard to do, too. The production designer is the person who is responsible for everything that you see on the film, what is there and how it looks, what's the reality of it. A good production designer can carry a weak director. Does it look like a room? Is it interesting? The director doesn't say to a production designer, "Put this here and that there." He hires a production designer and prays. Nobody messes with *their* work.

The only one who gets screwed around with basically is the writer, because, as I say, everybody knows the alphabet. And the producer makes contributions, and so does the actor's mistress, and so does the agent, and all that. That's why I say the first draft of the screenplay is all that gives me pleasure. The rest of it is basically dealing with exigencies that you know are going to happen. I am making this up now, but suppose you have a part in your script and suddenly someone says to you, "I hear Ali MacGraw wants to go to work. If we can build up the girl's part we have a shot at getting Ali because I know she wants to do a movie in the jungle." So that part *balloons*. Or this happens, and that happens, or Jack Nicholson doesn't want to play a loser, or . . . you get the idea.

One of the great examples of how Hollywood louses up things is Richard Brooks' film *Lord Jim,* and I don't say Brooks did it intentionally. But the novel is about a man who has a moment of cowardice and who spends the rest of his life trying to explain that moment of cowardice. Well, nobody would have played the part. All those stars would say, "I'm not a coward." So the movie is about a guy who *doesn't* have a moment of cowardice, and then explains his moment of noncowardice, right? It's really madness, but you're dealing with performers of talent and enormous egos. We all have that. And they are not going to play losers.

BRADY: From the way you describe doing a first draft—with that enormous sense of choice you have with a book like *A*

Bridge Too Far—it would seem that the kick is in predirecting the director.

GOLDMAN: Oh, yeah, sure. But I would never say that. The director is extremely essential. But the media keeps needing heroes. In the thirties, when sound was really starting, the heroes were all heads of the studios. Thalberg was a genius. Zanuck was a fabulous man in the editing room. Louis Mayer had his admirers . . . according to the media. All these guys were great. Well, movies have *always* been a group endeavor, from time immemorial. And after we got bored with reading that kind of bullshit, we read about how marvelous the stars were. That was when Clark Gable was the king, and all those *fabulous* people. And that was all bullshit. Now we are in this period of The Director and what a genius the director is. And everybody in the business knows that that's also bullshit. Ultimately, as with your book, there is a certain interest, because of money, in screenwriters, and we will get an amount of individual attention which will all be bullshit, too. And in five years you will be reading that the editor is *really* the genius of the film. The bottom line is that everybody knows this. It's one of those terrible things. That's why everybody in show business has such deep contempt for everybody who writes about show business (in the media sense), because they *know* it's all bullshit. And there's a reason for that. There's an uneasy alliance between the media and films because —how can I put it?—if you are a schmuck who writes for the Dallas *Evening News,* and some girl comes to town publicizing *King Kong,* to justify your existence in the universe you cannot say that this is a young starlet. You have to say that this is the hottest girl in the business, the hottest thing to come along since Whatever Her Name Was, who has since disappeared.

Anyway, what I'm saying is cinematographers now get paid five thousand dollars a week. That's a lot of money, because they can work a lot of weeks. They are also starting to get a percentage. When we were working on *Butch Cassidy* they wouldn't pay Connie Hall fifteen hundred, so the rate today has tripled (as everything has tripled); but cinematographers are crucial to a movie. In other words, they wouldn't *pay* a cinematographer five thousand a week if he weren't worth it. And the same goes for the others on a film. The basic, bottom-line truth is this: We *all* of us are very helpful. I find it disconcerting to talk about screenwriting as if it's a thing apart from the rest of it, because I'm only as good as the others allow me to be. It doesn't matter how good a scene or how bad a scene I write, how skillful or unskillful a scene I write. If it's a bad shot, badly lit, badly acted, badly edited, badly directed, if the producer has not functioned to let the director try and be clear . . . in other words, we're *all* of us at each other's mercy. That's the truth, and everybody, if you get them alone, will say that's the truth. But when you get Robert Altman, he'll say, "Oh yes, I had this dream."

The only one who is different from everyone is, for me, Ingmar Bergman. It's like they used to say of Sandy Koufax: "He's pitching in a higher league." But for the rest of us it's all the same. It's a group thing. And the group has to function. One of the reasons why there are so many failures is that movies are essentially trying to buy past magic. Charles Bronson killing people worked in this movie, and he liked that director. "If I can get that director and Bronson back together, it'll make money." Well, there's no reason that it will.

Anyway, the main thought is that yes, screenwriting is very important, and so are those other jobs. It's the same thing in basketball. Basketball's a wonderful thing. They love to publicize scoring. But in reality the only thing that matters to anybody who plays basketball (and I know some pro players) is *winning*. Pete Maravich was never on a winning team, and I don't know that the scoring leader has ever been on the championship team. Maybe Jabbar once. But for the most part, scoring leaders are on teams that lose. They get the ink, they get the hype, but that's not what the game is about.

BRADY: And they often get the money.

GOLDMAN: They often get the money. That's correct.

BRADY: But the outcome is often failure.

GOLDMAN: Well, again, as in sports, you are dealing with egos. What the media wants to do is glorify. The media is looking for heroes. But the hero in a successful movie is *the group*. In most pictures that I have been connected with, for example, the director is very important, but he's usually not the crucial figure. He sometimes is, but he is not *always,* and not often. I don't want to go into specifics. But basically they're usually not. Someone else is: the star is, the producer is. But the director . . . well, right now I think we are living through the twilight of the director's time. Because we are running out of them. We are getting bored with articles about Martin Scorsese being an artist. You know, there's a limit to how long we can do that.

I'll tell you what drives me mad. Martin Scorsese is a very gifted director. He did a violent film starring the hottest new star in the business, Robert De Niro, called *Taxi Driver.* And before it came out there was a big article in the Sunday *New York Times* magazine section, a big article by some fool—headlined "Why Is Martin Scorsese Risking His Career on a Movie Like *Taxi Driver?*" when what he *really* wants to make, the article went on to say, is a movie about Mother Cabrini, or something like that. Well, that's such patent bullshit. The idea of risking your career making a violent film starring Robert De Niro for a low budget is like Francis Coppola saying, "I am really risking everything doing a *Godfather* sequel." That's like somebody saying, "I am risking my whole career doing a James Bond movie." It's madness, and if the press will *buy* that, if that fool on the *Times* would be so dumb and so unprepared in his interviewing that he would *believe* the publicity hype that Martin Scorsese was risking *anything* by doing *Taxi Driver*—well, when you consider that the *Times* is supposed to be the best that we have . . . think what it's like when you get into Kansas City, Missouri! That kind of *falseness* is one of the reasons why those of us in the business don't have a lot of respect for those people outside it, because nobody really is interested in the true story. Because the story essentially is very dull: We all work well together, or we all work badly together. But you can't sell papers or *People* magazine with that.

BRADY: Your first draft is titled *The Sundance Kid and Butch Cassidy.* Why the shift to *Butch Cassidy and the Sundance Kid?*

GOLDMAN: I always liked *The Sundance Kid and Butch Cas-*

sidy. It's a difference in where the rhythm on the word "Cassidy" comes. I always liked the Sundance Kid first. Newman liked the screenplay and was going to play the Sundance Kid. But Newman had a lot of script problems because secretly, in his heart of hearts, he thought that Butch was a better part, I think. And George Hill, when he read the screenplay and agreed to direct it, assumed that Newman was Butch. When he said that to Newman (I was not present at this—I was told this by Hill), Newman *leaped* to that assumption. His script problems vanished with the wind because he now had the part that he thought he was better for, and the title—because he was the star of the movie—obviously that day became what it became. That is why.

BRADY: Suspicions confirmed department.

GOLDMAN: Well, it would have been madness to have it any other way. At that time Newman was the star of the picture, and there was no other star.

BRADY: Right. Redford was just on the ground floor of his career then. In that script you open with the observation *Not that it matters, but most of what follows is true*.

GOLDMAN: Right.

BRADY: How far did you go with the truth? How much of what went on is historically accurate?

GOLDMAN: What's historically accurate and verifiable is that Butch was the head of a gang that was called the Wild Bunch, secondarily called the Hole in the Wall Gang. (The reason we use the Hole in the Wall Gang is that the Peckinpah movie changed its title to become *The Wild Bunch,* creating a moment of wild panic. Everyone wondered, *What was it about?* For a while, we didn't know.) Anyway, Butch was an extremely affable leader, not a shooter or a fighter or any of those things. E. H. Harriman, to stop the train robbery, formed what I called a super posse, and they were outfitted in a special railroad car. In truth, when Butch heard about that and heard who the enemy was, he and Sundance and Etta took off. The super posse never chased him. He *heard* who they were, and went. So I had to write that whole chase, which must be thirty, forty pages. I don't know. The whole justification of that was the fact that they became legendary twice.

(There's the line in *Gatsby:* "You can't repeat the past." "But of course you can." They *did* it.) They became legendary in South America. So it was crucial that I get them to South America.

In fact, when the screenplay was first made available to people, the criticism was "Get rid of that South American shit." And I would say, "But they *did* it. It happened." And they would say, "We don't care if it happened. John Wayne doesn't run away. You can't have your hero run away."

Well, I knew that it would be an *enormous* problem in having my heroes run away. So I had to try and justify why they ran away, and I made this implacable thing, this posse *machine* that was going to kill them.

A lot of things about *Butch* are very different and unusual for a western, none of which were intended by me. There is not a confrontation scene. There is very little violence. It is very chatty, a very talky movie. Not a lot happens. One of the panicky things in doing the film was, I felt there wasn't enough action for it to be an action film, and it wasn't funny enough to be a comedy; and if we didn't *like* those two guys, we were all in trouble. And so I felt that we had to like those two people, they had to be affable or that was it. The humor was Jack Benny-like, slow and amiable—you had to *like* the guy; not Bob Hope-ish, with punchline after punchline.

Anyway, in real life Butch heard about the posse and left. So that central part of the script—the whole chase—is all made up. The learning of the language is all made up. Robbing the bank in Spanish and not knowing how to speak Spanish is all made up. What is verifiably real, I suppose, is very little. I hope the *spirit* of the script is real. I hope the two guys are like what they were like. We don't really know much about Sundance. But Butch *was* the leader of this gang. They *did* rob banks. They *did* rob the Union Pacific. Woodcock *was* the railway guy, twice. They *did* put in too much dynamite at one point and blew the shit out of the railroad car. There *was* Etta Place. She *was* the Kid's girl. She *was* exquisitely beautiful. We have a photograph of her from 1901; considering the quality of the pictures at that time, she was a wonderful-looking woman. Nobody knows whether she was a whore or a teacher. It's my contention she was a teacher because life is very hard for whores always, but especially at that time in the West; and I can't believe she was as beautiful as she was to have led that kind of life. And they went to South America, and ultimately they were shot. And they *were* found by the Alpoca mines because of the brand on the mule. That's how they were in fact caught. But all the stuff, all the robberies in South America are made up. They did try to go straight, but I made up the scene with the mine owner and the irony of their defending a payroll from robbers. So ultimately I think a lot of it's made up; what *isn't* is, basically, these two guys experiencing this great sweep in their lives and dying someplace where they didn't speak the language.

BRADY: One story is that when Butch saw that Sundance was dead, he turned his six-gun to his own temple and fired. Did you encounter that in your research?

GOLDMAN: Yes. One of the troubles when doing research on the West is that there haven't been too many brilliant historians dealing with it. It's very hard to find what's factual, because most writers basically want to promote whatever the myths have been. You want to keep saying that Wyatt Earp was a neat guy, so you will write that kind of book. You want to say that Billy the Kid was really a terrific fellow, so you keep reusing false material. It's very hard to find out what in fact is true.

BRADY: What prompted the bicycle scene?

GOLDMAN: Oh, they *did* ride bicycles in the whorehouse district in some towns. Bicycles were a fad, like the Hula-Hoop, in the 1880s or '90s. There was a theory, a contention that they would put the horse out of business, and I thought that was such a marvelous idea, it just *felt* right. That's historically valid: There *was* a bicycle craze. The music in that scene is a marvelous example of what I mean when I say movies are a group endeavor. I wrote in my first draft screenplay a shot where Butch and Etta are riding along in a ghost town at dawn and you see them reflected in windows. George grabbed that and said, "Let's have a song. Let's make that a song." Burt Bacharach and Hal David wrote the song. George said, "I want a song like 'I'm Bidin' My Time' in rhythm." And "Raindrops" has that kind of beat to it. It's *breathtakingly* shot by Connie Hall. Jesus Christ, that's some of the prettiest photography ever ever ever in the history of westerns. And the whole mix works. But I certainly can't take credit for it. I can take credit for sparking it, and setting up the moment —but it could have just lain there like toothpaste. Everybody has to be working well. Newman was wonderful. Katharine Ross was so pretty.

Funny story here. I was told that they hired a stunt man to do all the bicycle stuff, and they found when he got there that the stunt man couldn't do anything. He was basically a phony stunt man. And so Paul did every stunt on the bicycle, except, if you look very carefully, there is one shot of him riding through the fence backwards just before he sees the bull there. And that shot, that little footage, is not Paul. But all the rest is. Paul turned out to be a bicycle addict. And all of that, if you liked that moment —it was everybody's moment. So I sparked George, George sparked Bacharach and David, Connie Hall was at the top of his form, we cast the movie wonderfully with all of the principals— and all of it worked. So I am not trying to shitkick and say, "Gee folks, I'm just along for the ride." But it would also be madness for me to say, "Ah yes, this is mine." None of it's *mine* in movies; it's all *ours*.

Talk to anybody in the movie business, any working figure in the picture business—whether it's a cinematographer, or a mixer, or a producer, or a studio executive—anybody inside the business, and they will all say the same thing (and I'll go to my grave on this): Everybody gets together and *everybody* makes a picture. Because of this madness with the *auteur* theory that started in France, "the director is the author of the piece"; and because there is a certain critical acclaim for that in this country, what the press and the media reinforce is something that is false. Some people like to grow up thinking, "How brilliant is Peter Bogdanovich." And the fact is, he's like anybody else. It's as if the press said the world is flat, and all of us who are geologists know that it's really round. Movies are a group endeavor. It's as simpleminded and moronic as that, and what a director does is gaspingly hard and gaspingly small in terms of what the myth is.

It's a very hard physical job, let me tell you; I sure as hell couldn't do it. I don't know about foreign films. I'm not sure how it works over there, but I know in Hollywood we all of us get together, and works are collaborative. But, you see, they never send me out with a movie; they never send Gordon Willis out with a movie; they never send Dede Allen out with a movie. Gordon is a great cinematographer, and Dede is a great editor. No, they send out the director, and they send out the star. And to reinforce the importance of the director and the star, the journalist has to make the director and the star more important than they really are. The journalist is asking himself, "Why am I interviewing this person?" And he answers, "Why, he must be *responsible* for this movie!" And so the myth all gets continually reinforced, and *The New York Times* ends up writing about Brian De Palma. Well, the wheel is always in spin.

BRADY: Some material in the published *Butch Cassidy* script doesn't appear in the film. What about the silent film scene in Bolivia toward the end when Butch and Sundance see themselves on a screen? Is that verifiable?

GOLDMAN: That's a scene I've always liked. It *may* have possibly been true. It *may* have been that they saw themselves in an early one-reeler. I wrote that scene, in which they see themselves getting killed, because for me it presages what was going to happen: They get upset, Etta leaves—nice notion for a scene. In rehearsal, Paul was unsure of it, and George Hill didn't like it because he thought it was *too* much of a coincidence at that stage of the film. They shot it (I've never seen it), and I think it's the one major cut George made after the first sneak preview; he made a number of minor ones, I know. You mentioned earlier the opening line *Not that it matters, but most of what follows is true*. It doesn't say that in the movie. What it says in the movie is *Most of what follows is true*. That's because at that first sneak the line got a laugh. A *good* laugh. But there was *too* much laughter at the first sneak, and so what George basically did was take out a lot of laughs because you had to have that balance.

BRADY: I see. He was going for plausibility.

GOLDMAN: Yes. I think it's a beautifully directed film. I really do.

BRADY: The opening scene in *Butch Cassidy* varies from draft to draft. In one draft it features Sundance shooting the mirror hanging from the ceiling. Another draft features Sundance shooting poker chips from the man who's challenged him, and then in the film version he shoots the holsters off the man. What goes on from draft to draft to draft that accounts for the shifting of props?

GOLDMAN: We are dealing with a man who may have been, in western mythology, the fastest gun who ever lived—and nobody's ever heard of him. If it had been Jesse James and Frank James, I would never have had the scene there at all, because I wouldn't have had to establish in the audience's mind that Jesse James could shoot a gun. Here we are dealing with two men who, for reasons beyond understanding, movies never dealt with. So I had to try and set up, as well as I could, some kind of awareness that this guy is some *bomb*, and you don't want to get him angry at you. And his name *means* something. That's curious because it's not a good scene. It was the best I could do. The producer kept saying, "You must fix this scene. Get rid of it. Do something." And I would try and try and try, and all the while Hill was whispering in my other ear, "Leave it alone. I can make it play, I can make it play." Well, what he did was, he had that incredible close-up of Redford. If George were famous for being an artistic director, which he isn't, they would be talking about that close-up shot. Phenomenal. It's like ninety seconds; it's maybe the longest single close-up I have ever known. That whole scene is played in the close-up of his face. The whole poker game is set up—it's all on his face. And the reason George did it that way is that nobody knew who Bob was at that time.

We had to establish very early in the audience's mind that this was a movie where the stars were Paul Newman *and* a relative unknown, Bob Redford. Redford wasn't going to disappear in reel three and come back in reel twelve. This guy was going to be in there along with Paul Newman. Usually that second guy isn't. He disappears to get water, and he comes back after the star has had all the action, right? So George shot it that way. He always knew he could make the thing play, and he did. The reason those props kept changing is, you think, "What can we have him shoot that will look good? Let's try poker chips. Let's try this. Let's try that." And finally you end up with the best you can. And we got away with it because it's so beautifully done. The scene works for the audience, though it's not a very skillful scene when you see it written.

BRADY: I understand that one of the funniest lines in the screenplay occurred when Butch, on their arrival in Bolivia, says, "Just think, fifty years ago nothing was here." I understand that was cut because Newman couldn't keep a straight face.

GOLDMAN: I was told that. It's a good line, isn't it? It's a nice line. I didn't know that. I'm not even sure. Is that in the printed script or not?

BRADY: It's in print.

GOLDMAN: I didn't know that. I guess Newman just basically got hysterical. Hill said it somewhere. I didn't know that.

BRADY: Paul Newman has called *Butch Cassidy and the Sundance Kid* a love affair between two men. What was your thought as a writer creating this relationship between two men?

GOLDMAN: Well, the movie has been, in the days of Women's Liberation, criticized as being one of the first of what they call "buddy" films, which we have been plagued with over the last ten years as women's roles have waned and there are mostly male stars. How can I put this? I tend to write male relationships. I have from my first novel on—*Temple of Gold*. One of the reasons I did *The Stepford Wives* was I've always avoided doing movies that had many central, crucial female roles. But I don't think I write women very well. And when I read the Levin novel, I thought, "Hey, I can make this play." The movie didn't work out very well, but the reason I did it, besides liking the novel, was that I thought it was an opportunity for me to try and write two women that I could make real. So I don't really know about Paul's statement. Certainly it's *his* statement. He can make it if he wants to. It may be valid. I was trying to write a western.

BRADY: In writing *The Stepford Wives,* in trying to get away from strong male roles, did you find out anything about yourself as a writer?

GOLDMAN: It was such an unpleasant experience, *Stepford,* that I remember little of it. Very often you block out when a movie is a rotten experience, and most of them are. That will sound terrible when you put it into print because people will say, "Who the hell is he to say that? He's getting paid X dollars and I am selling shoes." The reality is, again, you do those movies because you *want* them to be wonderful. It's a certain percentage of my life. I didn't *have* to do that movie for the money. I did that movie because I wanted to do that movie and not movie A, B, C, D or E. In the case of *Stepford,* this is not meant to be critical; nor is it meant to be evil. Bryan Forbes was brought over as director. Bryan is English, and he has always written those films he has directed. And Bryan rewrote *all* of *Stepford,* until the last twenty minutes of the film, which is mine. He would have rewritten that, too, but he didn't have any time. I'm not saying that it would have been better if it had been mine; but I'm saying it *isn't* mine, and I wanted my name off it, and they didn't take it off.

BRADY: Were you able to use your premise that *Butch Cassidy* is historically accurate as a defense against requests for rewriting on that project?

GOLDMAN: No. I tend as a screenwriter to think of myself as being supportive. The only thing about me as a screenwriter that makes me different from most other screenwriters—not better or worse, but different—is I don't want to be a producer, I don't want to be a director. I don't want any more power than I have. I don't know if I could *have* any more power than I have, but I sure don't want it, because in my heart I am a novelist. In my head I am a novelist who happens to write screenplays. I think there is an adversary situation between writers and directors, anyway, because directors *really* want to say it's all theirs. They *really* do, and they're frustrated because most of them can't write, and secretly they all wish they could. And I think it's true that most screenwriters really want to direct. They *want* to. I think I would, too, if I weren't a novelist. You would go mad. So I try to think of myself as being supportive. And if somebody asks for a rewrite, I will give it to them, if I feel I can. If I can't, I'll leave the picture. But usually you try to stay in.

You try to hang on as long as you are able to. You are hired to do a certain thing. They are paying me for whatever skills I have. I mean, I'll argue wildly if I think they are screwing up something, but the scene in *Butch* we talked about, I thought was a terrible scene. So when they said, "Let's get rid of this scene and improve it," I was only too happy to do that. If they had said, "I don't like the scene with Butch and Sundance on the rocks when they're talking just before they jump off into the water," I would have gone to the mat for that scene because obviously it works. I mean, I had that scene in my mind before I wrote the chase. The fact that Sundance can't swim is not an accidental discovery. I knew that before I wrote the movie. I knew the Sundance Kid couldn't swim, so I felt what a terrific thing—to make this terrific gun for hire so vulnerable.

BRADY: Is that historical?

GOLDMAN: No. I have no idea. We don't know if Sundance could read, write or anything. We don't know anything about him. That was a thing I made up. I may have, in researching, read that So-and-So couldn't swim, or that many cowboys were not good swimmers. And so I may have grabbed it and thought, "Gee, wouldn't that be good for Sundance." So you remember that.

BRADY: Whose thinking was it to open *Butch* in black and white, shift to sepia tone, then into color?

GOLDMAN: I assume Hill. The reason I say I *assume* Hill is I don't know. I'm only present for a certain amount of the film, as everybody's only present for a certain amount. It *might* have been that Connie Hall said something to Hill, but I doubt that. I think it was George's wish.

BRADY: The first draft of *Butch Cassidy* ends with the soldiers filling the patio where the two outlaws were holed up. The final draft ends with a freeze of Butch and Sundance apparently while they were still in the room. There is no indication that they are on the move, or running out into gunfire; and yet the shooting script ends with a freeze of Butch and Sundance breaking out. Which ending did you feel was strongest?

GOLDMAN: Oh, I loved the ending. I loved it. That's a very tricky shot. The two of them run out of the cabin, the little room they're in, and it freezes. Then the color bleeds out of the picture, and *then* you pull back. Very, very, very, very tricky shot to do. I don't know how they did it—I wasn't there for the shooting. My memory is that Hill said they had a guy who was the head of cameras for Fox, or it may have been an independent camera-genius type, who told him that they could do it that way. Technically it's quite a shot.

That's why I say the production designer is so crucial. I'll give you an example. One scene that nobody likes very much in terms of production is the shoot-out scene with the Mexican bandits. Butch and Sundance are above, and the bandits are down below. They couldn't find a decent location. They took the best location they could, but I remember George saying, "It never really lit very well. It doesn't look good. The contrasts weren't what anybody wanted." And when you look at the scene, it looks quite bland. I mean, ultimately the scene plays because of the action. It's so funny—you know all the slow-motion Peckinpah stuff? We were meant to come out before *The Wild Bunch,* but George wasn't ready. So we did not come out in June. We came out in late September. Had we come out in June with all of our slow-motion violence, Peckinpah would have been accused of copying us instead of us copying him, when in fact nobody was copying anybody.

BRADY: But someone was looking at *Bonnie and Clyde.*

GOLDMAN: Maybe they were both copying Arthur Penn. I don't know. As I said, the New York reviews of *Butch* were really rotten. And critics are such *fools* very often because the idea that two movies coming out at the same time could be somehow imitative is ridiculous, because movies are so slow and take so long, it's very hard to know who's copying whom.

BRADY: You say that you are a novelist who just happens to write screenplays, and yet you said too that you conceived *Butch*

Cassidy and the Sundance Kid as a screenplay and nothing but. Given that pure state of your writing at the time—as a screenwriter—were you satisfied with the film, the outcome?

GOLDMAN: Oh yeah, I think it's really a nice film. I really do. I like it. We opened on a Thursday. We had rotten notices. On Saturday, Hill and I had agreed to do a talk for some film teachers, and so we did a question-and-answer thing. They had seen the movie and I remember one of the questions was, "Did Burt Bacharach intentionally steal the 'Raindrops' song from Fellini's *La Strada,* or do you think it was just a case of unintentional copying?" And I remember my answer—"I can't answer for Mr. Bacharach, but I'm thrilled that you think any of us would have heard of Fellini." That kind of thing. I remember George and I walking with tears behind our eyes, because we really thought it was a nice movie, and it was a disaster. And we stopped by the Sutton Theater where it was playing at Fifty-seventh Street and went in. The manager was just ecstatic. And we said, "Why are you ecstatic?" And he said, "Because we are doing terrific business and the audience likes it." And it was also playing at a Broadway house. We said, "Is it doing well there, too?" He said, "I'll find out." So he called the Broadway house—and it *was.* Then we walked to Fifty-seventh and Park, where we split, and I remember one of us saying, "Maybe we haven't got a failure after all."

The first time I saw *Butch,* Fox did one of those awful opinion-making previews where they hired a theater that had no warm bodies, no people who pay. They had it filled with critics, people in the business and opinion makers. And the movie lay there like this great turd. Nobody laughed, nobody liked anything. It was just death. Then the reviews came out and they were bad. I didn't really see the movie again until it was revived very successfully a few years ago. I went with my kids and we sat and looked at it, and it was like Gilbert and Sullivan because all the audience had seen the movie before and they were reacting *before* the Kid says, "I can't swim." It was a wonderful experience. Yes, I liked the movie very much. The only two movies of mine that I like a lot are *A Bridge Too Far* and *Butch.*

BRADY: What happened to your other western, *Mr. Horn?*

GOLDMAN: In terms of the West, it's about the most talented man who ever lived—Tom Horn, who was very controversial. For a while it either was or was not going to go as a movie, and Robert Redford either was or was not going to do it. I had nothing to do with it at this point. I don't know what happened, but eventually it got to Lorimar and somebody timed it, which I had never done, and it came out to be three hours and twenty minutes —which is why I think someone said, "Wait a minute—that's a four-hour television movie." At one time a director was sent in to work with me, but then he got another job, and I never talked with the guy who eventually directed it for TV with David Carradine. I've not seen the movie myself, though I taped it and I will watch it sometime. That's such a fabulous piece of material; Horn's life is so incredible. It's a great story, if it can be well told.

For me *Mr. Horn* was my last western. When I think of myself as a movie writer, it is as a genre writer. I tend to do one of each. I doubt that I'll ever write another war movie. I doubt that I'll ever write another spy movie. I wrote my caper picture—*Hot Rock*. I want to do other things. I am very anxious to write a musical. And I want to write a romantic-comedy-thriller type. I want to write those kinds of movies for which I had great affection as a child, and for which I have great affection now. I want to try and write one of them and then try something else. Since *A Bridge Too Far,* I am getting offered a lot of big war movies. Well, the last thing in the world I want to do is write a big war movie. I've done that. I think it would be extremely dull to try it again.

BRADY: How much research did you do for *A Bridge Too Far?*

GOLDMAN: Six months. I'll describe the work habits. It was June and I was coming back from Paris, to London to New York, on locations for *Marathon Man.* I had read the Cornelius Ryan book, had met with Richard Attenborough. The meeting went not well. Personally it went fine, but we couldn't get the script going. Then he came to America and we met again, and the meeting went *very* well. (Attenborough, by the way, is the most decent human being I have met in the picture business.) And then we went back to England and I stayed for about two weeks and I found all these other books on Arnhem. We would meet in the afternoons, and I would read a book in the evening and in the morning. Very often they weren't *whole* books on Arnhem. If the Sean Connery part had written his memoirs, maybe half would deal with his days at Arnhem, so I'd just read that portion. And then Attenborough would come in the afternoon and I would say, "I read this. This is a good character, I think. Do you like that? Did you know he was air sick?" All kinds of stuff. And he would say, "I like that, I don't like that, we can make that work." Whatever. So for a period of two weeks I was reading a book a day. Obviously you can't read them very heavily, very carefully, but you know a lot.

BRADY: Using your colored-check-mark system?

GOLDMAN: No, I only do that on the original, on the source. That was June. And I guess I wrote the screenplay in October, November; the screenplay was done before Christmas. Six months.

BRADY: The planning stage of a script like *Bridge* strikes me as being like going through a telephone cable—with a book that has several stories and several dozen characters, all of some merit.

GOLDMAN: It was hard. For example, there were five Victoria Crosses awarded to the British at Arnhem, and we didn't use any of them in the script. *All* of them fabulous stories of personal heroism. None of them could be worked into the story. Ultimately, what you try to do—as I said before, structure is crucial —is to wallow through all that stuff and find what the story's going to be: the ultimate, basic thread that you can hang everything else on. In *A Bridge Too Far* the plot is this: The Americans and the British are being parachuted behind the enemy lines, and this giant armored corps under the command of General Horrocks is to march up this single road and go over these bridges —which the Americans and the English have paratrooped in and taken—and reach the last bridge, which is Arnhem, and then wheel into Germany and end the war. So it's a matter of bridge, bridge, bridge. It's a linear thing: sixty miles of bridges to be taken, and this armored corps is to punch up this single road, go over it, each successive bridge, and over the last bridge at Arnhem. Well, Horrocks has a speech to his men when he tells them what the plan is, and he says, "I like to think that this is one of those American westerns. The Germans are the bad guys, and the paratroopers are the homesteaders because they haven't got a lot of supplies and they are under terrible pressure. And we're the cavalry on the way to the rescue." Well, once I had that thought—that *A Bridge Too Far* is the ultimate cavalry-to-the-rescue story, except the cavalry ends up one mile short—once I had that, there was the spine of the piece, and everything that could be threaded to hang off that spine, that was it. And if I could use it, super. If I couldn't use it, no matter how good the material was, it had to go.

In *All the President's Men,* Bob Woodward was incredibly helpful and talked with me endlessly on it. I remember saying at one point, "What were the *essential,* basic, crucial things that happened?" And he listed something like thirteen of them. And I remember thinking, "Yes, I've used them all." The book runs about three hundred and fifty pages, and the movie ends somewhere near page one ninety, on their Haldeman screw-up. And the notion on that was since Woodward and Bernstein had become media darlings, there was no point in glorifying them. Wouldn't it be classier, maybe, to end on their screw-up and let the audience carry the fact that *they were right* out of the theater with them? Now, in doing that, we lost a lot of wonderful material, most notably Judge Sirica. But ultimately, we were doing a movie that could only run about two hours and fifteen minutes. There was a limit to how much you can do. So the structure of *President's Men,* however much Hoffman or Pakula like to ad-lib, is basically there. They can do what they damn well please with it. As long as they maintain the structure. That's what's essential.

BRADY: You're talking almost along the lines of architecture, and anything that's extraneous, nonfunctional, must go.

GOLDMAN: Yes. I've done a lot of thinking myself about what a screenplay is, and I've come up with nothing except that it's carpentry, it's basically putting down some kind of structural form that they can then mess around with. And as long as they keep the structural form, whatever I have written is relatively valid; a scene will hold, regardless of the dialogue. It's the *thrust* of the scene that's kept pure.

BRADY: Is *A Bridge Too Far* historically accurate?

GOLDMAN: Nothing *spectacular* in *A Bridge Too Far* is fabricated. There's a great deal that's fabricated and brought together in amalgamations of characters and things like that, but nothing that's spectacular is made up. And there's a great deal of spectacular action, people doing incredible things. There's a sequence where the Germans have a bridge set to be blown up. And we had seen an earlier bridge blown up. So we know they can do it, right? And the general calls up this commanding general and says, "They are trying to get across the bridge. I request permission to blow up the bridge." And the German commanding general says, "No, you may not blow up the bridge." So they hang up and the German general says, "I'm not going to have my ass in a sling in Berlin letting the goddamn English and the Americans get across the bridge. The minute I see anybody on the goddamn bridge I am blowing it sky high. Get the engineer."

So they get ready to blow the bridge. The Americans and the British *take* the bridge, and he blows it. Except the explosives don't work. That's fabulous material. And that's all valid. You can't make up stuff like that. I mean, when have you ever heard of a commanding general being disobeyed by another general for reasons of career prestige, deciding to go against this commanding general—which is a court-martial offense. And then the explosives don't work, for reasons we never knew. That's super material, I think. So I say that it's valid, yes, I think *Bridge* is accurate. It's as accurate as *President's Men* is accurate.

In other words, you are not doing a documentary. *President's Men* covered many months and a lot of peoples' lives, and *Bridge* covers ten days and maybe seventy-five thousand peoples' lives —the Germans and the Dutch and the Americans and the British. Is it like a Robert Flaherty documentary? Of course not. But I would suggest it's accurate in terms of the spirit of the piece. It's as accurate as we can make it and tell a story. There are no dancing girls.

BRADY: Do you use charts or organization materials on a story line so complex?

GOLDMAN: No, depending. On *President's Men* I think I had Woodward's list of crucial anecdotes . . . the break-in, the General Accounting Office scene, and so on. I think I had that. I don't use much. As I say, sometimes I'll write down a scrap of dialogue to remind me of a scene, but usually I have it in my head. Lately, I've been doing this. I'll write down a list of scenes —thirty, forty, eighty scenes. They won't be scenes really, but key words—like fifty words, and each word is supposed to remind me of a scene that *promotes* the story. Since we are dealing with structure, that's crucial.

BRADY: You spoke earlier of doing genre-type films. Do you study other films to get the *feel* of a genre?

GOLDMAN: No, one of the sad things about what's happened since I've been so involved with film writing lately is I don't go to the movies as much anymore. I am working off my childhood. I mean, I've *seen* a lot of westerns, and I know what a western looks like. And I have memories of John Wayne and Ronald Reagan in war pictures, so I know what war pictures look like. I remember them. I was an *avid* moviegoer, but not anymore; it's just too unpleasant. When I write, I write all day, every day. I come here five days a week anyway, if only to have coffee and read the New York *Daily News* and the *Times*. But when I am writing, I come here seven days, and I am here from morning till night. And if I've done that all day for a period of weeks or months, the idea of going out with my wife to a movie—well, it's got to be a very special movie for me to do it.

BRADY: Why do you pour your prime years into the movies when you consider yourself a novelist?

GOLDMAN: Well, the only one I really wonder about is Joan Didion, who I think is so fabulously gifted, I wonder why she wastes time doing movies. I assume her answer would be the same thing. First of all, I don't know how good a novelist *she* thinks she is. I've gotten into a habit lately. The novels that I write tend to be ideas that happened years and years and years ago, and seven, eight or ten years after the initial incident I'll want to write that novel. If I wrote novels every day, I wouldn't write movies. It's as simple as that. But I have to have something to do between the times I am writing novels. I've been a professional writer now since 1956. I wrote my first novel when I was twenty-four. But I've written ten novels. Well, that's one every two years and I have got to do something in between. Now what I have found to do in between is write movies.

I have a theory. In the early years of my career I used to write a lot of short stories, and I was not very good at it. Finally, in the late fifties or early sixties, I wrote a decent short story—but it was never published. Everybody turned it down. I think I got seventy-eight rejections on it. I thought, "They don't want me." I finally did something that was as good as I thought I could do, and nobody wanted it. There was no point in continuing. I had a certain skill and facility for screenwriting, and since my career has clearly gone so well as a screenwriter, I think I keep doing it because they want me. Does that make any sense?

BRADY: Absolutely.

GOLDMAN: I assume that if anybody had taken my short stories I never would have done screenwriting. I don't mean that to sound as simpleminded as it is. I didn't *seek* screenwriting.

BRADY: Have you ever had the fear that your reputation as a screenwriter might account for your name on the cover of your next novel?

GOLDMAN: Oh, sure. As long as I basically don't think of myself as being a screenwriter primarily, it doesn't matter what my publisher puts on the jacket of my books to try and make the books sell. Basically it's what's inside my head, and I don't think of myself as a screenwriter.

BRADY: You had stories rejected when you were in college, didn't you? Oberlin, as I recall.

GOLDMAN: Yes, that is correct. I never showed any signs of talent when I was growing up. I graduated from college in 1952; I went in the Army; then in 1954 I got out and went to Columbia graduate school, and in June of 1956 I had my master's and the hours for a doctorate, and I was sick of school. I am linguistically impoverished. I had to learn three languages to get a Ph.D., and there was no way I could learn three languages.

I went home to Chicago—Highland Park—and in early July I sat down and I wrote in wild desperation my first novel—*The Temple of Gold*—in ten days. I never had that experience before. I literally would go to sleep at night not knowing what was going to happen in the book the next day, but I had this desperate sense that this was it: It was fish-or-cut-bait time. I had heard of an agent, sent the book to the agent, and it was taken by the first publisher it went to. If that had not happened, I would be in advertising. Since I had shown such little sign of talent growing up, I never would have written a second novel. I never would have dreamt of it.

When I say "such little sign of talent" what I mean is I took two creative writing courses when I was in college, one at Oberlin and one in summer school at Northwestern—and I got the worst grade in class in both of them. I was the fiction editor of my college literary magazine. There were three of us who were editors. Things were submitted anonymously, then voted on. I would submit my short stories, but I could not get my own short stories in the literary magazine when I was the fiction editor of it! I had really no great encouragement. I always knew I wanted to try it, but if it hadn't happened, I would probably be in advertising and drinking heavily at this point. But I never would have written a second book. And that's not bullshit.

BRADY: Did you do some work on *Papillon?*

GOLDMAN: Yes, I was the original writer on *Papillon.* There's one line of mine in the movie—the last line of the movie. In a sense, it's my structure, my decision to end it *there.* (The book goes on for another couple hundred pages.) I don't know if I should say it's my structure. I probably shouldn't. I only saw the movie once, and I've forgotten it. I do *not* claim much of it. It was one of those awful situations where I was working with Franklin Schaffner, who, I think, was relatively pleased, or said he was relatively pleased, with what he had. I really worked a long time with *Papillon.* I worked through three drafts of it. And

Steve McQueen, I think, needed money, because the divorce was coming through and costs of the movie kept escalating. I was present at the meeting at which some guys said, "Dustin Hoffman is getting hot. If we only had a part for Dustin Hoffman, that would be terrific." And we scoffed because there *was* no part. Meantime, I moved on from *Papillon* to *Waldo Pepper*. But they needed another star, so they made an amalgamation of the secondary parts and gave them all to Dustin Hoffman to try and make a secondary role. And since the movie has become such an enormous worldwide success, they were right to do what they did. Yes, I worked for six months on it. That was my Devil's Island picture.

BRADY: Another genre fulfilled. What happened to *The Thing of It Is* as a screenplay in 1969?

GOLDMAN: Oh, anguish. I went through it twice. It's a lunatic story. It's a novella of mine from before *Butch Cassidy*. I don't know who gave the book to Redford; somebody did, and he said, "Will you do it?" So I did it on spec for him. He read it and he liked it. And I had a director. Then *Butch* opened. Eventually Bob called me from the Salt Lake City airport, saying, "Listen, I don't think I can do that movie anymore. I don't think the audience will accept me in that kind of role. The character is kind of weak." The next day we had, at the time when he was really hot, Elliott Gould; and we had Faye Dunaway; and the director was Ulu Grosbard. Then Ulu walked off the picture to do *Harry Kellerman,* which is what killed his career for six years. It really put him out of work. It's an interesting thing in the movie business. There are some hits that can actually not help you. There are some flops that cannot hurt you, and there are some flops that can really kill you.

BRADY: What are some of the distinctions there?

GOLDMAN: It's hard to say. I don't think, for example, that *For Pete's Sake* helped Peter Yates' career, because everybody thought it was such an abominable movie. Now I think Peter's got enormous success from *Breaking Away*—for which I am delighted, because he is a very nice human being. But I think nobody cared that *For Pete's Sake* did business. Everybody hated it so badly. The kind of flop that can hurt you? Stanley Donen's picture with Liza Minnelli, *Lucky Lady.* I don't know. They are like a pack Out There, and they decided that *Harry Kellerman* was one of those flops that hurt.

Anyway, Ulu walked off to do *Harry Kellerman.* We had terrible trouble getting a director. Eventually we got a director whom I am *not* a fan of, and who behaved badly. He walked on the picture and then walked off the picture and then walked on the picture and then walked off—and then he came back on on the condition that I was forced off it. So I self-destructed the project. The director I *wanted* for the movie was Stanley Donen, who had done *Two for the Road,* which I adored, and all those other things. But—and this is an example of how the movie business works—when I mentioned Donen to an agent, he said, "Stanley's gone around the bend. He's not directing anymore. There's no point in going to Stanley."

The next year Stanley came to town, called me, and I gave him the screenplay. He loved it, wanted to do it, and I found out the truth—which was that Stanley was not this agent's client. And so he lied. I mean, this man actually said, "Stanley Donen is insane, is in an asylum and cannot work anymore." If I had *known* more at the time, I would have called up Stanley Donen and given him this script. Elliott Gould was a client, Faye Dunaway was a client, and the director who behaved badly was a client—and the agent was making a package. Which is why I am so happy being with Evarts Ziegler because I am not a loss leader, which is all I would be if I were with some of those other people.

Anyway, Stanley came in the second year. The movie happened again. We had a girl, we had Mia Farrow. Bob Evans at Paramount was to produce it. But we needed a guy. Bob Evans turned down Jimmy Caan, who wasn't "box office" at that time, according to Evans. I think he would be very happy to take Jimmy Caan now. Alan Alda wanted to do it, and would have been wonderful—this was before *M*A*S*H.* Evans didn't want him either. So we couldn't get a *man.* What happened was, Evans needed a picture for Ali MacGraw, and Mia Farrow was preempted to do another movie, so *The Thing of It Is* became an Ali MacGraw vehicle. She and Bob were having trouble, and she was up with McQueen, and Evans was desperately looking for something; then it went to MacGraw, and she didn't want to do it. And that was the last of *The Thing of It Is*. Evans lost interest. Donen went on to other things. And all the various versions of the movie, if my agent has anything to do with it, will never happen. Never ever. I went through a great deal of grief because of that movie.

This is not to knock L.A., which is beautiful and peaceful and all that—but it's also, in a superficial way, deals. It's "take a meeting." (That's a funny line in *Annie Hall:* "All the good meetings are taken.") Writing, ultimately, is really about one thing: going into a room by yourself and doing it. No one is going to do it for you. But out there if you are having lunch with someone, they'll say, "We'll make a development deal."

There are directors out there who will have eight, ten development deals going—and they'll do the eleventh movie; not any of the ten. And what's incredible about it is that the people who make the development deals with them *know* they aren't going to make any of the ten! But the nature of the business is to be able to say, "Well, I had lunch with John Brady the other day, and I think he's really interested in that *Craft of the Screenwriter* project." So all of a sudden we'll spend twenty-five thousand dollars, and you will "develop" it, as they say. It's frightening. One can get seduced so easily out there. I have on my wall a great quote from Sir Laurence Olivier. He and Charlton Heston had done a play somewhere about twenty-five years ago, and they'd gotten slaughtered. Heston said, "Well, I guess you've just got to forget the bad reviews." And Olivier said, "No, you've got to forget the good ones." I subscribe to that theory.

There's part of us that wants to be flattered, part of us that wants to believe we're wonderful. And the fact is, of course, we're not. We're all of us just trying to get through the day. I believe that what's dangerous about being flattered is you begin to believe it, and then you begin to expect it; and then all of a sudden it takes you farther and farther away from going into a room by yourself. I think it's very important to remember who we were while we're being what we are. I think that's terribly important for writers. I think our strength, our core, our *dramatis personae,* everything we write about is formed in those early years; and if you forget that person—those early eight or ten years of your life—and become what contemporary success will bring you, it cuts you away from where your strength is as a writer.

The standard cliché thing for an actor is, you make it in New York, you divorce your wife, and you marry somebody new in Southern California. The reason you do that is because your wife in New York, where you were an off-Broadway actor, remembers who you were before people were stroking you. She's the one who says, "Will you go to the door?" or, "Please go and do the shopping." But if you're an actor, you're a role player; and you *want* this new role. It's better, if you're an actor, to go through life and have nobody disagree with you—which is what happens to stars. Stars go through week after week and nobody ever says boo to them. I think star directors go through the same syndrome. And for a writer, I think it's frightening.

BRADY: Do reviews contribute to the headiness, or can they bring a writer down to earth with a crash when a movie is in release?

GOLDMAN: I don't know. I don't read them. I have a defense against any of that stuff: I do not read those things that I don't ordinarily read. I read in my ordinary life—besides *Sports Illustrated, The Sporting News,* and *Variety—The New York Times,* the New York *Daily News* and the New York *Post.* But I tend to get bad reviews—I have for twenty years—in New York, in particular; and it would be madness for me to seek out what *The New Yorker* or *Time* said about me. I try not to read reviews. It has nothing to do with writing.

Once I was in my dentist's office, and I saw a review of *Slap Shot.* I wanted George Hill to do well, so I read it. It was by John Simon. The opening sentence was something like (I'll misquote it), "George Roy Hill is a very careful director who makes very good movies when he is not working with William Goldman."

Well, I had *nothing* to do with *Slap Shot*. You know what I mean? So I don't read reviews. It's one of my salvations. I don't read them, good or bad. But I read that gratuitous cheap shot, and I said, "Jesus Christ, don't do that."

I told you earlier about the compliment given me by Stanley Donen. The other compliment which I treasure is from a friend of mine. These are the only two. A friend of mine said to me, "Whatever part of you is a writer you really protect." It seems to me that's essential, because the minute you start getting involved with reviews, or interviews (like this), or hype on movies, or any kind of extracurricular lecturing or answering fan letters or *any* kind of stuff like that—it has nothing to do with writing. And you can begin to become Peter Bogdanovich and believe your own press clippings, and then it's disaster time. It seems to me that it's essential to maintain a low profile and go about your business as quietly as possible.

BRADY: You said of Broadway critics in *The Season,* "You get the dregs, the stagestruck, the untalented neurotic who eventually drifts into criticism as a means of clinging peripherally to the arts. They fail and they are going to do their damnedest to see that everybody else falls flat, too." Are film critics also failures in your mind?

GOLDMAN: I don't read them.

BRADY: Are they influential?

GOLDMAN: On *some* films. I don't think it matters remotely how bad they said *Poseidon Adventure* was (they all said it was terrible). I think the reason people go to—quote—"big films" is that they hear they're fun or they hear they're good. I think reviewers are crucial to a foreign film. I think they are crucial to a small film, although Vincent Canby didn't write a worse review than the one he wrote for *Rocky*. It didn't matter very much, did it? Word of mouth is important. Everybody would *rather* have good reviews. Nobody likes to be criticized in print. But it's still word of mouth. I mean, why didn't people go to see *Nashville?* Because they heard it was dull, and they were right—it was dull. Very, very slow and tedious and pointless and arbitrary. But it got the reviews of the decade. In essence, reviews are mostly cosmetic for a major American film. They may help to form, in a crazy way, word of mouth. But I don't know of anybody who's ever said, "I'm going to see this movie because John Simon said it was wonderful."

BRADY: Here's a quote from Pauline Kael on *The Great Waldo Pepper:* "Goldman writes in a make-believe world where heroes play boyish tricks on one another, and where they are masters of repartee one moment and strong, silent men the next." In the same review she says the *Waldo Pepper* screenplay is "coldhearted and clever." Do you have any comment on that?

GOLDMAN: No. I don't know that she is wrong. Ultimately, I don't know what it means. Has she read the screenplay? It's very hard to know (not to say that Kael is right or wrong in that quote) who did what. *Waldo Pepper* had a screenplay by me, a wild fight between me and George Hill, a year in which we did not speak to each other (Universal sent a guy to New York with George's instructions; he would then tell me what George said, and I would tell him what to tell George when he went back). A rewrite by George was so terrible that the project was in trouble and was not going to get off the ground. Finally I was brought back in to salvage it, because Bob Redford wouldn't do what George had written. George and I are now speaking, and I hope to work with George before I die. But we are both very abrasive, George and I. So when you say that the screenplay is "coldhearted and clever," does Kael know all that? Is she talking about the *movie* being coldhearted and clever, or is she talking about the screenplay? It's very hard to say. It's a group thing. *What* was coldhearted, and *what* was clever? I am not saying that she is wrong, but I just don't know what she is referring to.

All that I would ask of any critic is that the critic go in unbiased and be honest. Where the *auteur* theory of directors falls to pieces for me is not that it's just madness as far as American films are concerned—because movies are a group endeavor—but . . . which Mike Nichols are you getting? The guy who did *The Graduate,* or the guy who did *The Fortune?* It's not the same guy. You catch one at the prime, you catch one at an off period, maybe? I don't know why. I'm not out to knock Mike Nichols.

What I am saying is I like *M*A*S*H*, and I thought *Nashville* was a snooze. Which Robert Altman are you getting? Are you getting the one who does *Images* and is very pretentious, or are you getting the one who does *McCabe and Mrs. Miller?* What I'm saying is, Shakespeare wrote *King John.* If you were an *auteur* critic, every Shakespeare play would, by its very nature, have to be a great play because it was by Shakespeare. And that's madness. We all know that some of the worst plays ever written were written by William Shakespeare. That doesn't affect the fact that he's the greatest writer who ever lived. Some of the *worst* films ever made are made by great directors. I think that Ingmar Bergman is the great contemporary figure. One of the worst movies I ever saw was a picture of his called *All These Women.* He's made a couple of awful, awful films, but that doesn't affect the fact that he is a . . . I don't know, I have no words for what I think he is. But ultimately he has good and bad days, just like the rest of us. That's what I object to in the *auteur* critics: They often are blinded by favoritism. All that I expect of any decent critic in films is that there be honesty.

BRADY: What do you mean by honesty?

GOLDMAN: Most critics don't go in with an open mind. *The Village Voice* listed their Ten Best Films of All Time, right? It's so screamingly funny that you wouldn't believe it! Their pick of the greatest film of all time is *Vertigo.* Well, you have to understand what that means. In the first place it means that they don't care about acting, because no film in which the female lead is Kim Novak can *possibly* be the greatest film of all time. OK. That's thing one. Thing two, Hitchcock is a demigod in their pantheon. If you're an *auteur*ist reviewer like all those people are on the *Voice*, Hitchcock is this giant. Well, you can't pick *Psycho*, you see, because lots of people pick *Psycho*. And the Orson Welles movie they pick—they don't pick *Citizen Kane*, they pick *Ambersons*, because *everybody* knows *Citizen Kane* is good. So look at the *Voice*'s list of the greatest movies of all time, and you know they had their minds made up. It has nothing to do with any kind of honesty.

BRADY: Your book *The Season* is a devastating profile of the business of Broadway. Now that you are on the inside of the film business, have you given any thought to a nonfiction book?

GOLDMAN: No. *The Season* came about for reasons that I won't go into, but I had been too much with the picture business, and I had made all that money on the *Butch Cassidy* sale, and I expressed quite vulgarly to you earlier how inaccurate most show business writing is. I was *passionate* that *The Season* should be accurate—and there are *still* a number of people who won't speak to me because of it. I was appalled. I hadn't expected that reaction. I was really stunned. I mean, actresses and directors and such who do *not* speak to me. So, to answer you, we are all of us very sensitive about people saying negative things about us in print. I think it would be suicide to try and write a nonfiction book about the movie business. People don't want it. People are very sensitive to criticism. Everybody is.

BRADY: Has *Tinsel* created any resentment from the Hollywood community? Though fiction, the book has its share of lifelike personalities.

GOLDMAN: *The Season* created a tremendous amount of flak, but the feedback on *Tinsel* was different. My agent circulated it to see if anyone wanted to buy it as a movie, and I was worried about reaction because I don't want to insult anybody or hurt anyone's feelings. But the feedback that Zig got was that people felt it was not a zap book on Hollywood. I'm very pleased about that. I want it to be accurate and authentic, but I don't want to run into comments like, "How could you bite the hand that feeds you?" I don't think it's that kind of book. As I think on it, *Tinsel* is very much like *Boys and Girls Together*—it's about five people in a town and how their lives develop and interact, and it's fairly long for me, longer than novels I've been doing lately.

BRADY: How did *Tinsel* come about?

GOLDMAN: I turned forty-five in August of 1976, at which time I promised my family—and because I wanted to do it, too—I would slow down. In the three years prior to that, I had written two novels (*Marathon Man* and *Magic*) and six screenplays, plus all of the rewrites. I was simply working way, way too hard. And so in August of that year I tried to slow down. What I didn't know was I *couldn't* slow down; I could only stop. And I was going crazy. I was doing some work—rewriting a screenplay, say—but there was no real writing going on for a period of time, so I arbitrarily said that on April Fool's Day of 1978 I would begin a novel, no matter what, because it had been almost two years since I'd written anything of my own.

I was so desperate to write a novel, I started two. I wanted to write a Hollywood novel, but it turned out I wasn't ready for it. *Tinsel,* though it is a Hollywood novel too, isn't the one I thought I would do. Through the first week I alternated on the two books —three pages on one, three pages on the other—and at the end of the week the second novel, the one that became *Tinsel,* was working all right, so I gave up on the other and just worked on that from April through August.

I also wrote an original screenplay for Joseph Levine—a pirate movie, *The Sea King.* I don't know what he'll do with it. Movies are so expensive now. It depends on someone saying, "OK, we'll spend the fifteen million dollars and make this pirate movie." It's a big investment, and everything has to be propitious, or you can get into terrible trouble. It's a potentially dangerous project, because so much of it takes place on water. An old unit manager once advised me, "Never do movies with *waak:* water, animals, airplanes and kids." Those are four things you can't control. You can't say to the water, "OK, smooth now. We're gonna do a retake." You have to wait for the water to smooth. And airplanes are a bitch, because you have to get the clouds just right . . . et cetera. In terms of technical stuff, stay away from *waak.*

BRADY: Will you ever get back to doing that other Hollywood novel now that you've done *Tinsel* instead?

GOLDMAN: Well, I would like to. I've always been intrigued in writing a novel about stars. And if I write another Hollywood novel, it will be that one. But I am so totally instinctive as a writer at this point, I don't know what's going to happen. It's funny how an idea from six or eight years back will suddenly press itself upon you. I'll put on the wall in my office every year or so little notes with my squiggles, labeled: "I Want to Write" —and then I'll list the movies, books, nonfiction, whatever I want to write. Sometimes I'll look back at one of these old lists —what I wanted to write in 1973, say—and I don't remember what most of them are. I'll look at "old man in detective story," and wonder, "What in hell was that?" On the other hand, I remember a note in 1970—"Bormann to New York"—that became *Marathon Man*. Like any free-lancer who is self-employed, I never quite know what I am going to do as my next project.

BRADY: What does being a free-lancer mean to you?

GOLDMAN: I'm a somewhat nervous individual. I would probably be much more secure emotionally if I were salaried. But when you're a free-lancer, some money will come in January; then nothing will come until April. And you fret. It's so inconsistent. I always thought it would be lovely to have a Broadway hit, to have a check coming in weekly. It would give you a great sense of security. I'm older now, but that was true of me emotionally when I was younger. Before I got into the movie business, I was writing novels. And I'd go nine months without any money coming in.

Another little fear comes along with age. Nobody knows when it's over. Except perhaps for Henry James, nobody thinks, "Well, this is my last novel, my last piece of writing." Unless you drop in your tracks, most writers go through that terrible period at the end of their lives, which can be five years or forty years, when you don't write anymore. I think there's that uncertainty in all of us free-lancers. I'm certainly aware of it. You just don't know when it's going to stop.

BRADY: Are you hearing winged chariots at your back?

GOLDMAN: I suppose I'm trying to prepare myself in advance —like in the old days, I used to bet that the Chicago Bears would lose, because I thought I wouldn't be so unhappy if they did lose. Except it didn't work that way. I was always so miserable when they did lose, I didn't gain a damn thing. But I think you have to prepare for the end as a writer, in a sense. I mean, you just don't know when it's going to occur. I can tell that there's a certain slippage in energy. I'm approaching fifty now. I used to be able to watch baseball on television and talk with the kids at the same time. Now I can't split my concentration that way. I'll get caught up in the game, and my kid is saying, "Dad, you're not listening," and I'll say, "What?" That's slippage. I'm not ready for senility yet, but I'm running into things that I can't do now that I could do ten or fifteen years ago.

BRADY: It sounds as though the agreement you made with your family—to slow down—hasn't been lived up to.

GOLDMAN: Well, I think it's been lived up to somewhat. I am certainly not the hard-driving writer I was a few years ago. In 1973 I got a rare disease—a strange kind of pneumonia, which put me in the hospital for a few days. I also had double vision for a long time, and a lot of blurred vision in the right eye. It was also the very first time I was aware of my own mortality. I suddenly thought: Jesus, I've got to get my money for my family. Once I got my health back, I went into that overdrive period— six screenplays in three years. That may not sound like much, but with rewrites it was probably closer to eighteen; plus the novels and the rewrites of the novels. I was working seven days a week. It was really very silly . . . and draining for me, draining for the family. The kids were growing up, and I was too busy working to notice. Since I decided to slow down, though, I haven't worked weekends (except when I was working on *Tinsel*), and now I stay home more. Earlier, though, I used to work all the time. I was never home. I was very driven, because I was so shocked by the disease.

BRADY: Did such overdrive writing affect your quality control?

GOLDMAN: I don't know. I'm no judge of that since I'm someone who generally gets slaughtered when reviews come out anyway. But I've never written anything I didn't *want* to write. I mean, I wasn't trying to write strictly for the money. It was a very fertile period, and I didn't put a governor on it. I just wrote a great deal in that period, and I'll never do it again.

BRADY: Even at normal speed, you turn out a lot of words.

GOLDMAN: Yes. I recently picked up a copy of *Tinsel* and read the little blurb about my writings, and I thought, "That's not something to be ashamed of. That's a reasonable amount of work. Why do I feel that I haven't done anything?" And it's because one is inside one's own skin, and I've got to get through the day the best way I can—and I *have* to keep writing. That's all that I do. I don't have a hobby. If I had a hobby, if I had something else that I enjoyed doing, things might be different. But I don't do things with my hands, and I don't paint. I write.

BRADY: How did you like the film version of *No Way to Treat a Lady?*

GOLDMAN: As I said earlier, it was about two stranglers, one of whom is jealous of the other. Well, they *cut* all that. So, I don't like it very much. I mean, they miscast. There are three roles. Lee Remick is wonderful for her role. The killer was a very mercurial, quick-talking, slender, funny guy; and the policeman is a big, ugly human being. So they cast Rod Steiger, who was not beautiful, for the mercurial, funny-guy killer, because he was hot. He was coming off his Academy Award–winning role in *In the Heat of the Night.* And George Segal was the cop. If the two had switched roles, the movie would have been better.

Again, nobody meant to make a rotten picture. Jack Smight was a perfectly skillful director. Elia Kazan said once, when I interviewed him about a play, something that I really agree with on movies. Kazan said that really your success or your failure is set by your first day of rehearsal; he felt that in a play the preparation of the script and the casting were everything. And I'm not sure I don't think that's true in a film also. By your first day of principal photography you have prepared your script and you have got your players, and if you have done that badly, it doesn't matter what you do—the film will fail. And I think *No Way to Treat a Lady,* and *Hot Rock,* were films that were basically—I'm not saying they were well written—not cast well.

BRADY: Your early novels seem somewhat autobiographical, but your screenplays and your later novels are not. They seem to be suspense stories. Are you as a writer moving somewhat away from yourself?

GOLDMAN: Boy, I hope not. I tend to be very, very good at hiding real events when I write, because it is just too embarrassing for me to have somebody come up and say, "Oh, I know who So-and-So was. It was really Such-and-Such." So I am very good at *not* having that happen. I would say that in a sense *Magic* is probably just as autobiographical as *The Temple of Gold*. I'm just a better dissembler.

BRADY: Really?

GOLDMAN: Maybe not. But I think probably. I mean, they all basically are. That whole question about autobiographical novels —once you get past Thomas Wolfe, who gave the street names, I don't know really what it means. Obviously everything we all write is autobiographical in the sense it's all *us*. Obviously, my adaptations are not in that sense autobiographical, because you feel it is somebody else's source material. The *choice* of doing this instead of that is purely autobiographical. The reason I choose to do this movie and not that movie is because something moves me in one project that doesn't move me in another, because of my own taste and the kind of person I am.

BRADY: Were you satisfied with the film version of *Magic?*

GOLDMAN: Yes, I thought it was a nice movie. A lot of people didn't. I thought Ann-Margret was wonderful, the acting was wonderful. I don't read reviews, but, look: It was never meant to be *Citizen Kane*. It's a genre picture. I remember talking with George Hill when we were preparing *Butch*. "I hope that in twenty years, when they mention *Shane* and *The Gunfighter*, they will mention *Butch*," I said, and we agreed. Likewise, when I was working on *Magic*, the great classic of this genre for me is Hitchcock's *Psycho*, and I hope that in twenty years it will be as scary as that movie. If it is, fine. If not, then it failed. I thought it was well acted.

I have this theory: I don't believe that movies are good or bad when they come out. I think that they work or they don't work for a mass audience, and you like them or you don't like them personally. But we won't know about the good or bad for a long time. Everybody raved about *The China Syndrome* and *Hair*, for instance. Well, they may be wonderful movies, but I don't know if they'll be wonderful in twenty years. Very often they break down, they get old-fashioned, and I think time is the only esthetic test of a movie—for me. Meantime, it either works or it doesn't work. *Magic*, in terms of audience, was very successful.

BRADY: Did you have Ann-Margret in mind for the screenplay even as you were doing the novel?

GOLDMAN: No. That story got out, but when I was writing the novel, all I was hoping was that I could finish the goddamn novel —never mind casting the movie. I never think, "Oh, boy, if I can get Burt Lancaster and Paul Newman, I'll get rich." I suppose, if I had been pushed, and if someone had said, "There will be a movie of this novel. Who would you like for Peggy Ann Snow?" I would have said Ann-Margret, because she has that sense of time: She's been around for so long . . . I just think she's terrific, and eventually she will get her due.

BRADY: Do you work best under pressure?

GOLDMAN: I don't know what "best" means. I don't know what "pressure" means. I am *compulsive* about deadlines. I am compulsive about time.

BRADY: I noticed in one of your drafts of *All the President's Men* you said, "I want everyone to know that this is delivered one week early."

GOLDMAN: Yes, I've been early every time. I'm compulsively early. If you invite me to your house at eight o'clock, I am walking around the block outside at five of eight. I have a hatred of being kept waiting, to the extent that the first time I met Hiram Haydn, who was the editor I wanted to be with, he kept me waiting for fifteen minutes. And the first thing I said to him was, "You must not do that to me again." I mean, I *hate* it. I am neurotic about time, and I am also neurotic about deadlines. I will do *anything* to be early. I may have to do crazy things to make it happen. If I'm panicked that I won't be able to make it, I may have to ask for an extension, and *then* beat the deadline.

BRADY: What about other pressures, such as when projects overlap? For example, you wrote the screenplays for *All the President's Men* and *Marathon Man* at about the same time, as near as I can judge.

GOLDMAN: I was moving from one to the other. They overlap. They *had* to overlap. But you don't intend it that way. I don't remember the specifics of that, but what I am guessing is one was due in January, one was due in June, so you hand in your January one and suddenly you don't get a director on that until August. So you are doing rewrites on the one you handed in in June, let's say, because they're prompt, and then suddenly from out in left field someone from January comes in and says, "Hey, we have got to have this, too." In other words, it was because of the exigencies of the business that I got caught up in that. Ordinarily you try not to.

I don't think I am a very good rewriter. I don't like to rewrite. I don't enjoy it. One of the reasons I left the theater is that I hated the on-the-road experience in Broadway. I hated being out of town and that kind of thing. That's one of the reasons I don't like being on the floor of the movie. I'm there as little as possible when they are shooting. On the other hand, I have always wanted to do script doctoring, though I have never done any. It must be a terrific thing. When you're the screenwriter on a project, you are always the villain: "Why isn't it better? Why isn't it quicker? Why is it so long?" If you're the doctor, though (a) the movie is already in trouble, and (b) you can't hurt it. They *love* you! All you can do is help them, either way. I've never done it.

BRADY: Are you able to work comfortably under those battle-field pressures and hurry-up conditions?

GOLDMAN: I'm really crazy. How can I put this? I *don't like* my writing. I like almost nothing I have ever written. I like one book, which is *The Princess Bride*. And I like my children's book, *Wigger*. I don't really like anything else that I have ever written. There are individual scenes that I think are nice, but as a rule, I don't ever go back and look at what I have written because it is too embarrassing. One of the reasons I write so fast is that, since I don't really like what I am writing, one of the pleasures is *getting done* with it, if that makes sense. Basically I think that accounts for a great deal of the way I write. I suppose one of the reasons why I am so good about deadlines is the fact that meeting deadlines is one of the few prides that I can have: Since the writing is sure as shit not Shakespearean, the least I can do is get it in on time.

BRADY: You say you dislike much of your own writing. Exactly what do you *dislike* in your screenplays?

GOLDMAN: It's that horrible thing that your writing never really is as good on paper as it is in your head. That utter sense of failure. If we're talking about movies—I'll use *Butch Cassidy* because most people that are going to read this book have seen it —there are only two scenes in *Butch Cassidy* that I can read with a certain amount of pleasure: the scene just before the jump on the cliff, and the scene after the shoot-out. That whole dialogue about "I got a great idea about where we should go next"—I think that's really very solid writing. And I can look at that and say, "Yes, I am proud of that scene." They are dying, and they don't mention that they're dying—all that stuff. But for the most part you are confronted with your own inadequacies—and it's much more evident in fiction, because in movies other people can cover for you, or can ruin things for you. So it's not just you. Remember I said I don't really like talking about a scene in a movie, because it's always what everybody *does* with the scene. But in books, in *Marathon Man* for instance, I really only liked the run. That's the scene in the book that I like, when he's running away from the "baddies." I can look at that scene, and I can think that's as good as I can do that. That really came out nicely. For the most part you go to work thinking, "Oh, boy, I'm going to really do something today." And then you end up at the end of the day, and it's done, and it's done as well as you can do it. It's just disappointing.

BRADY: After steeping yourself in a novel like *Marathon Man,* how can you stand to relive the story again and again for several drafts of the screenplay?

GOLDMAN: I can only answer this by sounding arrogant, and I don't mean to. There is a certain interest in my novels *if I do them as screenplays* that is greater than the interest in the novels alone. In other words, it was understood when *Magic* was sold that I would do the screenplay of *Magic*. It was understood when *Marathan Man* was sold that I would do the screenplay of *Marathon Man*. It's very hard, because one is not *ruthless* enough doing screenplays of your own novels. There's that wonderful Faulkner phrase about writing: "You must kill all your darlings." Well, if I'm adapting Cornelius Ryan, and there's something that I want to cut and not use, I don't have to deal with his anguish or how many hours or months it took him to write those thirty pages. I just say, "Off with it. Lop it off." When it's my *own* novel, it's very hard to say, "Off with it." You think, "Oh, Jesus, that was so hard to write, and it took so long to do this right, why don't we just try to keep . . ." You are not as ruthless with yourself on your own screenplays. So I suppose, in a sense, that in an ideal world I would rather not write the screenplays of my own novels. If that severely affects the possibility of the sale of a novel, I'll write the screenplay. I don't know, for example, if either *Marathon Man* or *Magic* would have sold as movies if it was clear going in that I was not going to write the screenplays. They *might* have. But I don't know that. I know that certainly it was an advantage from Zig's point of view to be able to say, "Yes, he is going to do his own adaptation."

BRADY: Where did you get the idea for the dentistry torture scene in *Marathon Man?*

GOLDMAN: First of all, Szell is modeled on Martin Bormann, who was called, what?, The Angel of Death. Bormann, I think, was a doctor, or had two doctorates, and did crazy experiments on people. He was the one who tried to grow tits on men, and stuff like that. Terrible things. And I've always been panicked by dentists. There is something in *Psycho* (the ultimate horror film for me) beyond speech about that shower scene. You are naked, you are helpless. There's a curtain. You stand. In a crazy sense, the only fear that I have that I can write about that's equivalent to that is something awful about dentistry. There's the pain. It doesn't exist, though, for kids anymore. Dentistry is the one thing that's really gotten better lately. Now you have music, and it doesn't hurt. But when I was a kid, you know, there was something about somebody invading your body, strange things going in on drills. I don't know. That's basically where it came from.

BRADY: What is your attitude toward violence in screenplays?

David Seltzer says of his writing *The Omen,* "I was very conscious of including the most repulsive scenes I could imagine. I wanted to write a commercial movie." Is that the way it is?

GOLDMAN: I don't know. It's *his* thing. That's *his* statement. I am trying to think of a violent film that I have been involved with. Obviously, *Marathon Man* is really what we have to deal with, isn't it, in answer to your question?

BRADY: Yes.

GOLDMAN: I wrote the novel. I was writing a spy thriller, because I love Eric Ambler and Graham Greene. I had no intention or notion when I was writing that book that it was ever going to be a movie. Never ever ever. There was nothing really gory about the dental scenes, which are, I guess, the crunch violent scenes in that script. I mean, it's not like Roger Corman's doing them. You don't see a drill going into a tooth. But the *material* is explosive. John Schlesinger did it quite delicately. I'm very dubious about violence, and I think one of the wonderful reasons why a movie like *Black Sunday* flopped was that the public is tired of mindless violence, bored with it. They've had enough.

BRADY: I'm talking about violence, not special effects, and one of the most violent scenes to me in *Marathon Man* was when Doc was killed by Szell. Just that shot of his face, and the awareness that a blade is going through his entrails, is enough to make one turn away.

GOLDMAN: Well, I'll tell you. The way Schlesinger did it is not the way it was originally done. The way it happens now is Doc and Szell are talking, and suddenly the talking gets heated, and Doc (Roy Scheider) goes, "Oooh!" And there's not a *sign* of blood or a weapon or anything. It's done as delicately as it could possibly be done. You don't see the blood until he comes to the apartment door and yells, "Babe!"

If you look at it very carefully, there's not a *speck* of blood. There isn't. Now, I was not present at this, but I will tell you the story. It was originally not done that way. It was originally shot with great blood coming out of Scheider's stomach onto his shoes. His shoes were turning red, OK? They had a sneak in Clint Eastwood country, and they had, from what I am told, what was, along with *The Godfather,* one of the two most successful sneaks in the history of Paramount. And euphorically they flew the next night up to San Francisco for the second and final sneak.

San Francisco is noted as being a very sophisticated sneak town; also extremely homosexual, and very smart. There was some difficulty. It was hot; there was trouble with the air conditioning. Dustin Hoffman, I think, arrived late and the lights had to come up and down, so there was a certain discombobulation with the audience before the movie started. (This is all second-hand. I'm not sure if this is true, but I was told this.) The movie went along, and in the middle of it a homosexual stood up and screamed at the audience, "Sadistic shit!" and left. There was a very strong feeling among that audience that the movie was too violent. Now, they then went back to work and cut three minutes of violence out of the movie. They also publicized what had happened in San Francisco, so that *Marathon Man,* which actually has only one shot that I think is relatively violent—which is the blood spurting out of Scheider's hand—had a reputation as being extraordinarily violent, which, in fact, it really isn't. And one of the reasons it didn't do better as a film is that I think a lot of people had heard how violent it was and stayed away. *Marathon Man* came out when interest in violence was slowing down. *Black Sunday* suffered even more so.

They get very upset in the movie business, as they should, when they guess wrong. They don't mind so much if *Nickelodeon*'s a disaster because they knew *Nickelodeon* was a piece of garbage before it opened. Columbia knew it, OK? Where they get very unsettled is when they have a *Jaws* and it turns out as a flop. And *Black Sunday,* they thought, was another *Jaws.* A disaster. When *that* happens—when a movie that they've *seen,* and they *know* is going to be commercial, fails—that sends shivers because it means people are going to lose their jobs. And I think what it means is that right now, as we speak, mindless violence is basically terminated. We have had our streak of it, and it's over. I think 1968 was the last year that Julie Andrews was the top box-office star, and the first year that Clint Eastwood was. I would like to think that *that* was the end of one kind of sensibility for movies—the end of *The Sound of Music* and the start of the spaghetti western. So the violence run has gone from 1968 to the late seventies, and I think we're done with it now.

Of course, I'm just guessing—and that's the crucial thing about the picture business: *Nobody knows what will work.* It's *all* blind guessing. You are guessing public taste two and three years down the line. You don't know who's going to be a star and who isn't. If we *knew* what was going to work, we wouldn't spend eight million dollars making *Nickelodeon* and one million making *Rocky.* We'd make nothing but *Rocky*s. Nobody knows. And that's one of the things about the picture business—that, regardless of what happens, there's that wild insecurity that we feel: *Nobody knows what will work.* Nobody has the *least* idea of what'll play.

BRADY: Perhaps nobody knows what will work in a movie, but judging from your notes on the first page of the first-draft screenplay for *A Bridge Too Far,* you work hard at eliminating obstacles.

GOLDMAN: I wrote those notes while discussing the script with Richard Attenborough. They are his thoughts pertaining to the second draft, which would follow. The screenplay was written November 10, 1975, according to the cover sheet; and these notes are from a meeting on January 4, 1976. I'll get to specifics in a second.

We were always under terrible time pressure on *Bridge* because we knew from the start it was going to be a monster movie. It had to be. Also, the great enemy of all location films is weather. We knew from the Dutch weather that the filming had to end by early October of 1976. Mr. Levine always had a mystic notion that we were to open June 15, 1977. When I first met him in 1974, he said, "We are going to open June 15, 1977." I don't know *why,* but we *did,* and in order to be done shooting in the fall of 1976, we had to *begin* shooting in April of 1976, because that's when the weather clears in Holland. So Attenborough and I came to an agreement very early on, that in order for me to make that deadline, in order for me to have a screenplay that they could use to *do* all the things they had to do, including *casting*, there was certain research that I should not bother with.

Under ordinary conditions I might have tried to read all kinds of stuff dealing with 1944 British slang, for instance. We agreed that I shouldn't bother with that. We agreed that if there were any errors, he would make things accurate. One of the things, for example, that I also didn't worry about because there wasn't time was the British military structure. I don't know to this day what the various RAF career military grades are; I would put down the equivalent in American, and if it was incorrect I didn't care because that would be changed. The first draft was the one, I guess, we got the cast on. My goal was to make a reading experience of the screenplay, to make the reader on this draft *feel* something. The second time around, though, we had to go to the generals, we had to go to the British Museum, and we wanted them to think of us, as we were, a deadly serious operation.

This is *really* a major Roman numeral one that I am getting into now, which you didn't ask about, but it would come up anyway. Each assignment that I am given is different, and I feel I'm doing my job successfully if the picture shoots. If the picture is good, that's terrific. If the picture is successful, that's terrific. But *basically* my job is to see that the film starts. My screenplay is a catalyst. So you alter what you do for each particular screenplay. For example, let's take two adaptations—*A Bridge Too Far* and *All the President's Men*.

Both have very strong similarities: a lot of living people, very complicated historical data, trying to simplify it, trying to find the structure, and so forth. The differences are, for example, in *All the President's Men* we had a producer, we had no director, and we had one star who was also one of the producers—Mr. Redford. It was clear to us going in that, although Redford was very much aware that conceivably he was miscasting himself, and that maybe we should have done it with two unknown actors, we were stuck, since it was his baby, with Bob Redford as Bob Woodward—which meant we *desperately* needed somebody to play Carl Bernstein who was of equivalent stature. If we had gone with an unknown as Carl Bernstein the feeling was that everybody would have thought that Robert Redford was basically stealing the movie for himself. Well, the two choices were Dustin Hoffman and Al Pacino. We *had* to have one or the other. Those were the only two ethnic choices that are comparable stars to Bob Redford. Well, we got Dustin, but I was *very* much aware when I wrote that screenplay that the Bernstein part had to not just be *good*. It had to be *good enough to try and nail a major star*. And since major stars get offered hernia-producing tons of material weekly, it had to be a very, very special role if we could make it such, because not only was he going to be acting against Bob Redford—Bob Redford was also the producer. And when you act against Barbra Streisand and she's the producer, you disappear. So the part had to be as bulletproof as one could make it. *That* was my feeling, along with the hope that the picture would go forward. But my principal craft job in the screenplay of *President's Men* was to make the Bernstein part *appealing* enough to nail Dustin or Al Pacino.

In *A Bridge Too Far* I knew going in I had to write a dozen parts that would attract stars—so you had to come on very, very big when I introduced each of those guys. And you bullshit, you know, when you introduce a character in the script. The opening sentence describing Major Julian Cook, which is the Redford part, goes something like: "If this man had been an actor, he would have been a star." Well, a star reads that, and he says, "Ah, this is a star role." In other words, that's all there very consciously. In addition, there were enormous craft problems on *A Bridge Too Far*. None of the main characters die. None of the historical figures die. You can't have a war film in which everybody lives. So I had to try and invent a sufficient number of *secondary* characters. I mean, I can't have James Gavin dying. He's alive up in Boston, right? Since we *had* to be authentic, one of the craft problems, in addition to making a dozen star parts, was inventing memorable small characters that I could in fact kill so that the audience would be moved. The problem is finding air space amid all the material for a three-scene role of someone who can die.

Another problem of *Bridge* is it had to *not* be a British film. Ultimately, the heart of *Bridge* takes place at Arnhem, which is the bridge that is too far. And that's where Sean Connery and Anthony Hopkins are; they are British and they have the two largest roles in the film. So the American roles—Ryan O'Neal, who plays Gavin, the third-largest role in the film; and three spotted American roles for Elliott Gould, James Caan and Redford—are intentionally written quite spectacularly to give weight and a feeling of American balance to the script, because Joe Levine kept saying, "Don't give me *The Battle of Britain*," a big foreign *British* film with all kinds of British stars that died in America. In other words, it *had* to be American as well as English. And it was Joe's contention from the beginning that whoever he hired as a director, the screenwriter would be of the other nationality. If he hired an American director he would have tried, I assume, to get Robert Bolt, or Frederic Raphael, or . . . I don't know. But because he had a British director, he insisted on an American screenwriter.

What I am saying is that although all screenplays are essentially the same—one hundred and thirty-five pages, the usual form—the task of the screenwriter, at least in my eyes, varies *enormously* according to the individual needs of the production. And that is instrumental. Now, as I say, this is the second draft of *Bridge*. A note here, for example, says "red beret canister." It's a scene that Attenborough always liked that I didn't, because I didn't know how to shoot it. It works wonderfully in the movie. It's a little sixty-second sequence of shots. The British are trapped up at Arnhem. They are getting supply drops from Britain, but their radios are dead, so they can't contact anybody outside of Arnhem—that's one of the screw-ups in the story. The British do not know that the drop zones where they are dropping their material, food, ammunition, etc., are now in the hands of the Germans. And the British on the ground at Arnhem tried fires and screams to alert the aircraft, but the aircraft was under strict instructions to ignore everything on the ground because they might be Germans. The British division at Arnhem is known as Red Devils. They wore red berets. It really happened that when they were trapped one of the young boys snapped and went running out into an open field after a large canister. They were so short of food and ammunition that he went out running at great risk to his own life, in spite of the fact that there was sniper fire covering the field. He grabbed the giant canister, lifted it up, and ran back to the British lines with it. Just before he got there, he was killed by a sniper, and the canister fell open—and it was filled with red berets.

Now, I was always against that sequence because I thought it would take too long. I did not know how to make it, how to shoot it. It's a *moment*. There's a fabulous piece of material in the movie. There's a woman whose house is taken over, and she gradually goes insane because of the noise. The last time you see her she's in this house in the middle of this *wild* action—Germans all over, etc. "I want a taxi," she says. She's Dutch. "I want a taxi. Get me a taxi." Nobody will get her a taxi, because they're all frantically trying to take cover. So she says, "I'll get my own taxi." She goes walking out (and the way Attenborough's done it, it's just brilliant); I swear to Christ she walks out in the middle of this *maelstrom*. You think she sees a taxi. And she says, "Taxi," and she starts for it. All of a sudden boom-boom-boom, and there's a balletic thing and she dies.

Well, that's in essence the same kind of material in the red berets canister scene. So I argued that we didn't need them both. And Attenborough *loved* that red berets thing. I find that when you are dealing with a talented director, you go with it. Remember when I talked about George Hill saying that he could make that rotten scene introducing the Sundance Kid play? Ultimately, if a director knows how to make something play and has talent, you *go* with it. What I didn't realize is how economically Attenborough could shoot the red berets scene. He does the whole thing with the boy running back, getting shot, falling, and the canister opening in one. What happens is the boy runs, runs, runs with the canister, is shot. As he starts to fall you see a reaction of one of the men who's screaming, "Come on, run, bring it, bring it, get going, get going!" and you cut back to the kid and it's a pull-back shot of the kid lying dead and the canister open as it fell, the red berets rolling on the ground. And it's very economical. That's something that *he* wanted in, that he could make play.

These other notes: "Four basic worries about the movie. One, the end doesn't work. Not as poignant, not as devastating as possible. Solution, have more people that we know before left behind wounded." These notes just say the end doesn't work. Clarify.

BRADY: The second note here is: "Two, clarify what's happened with all the people who didn't get to the bridge."

GOLDMAN: In other words, one of the fuck-ups that happened was that ten thousand British paratroopers landed eight miles from Arnhem bridge. And only a couple hundred of them got through to the bridge to try and take it. And it had to be clear why the others didn't get through. In fact, the Germans left one road—for reasons nobody understands—totally unwatched, and those guys got through. So that's what that note means: Make clear what is unresolved in this draft.

BRADY: Note three: "Three, film is told through eyes only of officers."

GOLDMAN: Yes, that's really an adjunct to what I said earlier: that none of the main characters die. Here's another note—"Add someone where possible to identify with non-coms." In other words, that's making characters more vulnerable, more human. Basically, Cornelius Ryan was an elitist and told his story through the eyes of the various generals. I don't mean that as a criticism of Ryan, because Ryan did hundreds and hundreds of interviews with enlisted men. But ultimately, it's my feeling that Ryan takes the point of view of the officer in his book—and all of the officers survived Arnhem. But the film had to have people who died. It also had to have ordinary soldiers as well as officers. It had to be that mix of all those people who were involved in battle.

This is now the end of that large Roman numeral one that I started on, meaning each job is different. Although you always do the best you can, each job is different because the *requirements* of each particular job are different. For example, on the first draft the requirement is to hope the movie gets made. Once you go into the second or third draft, usually the movie is set. Usually there is a director involved, or if there *was* a director involved, now there is a star involved. With each draft, things are more and more complex for the screenwriter. Maybe there's a budget thing. Maybe instead of making an eight-million-dollar picture, they'll do it at only six million. So we have to cut out certain stuff, or add certain stuff, or whatever.

Usually whoever has hired you will say, "They're not so sure about this. I hope you can get a woman's part in it. I think they'll go for it." And then you find out that's valid. So you have to know what the opposition is. You also know that in fact executives would always rather say no than yes. Once they say yes, they get hooked.

BRADY: How so?

GOLDMAN: I mean, whoever said yes to *Nickelodeon,* whoever said yes to all those disasters Columbia had a few years ago, was thanking God Columbia also had *Fun with Dick and Jane,* which did some business. But what I'm saying is, it is much easier once you say no; then if *everybody* says no on the same project, you're in good shape.

BRADY: What was your reaction to *Bridge*'s critical reception?

GOLDMAN: The reviews were mixed, but one of the things that is crucial to an understanding of movies today is that movies are international. While it was disappointing in America, considering what our expectations were, it won a popularity poll in England from one of the big newspapers as Film of the Year. The film was an enormous success, I *think,* almost everywhere in the world except America.

BRADY: Why?

GOLDMAN: One, I don't think Americans want to see a movie where we don't win. That was always Mr. Levine's gamble: Would Americans *want* to see a movie in which the calvary doesn't get there? That was always the iffy part. The iffy question on *All the President's Men* was, "Would anybody *care* to see a movie about Watergate when we have been inundated with Watergate stories for so long?" The answer was, "They did." In the case of *A Bridge Too Far,* the gamble always was, "Would Americans want to see a movie in which they don't win?" And the answer was, "They did not."

BRADY: Do you ever think that the truth of *A Bridge Too Far* may have been blurred by the Cast of Thousands approach?

GOLDMAN: It could have been that. Yet Vincent Canby, I think, said in his *New York Times* review that the cast of thousands worked here, because if you *didn't* have those famous faces, you wouldn't know where the hell you were. It's a complex story with a sad ending. And ultimately it didn't do that badly; the movie is a much more successful commercial film worldwide, for example, than almost anything else I've been connected with, including *All the President's Men.* I mean, *much* bigger. Much bigger than *Marathon Man.* So it's one of those crazy things. It's as if you said to the director of *Smokey and the Bandit* in New York City, "Well, Jesus Christ, I hope you get another picture; I'm sorry this one didn't do well." He would say, "Are you out of your mind? It was one of the biggest movies of the year, after *Star Wars.*" *Smokey and the Bandit* may have stiffed or disappointed in New York, but it was bigger than *The Deep.* But people who live in media-centered areas like New York and Los Angeles don't know that.

Everything is very fragmented today. Almost nothing, except I guess *Star Wars,* breaks through everywhere. And that was always the gamble on *Bridge:* Was it too long? Was it too sad? I think the quality of the film, the stupendousness of it in terms of what you see on the screen, for me is still glorious. Why was this movie a giant hit in Great Britain and Australia, etc., and a disappointment in America? First of all, it's a comparative disappointment. I mean, it was bigger in America than *Marathon Man* was. And *Marathon Man* didn't do badly, so a lot of it is hype, and a lot of it's what your expectations are.

But that particular question, "Would this country go for an unhappy movie?" We never have. I still think—this is not after the fact; I'm not saying this seriously—if we had ended the movie after the Redford sequence, when he crosses the bridge successfully about two hours and ten minutes into the movie . . . if we had ended the movie there and flashed a card on that said, "But the rest of the battle was a bitter disappointment. The Allies tried to go a bridge too far," and you ended the movie five seconds after he has crossed the bridge, the movie, I think, would have been an enormous commercial success in America.

BRADY: I don't see how.

GOLDMAN: Well, when I saw the movie in various capitals around the world, at that moment they were clapping. They were with it, they wanted it to work; and the last forty minutes are very grim and harrowing. Everybody gets slaughtered in that last forty minutes. We had an experience when we had our sneak on *Waldo Pepper* in Boston that had similar overtones.

Waldo Pepper came at a strange time in our careers. George Roy Hill's last movie had been *The Sting*. Redford was at the absolute hysterical peak of his heat—it was just after *Gatsby, Sting* and *The Way We Were* had all come out within a span of five months. Plus the reissue of *Jeremiah Johnson,* plus the re-issue of *Butch*. In those twelve months more money was spent to see his visage than has ever been spent on any star before or since, I think. He was the hottest thing that ever happened. And this was the first movie afterward. We had a sneak in Boston, and you must believe what I'm about to say is true.

They loved it. They were laughing and clapping and eating it up with a spoon—until the girl dies going off the wing. All of a sudden you could sense this glacial hatred coming from the audience, and we never got them back. There was an anger, a sullenness as they walked out; they were making crappy remarks to the people who worked for the studio, because we had not given them what they wanted. Now, from my point of view and certainly from Hill's, it would have been nauseating and unforgivable on our part to have the sequence when he tries to rescue her on the wing if we knew the rescue was going to work! Because that's Errol Flynn time, and we don't believe that anymore.

You generally give an audience what it wants, but sometimes

you can't do that. Sometimes you hope you'll get in what *you* want and the audience will want it, too. I guarantee you (no one can ever prove me wrong or right) that if we had reshot that business of *Waldo* so that we had a shot of him holding onto a dummy on the end of a wing, and then he had gotten suspended —not for letting the girl die, but for stunting over a crowded area —the movie would have been infinitely more successful.

We're not talking about a stiff either. *Waldo* did reasonably good business. What I'm saying is that up until that point, about an hour and twenty minutes into a two-hour film, when it was fun and games, they loved it. But we could not shake them. *Waldo Pepper* begins with a whole bunch of shots of plane crashes, the most glorious sad tune in the world played in a minor key, and shots of dead pilots with their birth and death dates. Now what we're saying to the audience is, "OK, fellas, get ready; it's not always going to be fun and games. It's gonna turn dark." That's why we started that way. But there was no way we could make the audience accept the fact that the girl goes off the wing and that Bob Redford didn't save her. I am convinced, even though the film was written for Redford and I thought he was wonderful in it, that if we'd had Jack Nicholson or Al Pacino—I don't know if any of the *rest* of the movie would have worked, but the falling off the plane would have been acceptable because there's something dark about Nicholson and Pacino. They bring *with* them, somehow, a sense of failure.

BRADY: In *A Bridge Too Far* there's a scene in the script—this is the second draft—in which Ludwig says, "Market Garden was a stupid plan. If it had worked, it would still have been a stupid plan." That scene is cut in the movie; yet it seems to put a useful perspective on the whole Arnhem mess. I guess I get the feeling that the script editorialized a little more than the film ultimately did.

GOLDMAN: In that particular case, I'm going to guess that that was not shot because the feeling was that the story said that. Every little scene that you can cut, you cut. When you're dealing with the kind of costs that movies deal with, if you can cut a forty-second scene or a minute scene, that's three setups—that's maybe half a day or half a morning's work, and you just *do* that. It did not add to the spine of the piece.

BRADY: I thought one of the strongest moments in the film was when one of the first of the wounded in Kate Ter Horst's house drops blood in the middle of her children's toy train track. Do you remember the origin of that?

GOLDMAN: Yes, I think that's probably in the first draft. We were trying to show how terrible it was (like the lady with the taxi) for the civilians. And what I wanted in writing the screenplay, what we wanted in the movie, was that the first time you would see the house, the house should be just lovely and sunny with lots of pretty children; and then there was that one little drop of blood in the kiddy's game that's supposed to presage, give an indication of the gore that is to come. There were all those men who died in that poor house. There's one moment that I still jump at—it's when they're bringing in a wounded guy and the gunfire goes *through* the house. A guy who's bringing in the stretcher just falls dead. That's so terrifying—the idea of gunfire going *through* a house, because you think once you're in a house, you're safe. And you're *never* safe. I'm glad the moment worked for you.

Let me tell the super story that Cliff Robertson told me a dozen years ago, and I think I'm giving credit properly. It was a story he had been told by Rosalind Russell. I think he met her during the filming of *Picnic*. She said, "Do you know what makes a good movie?" And he answered something like, "I don't know —good script, good actors, good cameramen and good directors, etc., etc." "No," she said. "Moments." She said, "A couple of moments that people remember, that they can take with them, is what makes a good movie." And I always thought, gee, when you think of *Gunga Din,* for example, which is my favorite movie, there are certain *moments* that you think of. Or when you think of *8½,* you think of certain *moments*. It's like when somebody says to you, *"The Maltese Falcon,"* certain *moments* jump to your mind—bing, bing, bing. And if there are *enough* of those moments, I guess, Miss Russell's point was, the movie would remain in the people's memory. And that's really what you're after. What brought this to mind was your saying you liked the little drop of blood in the toy train going around. That's a moment.

One problem we had, which we *never dreamed* we would have in terms of reviews, was acceptance of the truth. What drew us to the material was the phenomenal quality of the material: all these weird, nutty, loony things happening, *really* happening—right? Well, some of the reviews, I was told, said, "How dare they actually ask us to believe that a general of Browning's character and stature would actually know of rumors that there were German tanks in the area and allow the plan to continue?" Well, the whole point was, he *had* it! He had the goddamn pictures! Even some of the brightest people I know thought we threw in the Jimmy Caan sequence to add some pizzazz. The fact is, it's all from the book! *Nothing spectacular is made up.* One of the things that dogged us was, we never got that *through* to the people. They thought we were not being as truthful as we were being, and I don't know how we could have done it any better. There was a reluctance on the audience's part to believe what we thought was the gold of the story: the horrible truth of it all.

BRADY: In one of the most moving moments, to use Roz's expression, the Dutch Underground leader's son is shot on the street, and he puts the boy on the dead pile used to block the German tanks. But in the script, both father and son are shot, and other hands put them on the pile.

GOLDMAN: Oh, is that right? What draft? That surprises me, but, as I told you, I only read things once. If anybody is moved by the movie, they're moved by that moment. You don't need them both shot. It's better with the kid.

BRADY: In the first draft of the script, Dolan (Jimmy Caan) orders the colonel to examine his captain. He says, "Right now, or I'll kill you where you stand."

GOLDMAN: Right.

BRADY: In the second draft, this line is changed to "Right now, or I'll blow your fucking head off."

GOLDMAN: I think Richard wanted "Blow your fucking head off."

BRADY: Just to punch it up?

GOLDMAN: I think "kill you where you stand" may be from the book, or maybe that's from me; but I remember somehow that that's Richard's suggestion. I don't know. I like it very much: "Blow your fucking head off." I suppose a lot of it comes down to what kind of a rating you are going for—which is not something you think about a lot, because you almost always know it going in. Are you going to be a G or a PG or an R? I don't think I'll ever do an X picture, and I can't see me doing a G picture. People don't want G's now; it's so strange—I think *Star Wars* could have had a G and took a PG instead. I'm not sure that's true, but that was the rumor because G has somehow come to stand for Disney and *Benji*. Until *President's Men* the word "fuck" meant an automatic R. I think that Redford made a personal plea to the board on *President's Men,* whoever decides what your rating is, because, for example, to change "rat fucking," which was the Nixonian phrase for *skullduggery,* to "rat humping" or something to get a PG would have been so *false,* that it was built into the material. Also there's the Johnson story with the line "Tell Ben Bradlee, 'Fuck you.' " That's a *direct quote* from the President of the United States. So we weren't making up dirty language to be scurrilous. I think *President's Men* set a precedent in that it was the first time in my memory that a movie with a "fuck" got a PG. A PG is always preferable if you want any young audience at all; an R limits you so. I know Mr. Levine made a very strong stand that we wanted a PG on *Bridge Too Far,* because we wanted to have young people be able to see it so they could know what war was all about. And he got it. We were originally given an R, and then we were switched I think unanimously to a PG. That may seem all very internecine and stupid, but it isn't.

BRADY: In the second draft of the film, why did you add details about the kinds of cars that Von Rundstedt and General Browning drive? You have Von Rundstedt in a Mercedes and Browning in a Humber Snipe.

GOLDMAN: Oh, that was probably Richard. I assume that Richard found we could get a Mercedes and we could get a Humber

Snipe. It's like having to do with the manner of dress and manners of addressing each other and what rank are people. You overlook details in an early draft sometimes, knowing that they'll come into play later.

BRADY: Isn't this more a matter for production than for the screenwriter? Do you commonly sprinkle props through your scripts?

GOLDMAN: You never know where that kind of thing comes from. I don't know anything about automobiles. I'm a terrible driver. I don't like to drive. In *Harper* that character had a certain kind of car—an old, beat-up Porsche, with the unfinished door. That was Newman. That was Newman's character. I remember him saying, "I want to drive an old, beat-up Porsche, and I want to wear short-sleeve shirts and . . ." That's the actor dealing with character and feeling comfortable. Very often it comes down to production design. It also comes, in the case of something like *Bridge Too Far,* to: What can you find? You're dealing with a period. Can you find a reasonably priced, beautiful-looking 1940 Mercedes that a general might ride in? And if you can't, what are you going to do? You have something else. One of the awful things about movies is there has to be this kind of accuracy, because if we'd put in a Mercedes that was one year off, there would have been letters from all over saying, "You had a 1943 Mercedes, and they did not make them that year because that was the year that the Bonn factory burned. . . ." I'm making all that up, but you try to be as deadly accurate on that kind of stuff as you can.

BRADY: The insertion of one exchange causes a little confusion in *Bridge* about Browning's character. When Urquhart asks Browning, after Arnhem, what he had thought of the operation, Browning says, "Well, as you know, I've always thought we were going a bridge too far." Yet early in the film, Browning seems to be gung ho for the project, and even ignores, as you said earlier, the photos of some tiger tanks to proceed with it. This makes Browning look two-faced, like a political general. Was that your intention?

GOLDMAN: Well, Browning, you see, *did* say the famous line about a bridge too far. He said it to Montgomery before the battle when Montgomery got the OK from Eisenhower. I wanted desperately to end the movie with the title. And we fussed terribly with how that last line should go. I think in the beginning I had him saying something like, "Well, I always thought we would go a bridge too far," which was just too horrible and calculating. I think Richard may have given the version which now stands, which is, "Well, as you know, I've always said . . ." Because at least that's true, because he *did* always say they'd try to go a bridge too far. He did also have the information on the tanks. He was a very controversial and a brave and desperately well-dressed soldier. His widow felt very bad about the film. We've talked to people since, very high-ranking in British military during World War II, who felt it was not at all defaming to Browning. So I don't know.

BRADY: This note prefaces a couple of the early drafts of *All the President's Men:* "The film is written to go like a streak."

GOLDMAN: Yes. Now that *President's Men* has become what it has become, everybody assumes it was always going to be a film, etc., etc. There's *no way* anyone wanted to make the movie. I mean, they were willing to develop it because Robert Redford is Robert Redford. And they were willing to buy the book, and they were willing to pay for me. But ultimately most movies are not go projects until there's a script. That's one of the madnesses about the business. In other words, if Steve McQueen, God rest his soul, said, "I want to play *The Baryshnikov Story,*" they would say, "Great, Steve baby, that's a fabulous part for you. You've always been balletic on screen. We'll develop a hundred thousand dollars' worth." Or, "We'll develop two hundred and fifty thousand worth." *That's basically to keep Steve McQueen happy*. I mean, ultimately what they're probably doing is going into the executive washroom and saying, "Fucking McQueen is off his rocker. He wants to play Baryshnikov. Well, we want to have a nice relationship with him. Maybe he'll want to do a bang-bang picture next year. Let's develop it, OK?" But ultimately, the go-forward, the decision to say, "We'll spend five, six or ten million" doesn't come off some star's interest. It doesn't come really until there's a screenplay.

"This picture is written to go like a streak" was an intention to indicate *whoooosh*—to tell the reader that this thing is going to rocket along. It was to try to indicate to the people at Warner Bros., "Hey wait a minute. This could be a commercial entity. *Make* the movie." In other words, that's me selling.

BRADY: Second point. In your script preface you refer to "the black and white feel that I hope it has."

GOLDMAN: One was aware because of the fame of the book and the fame of Redford that it was going to be a movie that cost a lot. But the feeling was that of a little black and white 1930s Warner Bros. film. It *should* have been a movie made with unknowns, or it *could* have been a movie made with unknowns in the thirties—all of it in that one set. Black and white. Before color. Before we got big. And that's what I mean by "the black and white feel." It was always a little picture. The fact that it cost eight million is mere accounting: It went over the budget by a lot, and also had expensive stars and other people that were costly.

BRADY: *All the President's Men* as a script is very close to recent history, and most, or all, of the people who were prominent in the film are alive today. How close did you work with the individuals depicted on the screen?

GOLDMAN: I spent time in Washington. I spent days on the fifth floor of the *Washington Post*. I sat at a desk near Woodward's desk and watched what happened. I interviewed and had dinner with Ben Bradlee and talked to Howard Simons and Harry Rosenfeld. I was present at "budget meetings," when they discuss what is going to go on each page in the newspaper. And a lot of talk. Woodward was wonderful on it.

I went to a number of budget meetings, maybe four, maybe six. I don't know. And Harry Rosenfeld (who was the part that Jack Warden played) was not present at the first budget meeting. There were two each day, early and late. He was not present the first two that I was present at, and several of the top people, almost *all* of the super top powers of the *Post* came up and said, "This wasn't really good today. It wasn't really a good budget meeting. Harry wasn't here. Harry's so funny. Harry's got so many one-liners. Harry's one of the great unacknowledged comedians in the world."

Now at the next budget meeting Rosenfeld *was* there, and he was hysterically funny. And I wrote down *tons* of his lines that he would say in a budget meeting—which I used in the first draft of this screenplay. One of the things that caused *hysteria* about the first draft of this screenplay was, "What the fuck are all these gags doing in the budget meeting?" Now these same men who objected to it—Howard Simons, Ben Bradlee, etc.—all those people were the ones who came to me and said, "This wasn't a good one. It wasn't really funny today. Harry wasn't here."

Now, what I'm saying is everybody has a legitimate reason to be panicked when they are going to be depicted in a film, because it's *their* life, and if we had made Harry Rosenfeld an ass or Ben Bradlee a fool or Howard Simons a jerk, they've got to live with that image. My guess would be, having gone through *A Bridge Too Far* and having gone through *President's Men*, I ain't about to do any movies for a long long time in which anybody's alive. It's not worth it.

BRADY: Many scenes in the early drafts of *All the President's Men* don't make it to the shooting script. There is a scene that shows Woodward as a pretty good gambler with some guys on the *Post*. It tells me that Woodward was cautious, but when he played for stakes he could win. I found this illuminating.

GOLDMAN: Yes it was.

BRADY: Why was it dropped from the shooting script? Do you recall?

GOLDMAN: Well, again I don't know. I wrote four versions of that, and I was cut away from the herd the first day of shooting. Once it started shooting I never had anything to do with the picture. I don't know why a lot of things were cut. Woodward *was* a gambler. It was a good character thing. My guess is there wasn't time. My guess is also the parts had to somehow in a crazy way be balanced.

BRADY: The role of Bernstein seems to have a little more flavor to it in the film.

GOLDMAN: Redford I think emotionally is much closer to what Bernstein is in real life than to what Woodward is in real life. And Redford, had he been given the choice before it was a script, would rather have played Bernstein, because Bernstein was a more colorful character on first meeting.

BRADY: In the film, when Bernstein goes to Florida to see Dardis, he telephones from across the hall and calls the secretary away from her desk. Then he slips in behind her to see Dardis. In the book, Bernstein does not do this. He doesn't really misrepresent himself. Instead, he goes to Dardis' boss. He goes in from above, instead of through the front door, so to speak. What changed this?

GOLDMAN: I did not write that sequence. I think the feeling was it was cuter and quicker and it played better. It *played* better. It did. One of the problems with the movie always was there was so much talking. It was talky and filled with names. The whole Dardis sequence was complicated anyway. It was just an expeditious way, if that's the word, of getting him in, a quicker way of doing it. It doesn't in effect alter anything. It's a nice character thing for Bernstein. It shows him thinking on his feet. We know he's got a big mouth. So him yelling at Dardis' boss couldn't tell us anything about him. And it *is* more cinematic; it's less talk. You have a little laugh in the audience when it worked; and it doesn't affect anything, it doesn't matter. He got in to see Dardis.

If he had not gotten in in real life, and we had faked it that way, I think it would have been morally wrong. This is one of the things you do when you are dealing with real events and you are trying to truncate, you're trying to make things as quick as possible. I did an interview with somebody who was talking about *Marathon Man*. In the movie Olivier goes into the diamond district and is discovered by some Jews, and this guy was objecting to this scene. He was objecting to the logic of Olivier going into the diamond district, and I said, "I don't want to argue with you whether you are right or wrong. The reality is, did you like the scene of Olivier almost being caught?'' And he said, yes, he thought it was the best scene of the picture. And I said, ''OK, then I would argue with you: Since it does not affect the general structure of the film, it *doesn't matter* why he goes into the diamond district.'' In other words, if the diamond district had led to his being caught by Dustin Hoffman, then you could say, ''Hey, wait a minute. This really is a crucial part of the plot. It's wrong.'' But in essence, that scene is like ''Ol' Man River'' in *Show Boat*. It's a turn. ''Ol' Man River'' does not advance the plot, the story. It just makes the trip more pleasant. And that's what that scene in *Marathon Man* was. It's just a very exciting piece of cinema. I'm getting at the same thing in this. In *President's Men,* I don't think that this kind of change of the truth matters because the fact is Bernstein *got* in to see Dardis, he got information, and then we're back accurately again. I don't think that's a cheat. The most bland way to do it would have been to have him walk up and say, ''I'm here to see Mr. Dardis, please. My name is Carl Bernstein.'' And the secretary would say, ''Go right in, sir.'' Now *that* didn't happen, either.

BRADY: There's a scene with Katharine Graham in one of the middle drafts. She's sketched rather dramatically and heroically, and she also seems to probe for the identity of Deep Throat. What happened to that?

GOLDMAN: It's a good scene. It's in the book. I don't know. I think maybe that Mrs. Graham didn't want to be in the movie. There was talk at one point of Alexis Smith playing Katharine Graham. But I don't think the scene was ever shot. The movie always had a problem—it was long. And so tons of stuff went out. One of the things that I still miss desperately in the movie —and I began it in the first draft this way, and I went with it through several drafts before I was forced to give it up—is that the June seventeenth break-in was their third or fourth one. And nobody knows that. Once the burglars got stuck in a hotel corridor. They had to spend the night. Another time the key wouldn't work.

At one point I had the movie beginning with a shot of the Watergate, the most corny shot (intentionally) in the world, then a shot of a bunch of burglars. Viewers would say, "Ah, Christ, they're beginning with the break-in. This is a bore," right? And then we have a guy say, "It's the wrong key. I've got to go back to Miami and get the right key." And another burglar says, "But you got *this* key from Miami. Why do you have to go back?"— which I thought was *super* material because it would make the audience think, *Wait a minute.* What I wanted the audience to feel was, *Oh, I didn't know that.* Because that was what we figured the enemy was—the fact that everybody felt they knew the story. So the more we could jab them off balance at the beginning, the more they would pay attention. That was the logic. I *still* think it's a good idea.

BRADY: The script as shot seems to be a hard compression of a lot of good scenes, with many dropped by the wayside.

GOLDMAN: Many scenes were shot, but never used. There was a lovely scene that was Alan Pakula's idea, for instance. It was always a desperate, desperate desire on Redford's part to have women in the movie. Now that's funny, because we are praised greatly for *not* having women in the picture, but social lives were involved. And there was a very, very sweet scene when Bernstein's wife or ex-wife or ex-girl friend comes to see him before he goes to Florida; he can't find his bicycle and it's been stolen —all of which is true. But apparently it shot just rotten. Dustin ad-libbed. The girl was nervous. The movie was overlong. The scene was unusable. So there's a lot of stuff that was shot, I am told, but was not done. I think the first sneak ran two hours and thirty minutes. They then cut out twelve minutes. I don't know why. But the great problem with that film was always compressing it. Compressing it and having it make sense.

BRADY: What about the scene in which Woodward and Bernstein help Sloan with some housekeeping? That is not in the book and it is not in the film, but it *is* in your screenplay draft. Now, how would you get that information?

GOLDMAN: Woodward.

BRADY: Your interviews with him?

GOLDMAN: Yes. Nothing like that is made up. You wouldn't dare. I mean, we might compress something, but you would never manufacture. They helped Sloan with his housekeeping. One of the things that drives you mad is people saying, "Is it authentic, is it authentic?" The reality was there were four editors involved in *All the President's Men,* and one of them was really, really important. His name was Barry Sussman. And Barry Sussman was more important than Ben Bradlee by miles.

BRADY: He was the Watergate editor at the *Post.*

GOLDMAN: He was the crucial figure. I remember Ben Bradlee and I were having dinner, and I said, "There's too many goddamn editors. We'll have to compress." And Bradlee said, "Get rid of Sussman. He is known as the First Casualty of Watergate —crushed because he was left out of all the hoopla." That is what Bradlee told me. I never talked to Sussman. So when people say, "How authentic is it?" The answer is most of the stuff dealing with the editors is really, I suppose, Sussman dealing with Woodward and Bernstein, not Bradlee or whoever.

BRADY: Ouch.

GOLDMAN: But you get material any way you can. There's a wonderful speech that Bradlee has about when he was at *Newsweek* and he wrote that J. Edgar Hoover was going to be replaced by LBJ. And then Johnson called a press conference the next day and said, "I am appointing Hoover head of the FBI for life." It's a lovely speech that ends with Bradlee saying, "I fucked up, but I wasn't wrong," which Woodward comes back with at the end: "We fucked up, but we weren't wrong." Well, that entire speech was given to me by Woodward. It was an off-the-record interview he had with Bradlee, which I was allowed to use. And that whole story is Bradlee's dialogue: "You did it to us, Bradlee. You got us stuck with Hoover for life." Now the "I fucked up, *but I wasn't wrong"* at the end is me; I wanted to use it again to make a full-cycle effect. Anyway, when you are doing research, you get it from anywhere. Anything you can use, you use when you finally have your structure in your head. Or if you are trying to find your structure, you remember stuff. It's terribly helpful. I mean, Woodward's giving me that Bradlee interview was terribly helpful.

BRADY: Were there any legal objections to the screenplay?

GOLDMAN: I think the feeling from the beginning was that there had been no legal objections to the book, and Woodward and Bernstein did nothing in the book that they didn't have notes on, so as long as we stayed pretty much with the book material we were OK. The script probably had to be read carefully by the Warner Bros. legal department, but for the most part I think the feeling was we were relatively safe because most of the main characters were on the *Post*. We were using a lot of false names, as did Woodward and Bernstein—so we didn't have to have the bookkeeper's consent, for instance, because she was never called by name. That was a minor problem, but certainly something to be considered at all times.

BRADY: Redford had a first draft screenplay of *President's Men* written before he selected a director, which suggests that he wanted to shape the story. Is this true? What was Redford's impact on that first draft?

GOLDMAN: Well, he behaved like a producer. We had meetings. We knew the kind of things we had to do. *Marathon Man* and *President's Men* overlapped because we didn't get a director for a long time. There was a lot of trouble getting a director for *President's Men* because in the first place there were only a few people Bob Redford wanted; and in the second place, just as it was complicated getting a costar (since the other star was the producer and had the muscle), most big directors would not want to be put in a situation where they would be directing a film where the star of the film was their boss. So you find yourself in a very limiting situation.

BRADY: Carl Bernstein's been criticized for doing a screenplay based upon the book after your screenplay was already in. What was he so unhappy about?

GOLDMAN: You'll have to ask Carl.

BRADY: The teletype ending to *All the President's Men* seems more of an appendix than a dramatic conclusion to me.

GOLDMAN: I felt it was good. My draft had mug shots, remember?

BRADY: Yes. Guilty, guilty, guilty . . .

GOLDMAN: I wanted to see all those faces coming at me with

guilty across them. I thought it would be very impressive to see the thirty-five or thirty-seven men starting from those few Cubans and working up to the White House. They went with the teletype machine, which I think is better because it is more newspapery. Ultimately, it's the same ending. My ending was the two reporters working in a room, with the mug shots superimposed.

BRADY: Is there sometimes temptation for the writer and perhaps the director to emphasize pacing of the film at the cost of motivation and clarity? In *Marathon,* for instance, it isn't always clear what the hell is happening or *why* it's happening.

GOLDMAN: OK. We had a director who was one of the best directors now working, who had never dealt with this kind of material before. I suspect John Schlesinger only did this movie because he was frightened about the possible reception of *Day of the Locust* and he wanted to do a commercial film. I'm guessing. I don't know if that's true.

Anyway, when it comes to *Marathon Man,* whatever John Schlesinger can make play, he makes play. When we would talk, John had all kinds of dazzling ideas—John loves texture, OK? —all kinds of marvelous visual notions that I put in the screenplay, some of which stayed and some of which were just too confusing and too complicated and didn't work at all. Like, John had the notion of cities in crisis. Everything was chaotic—garbage strikes, luggage strikes—everything was fucked up except Szell, who is living in South America, where the air conditioning is beautiful, the music is lovely, and everything is terrific.

Well, it's too expensive to shoot all that. Some of it was lost, and a lot of it was just very confusing in the film. Nobody understood what that was with the luggage, with the garbage. What are those people complaining about? It didn't work. So a lot of what's confusing is because of notions that didn't play. But I am not a director, and when Schlesinger wants to do a certain kind of thing and thinks he can make it play, I am very happy to have a man of that caliber do a genre piece. And so you give him as much as you can that will make him confident. So a lot of the confusions in *Marathon Man*—well, I can't tell what's confusing, because I am too familiar with it. I literally don't know.

BRADY: Some of the backdrop certainly becomes camouflaged.

GOLDMAN: Yes. One of the things that is altered is a lot of the trips in Europe. In the book the Roy Scheider part is set in four or five different countries. That's all combined in the film in one little scene in Paris, which is not, believe me, a Shakespearean episode. On top of that, the reason I think Scheider took the part, if you remember the book, is that long early scene in the bar where he meets the old legendary over-the-hill spy . . . and the guy is killed in the men's room. Scheider savages the men who killed him, but he also realizes that he's panicked himself.

BRADY: Yes.

GOLDMAN: That was all shot, and apparently it was wonderful —and they cut it all.

BRADY: I understand it was quite violent.

GOLDMAN: It wasn't so much that it was violent. It was long. It was an eight-and-a-half-minute sequence, but what it did do was give some underpinning to the story. It meant that when you later saw Scheider in Paris, you were seeing a man you knew was cracking and over-the-hill—*not* a man who looked terrific and was capable of killing everybody. In other words, everything that basically happens to the Scheider character from the cut scene is altered. When he grabs the boy in the restaurant and says, "Don't go after the girl"—everything about him, the way he's talking about their father . . . all the way Roy *played* it . . . the scene with Dustin when he comes in the room . . . all of that vulnerability is *gone* because you don't *know* he's a guy who's dead but won't lie down. You don't know it. Without that eight-and-a-half-minute scene, you see a superstud. And it affects terribly what happens after. I'm not saying they were wrong to cut it. What I am saying is it was a *grievous* cut. Maybe it would have been less confusing if it had been in, and if the movie had been eight and a half minutes longer. I don't know.

BRADY: I think it would have added a basement to an awful lot of scenes that followed.

GOLDMAN: Well I think so, too. But I was not there.

BRADY: The murder in the opera puzzled me in the film—discovering the man dead in his opera seat.

GOLDMAN: Yes, all of that. Basically John's an opera nut, and he always wanted to shoot the Paris opera. Another thing that may have clouded the story is we had to fabricate because of budget. We had to fabricate *one* incident to cover all the European trips that the original story had. So we used Paris.

BRADY: The telescoping, I am sure, is practical—but does it make story-line sense? First of all, I guess I am comparing the film with the book, and—

GOLDMAN: *Always* a mistake. They are different. Whether it's my book and movie, or anybody's, it's *crucial* to remember that. When people say, "Is it like the book?" the answer is, "There has never in the history of the world been a movie that's really been like the book." Everybody says how faithful *Gone With the Wind* was. Well, *Gone With the Wind* was a three-and-a-half-hour movie, which means you are talking about maybe a two-hundred-page screenplay of a nine-hundred-page novel in which the novel has, say, five hundred words per page; and the screenplay has maybe forty, maybe sixty, depending on what's on the screen, maybe one hundred and fifty words per page. But you're taking a little, teeny slice; you're just extracting little, teeny *essences* of scenes. All you can ever be in an adaptation is faithful in spirit.

BRADY: You are willing to accept that even as the man in the middle on your own creation?

GOLDMAN: Absolutely. That's what's hard about doing your own screenplays—you are often not ruthless enough. Also you are punchy. I don't know what makes sense in *Marathon Man*. I've been through it too many times: four screenplays and two versions of the novel. So I don't know if this guy did that in what version. And as I told you, I don't reread them.

BRADY: I understand because of the deletion why there is a lack of logic that would be there otherwise in the screenplay. There are also some character traits deleted in the screenplay, and I wonder why. In the book, for instance, Doc (Roy Scheider) is homosexual.

GOLDMAN: Yes.

BRADY: I think that maybe a *close* view of the film would give you a mild suggestion that Doc is homosexual, but it's barely there.

GOLDMAN: I wanted to drop it out of the movie altogether. It was one of those things that never really picked up. I don't see any reason for it, and the way that William Devane delivers the line "Call me Janie. All my friends do," it's almost in long shot. In other words, the only way you can make it clear is to go in *close,* and I'm sure John shot it that way. But they must have decided not to pick up that strand in the film. I don't know. I was not involved.

BRADY: It's lost. It's there only for people who've read the book, too.

GOLDMAN: Right. It's very hard to answer some of these questions. Let me try to make a point. You can ask me a lot about *A Bridge Too Far,* because I know a lot about *A Bridge Too Far.* But I know really nothing about *Marathon Man* or *All the President's Men* once they started shooting. I saw them in theaters like you did. On some movies you have a close relationship throughout, and on some movies you don't. And sometimes when you don't have a close relationship it doesn't mean that you are fighting with the people who are doing the picture. It just means they don't *need* you anymore.

BRADY: Were you trying to write Babe in the film as a softer person than he is in the book?

GOLDMAN: No.

BRADY: He strikes me in the novel as being initially innocent. In the movie though, this transformation seems to be diluted. For example, he doesn't shoot his girl in the movie; nor does he kill Szell in the movie—both of which occur in the book.

GOLDMAN: I don't know why they did that. I don't know why. Maybe Dustin didn't want to play it. Maybe Evans thought it wasn't a good idea. Maybe John felt what they did was better. I wasn't there. I don't know. Start with the basic fact that if there is a change in character, it wasn't in my mind since Babe is Babe in my mind. Ultimately, Dustin's too old. I mean, Dustin's probably in real life forty, and looks . . . thirty?

BRADY: A little more, perhaps.

GOLDMAN: He looks thirty, anyway. And that was always a problem of Dustin's—that he was too old for the part. Babe, the kid described in the book . . . oh, I don't know who he was like —Jimmy Stewart when he was twenty-four? Tall, gawky, awkward kid. He runs a lot. Schlepper. A schlemiel. Young. Bony. Brilliant. Brilliant. Dustin was always, I think, quite legitimately worried because he was too old.

As a general rule I would say if you could corner every director in the world and say, "This is off the record, and I'll go on the cross if anybody finds out, but you must answer truthfully: If you can make your next picture (and you have the same budget) but in one case you have a star and in one case you don't have a star, in one case you go with a famous name, and in the other case you go with an unknown, but it won't affect in any way, shape or form how much money we give you to make the movie . . . would you rather have a star or would you rather have an unknown?" There may be *one* director in the history of the world who would rather go with the star, but for the most part none of them want to. Stars are a pain in the ass to a director. They have to be coddled, they need to be stroked. Ultimately what they do is waste time, and time is the enemy of all productions.

I would say stars very often, if they're properly cast, are wonderful. They are very, very helpful. Whether they are worth what they get is something that we can argue about at some other time and place. When the director's on the floor, he's being eaten alive by the company. They say, "You're one-half day behind schedule. You know how much money that costs? You're talking fifty thousand dollars a day."

OK, let's say you're talking fifty thousand dollars a day on an ordinary picture for each day you shoot. If you and I are doing a scene for the director, the director will say, "John, do it again. Give me a little more left profile and be a little louder, and, Bill, just do what you were doing but more." And we'll say, OK. And he'll do it eight, nine, ten times . . . whatever it is. "John, you do this; Bill, you do that." *Zap*. With stars, though, it's "Oh darling, that was brilliant. Jesus, that was marvelous. Keep doing it." They're stroking. They have to be stroked because a star can cause trouble. All productions, *all productions*—underline—are at the mercy of a cranky star.

In rehearsals of *Marathon Man* I saw Dustin Hoffman take one solid hour to discuss the rightness of a flashlight. The scene was Doc's entrance into Babe's room. It's written with Babe flashing around with a light. Dustin said, "I don't think I'd have a flashlight." We wasted an *hour* talking, trying to *justify* to Dustin why he would have a flashlight by his bed, or under his bed, or wherever it was. Ultimately he kept the flashlight. If he had not wanted to keep the flashlight, there ain't no way he was going to have a flashlight under his bed. Now, if Dustin had not been a star, but had been an unknown actor and he had said, "Gee, I don't think I want to have a flashlight under my bed," Schlesinger would have said, "Well, we'll worry about that later. It's not important. Do what's written *now*, OK?" But with a star, you have to stroke him. And if a star really wants something, you *give* it to him, because you can replace a star *until you start to shoot*. But once you are shooting, you give them what they want.

One of the miracles of *A Bridge Too Far* is that none of the stars misbehaved. Fourteen stars and they all behaved. Nobody messed around. I mean, you don't know how insecure, legitimately, most stars are. It always comes as a shock because God has usually given them such beauty and such charm, and we are always amazed that they aren't what they seem. But they're *not* what they seem. And they basically waste time. Very often they're worth it. For a writer, very often it's a terrific thing having a star do your script. But from a director's point of view, I think stars are a pain in the ass. As always, to stupid statements like "Stars are a pain in the ass," there are exceptions. For the most part, though, stars are very difficult. They are very insecure; and they know, they are aware of, their power.

BRADY: For the ending of *Marathon Man* your early drafts stick to the book—namely, Szell slashes at Babe, and Babe shoots him. But in the fourth draft Babe tears up Szell's passport and leaves him to the authorities, and Szell then kills himself. In the movie, of course, Babe forces Szell to swallow diamonds, and he then falls on his own knife.

GOLDMAN: Dustin didn't like the ending. I don't like what they ended up with. I don't know who wrote it, but it wasn't me. I wrote four endings, plus the ending in the book. I know the ending with the passport was one we came up with one lunch because Dustin was upset with the ending. Now, I was on another picture, so whoever came in to rewrite that last scene to eat-the-diamonds, they did the best they could. I don't like it, because it leaves out two crucial pieces of information.

The whole last scene has always been constructed for two things: One, the hero does not know that the villain killed his beloved brother. And when he finds that out, the dialogue is something like "You killed my brother." And Szell says, "I didn't do it." And then Babe says, "Janeway told me you did it." And Szell says, "I had to. I had to. You're very smart, but not yet wise." And Babe says, "Janeway didn't tell me anything, so don't worry about me. I'm fucking wise." And that kicks it up to a whole different emotional thing once Babe has that information. That's point one.

Point two, the hero is armed, and the villain is *secretly* armed. I have just seen him use it in the diamond district, and the villain is *very* much armed—so the whole sequence is very linear. *Don't get too close. Jesus Christ, stay away*. That's the way it all should play. Babe doesn't know, so when Szell says, "Let me show you what I got," for Christ's sake *that's* the way the tension should play. In the movie, both those factors are negated or forgotten or not used very heavily, and I think since the bulk of the book was set up for those two facts to be crucial, and then they're ignored—that's one of the reasons I don't like the diamond scene. I mean, if I had known early on that we were going to have an eat-the-diamonds scene and he was going to fall on his own knife, it's a whole different ball game. You know what I'm saying? You shepherd, you husband, you keep little pieces of information in a piece, and when you release them they have an effect. When Babe finds out that this monster killed his brother, that should make him able to do *terrible* things.

BRADY: Yes.

GOLDMAN: All gone, all gone.

BRADY: Well, that's the power of the book. And the fact that Szell, who never makes a mistake, sticks it to himself at the end of the movie . . .

GOLDMAN: I did not write the ending, and I think it's shit. Let me say again, though, that they didn't make it that way because they thought they were doing it wrong. Everybody's under the gun. The pressures of making a movie are tremendous. The writer gets a certain chance at tranquility because there's nothing till the screenplay is in. But when you are on the floor the pressures are murderous. They are *murderous*. So when they came up with that ending, nobody sat around and said, "How can we ruin the ending of this thing?" I happen to dislike it. I happen to know a lot of people who *loved* the ending. And they may be right. What I am saying is, personally, I think it leaves out certain emotional stuff. But they were doing the best they could.

BRADY: When you know who the director is on a project, do you attempt to tailor the screenplay?

GOLDMAN: Absolutely. One hundred percent. Because directors are just like the rest of us. One of the things that drives you crazy when you read about how brilliant they are is they are just like all of us. They're human and they are frail and they have strengths and they have weaknesses. You absolutely tailor toward a director's strength. You absolutely do. If you were writing an Alfred Hitchcock picture, you knew you didn't want to give him scope. He couldn't shoot scope. And if you have David Lean, you don't give David Lean a scene in a room. You give David Lean scope and he can *shoot* it. He's willing to, and he has the skill and brilliance to shoot it. Hitchcock, no. And I use those examples of two extraordinary directors that do different things. Directors *do* different things well.

Richard Attenborough is one of the three directors of the world with a genuine expertise in scope. The other two, I think, are Lean and Frank Schaffner. And if you have a big scene, you can give it to Attenborough. I mean some of the stuff in *A Bridge Too Far* was *awesome*. I guess the parachute drop is the single most stunning use of camera and the biggest scene I ever was involved with in my life. It's just an incredible sequence. Now that was four days. It was nineteen cameras. It was God knows how many planes, and God knows how many thousands of men. But if you gave that sequence to Alfred Hitchcock, he would say, "I can't be bothered with that." That's not where his heart was. I once asked Attenborough about that ability for size, and he said, "Well, you have to be willing to do it." You have to be patient enough. If you are David Lean, you have to be willing to say, "OK, this is the next five years of my life."

So yes, you absolutely tailor for a director—because you are mad not to. George Hill is one of the few directors in the world who can do action and who can do comedy.

BRADY: I don't know about the comedy.

GOLDMAN: Well, I think *Butch Cassidy* has a lot of comedy. I think *The Sting* has a lot of comedy in it, as does *The World of Henry Orient*. He has a skill for that. And he can also do action. Most directors can do one or the other. I would not want to give Mel Brooks an action scene, or Woody Allen; and I would not want to give Robert Aldrich a comedy scene. So, basically, I am *very* much aware, once a director comes in, of trying to write for what I think their strengths are.

BRADY: True or false: "The rightness of a writer for a given project will hinge in nine cases out of ten not on his rapport with the material but his rapport with the director."

GOLDMAN: I think that's wrong. Did I say that?

BRADY: No. Larry McMurtry said it.

GOLDMAN: That didn't sound like me. No, because most of the time when I do a screenplay I am the first element. There's no director. When I wrote *Butch Cassidy* there was no director. When I wrote *Hot Rock* there was no director. The next one was *Waldo Pepper*. There *was* a director. *Marathon Man* there was no director. *President's Men* there was no director. *Bridge Too Far* there was a director. *Harper* there was no director. *Magic* there was no director at the time I wrote the screenplay. So ultimately I think the rightness of the writer for the material is crucial. That's the first draft. That's what either gets the movie off the ground or not. In a crazy sense you can almost say there are two entirely different versions of any screenplay. There's the stuff written before the movie is a go project, and there is what's written when the movie is actually going to be shot. And sometimes they have very little to do with each other. The purpose of the earlier version or versions is to make it happen. The purpose of the later version or versions is to be as supportive to your director as you can. You want to make the performers relaxed. You want to make the movie as good as you can make it.

BRADY: Do you support a director by rewriting on the set?

GOLDMAN: No. I am not on the set. I don't want to be on the set. It's boring on the set, and I make the actors nervous. The most exciting day of your life is your first day on a movie set, and the dullest day of your life is your second day on a movie set. The first day it's all *Alice in Wonderland*. You think, "Oh my God, it's really happening. Look at that beautiful girl. Look at that handsome man. Look at all those cameras and all that light and all that heat." And the second day what you realize is that they may shoot ninety seconds of finished film. They may do four- or five- or nine-take setups, and between them there will be an hour and a half wait in which you are not doing anything. You just sit on your ass and wait. Stars go to their trailers. The director sits around. The only ones who work are the script girl and the cameramen changing lights. So, no, I don't. I have been called—like on *Butch,* sometimes Hill would call me and say, "We can't get this location," or, "I need some dialogue for this or that." But I try not to be on the floor very often.

That's peculiar. Most screenwriters would say I am just insane on that. I am not saying I am right or I am wrong. My personal preference is not to be around. I try to be as helpful as I can be, and if there's any reason for me to be around, obviously I'll do it; but as a rule I would not like to be because I think (a) usually I've done the best I could by the time we come to shooting, and (b) I'm on to something else, and I think I'm a disturbing force on the floor for the actors.

BRADY: *American Film* quotes you as saying, "Screenwriting is the equivalent of what the women's movement people call shitwork. It's a craft that's very occasionally raised to the level of art.'' Admittedly, screenwriting usually *is* a craft, but does that really make it shitwork?

GOLDMAN: I can give you a very good example. Shitwork in the Women's Liberation Movement, at the time when I was researching Women's Liberation for *The Stepford Wives*, is a phrase that women use for work that when it is done well is ignored and is only commented on when it is done badly; i.e., housework. No husband walks in and says, ''Oh, how beautiful. You've dusted the top of the refrigerator.'' What you say is, ''What is this? A pigsty? I work my ass off and I come home and there's filth all over.'' OK. I'll give you a great example of this. When *Waldo Pepper* opened in New York, there were two raves and one pan. The two raves did not mention in any way, shape or form my name; but you better believe my name was mentioned very prominently in the pan. *Even George Hill's great skill and love of airplanes could not save this turgid piece of shit by Bill Goldman,* right? But the raves all went to the director, the actors . . . that's what I mean. Yes, screenwriting is shitwork.

The trouble with that quote, which is a quote I will stand by, is sometimes it gets *mis*quoted, and people think I said screenwriting is *shitty* work. I don't mean that. Shitwork means work that when it is done well is ignored. When the piece is very good, very often the writer will be ignored. When the piece is rotten, they will say, ''How could Arthur Penn have done *Night Moves?*'' Or, ''Poor Arthur Penn, Marlon Brando and Jack Nicholson. Why did they get hoodwinked into doing this awful script by Tom McGuane—*The Missouri Breaks?*'' I do not know that I am speaking the truth, I only know people who have read the McGuane script. It was apparently a very taut, terrific western, which was *totally* distorted by Brando, Penn and Nicholson. I mean, Tom McGuane is a really respected novelist, and no one says, ''Jesus Christ, how did this terrible thing happen to Tom McGuane's work?'' What they said was, ''Oh, Arthur Penn, poor man, how did he get suckered into taking this script so seriously?''

There's a quote about *Night Moves* which I love. I have it on my wall here: "I can't figure out whether the screenplay by Allan Sharp was worked on too much or not enough, or Mr. Penn and his actors accepted the screenplay with more respect than it deserves." One of the things that drives you crazy when you are dealing with a powerhouse director is they are like a giant ape: You feed them what they want. So when you see a Mike Nichols disaster or an Arthur Penn disaster or a Robert Altman disaster, that's *their* fault. When Clint Eastwood is in a crummy movie, the script is as good as he would accept. Whatever problems there were, he tried to solve for *his* satisfaction. In such cases the screenwriting goes by the boards. Maybe it will be better. Maybe it will be worse. But it won't be what's written.

BRADY: You're more caustic than other screenwriters I've spoken to. You once referred to your craft in an interview as "something that's denigrating to the soul." Why would you say that? Is it that dishonorable?

GOLDMAN: If *all* you do is write screenplays, then it *becomes* denigrating to the soul. Which I think is true. I don't go to Hollywood very often, as I said to you earlier. I remember once I was at a gathering at which most of the people in the room were screenwriters. And they were the most despair-ridden people. I mean, all you had to do was say "rewrites" or whatever and they had horror stories to tell; because ultimately if you are *just* a screenwriter, it *is* denigrating to the soul. If that's all you do in your life, your life is constantly tromped on by directors who are insecure or stars who want to have their parts made bigger. Nobody in the world—how can I put it to you?—maybe it's too strong a statement, but there's almost nobody in the world who wants to be *just* a screenwriter. They *want* to be producers, they *want* to be directors. They are using screenwriting as a stepping-stone to some other source of power. You can go through careers. The most successful screenwriter of our time and maybe the best in the last thirty years is Ernest Lehman. I mean, Ernest Lehman's first eight or ten credits are just *fabulous: Somebody Up There Likes Me, North by Northwest, Sabrina, Executive Suite* . . . just an incredible list. And he became a producer, then a director, and now he is back doing screenwriting. Daniel Taradash wrote *From Here to Eternity,* became a director, back to screenwriting. I mean, generally they try to get *out* of just screen-writing because they get tired of the alterations, because often the alterations improve things, but often they don't. And often the reason behind the alteration is valid, and often it's not. Often it's ego.

BRADY: Ernest Lehman said, "My advice to the writer is to be smart enough or lucky enough in all these creative battles to lose the right battles."

GOLDMAN: That's a wonderful quote, isn't it?

BRADY: Do you try to lose the right battles?

GOLDMAN: No, I don't. Basically I'm not tactful. I'm not proud of that either. Even in talking to my wife and my children, I am not by my nature tactful. I don't like being stroked. It's a waste of time. I don't want to have to bother stroking you. If I think you have a bad idea, rather than say, "Gee, I think that's a marvelous idea, but what if we did A, B, C and D instead of X, Y and Z?" I would rather say, "Blah." It saves a lot of time.

BRADY: Dino De Laurentiis says a book writer can never write a screenplay. Do you find any of that attitude in your Hollywood travels?

GOLDMAN: There tends to be a certain lack of high esteem in everybody's view of screenwriters. As I say, we're coming a little bit more out of the closet into the sun now—at least into the shadows, if not the sun. So that kind of statement by someone like De Laurentiis is simply moronic. People think that novel writing and screenwriting don't go well together. It's not really true. Screenwriting *is* a craft, a strange craft. You don't have to be a good writer. I don't have even very much respect for anyone who is *just* a screenwriter in terms of writing. Writing a poem is hard. Writing a sonnet is hard. Writing a novel or a play is really hard. But writing a screenplay . . . it's not that it's easy . . . it's *different*. It's *not* hard. *It's not hard.* It's basically a skill. Writing a sonnet is only a skill to sonneteers. To most of us, it's awe-some. How do you make the lines rhyme? How do you make it so concise?

Screenwriting is a peculiar thing. I mean, we're this appendage in the business. They would like to do without us, kind of, but they can't get a movie made without us. And most screenwriters, most of us are not very good. We really aren't. But basically we are very important, and everybody in the business knows we are important. And everybody outside the business doesn't understand what we do, and there's no reason to really know what we do. Nobody understands what a cameraman does, and they shouldn't. Do they like the movie? Did you have fun at *Jaws?* is really all that matters. It doesn't matter who made the monster.

BRADY: Robert Towne says that strangers coming together on a film rarely make anything good. Do you prefer to work with friends?

GOLDMAN: Not anymore.

BRADY: Do you want to amplify that?

GOLDMAN: It's just that I went to work on *Waldo Pepper,* for example, having a good relationship with George Roy Hill. Then we had a terrible, terrible fight. It may or may not have damaged the picture. It may have helped the picture, I don't know. But it's always a painful thing when you don't speak to someone you like for a year of your life. I would never have done *Waldo Pepper* except that it was by George. George is the one who had the love for old airplanes.

It's often more expeditious if you get on with the people you are working with, perhaps. I would disagree with Towne's statement, but it works for Towne. But you see, Towne's very much on the floor. Towne's *there.* Towne wants to work with Bob Evans and Jack Nicholson and Warren Beatty and those people, I assume. He's a friend of theirs. He's in the business. He's part of the Hollywood community.

BRADY: If you were a scrambling young writer, what would you do to break into films today?

GOLDMAN: I would write an original screenplay and use any contact that I possibly had to get me in to see anybody to have somebody, anybody, read it. Anybody who your second cousin Sadie went to high school with thirty-five years ago who knows somebody who works in the mailroom at William Morris is a help. Anything to cut yourself away from the herd. If I were a young screenwriter today, I would try to find out what kind of films seem to be meeting with public acceptance that I felt I could write with some passion, and I would write an original screenplay and then flog the shit out of it and use any contact that I had. I remember once in my career driving up to see Paul Newman after Paul had agreed to do *Harper*. He agreed to do *Harper* with great quickness because he had been given the script when he was in Europe in agony doing a disastrous film directed by Peter Ustinov, costarring Sophia Loren. *Lady L,* or something like that. Newman had to wear tights, and he felt all wrong for it. *Harper* was a very Americana kind of thing, and he felt strongly: he *jumped* for it.

I remember Elliott Kastner, the producer, looking at me and saying, on the way back from the meeting with Paul, "You don't know what's just happened, do you?" And I said, "No." He said, "You jumped past all the shit." Which was true. Automatically I wasn't a nobody anymore. I was a somebody who had written a Paul Newman picture. My agent could then say, "This guy has written for one of the number-one box office attractions." So when I say flog it with everything you can, I also mean do the best you can. Don't write stuff you can't handle. If you don't like romantic comedies, don't write *Annie Hall*. You have to always write your best, or you're dead.

It's very hard. You get asked that all the time: "How do you break in?" The answer is a wonderful quote from a great basketball player, Ed Macauley: "When you are not practicing, remember, someone somewhere is practicing, and when you meet him he will win." The same is true in writing. You have to get up very early in the day and work very hard. It's not like selling shoes. You can always get a job in New York driving a cab. But everybody would like to be in the movie business. There's *severe* competition. *Grotesquely* severe competition. So when you say, "How do I get in the movie business?" I don't know. You just hustle your ass off, and get lucky.

BRADY: Have you always wanted to be a writer?

GOLDMAN: Yes. Irwin Shaw is the reason I am a writer. I always wanted to be a writer when I was growing up, and when

I was seventeen or sixteen or eighteen, somebody gave me a copy of *Mixed Company*. Shaw's a *great* short-story writer. He's one of the best in American history, I think. And I couldn't believe that they seemed so easy; they were such marvelous stories—that was the thing that really made me think, yes, I really want to be a writer. And Raymond Chandler, Ross Macdonald, Dashiell Hammett—those three. And Chekhov, and the Russians, and all the people you loved growing up. Dumas. In terms of movie writing, I feel influenced by all of the wonderful fantasy adventures you read when you are a kid—*The Three Musketeers,* that kind of thing. My favorite movie of all time is *Gunga Din*. I still can't see it without weeping. Nothing in second place. *Shane,* perhaps. I'm not saying that *Gunga Din* is the greatest movie ever made. But it's my favorite.

BRADY: Do you have a masterwork in mind? Anything that's in the midnight of your mind somewhere?

GOLDMAN: No. I don't understand the creative process. All I know is it's been working, and I don't want to mess with it. I don't know what I'm going to write next. There are always things on some back burner, and you don't know when they will percolate. Then one bubbles up and I want to write. They force themselves into my consciousness.

BRADY: You like to keep it spontaneous.

GOLDMAN: Yes. Very, very.

BRADY: And ultimately, how would you like to be remembered?

GOLDMAN: Storyteller.

ERNEST
LEHMAN

BARNABY JACKSON

Ernest Lehman was born on Ninety-second Street in Manhattan during the early days of the prosperous twenties. He spent his youth in Woodmere, a wealthy suburb on the south shore of Long Island, and attended a private academy. Then came high school, and the life-changing Depression. The Lehman family mansion was replaced by an apartment in New York City, and young Ernie entered the free City College of New York. He planned to become a chemical engineer but fell under the influence of the literary department's Professor Theodore Goodman (who also taught Paddy Chayefsky), and halfway through college Ernest Lehman decided to become a writer.

Professor Goodman gave Lehman a B+ for the narrative writing course but warned him about a definite "slickness" in his short stories. That slickness, when tempered, was later to lead to numerous fiction magazine sales for Lehman, and then to a job with a publicity agency that specialized in theatrical and motion picture accounts. "This was my introduction to show business," the screenwriter recalled in Roy Newquist's *Showcase* some twenty years ago. "I was truly struck by the glamor and the behind-the-scenes skulduggery that goes on in the world of Broadway pressagentry, Broadway column-writing, night club life, Hollywood personalities on safari in New York, etc. I must have been quite impressionable at the time because I was moved to make this my world of fiction, and I went on to write many short stories and novelettes about the denizens of Broadway."

Ernest Lehman's novelettes included *Sweet Smell of Success* and *The Comedian,* both of which appeared in *Cosmopolitan* before being published in book form. Quickly, Lehman was called to Hollywood by Paramount Pictures. "It was like taking 'The Last Train from Berlin,' " he told AP columnist Bob Thomas. "The picture business was falling apart, and I was one of the last contract writers brought out here."

Ernest Lehman is one of the earliest of the new breed of screenwriter. With credits from the fifties that included *Executive Suite, Sabrina, The King and I, Somebody Up There Likes Me, Sweet Smell of Success, From the Terrace* and his first original screenplay, *North by Northwest,* he moved to the top with quiet competence, commanding respect, a high salary and a slice of the profits. He also became the master adapter of Broadway properties to the Hollywood screen in the sixties, doing scripts for *West Side Story, The Sound of Music* and *Who's Afraid of Virginia Woolf?* Few screenwriters have been part of so many projects that have become major movies of their time.

Today Ernest Lehman splits his time between fiction (his

The French Atlantic Affair was a 1977 best-seller) and screenwriting. Recent credits include *Black Sunday* and Alfred Hitchcock's last film, *Family Plot*. He is currently working on a novel, and recently completed an adaptation of the Brenda Starr comic strip for the screen.

Our conversations took place at Lehman's home in Brentwood in the western end of Los Angeles. It is a bright, friendly home in an oasislike setting at the end of a long drive that is sliced between two other pieces of property. The house itself could have been transported from Southern France—white with dark gray wood shingles, rooms filled with white and yellow tones, and an airy, flowing feeling. A gray Siamese cat named Dolly roams the grounds. The wooden swing that was used in *Virginia Woolf* hangs from a large mulberry tree, and a basketball hoop and backboard hang over the garage door.

To the left of the main house is a wing with a separate entrance to the game room. Here there is an old-fashioned billiards table, comfortable chairs, a red vinyl couch, walls splattered with posters from France, and in a corner a white enameled barber chair with a red backrest, a prop from an ancient movie.

Like an Ernest Lehman script, the author is trim and meticulous. He looks ten years younger than he is, and only the reading glasses on a gold chain around his neck even hint at the years he has seen as a screenwriter. He climbed into the barber chair, tilted it back, and we commenced with a discussion of the importance of a script to a movie's success.

———————————

BRADY: Do you think that most bad films can be traced to a bad script?

LEHMAN: I just happen to be one of those irrational persons who think that a film cannot be any good if it isn't well written. It just *can't* be. And in all likelihood, if it's bad, it was badly written. Most, but not all bad movies, can be traced to a bad script.

BRADY: You said of your own work once that the screenplay for *Portnoy's Complaint* was rather well written, that the screenplay read well. What happened there?

LEHMAN: I said that *others* felt that it was well written. I didn't say that *I* thought it was well written. I don't go around saying *any* script I've done is well written, even if I secretly think so. I think I said that most people who read the script of *Portnoy* felt that it was well written. Most people aren't capable of reading a screenplay and knowing that, even though it seems to be well *written,* on *paper,* it might make a bad *picture.* It's a very difficult thing to spot. And sometimes it's very difficult to read a script which seems to be almost unintelligible and realize that it's going to make a hell of a movie.

BRADY: Well, in the case of *Portnoy,* would you say it was a bad script?

LEHMAN: In retrospect, looking back on that whole venture, I would say that it *was* a bad script. I don't think that some other director could have taken that script and made it *appreciably* better than it was. I still feel that there were some damned good scenes in that picture, well written, well directed (by me) and well acted. *Really.* But the whole approach of the screenplay produced a film that didn't work. Charles Champlin of the L.A. *Times,* in one of his follow-up pieces on the picture, said that in retrospect, he felt that no one could have made a good picture out of *Portnoy's Complaint.* He said the novel was essentially undramatizable, and in a sense it *was* undramatizable. I made the choice of deciding that the only part of the novel one could really dramatize was the story of what happens when thirty-three-year-old Portnoy meets the girl called The Monkey, with enough material up front to explain why he was the way he was at age thirty-three.

And that was not really what made the novel such a brilliant work. The novel was at its greatest during Portnoy's early life, and all of it was done as interior monologue, a man lying on a couch talking to his analyst. Let's say it just didn't work as a film, OK? And not necessarily because the direction was lousy, although I am sure there were some scenes that were poorly

directed. But that wasn't why it didn't work. It didn't work because, as a screenwriter, I never found the right way, if there
was one, to dramatize that novel as a film.

BRADY: When did you realize it wasn't working?

LEHMAN: After the first review, which was a rave in *Daily
Variety*. I still have it. It came out on a Friday, and I had exactly
one weekend in which to dream that maybe this picture was
going to be OK after all. And then the roof fell in, with the
exception of a few *good* reviews here and there throughout the
country (Archer Winsten of the New York *Post* gave it an excellent one). It got to the point where I decided it would be better
for me personally not to read the awful reviews, because I wasn't
going to learn anything from them that could help me. You *rarely*
learn from reviews, because each picture is different, with its
own specific and different problems. I decided that it would be
better for my future life not to have the horrible words that were
written about me and the picture grooved as brain traces. You
know, if you *hear* that Rex Reed said the picture was indescrib-
ably terrible, well, that isn't the same as *reading* it. Summing it
all up, *Portnoy's Complaint* is a perfect example of a picture that
failed because the screenplay did not solve its problems. That
those problems might have been unlickable is beside the point.

BRADY: And yet when you were in there writing the best
screenplay you could, did it ever occur to you that maybe this
film was not going to go?

LEHMAN: Of course it occurred to me. It always occurs to me,
every time I work on anything, that it could be a calamity. You
never know if it's going to work. Never. You must never have a
feeling of elation, triumph, optimism and all that, beforehand.
Never. Never. That is foolhardy. It is inviting disaster. Much of
my effort as a writer is spent trying to avoid failure, because
failure is almost the name of the game in the film world. Most
pictures are failures, artistically or commercially or both.

BRADY: When you say your efforts as a writer are to ward off
failure, it sounds as if you are never really certain of a scene or a
line.

LEHMAN: A scene or a line does not a picture make. Quite

often I like something a lot that I've written; but you never know whether the whole picture is going to come off, because there are so many slips twixt the finished screenplay and the first screening. How is it going to be cast? Who's going to direct it? The scenes that are playing in my head—how do they *really* play on the screen? The amazing thing about screenwriting is that the screenwriter does not, like the stage dramatist, hear his dialogue spoken until it's too late (for him) to know whether it plays or not. He seldom sees actors performing his scenes, so that he can say, "Hey, wait a minute. I wrote that wrong. That's no good. It doesn't work. I have to redo that. I'll do it tonight. Tomorrow we'll do a new scene. I'll have it for you in the morning." No. Maybe he goes to a preview, at best. Usually when I finally see the film I mutter things like "My God, why did I make that speech so long? It's *interminable.*"

Sometimes I know way ahead of time that scenes are too long and I can't do anything about it—like in *Family Plot,* I couldn't bear the idea of that seance scene that opens the picture going on forever and ever with all that exposition. I wanted to do it as *several* scenes, but Hitch, with good logic, wanted to get it over with in one gulp. So I wrote the damn thing as one unbroken scene, and plenty of my best friends complained afterward that the scene was too long. Why argue with them and explain to them that there were good reasons to do it that way? They were right.

BRADY: There's a lot of information in that scene.

LEHMAN: I know, but one of the most important feats in screenwriting is to convey exposition not only without it appearing to be exposition, but also without wearing the audience out, and there's a limit to how much you can do in one long, sitting-down scene.

BRADY: What are some of the methods that you use to convey information without its seeming expository?

LEHMAN: One of the tricks is to have the exposition conveyed in a scene of conflict, so that a character is forced to say things you want the audience to know—as, for example, if he is defending himself against somebody's attack, his words of defense seem justified even though his words are actually *expository* words. Something appears to be happening, so the audience believes it is witnessing a *scene* (which it is), not listening to expository speeches. A scene, to me, has to have some element of conflict in it or some cross-purpose. It doesn't have to be a quarrel, but there should be some kind of tension. The most obvious are scenes involving opposing viewpoints. If it's a two-character scene and both characters have the same goal, usually to make the scene work the goal of one has to be either slightly different or more powerful than the goal of the other. If two people are in total agreement about anything, usually there's no scene. To answer your question, conflict is an excellent device for conveying exposition. Humor is another way of getting it across.

BRADY: In the scripts you did with Hitchcock, I sensed that you really underplayed the exposition because you felt that the viewer knows that in a Hitchcock film, every little detail somehow or other adds up.

LEHMAN: Right. You got a lot more attention paid to every little thing you did and said in a Hitchcock picture. It's amazing, you know, how he could manipulate an audience. Take *North by Northwest,* for example: the beginning of the crop-duster sequence, in particular, when Cary Grant is standing alone by the roadside waiting for a man he has not met (but has been mistaken for) to show up. Most directors would have had maybe one or two cars whiz by, and figure that that was about all an audience could tolerate. But Hitchcock knew better than that. He had a car come from one direction, zoom by and disappear in the distance; then he held on a long interval in which nothing was happening; then he had a car come from the *other* direction, and zoom by and disappear in the distance; and then *another* long interval of silence with nothing happening; and then a truck came by and merely blew dust all over Cary Grant and disappeared in the distance. And still nothing had really happened. Hitch knew how to milk that sequence in a way that no other director would have known how to do, or would have had the guts to do. There was an awful lot of ominous *nothing* going on for a long time before the stranger appeared on the other side of the road. That was just one aspect of Hitchcock's unique style.

BRADY: What other earmarks would there be in that style? *North by Northwest* struck me as being a highly readable script, lively and filled with delightful lines.

LEHMAN: If you didn't try for that, you weren't writing a Hitchcock picture. There had to be a certain amount of wit, or an *attempt* at wit. No matter how melodramatic the goings-on were, the characters had to have a sense of humor. They could not take themselves too seriously. And they had to speak in circumlocutions—those were the rules. The James Mason character in *North by Northwest* is typical of a Hitchcock heavy. They never talk "nasty" talk; they talk silken, suave, professorial talk while they tell you they are going to have to kill you. The vocabulary of a Hitchcock villain contains many expressions like "I'm afraid that," or "Unfortunately, my dear fellow," or "I regret to tell you"—you know, do away with him but be a gentleman about it.

BRADY: There's a great line by Cary Grant in the film when he says that the girl uses sex the way some people use a flyswatter.

LEHMAN: You liked that, huh?

BRADY: Do you work hard at developing such one-liners?

LEHMAN: I must say I find writing that kind of dialogue a little less than difficult. If I have a style, it tends to have people, maybe to their detriment, display a predilection for the wisecrack, repartee, the flip manner. And I myself tend to be a little bit like my characters when I'm writing—not a tongue-in-cheek attitude exactly, but I don't seem to take writing as seriously as some writers would, or should.

BRADY: Could that perhaps explain why your successes for the most part have been what might be called entertainments?

LEHMAN: I think calling my films "entertainments" might be too much of a generalization, and perhaps very slightly unflattering. Part of *Somebody Up There Likes Me* was entertainment, and part of it wasn't; very little of *From the Terrace* was an entertainment; *Executive Suite* was not an entertainment. And what about *West Side Story,* and *Who's Afraid of Virginia Woolf?,* not to mention *Black Sunday* and suchlike? I'm trying to think of what your definition of the word "entertainment" would be.

BRADY: I'm speaking of *tone,* perhaps. You took a rather entertaining approach to *The Prize,* I thought, given the rather somber, almost heavy-handed nature of the book.

LEHMAN: I would say that the book was serious, and quite properly took itself seriously. It was my own choice, right or wrong, that the serious subject and serious approach would not be viable film fare. Maybe I didn't know how to do it as a serious film. Maybe I felt people would not go to see it as such. I wanted it to be a success as a film, and I felt that in order to make it work (we use words like that: *How do we make this work?*), it would have to be made into a *movie* movie—amusing and nonserious. I made the Paul Newman character pretty flip. I think I was stealing from myself, sort of road company Hitchcock. *Very* road company, I'd say.

BRADY: Was it your doing? Or was it done in collaboration with director Mark Robson?

LEHMAN: If it was bad, it was my doing. If it was good, it was the producer's and director's doing. Robson came on as director of *The Prize* after the screenplay had been written. The producer was Pandro Berman. He worked on the picture for two years.

BRADY: How did you feel about someone else making a screenplay out of your novel *The French Atlantic Affair?*

LEHMAN: God, it was neat to be on the other side of the fence. Some other screenwriter had to sweat and say, "Oh, my God, this is ridiculous. How am I going to make a movie out of this?"

BRADY: You liked that?

LEHMAN: Sure I did. Everybody said, "Why don't you do it yourself?" The answer was simple. I spent years writing that novel. I wasn't going to do to *it* what I had done to the novels of others, because I know what you have to do. You have to be *merciless.* It would have been painful for me to have written a scene for the novel, liked it, and now have to say, "Uh-uh, out. Can't have a ten-page scene here. We'll have to do that in a page and a quarter." And I'm sure I'd have found a million ways to do the picture better than the book and say, "God, why didn't I think of that last year?" Anyway, we now know that MGM's succession of screenwriters failed to come up with a makable theatrical film, and so it was done as a six-hour miniseries on TV, and failed to fill me with joy.

BRADY: Do you really think you've "done it" to others, though? You make adapting sound almost vicious.

LEHMAN: Well, I exaggerate for effect. When I say I have done it to others, really the only embarrassing adaptation was on *The Prize,* because Irving Wallace is a very close friend of mine. I mean, we've been very close to each other for many years. It was a rather strange situation for me to be in, doing this screenplay based on his novel, and I know he regarded his novel as a serious work, as who didn't, because that's what it was, one of his very best. And so he went off for a summer vacation knowing I was working on the screenplay, thrilled at the whole idea. While I, unfortunately, could find no way of writing a screenplay that would *work.* That summer I went to Sweden and Denmark and phumphed around for a month doing research, trying to determine how to do the picture. I got back, started making notes, pushed ideas around, and Pandro Berman was very nice about it, didn't bother me at all. "Whatever you're doing is OK with me." This lasted for three months. Finally I realized: *I can't lick this. I can't do it. I don't know how to do this as a movie.*

Now Irving comes back from his trip to Europe and comes over to the house and sits by the side of the pool with me, and we start talking about his trip, all the fun he has had. An hour goes by and he says, "Ernie, how come you haven't mentioned *The Prize?*" This was a Sunday, and in my desk at MGM—handwritten on a legal pad (I hadn't typed it yet)—was a letter of resignation I was going to give to Pandro Berman the next day, Monday, telling him why I had to leave the picture. *I just don't know how to do it. Sorry, et cetera, et cetera.* So I told Irving, "I haven't been able to lick it. I'm sending Pandro Berman a letter tomorrow. It's kind of embarrassing, Irving, but I just can't

make a go of it.'' And he said, ''Gee, I'm sorry. That's a shame.
I hate to hear you've had a bad summer. What kind of ideas did
you come up with?''

So I started telling him all the stuff in my notes, the idea of
making it a Hitchcockian kind of thing and making sport of a lot
of the novel's seriousness. And he said, ''That sounds like a
movie to me. That sounds like a *good* movie.'' And I said,
''Really?'' And he said, ''Yeah, it sounds like a *movie*.'' So, the
upshot was, on Monday I called Pandro Berman, who, to this
day, doesn't know there was a resignation letter waiting to go to
him, and I said, ''I'd like to have a meeting with you.'' I met with
him that day and said, ''Look, I haven't written anything yet, but
these are the ideas I've had.'' And I told him everything I had
told Irving, and Pandro said, ''Great, terrific, write it, go!'' And
that's how I found myself locked into *The Prize* for almost two
years. I mean, it took me forever. It was so hard to write, painting myself into corners and trying to write myself out of them. It
was all so complicated, so full of intrigue, and not all of it came
off too well, though some of it was damned good. It's on television a lot these days, he said, grasping at straws.

BRADY: You strike me as being an extremely sensitive human
being in a business that requires the insensitivity and the thick-
ness of . . .

LEHMAN: An elephant's hide. How many writers have you met
who could just bull their way through all this? I have never met
one. In my day I did some pretty wild things, starting with the
very first picture I wrote. By then I had written for publication.
I was used to seeing my by-line in national magazines—*Collier's,
Cosmopolitan, Esquire*—and my attitude was: That's *my* story.
Nobody was talking about who the editor was, or the publisher.
Then came Hollywood. I write my first movie, *Executive Suite,*
and I see a cover story on the film in *Newsweek*—a five-page
takeout inside with a big glowing review, and everybody is mentioned—the head of the studio, the name of the dog in the picture, *everyone*. Except me. Nowhere is there the word
''screenplay.'' Nowhere is my name. I was new. I didn't realize

that it was par for the course. And I was furious. I fired off a telegram to the editor of *Newsweek*. He not only printed my wire, he printed a box in a subsequent issue apologizing to me for not having included my name in the review. That was just the beginning.

I used to phone film critics. I'd get their home telephone numbers. One poor lady who used to review for a local evening paper in L.A. wrote this great review for *North by Northwest*. Not a mention of me. I called her at home. She started *weeping* on the telephone. "What can I do? You're so right. Let me write something immediately." No. I said I didn't want her to write something immediately, but to remember, the next time she reviewed a picture, that pictures are *written* as well as acted and directed and photographed and edited and scored and all that. The screenwriter determines what scenes are in and what scenes are out; decides whether that bit of information is dramatized or just referred to; whether it takes place on or off screen. There are a million decisions made by the screenwriter. When he's adapting someone else's work, he's the one who looks at a sequence in the book or play and decides: *It won't work in the movie. We'll just have to forget it. Or change it from a ship to a plane.* The director doesn't say, "I've got an idea. Let's shoot the scene in a plane instead of a boat." No, it's written. It's *written*.

I remember the *Newsweek* review said, "Director Robert Wise then moves his drama to the boardroom for the final sequence," and I said to myself: *No. The director doesn't move the drama to the boardroom; the screenwriter moves it to the boardroom because that's where he and/or the novelist thinks it should be.* All those decisions are screenplay decisions, and those reviewers simply don't know it. Some of them still don't even know how pictures are made.

BRADY: The situation seems to be changing for the better today.

LEHMAN: Yes. I think so. Screenwriters like Bill Goldman certainly have become very well known. Paul Schrader with a slew of startling pictures also got to be well known. But still, largely only in the industry. They still are probably Bill Who and Paul

Who to the public at large. Me? I have *two* names—Ernie Who and Ernest Who.

The public knows more about the director than anyone else because film critics, in order to be able to write reviews, apparently have to personalize and channel the creative forces into one persona. It's just too difficult for them, or too much work for them, to review a film and find out who did what to whom. They make it easier for themselves by unconsciously falling into the *auteur* theory, and that perpetuates the *auteur* theory, and it then becomes an untrue fact of life. So when films are listed in various magazines, it's Robert Altman's So-and-So and John Huston's So-and-So and George Roy Hill's So-and-So—insert the title. The magazines don't say So-and-So, directed by Hal Ashby, written by So-and-So and produced by So-and-So. It's the director's film. Magazines use the directorial possessive almost exclusively.

I used to play a little trick on interviewers. I would say: There was this writer and he read a novel which he thought lent itself very well to the medium and he decided to take an option on it and went to a producer and the producer was enthusiastic, too. And they got a director who was interested. So the writer took a ream of paper and a typewriter and locked himself in his study for three or four months and wrote a first draft—and the producer and director were *very* enthusiastic. Anyway, to make a long story short, the script was produced and, oh, they got this star and they got that star, and it was a smash hit. Then I'd say to the interviewer: What am I talking about now? Am I talking about a *movie?* Or am I talking about *Teahouse of the August Moon* on the *stage?* Or am I talking about Goodrich and Hackett's stage adaptation of *The Diary of Anne Frank?* Or am I talking about the musical play that was done, based on the novel *7½ Cents* and called *Pajama Game?* I had made the interviewer think I was talking about a movie. See, I was trying to show him there really is not all that much difference between writing a movie and writing a play, because in both cases you wind up with a dramatic manuscript which is then *produced*—the difference being that in movies it is photographed and edited and scored. But the *writing* process is very much the same. Now, I wasn't even talking about *original* screenplays, because with them it's even *more* similar to writing a play.

BRADY: Isn't it true, though, that in the theater the playwright has approval of script changes that a screenwriter would not have?

LEHMAN: That's true. Also, the playwright can't be replaced or rewritten without his approval. And the actors can't change their lines without his approval. But I was just trying to convince this journalist that there isn't that much difference in the *creative process* of writing the two forms of drama, except that one of them is to be put on the screen.

BRADY: Though you have produced and directed films, do you take yourself by and large as a *writer?*

LEHMAN: Yes, of course.

BRADY: And the other hats you've worn?

LEHMAN: The other hats were worn only three times.

BRADY: For better or for worse?

LEHMAN: Two of the three films I produced received best picture of the year Academy nominations and nineteen other nominations. What's so worse about that? It was an experience, producing as well as writing, and then producing, directing and writing. It was a heady sort of ego trip. Very strange to be in a position of so much weight. I hesitate to use the word "power," but . . . so much *influence.* For me a director is somebody everyone looks to as though to say, "What do we do next? Where do you want the camera? Is that scene OK? Do we shoot it again?" But if you are the producer, too, as *well* as the director and the writer—that's the ultimate in making a film, I guess. What a shame that *Portnoy* wasn't a good one, although *while* I was doing it it was very exciting. Exciting and exhausting. I had the opportunity in rehearsals, you know, to say, "I can't direct that. That scene doesn't work. It's undirectable. It's got to be rewritten." So I could rewrite it. I was *there.* I was the director and the writer. And there was no one there saying, "No, you can't do that. I want it *this* way." I was the producer.

BRADY: That whole experience must have had much fatigue for you.

LEHMAN: Oh, it was physically exhausting, as it is for all directors. It really is. I'm amazed that I went through it. A lot of location stuff. God, you should have seen me directing on the streets of Rome. Somebody who had never directed *traffic* before is directing on the streets of Rome, is directing on Fifth Avenue in New York City, is directing in Tel Aviv, in Vermont. It was some experience, really. I mean physically. Climbing roofs and . . . every part of it was just amazing. I'm somebody who sleeps late—and I had to be up every morning at six-thirty!

BRADY: How can you sleep late in this business?

LEHMAN: That's the reason I became a writer. I can't get up to be in an office at some ridiculous hour, like nine-thirty. I really can't.

BRADY: Do you work late, or do you just like to sleep late?

LEHMAN: I'm a late night person, whether I'm working or not. Producers and directors and other colleagues have been trained not to call conferences with me at nine in the morning. Or at ten either.

BRADY: Are you writing any memoirs?

LEHMAN: No. But I *did* keep a log on the making of *Virginia Woolf,* three hundred and seventy-five thousand words. If it ever saw the light of day people would say: *I don't believe it.* The whole thing is better off buried, believe me.

BRADY: That seems to be the tendency now, to write a book about the making of the movie.

LEHMAN: Well, in some ways it can be a betrayal of other people's trust. You know, if you are working closely with people on a movie and they don't know you are recording everything they do and say, or writing about it each night, waiting for the day you can publish it—a lot of things they do and say aren't going to look all that good. And that includes the behavior of the diarist, too.

BRADY: When did you first begin to see yourself possibly becoming a screenwriter?

LEHMAN: While I was writing magazine fiction in New York, I wrote to my agent and told him that one of my ambitions was to become a screenwriter, because I felt that I would be good at it, and a few years later, through no efforts on the part of a literary agent or anything like that (he was no longer even my agent), I was tapped by Paramount Pictures as a result of my novelettes appearing in *Cosmopolitan*. First was *Sweet Smell of Success,* which appeared under the title *Tell Me About It Tomorrow* because the then-editor of *Cosmopolitan* did not want to use the word "smell" in the magazine. (He admits it was one of his few mistakes.) *The Comedian* was also published there, and within a month after that, a telegram from the West Coast arrived at the New York office of Paramount: See if Ernest Lehman is interested in coming out to California as a film writer. I remember every bit of that day, the day that was going to change my life.

BRADY: What did Paramount want you for?

LEHMAN: Nothing specific.

BRADY: What was the impetus for that telegram?

LEHMAN: Well, the real impetus for the telegram, I think, was in part the published fiction itself—which was pretty damn good, if I say so myself. I don't think there was a word in either of those novelettes that I would change today. And I've reread them many times. They were *good*. And considering that they appeared in a slick magazine, it was kind of amazing. They were really hard-bitten stuff. Both of them. But I think what helped enormously was a column published by a former employer and friend of mine, a famous press agent, the late Irving Hoffman, who was also a columnist for *The Hollywood Reporter*. Through the intervention of a mutual friend, he ran a whole column in the *Reporter* about me and *The Comedian* and what a hell of a screenwriter I would make, and within a week there was a phone call from Paramount. This was in 1952.

BRADY: Hadn't you done work on a screenplay earlier?

LEHMAN: No, I had sold an original story to Hollywood which came out as a picture called *The Inside Story*. But I never regard that as my film work. That was just an original story that I sold and someone else wrote as a film. The irony of what I just told you is that for about a year and a half before Irving Hoffman ran that column, which helped a lot in my being summoned to California, he was not talking to me. We were on the outs because he felt—and I won't say rightly or wrongly until I think about it some more—that I had betrayed him in a way by writing *Sweet Smell of Success*. He felt that others would think that the fictional columnist was Walter Winchell, and that *he* was the press agent character, because Irving Hoffman *was* very close to Walter Winchell and there were many aspects of my fictional columnist that made people think of Walter Winchell. I'm not talking about the movie. I'm talking about the novelette.

And so we were on the outs. I had worked with Irving as a press agent. I had been one of his staff, a Broadway press agent, and I was fascinated with that underworld of nightclubs and columnists and press agents—how some people killed others with words instead of bullets. Irving and I had a few bitter confrontations in which I tried to make him realize that the only world I knew was the world that I *knew,* and a fiction writer uses his material. It's all he's got. I made some changes in the manuscript at his request before it was published, and in our confrontations I must have made him feel guilty about something, too— just as he made me feel guilty for having written *Sweet Smell of Success*—because, after the mutual friend intervened, Irving did me this big favor, he ran this column in praise of me. The fact that I wrote the entire column myself is, I suppose, merely incidental.

And for quite a few years after I arrived in Hollywood, I was quite leery about having anybody make a movie of the novelette. I didn't feel at all safe. In fact, once I was going to make the columnist a woman. I thought that was safer. But I never did. And then eventually I sold the property to Hecht/Lancaster. I wrote several drafts of the screenplay. Then, when I still had some scenes to rewrite, I fell ill with a pain in the gut, and Clifford Odets took over for me. My doctor ordered me to leave the film and the country.

BRADY: And the country?

LEHMAN: Yeah. Get away from pictures, he said. I went to

Tahiti, but only for three weeks. It was enough to clear the pain in my gut, though. It was a spastic colon, brought on by tension. I had had a lot of problems with the people involved in the making of that picture, which I'd rather not go into.

BRADY: And the work had high emotional content for you from the start.

LEHMAN: Oh yeah. First of all, I had lived through most of that story, and the publication of it had caused all kinds of bad vibes, and there were always dreadful fears of retaliation from Winchell, even though he would tell people, "I don't take on the Lehmans of the world. I take on the Peglers." He wouldn't fool around with small fry like me. Anyway, that's how I came to California. Paramount brought me out here on a seven-year contract with six-month options. And here I was. And before I could even get a Paramount picture on the screen, I was borrowed by MGM to write *Executive Suite*. And while I was working on *Executive Suite* at MGM, Paramount dropped their option on me, although my next picture was back at Paramount. They brought me back there to work with Billy Wilder on *Sabrina*. And after that I went to Twentieth Century-Fox to do *The King and I*.

BRADY: How did *Sabrina* go? As a young screenwriter that must have been a rather heady experience.

LEHMAN: Fantastic experience. Fantastic. I had no picture on the screen yet. They were shooting *Executive Suite* at MGM, and Bill Holden, who was Billy Wilder's close friend, and who was going to be in *Sabrina*, used to come over to Billy's house at the end of his workday, where Billy and I were still working on *Sabrina*. Holden would come over to have a drink with us and take me aside in a corner and tell me how the day's shooting had gone. And it used to irritate the hell out of Billy. What was I doing in *his* living room talking to *his* buddy Bill Holden about some damned picture at MGM *not* called *Sabrina?*

Sabrina was a problem picture from the word go. Absolutely. You'd never know it, looking at it today. It's a dream up on the screen. Billy was shooting all day, and we were working on the script all night and during lunch hour—always one day ahead of the shooting. I sort of collapsed on the set one day, and Billy sent me home. The doctor put me out for thirteen hours and said, "You stay in bed and don't work." Billy would sneak over to the house at night, though, and I had to hide him in another room when the doctor came.

The whole picture was *such* a strain, and I was such a neophyte in this heavy atmosphere, even having fights with Humphrey Bogart on the set. Bogey resented the fact, I believe, that I was part of a little clique—namely Billy and Audrey Hepburn and Bill Holden and myself—and Bogey was sort of on the outside and felt he wasn't being treated properly. Quite often he'd be irritated with me. Once I was upstairs in my office rewriting a scene while they were shooting on the stage. I came down, and I hadn't made enough copies of the scene to go around. I gave one to Billy and one to Bill Holden. I didn't have a copy for Bogey, so he started screaming at me. I really mean *screaming*. "Get this City College writer out of here and send him back to Monogram where he belongs!" I don't know what "City College writer" means. It didn't mean anything *good*, believe me. And Billy said, "There will be no further shooting on this picture until Mr. Bogart apologizes to Mr. Lehman." I'm shrinking and dying in front of a hundred and fifty people. Who *needs* this? Ridiculous. Bogey came over finally. "Come on, kid, let's go in my dressing room and have a drink."

When you see the picture on the screen it's a delight. It got me my first Academy nomination for best screenplay, my first Writers Guild award. And the picture was on everyone's Ten Best list. But the public doesn't know the pain and heartache that go into bringing enjoyment and entertainment to the screen. People *kill* people behind the scenes.

BRADY: You've done some landmark films. Which one gave you the most satisfaction as a script and as a film?

LEHMAN: *Somebody Up There Likes Me* with *North by Northwest* a strong second.

BRADY: Why would *Somebody* share honors with *North by Northwest?* Is a good adaptation of a book as rewarding to do as an original?

LEHMAN: Well, you'd have to read Rocky Graziano's book

before you'd know whether I had done a *good* adaptation. But I liked the screenplay because I had done research and felt I had found the *real* story of Rocky, which I didn't feel was totally revealed in his autobiography. Nevertheless, some of my screenplay was fiction, you know. I just had to make some of it up in order to make the drama work, because the district attorney of New York City didn't want to cooperate with me. A couple of assistant DA's threatened to sue me *and* MGM if we tried to portray them in any way. And the whole third act depended upon Rocky losing his boxing license. I still see it on TV and still think it's a good picture and a good script.

BRADY: What sort of research did you do for *Somebody Up There Likes Me?* Did you know much about boxing previous to that screenplay?

LEHMAN: I had never seen a professional fight before I started on that film. I had listened to them on the radio, but I had never seen one. I went to Stillman's Gym in New York and hung around. Rocky took me to all the places he had lived in, and the places he had robbed. I went to his local police station and had long sessions with DA Frank Hogan, and with the very people who had tried to prosecute Rocky, including the assistant DA. I talked to Rocky's wife, because I wanted to find out what his relationship had been with his father, which I had suspected was at the root of his delinquent criminal life. That's the kind of research I did. Oh yes, I went to a couple of professional fights, too. And hated them.

BRADY: From what you said earlier about *The Prize* and from what you are saying now about *Somebody Up There Likes Me,* it sounds as if you take the title and use it as an umbrella when adapting, but that one is not likely to find too many lines from the original property in the script.

LEHMAN: That's accurate only if the property I'm working on doesn't have the kind of material that, in my opinion, would make for a good film. It wasn't true of *West Side Story,* and it wasn't true of *Who's Afraid of Virginia Woolf?* There was an awful lot in those two plays that was brilliant on stage and equally brilliant when used for the screen version. I always regard myself as a person who stands guard over the original work: "No, I'm not going to take that out. It's *good*." It was one of the reasons that Bob Wise was eager to have me do *West Side Story*. He felt that I wasn't going to throw anything out just to prove how good I was, that I had enough confidence in myself not to have to *prove* anything.

It's quite difficult when you adapt a famous work. There is a tendency to say, "I have to justify my existence," a tendency to say, "Look at what *I* did." Still and all, I do think I did my share to improve on the original works. Things I did with *West Side Story* people don't even know about. To me the picture is infinitely better-structured as a film drama from beginning to end, with proper places for the music, and things like that. *The Sound of Music* was a famous musical play, but its success in the theater was far more commercial than artistic, and I had to take drastic liberties with it to make it a movie. It's much better as a movie than it is on stage—in *my* opinion, of course.

Albee's work is unusual in that there are places where he departed from the dramatic line completely; yet his verbal music was so dazzling that it worked on the stage. But I felt you couldn't always get away with that in a film. I would take those detours out, or they would appear in another scene instead of where he had placed them. But people are not aware of those things, fortunately. The less the seams show, the better.

BRADY: What do you mean by verbal music?

LEHMAN: Dazzling language, dazzling ideas, very esoteric at times. Something brilliant, affecting an audience's subconscious. Sometimes they didn't even know why they were feeling the emotions that were overwhelming them.

To change the subject, can you imagine my doing research before writing *West Side Story?* It might sound crazy, but I did. Bob Wise and I went touring the east side of Harlem, visiting gangs, talking with gang leaders, talking with police, cruising in police cars and all that stuff, not knowing what it would do for us. You just feel more secure if you feel knowledgeable about the world you are dealing with in a particular movie. For *North by Northwest* I practically went through Cary Grant's adventures before writing the picture. I spent weeks in Salzburg before starting *The Sound of Music*. The picture would have been totally different if I had never gone to Salzburg. I got many ideas for the screenplay just from seeing locales and thinking of ways of working them into the movie.

BRADY: *North by Northwest* is such a picaresque script—and you say that you practically lived the Cary Grant role?

LEHMAN: I'll tell you what I did. I went to New York, went to the United Nations and spent five days there. I knew there was going to be a sequence in the United Nations, knew I needed a murder to take place there. I spent time in the Delegates' Lounge, sat around listening to people being paged on the public address system, watched colorful figures come and go. I thought, "Good, it's perfect." It's a great-looking room. It could be a *great* place for a murder. Well, that stuck in my head. In the script I called it the Public Lounge. Then I went out to Glen Cove, because I knew the Soviet Union's United Nations delegation lived in a mansion there. I met a judge in Glen Cove who happened to have gone to school with somebody I knew in California. He proved most cooperative. I didn't drop in on him unannounced. I told him I was writing a movie and needed a sequence in which a man gets picked up for drunk driving—would he please put me through the whole thing? And he did. I went through the whole damn experience that I wrote for Cary Grant later. They brought in a doctor who gave me an examination as though I were drunk, and I learned the tests he would give me, and whether they would allow me a telephone call, and what words they would use as they bring you into the station house. To me that's good research, and helps in the writing of a screenplay.

Then I went to Grand Central Station, roamed around, got on the Twentieth Century Limited, went to Chicago, checked in at the Ambassador East and hung around the lobby and looked the place over and got familiar with it. Then I took a train to Rapid City, South Dakota, and hired a forest ranger on his day off and told him I wanted to climb Mount Rushmore to see what was on top. I got halfway up and realized how dangerous my predicament was. I looked down. One slip and that was it. I said, "Look, I'm not going one step farther. I'm a screenwriter, not a mountain climber." I went down and bought him a Polaroid camera, and *he* went up the next day, photographed the top in all directions, and it turned out there was nothing up there. It was impossible. No way you could do a sequence on top of Mount Rushmore. But I wrote it anyway, and Hitchcock constructed it at the studio.

I also attended a few auctions to get the feel of the Chicago auction scene in the picture. This to me is writer's research. I can't write a sequence in which a man is picked up for drunk driving in Glen Cove if I know nothing about it. I've got to find out by going through it. I can't write a murder sequence in the United Nations if I've never *been* in the United Nations and don't know what the sounds are like or who the characters are or what a receptionist would say. I have to go through all that.

BRADY: Where did the idea for the Mount Rushmore setting originate?

LEHMAN: Hitchcock always wanted to do a chase across the faces of Mount Rushmore. You might say in a way it was . . . a goal we had to get to. Who was getting there, and why, who was chasing whom, and why—that was all a total mystery. Mount Rushmore was a shadowy, distant objective that, in a way, gave impetus to the creating of the movie. The sequence became one of the things you remember most about *North by Northwest*.

BRADY: So many scenes in that film seem to be a combination of private, intimate, possibly harmful things happening in public places. I wonder if there is some structural theme that you were after.

LEHMAN: I'd have to read what some French writers on films have to say about it, who interpret these pictures years later. I'm serious. I once saw a French film magazine filled with diagrams of the movements of the characters in *North by Northwest* and how they all have a meaning: going from left to right here . . . and scenes with circular movements there. Hitch and I used to laugh sometimes when we read about the symbolism in his pictures, particularly in *Family Plot*. By mistake a propman had two pieces of wood set up so that they looked vaguely like a cross, and the car goes downhill and crashes through a field, goes through a fence and knocks over the cross. So some learned New York critic commented: There's Alfred Hitchcock's anti-Catholicism coming out once again. When I was at the Cannes Film Festival with *Family Plot,* Karen Black, Bruce Dern and I attended a press conference, and some French journalist had the symbolism of the license plate in the picture all worked out: 885 DJU. He had some *elaborate* explanation for those numbers. When he got through explaining it, I said, "I hate to tell you this, but the reason I used that license plate number was that it used to be my own, and I felt it would be legally safe to use." So much for symbolism.

BRADY: How did you come by the title *North by Northwest?*

LEHMAN: The same way we came by the film itself—circuitously. We once had the working title *In a Northwesterly Direction,* which was never used—along with all the ideas we kicked around and never used. I said I wanted to write a definitive Hitchcock film—the Hitchcock film to end all Hitchcock films. Hitch said to me, "I always wanted to do something involving a chase across Mount Rushmore." Then he said, "I had an idea for a scene once where someone is addressing the United Nations General Assembly and the delegate from Peru is asleep. The man who is addressing the General Assembly gets insulted and says he will not continue unless the delegate from Peru pays attention. Someone taps the guy on the shoulder and he falls over dead. The only clue is some doodling he had been doing on a piece of paper which looked like antlers on a moose." I said, "That's very interesting." Of course, we never *used* that. But it was like I was saying to myself, "Oh, I see, maybe this picture will have something to do with the United Nations." Then Hitch said, "I've always wanted to do a scene along an automobile assembly line. You start with nothing on the assembly line, then the fender, and various parts come in. It's the longest dolly shot in history. The camera follows a whole car as it is being assembled, from nothing to the completed car, which is then driven off the assembly line, and in the back seat of the car there's a dead body—and it's all in one shot." I said, "That's terrific." Then Hitch said, "I always wanted to see something like a Moral Rearmament Conference in Lake Louise. Some very nice families seem to be gathered there. Suddenly a twelve-year-old girl pulls out a gun and shoots someone."

I was making notes on all these little Hitchcockian things, which we *never ever* used. I've got a whole slew of them, all kinds of situations. An Eskimo is fishing through a hole in the ice. Suddenly a hand comes up out of the hole. Finally I said, "Well, I see we are starting at the United Nations, and we are moving in a northwesterly direction. We wind up in Alaska, there's a tidal wave, and a plane is trying to take off. . . ." All these touches sound fascinating when you are talking, and though they came to nothing, that must have been what gave rise to our thinking about this picture—*whatever* it was going to be, moving in a northwesterly direction from New York on to Detroit, then on to Lake Louise and on to Alaska, whatever, whoever, whyever. So that title was around for quite a while.

Finally, when I started really working on the script, the head of the story department at MGM suggested that we call it, as a working title, *North by Northwest*. That's how that title came into being. That was only a working title, too. And I remember after I had finished (I called it *The Man on Lincoln's Nose* for a while), Sammy Cahn came into my office one day and said, "I've got the title song," and he *sang* for me a *love* song called "The Man on Lincoln's Nose." I mean it's like George S. Kaufman and Moss Hart writing a play about Hollywood. Here's this famous songwriter doing "The Man on Lincoln's Nose" in my office. No parody. He was *serious*. That's Sammy Cahn. Give him any title, he'll turn it into a love song, and it'll be a smash. Finally, Hitchcock called me and said, "We've *got* to find a title for this picture." Well, we never did find a title for the picture better than *North by Northwest*. And afterward, we found out that there *was* no such direction. And you should see the hundreds of thousands of words on *that* subject! Ah hah, symbolism . . . they used a direction that doesn't exist. . . .

BRADY: How did you develop the crop-dusting scene?

LEHMAN: My memory isn't *that* good. All I know is that it happened in Hitch's study at his home one afternoon, when we were discussing ways for the heavies to get Cary Grant killed after he arrives in Chicago. I remember Hitch kept talking about a cyclone, and how it menaces Grant from the sky. I said, "Hitch, that's not good." He said, "Oh, that would be wonderful. It's easy to do." I said, "Yeah, but *they're* trying to kill him. How are *they* going to work up a cyclone?" Anyway, now we are up in the sky with a cyclone, right? And I just can't tell you who said what to whom, but somewhere during that afternoon, the cyclone in the sky became the crop-duster plane. Before the day ended, Hitch and I were acting out the entire sequence. The plane making its passes, Grant seeing the cornfield, ducking into the cornfield, the various passes of the plane with a gun; then he sees a car, tries to wave it down, it ignores him, and he races into the cornfield. Crop-dusting poison is going to drive him out. He sees a diesel truck. I remember all that stuff. And that's where it all happened. In the study in Hitch's house. The next day I went to my office and wrote it, naturally with the greatest of ease. I had already seen it all.

BRADY: Do you ever use a storyboard when writing?

LEHMAN: Well, a storyboard is really done by an illustrator who is visualizing or drawing scenes that have been written. That's the director's work with his art director or his illustrator, his sketch artist. As a writer I used to storyboard my script at times, putting index cards up on a board with tacks and standing back and looking at the cards and saying, "Oh yeah, that scene, then that scene, then that scene" . . . all in order. "Gee, that's kind of long. Twenty-eight scenes in the first act. That's kind of a long first act, you know."

BRADY: Is it that mathematical?

LEHMAN: Not really. But sometimes you can see an imbalance. If I've got only five cards there in the second act, it's ridiculous. That first part is going to take an hour and ten minutes to play. And that little second part is going to take fifteen minutes. That's not right.

BRADY: Should the three acts be approximately the same time?

LEHMAN: I don't say anything is that mathematical. No. There's just a kind of feeling about imbalance.

BRADY: How visual is your thinking as a screenwriter? Do you try to set scenes as well as establish dialogue?

LEHMAN: Yes, definitely. I see everything. I occasionally put in an excess amount of direction, like "He turned and walked across the room and looked out of the window for a moment." It's almost like I'm playing the scene in my head. I never, just *never* put down only dialogue; I'm always acting it out in my head.

BRADY: *From the Terrace* is a huge novel. How did you cut it down to size for a screenplay that runs a hundred and sixty-five pages?

LEHMAN: I decided to make the movie about that part of the protagonist's life—Alfred Eaton's—which starts with his coming home from the war and ends up with his leaving his wife for the other woman. The novel starts long before Alfred Eaton was born. It starts I don't know how many generations earlier, and devotes several hundred pages to Alfred Eaton's antecedents, then follows him early in life through that portion that I did on film, and then it follows him into late middle age. I knew that I wasn't going to do that. I found the portion of the novel that I felt might have a movie in it, and used it.

What part of a long book do you dramatize? That, so often, is the problem. It certainly was with Rocky Graziano's autobiography, *Somebody Up There Likes Me*. What part do you dramatize? My most important decision on that one was deciding that the third act had to be Rocky's winning the middleweight championship from Tony Zale. Over and out. The book keeps going on. He loses the championship again and has a rematch with Tony Zale and loses and winds up in television as an actor. . . . What part of it should be the movie? Where do you start and where do you end? I asked myself those questions, and answered them. You *must*.

BRADY: What ingredients do you look for in each act?

LEHMAN: In the first act, who are the people, what is the situation of this whole story? Second act is the progression of that situation to a point of high conflict and great problems. And the third act is how the conflicts and problems are resolved. That's putting it a little patly, but that's the way it ought to be.

BRADY: So you go through the undergrowth and extract the three acts?

LEHMAN: Well, you try. You do it kind of unconsciously, instinctively. What's the drama here? Where's the conflict? What's the resolution?

BRADY: Why don't you write more original screenplays?

LEHMAN: I think that if somehow I came up with an idea that appealed to me, I would prefer to write it as a novel. I really would. I've got an idea now which I know would make a movie, but I would much rather write it as a novel if I can. It just seems so limiting to write it as a movie. It's got just that one market, and that's it. Either somebody likes it and wants to make it as a movie—or you've got yourself another manuscript to file away.

BRADY: But *North by Northwest* is such a brilliant original screenplay. That's the thought behind my question.

LEHMAN: Yeah, but that was back in 1958. I was exclusively a *screen*writer then, and originals were not smiled upon in those days, believe it or not. There was *very* little interest in originals in those days. That all came later. Studios, distributors wanted the assurance of someone else having thought a property worth publishing, or it had been on the best-seller list, or a hit Broadway play. They wanted that prior validation of the worth of the thing. In those days, if you went to a party in the Hollywood community and somebody would ask, "What are you working on, Ernie?" and you replied, "I'm doing an original now," the response would be "Oh." That was their reaction. "Oh." Like they were a little embarrassed for having asked. Your importance in the eyes of others was directly proportional to the importance of the source material you were working on. If you were working on a film version of some famous Broadway play, you were made to feel important. If you were working on something that you were going to create all by yourself, they'd secretly think, "He's in bad shape. Working on an original." That definitely was the climate at one time in this town.

BRADY: That would be the 1950s, and perhaps through the sixties.

LEHMAN: It started changing, I think, with Bill Goldman's sale of *Butch Cassidy and the Sundance Kid* for, I believe, four hundred thousand dollars. That was a breakthrough in a way. It served notice to writers that if they wrote a screenplay that someone wanted to do very badly, it would sell. However, it wasn't *just* that someone wanted it very badly. It sold also because Paul Newman and Steve McQueen *wanted to do it.* (Ultimately Paul Newman and *Robert Redford* wanted to do it.) *That* made it suddenly worth four hundred thousand dollars.

BRADY: Why haven't you written more originals in light of the changed attitude toward them?

LEHMAN: Well, *North by Northwest* would have been relatively nothing without its being *North by Northwest directed by Alfred Hitchcock.* It wouldn't have been much of anything in someone else's hands. The mere presence of Hitchcock, *plus* his particular skills as a director—and the fact that he could get a Cary Grant with the greatest of ease—was an enormous help. I am not downgrading my screenplay at all, but writing that film doesn't mean that I could have dashed off a dozen *North by Northwest*s thereafter and they all would have been successful. Oh, no. I had no illusions about that. I knew that the fact that it was a *Hitchcock* picture made it ultimately memorable. And there *are* no Hitchcocks anymore, God rest his soul. There really aren't. And it wasn't until years later that the picture came into its own. It was successful and highly regarded when it came out, but pretty soon thereafter the whole genre kind of fell into disrepute because along came the James Bond pictures, which were not Hitchcockian in any way, which depended entirely on other things, but they were hugely successful. The *North by Northwest* kind of picture was mild, during that era, compared to what you got in a James Bond picture. Audiences loved the Bond gadgets and the sex and the spoof, the whole number. And so I moved on to other fields, only to team up with Hitch again years later for *Family Plot.* It saddens me to talk about it. I never wanted that to be his last film. I'm grateful that I was part of it. But I returned to him again to write what was to be his next picture, *The Short Night,* because I suspected it might be his last, and I wanted it to be much better than the previous one. Sometimes I think we both knew, on this one, that we were going through the motions. Were we or weren't we? I'll never know. He *wanted* to make it, didn't he? I *wanted* him to make it—isn't that why I wrote it? But did either of us believe that he could? Did either of us ever admit that he couldn't, even to ourselves? Now that Hitch is gone, I think the script will vanish as he did. I don't think it should be made. Not without Hitch.

BRADY: You were originally going to direct *Sweet Smell of Success.* What changed your plans?

LEHMAN: They were changed *for* me. I went on a location-hunting trip, and when I returned, Harold Hecht called me into his office and told me that United Artists had gotten cold feet about the idea of a first-time director directing this picture because they hadn't had such good luck with Burt Lancaster directing *The Kentuckian,* his first and for all I know *only* attempt at directing. I was very upset—and very lucky, because I am sure I couldn't have brought it off at all, not the way Sandy Mackendrick eventually did. I don't know what made me think at that stage of my life that I was capable of directing.

BRADY: You had never done a musical, and yet you were asked to do *The King and I.* What sort of thinking went on, and how did you settle yourself into the job?

LEHMAN: That was quite a surprise. Charles Brackett was the producer of *The King and I,* and I don't know why, but in some strange sort of way I had a very good reputation very quickly as a screenwriter, and it was purely on the basis of *Executive Suite* and *Sabrina,* and the fact that they were very unlike each other as pictures. Charles Brackett did check with Billy Wilder to see what Billy thought of me, *then* asked me whether I'd be interested. I said I'd never seen the play. It had run for two years in New York before I arrived in town. So I went back East and saw the play, and returned, and got to work. And somehow I seemed to know what I was doing. To me there is so much craft that goes into writing a movie that I could never be typecast as somebody who could only write a *certain kind* of movie. I guess if you could say anything at all about me that might be unusual, it's that some of my movies are so unlike other of my movies that it is surprising I am attracted to them and know how to do them with so much apparent confidence.

I still have the telegram from Yul Brynner saying: "Congratulations on your double header in *Variety*." Because the review of *Somebody Up There Likes Me* and the review of *The King and I* appeared in the same issue of weekly *Variety*. Everybody was a little astounded that the same screenwriter could have done two such dissimilar pictures. I also have a letter from Oscar Hammerstein, suitably framed on my wall, thanking me on behalf of himself and Dick Rodgers for my adaptation of *The King and I*. I had had conferences with them both. They were out here making *Oklahoma*. I was pretty gutsy in those days, standing in a room with Richard Rodgers at one desk and Oscar Hammerstein at the other, with a handful of filing cards in my hands, outlining the movie I was going to do, telling *them* how I was going to do the picture version of *their* musical. And believe me, I knew who they were, too. They were pretty formidable, particularly Dick Rodgers. At one point I suggested something he didn't approve of in the "Shall We Dance?" number. He said, "Why do you have him do *that?*" I said, "Because I want to show the audience that it has really gotten to the point where he would like to go to *bed* with her." He said, "Ernie, there's something you don't know. There's a certain convention in musicals. When two people *sing* to each other, that means they are in love. When two people *dance* together, that means they would like to go to bed with each other. You don't have to have him do anything else." And so it is a big moment in the picture when the King puts his hand on Anna's waist, and they start dancing. In fact, we did a *close shot* of his hand on her waist. Perhaps that means something unmentionable.

That picture was shooting at the same time as *Somebody Up There Likes Me*, while I was working on *Sweet Smell of Success*. You couldn't ask for three more dissimilar pictures. I was at MGM using my office there to work on *Sweet Smell of Success*, which was really a United Artists picture. Bob Wise was shooting *Somebody Up There* down on the MGM stage, and needed a change in a scene. So I went down on the set and did it. Then Charles Brackett called me and asked me to come over to Twentieth Century-Fox because Yul Brynner had to walk across a very long set and the dialogue I had written didn't get him across properly. So I went over to Twentieth. Those were good days, working on three different pictures in one day. I remember Yul Brynner calling me sometime later and saying, "Ernie, I just saw a rough cut. I think we have a movie here. I *think* we have a movie." And over twenty years later, he called again, from New York. He was on the road with the stage revival of *The King and I.* "I'm gradually working into the play everything you did in the screenplay. But before I come into New York with it, I want your permission to do that." I said, "My permission? Of course you have my permission. You don't have to ask me. First of all, it belongs to Twentieth Century-Fox, that screenplay, not to me." He said, "I don't want their permission. I want yours, as a writer." I said, "You've got it." So I sent him a wire saying I was thrilled to be able to help, and I got a telegram back: "You are a prince," signed, "King." What a character.

BRADY: You've adapted *The King and I, The Sound of Music, West Side Story* and *Hello, Dolly!* How would you rank them personally in terms of difficulty and achievement as a screenwriter?

LEHMAN: Most difficult was *Hello, Dolly!,* which was the lowest as an achievement. They are all so different. I saw *The Sound of Music* a few years ago when it was rereleased and we had another "premiere." Almost the whole company went, including Julie Andrews. Also Bob Wise, Saul Chaplin, and all the children, who are now grown up and beautiful young adults. And my overall impression was, Jesus Christ, I never realized it was such a good picture. Beautiful to look at. The scenes play, the people are perfect; it's just a *good picture.* That's why it was so successful. I don't see pictures like that anymore. I really don't. I've seen a thousand pictures since that picture came out, and I realize that they're different now. I mean, there are a lot of fine films

—but that one had something about it. Every frame was just right. Bob Wise did everything perfectly. Julie was so good. Chris Plummer, despite his hating the picture and not wanting to be in it and all that, was very good. He brought a lot to it.

The musicals were all difficult to do, in some sort of way. But *West Side Story* and *Sound of Music* certainly rate number one and one-A, whatever order you want in terms of achievement; and *The King and I* would come right after them; and *Hello, Dolly!* would be at the bottom. There *is* no way to make a really good picture out of anything based on *The Matchmaker*. I'm convinced of that. You know why? Because half of it is about these two silly young clerks and their romantic adventures. There was never enough about Dolly Levi. I realized that when the picture flashed on the screen at the Broadway premiere of the movie at the Rivoli Theater—you know, this big gala premiere, and it suddenly occurred to me, Oh my God, all these people are here to see a *Barbra Streisand* picture. And I know how much of this picture doesn't have her on the screen. The show's title was sort of a misnomer in a way, *Hello, Dolly!,* because there was not very much about Dolly Levi. I remember when I saw the play and Carol Channing came out at the end and was taking all these tremendous bows, I kept thinking, "Hey, wait a minute, you're acting as if you were the whole show." Gower Champion was as much the show as she was, as far as I am concerned. It was the *staging* that made it magical on stage—so, as a movie, I tried to overcome this flaw in the story with production values —gargantuan sets, beautiful costumes and everything.

I don't know how I could have solved the problems of *Dolly.* I'm serious. I'm not defending the screenplay in any way. Apparently, it wasn't very good. I think that what was built in there was the unfortunate structure of the story, which works on the stage. It *works.* The stage has different requirements. But it wasn't a marvelous show specifically because it was brilliantly written, which is not to detract from Michael Stewart, who wrote the book. He wrote one of the most successful musicals of our time. His book worked to perfection. But the show did not succeed because it was brilliantly written. It succeeded because the character of Dolly Levi was great on the stage as played by Carol Channing. The score was terrific, and Gower Champion staged it beautifully. He made it all come off.

Now, lurking in that huge hit that was playing all over the country, lurking in it were what I regard as flaws fatal to the possible success of a movie version. If we had made the movie for six million or seven million dollars, it would have been a commercial success because its grosses were big enough. But there was no way of recreating old New York unless you spent money. There *is* no old New York. There is no way of doing "Before the Parade Passes By" without having a parade and some people there, extras. There is no way of doing *Hello, Dolly!*, which is known by so many people because of the success of the show, without including the story of the two clerks who go to New York in search of adventure and find love with two women. Silly characters. And when you're doing their story, it's very hard to keep the star on screen who is Dolly Levi, who is Barbra Streisand. You are supposed to go with the money. If you have a star, you don't concentrate on the featured players for thirty minutes. And every time you cut away from Streisand (there are a lot of Streisand fans, you know) audiences lose interest. They are thinking, "Where's Barbra?" Well, what do you want me to do, folks? This is *Hello, Dolly!* This is about two clerks who go to New York and go into a hat shop and meet two girls and have adventures, and *occasionally* we get back to Dolly. And that was so clear to me when the picture screened in New York. I suddenly saw the whole thing . . . trouble, trouble, trouble.

BRADY: Why did you go for a younger Dolly?

LEHMAN: I didn't think Carol Channing could photograph well enough, talented lady though she is, and a *wonder* on the stage. But the camera is *merciless*. We would have used her in a second if she could have gotten past that damned camera eye. She never knew what a disappointment it was to all of us to come reluctantly to the decision not to use her. I can't blame her for having disliked us for what seemed to be our idiocy. Who *do* you put in it and make a viable movie out of it? And who's going to sing all those great Jerry Herman songs? It's true that Barbra Streisand was miscast (she knew it; I couldn't admit it), but to me it seemed like the best of all possible choices. Musically, she was tremendous in the picture. Walter Matthau was great. But I don't think the screenplay could ever solve the basic flaw. The whole impetus for that story was, you know, based on a play that started in 1826 in London and then was done as a Viennese play in 1857, and then was done as *The Merchant of Yonkers,* by Thornton Wilder, and then he rewrote it as *The Matchmaker.* And the movie made of *The Matchmaker* was *terrible.* And then *Hello, Dolly!* was written. And it was such a huge success on the stage that it didn't seem possible that it couldn't succeed as a movie. Well, it cost a lot of money, and we didn't succeed.

BRADY: What are your inner guidelines for weaving story with music in a film? In several screenplays you move numbers around, and you've had new songs written for film versions, too. What dictates these shiftings, these additions?

LEHMAN: I treat everything as though the story were a *non-musical.* If I come upon a song and it doesn't seem to be really a natural part of the story, I'm brought up short. Usually it has been dragged in by some left-field kind of lead-in. It didn't flow out of anything that was happening. So I either rewrite the scene, my objective being to make that song come naturally, or I look to see if the song is in the right place.

Sometimes even those who have seen the play don't know that my film version is different. I think the most notable examples were in *West Side Story,* where I shifted "Gee, Officer Krupke," shifted "I Feel Pretty," shifted "Cool," and removed a fantasy sequence. I shifted the point of view of the song "America," too. "America" in the stage version was about the conditions of Puerto Ricans in Puerto Rico. It was rewritten by Stephen Sondheim for the film so that it was about conditions that Puerto Ricans encounter in *America.* After all, the song is *called* "America."

BRADY: You also went to Richard Rodgers for two new songs for *The Sound of Music,* and you had two new songs written for *Dolly.* Do you get cooperation on these rewrites, so to speak?

LEHMAN: Oh yes. In the case of Richard Rodgers and *The Sound of Music*, the love song that Maria and Baron von Trapp sang in the stage version was called "Ordinary People." And it wasn't very romantic, even though it was lovely. Director Robert Wise and Saul Chaplin, his associate producer, felt it was wrong for the movie. I must say that I didn't agree with them at first. But they convinced me. I opposed them because I had heard it so many times that I was hung up on it. "Ordinary People" was replaced by another song which Richard Rodgers wrote called "Something Good." It was lovely. It never became a hit, but it really worked in the movie. Rodgers did part of another song that Saul Chaplin and I privately worked on and helped create, a number known as "I Have Confidence." Saul Chaplin took music from other parts of the show and did a brilliant job of writing a musical verse for the recitative. Then he and I wrote the lyrics for that recitative and all the stuff leading into the chorus. Then we used some of Richard Rodgers' chorus, and Saul and I wrote lyrics for the rest of it and just kept quiet about the whole thing.

BRADY: In *The Sound of Music* "Do, Re, Mi" on stage is a living-room song. In the film it trickles over several days. What were you after in that?

LEHMAN: That's one of the best things I did in writing the screenplay—thanks to my trip to Salzburg, where I saw all those marvelous locales. And I knew for a fact that we would have died with an eleven-and-a-half-minute musical number in a *living room*.

BRADY: Does it run that long?

LEHMAN: Yes. On stage it's eleven and a half minutes in the Trapp villa living room with Maria seated and the children around her. It worked beautifully on stage, but stage conventions are different. I used to play the stage soundtrack over and over again in my office, and I knew that we would have a problem with an eleven-and-a-half-minute sequence. I realized I needed something to show a growing relationship between Maria and the children, and a passage of time. The question was how do you make it *work*, how do you make it *move* on film? Well, Salzburg's natural beauty and the movement of the camera and the players over several days *compressed* into a fast-cut sequence *made* it work.

BRADY: That's an interesting consideration. Do you at some point in the musical sit down and clock all the music and then talk to the musical director and say, "Now, how long are we going to run this sequence?"

LEHMAN: Oh no. Not at this stage. Not when I'm writing the screenplay. I know that "Do, Re, Mi" is going to be done, period; we are not going to cut part of that famous number, because it works so well. Particularly once I decided how to do it. I started listening to it over and over, knowing it had to keep running as though it were one number; you can't pause at any place. So if you are cutting from one scene to another, there has to be a natural place to break the music. I just kept playing it over and over, and I noticed *there*—and I'd make a mark—and *there*—and I'd make a mark—there just seemed to be places where it *completed* itself for a certain segment. Then I recalled all the various places I'd been in Salzburg. I recalled being on a horse-drawn carriage, my wife and I. I had even taken home movies. I said, "That'd be good for the kids." I remembered certain paths. And I thought it would be good to put the children on bicycles. And I thought, *Change their costumes*. That proves it's a different time as well as a different place. That's going to give the impression that this all took place over a matter of weeks, rather than a few hours or eleven and a half minutes, so that when the scene starts, Maria has a certain relationship with the children, and when it ends she has a *different* relationship with them. Some of them have grown to like her. She's won over some of the children. And it gives you a chance to use some of that fantastic, beautiful scenery around Salzburg. And it opened the number up, and it was just terrific—the way Bob Wise staged it. Both he and the choreographers. Once in a while you get lucky and make a good decision.

BRADY: You mentioned seeing *The Sound of Music* in re-

release, where it did well. In addition to being a successful film twice, it was an influential film in that everyone was trying to make another *Sound of Music.*

LEHMAN: And losing a lot of money in the attempt.

BRADY: Yes. What is there about *The Sound of Music* formula that made all imitators weak by comparison?

LEHMAN: Nobody was too sure what the ingredients actually were that made it so enormously successful. *The New York Times* magazine section did a huge lead article on "How Come This Picture Is the Top Grosser of All Time?" This was before *Jaws* or *Star Wars,* before *The Godfather,* but after *Gone With the Wind,* which it surpassed. And there was no way of imitating that particular combination of ingredients, because we are not sure what the ingredients were. There were so many, you know. Was it because it was about children trying to get closer to their father, who was cold and aloof? Was it because it was about the church and children? Was it the music? Was it the beautiful scenery? There were so many things. There's a very moving moment when Baron von Trapp starts singing "The Sound of Music" with his children after he has discouraged music in his house. It was *very* moving on the stage. And I had always remembered that moment. In fact, when I saw the play on stage after it had been frowned upon by the critics, I started telling people even then that someday this is going to make a very successful movie, which is why I wound up doing it, because everyone knew that I had this feeling.

William Wyler was contemplating directing it at one time. I took him to see the play. He *hated* it. We were walking up Fifth Avenue afterward, and he didn't even want to face Darryl Zanuck, who was waiting for him at "21" to see whether he was going to do the movie. I was trying to talk Wyler into it. He said, "Keep trying, but I know I hated it." I said, "Let me ask you one thing. How did you react to that moment in the play when the Baron starts singing with the children?" He said, "You know something? I almost broke out into tears. Strange that you should bring that up. That moved me so, I almost started crying. Isn't that strange?" I said, "That's the big secret in this play. That's the moment that has such a universal tug. I don't know what it is. Maybe we all wish we had been closer to our parents, or we wish they were closer to us, or . . . there's some kind of longing there. Something strange and universal." And when the picture opened, it started being a phenomenon. There were some people who were seeing it twenty-six times, a hundred and thirty-two times. There was a woman in Australia who saw it three hundred-plus times. It was amazing. There were protests in some college towns because they wanted the picture removed: It had been there for a year. They wanted to see something *else*. They were sick of having that damn picture in their theater. And it was *all* because people went over and over and over to see *The Sound of Music*. When it was rereleased again eight years later, I think it grossed eight million dollars very quickly. There's something about it. Time cannot hurt it. Nothing. It's timeless.

BRADY: Comparisons are generally odious but I suppose inevitable for someone who adapts famous plays.

LEHMAN: Only if you say so.

BRADY: Is comparing a film to a play as misleading as, say, comparing a film to a novel?

LEHMAN: Offhand, I would say it's probably less misleading because at least they're both a dramatic medium for actors, whereas a novel is not a dramatic medium. And you can't have much interior monologue in either a play or a movie (other than Eugene O'Neill's *Strange Interlude,* in which the characters turn aside and reveal their thoughts to the audience). So a play and a movie are more similar than a movie and a novel. But it's usually more difficult to make a motion picture out of a play, because a play, particularly in times past, usually has one or maybe two sets; or, wonder of wonders, three or four sets. But usually one set. So you have the problem of making the story *move* for film, of getting it out of the house, so to speak. A novel, though, is usually all over the place—and there is a richness of choice for scenes and settings.

BRADY: Are adapters typecast? Have you turned down, say, some musicals in order to avoid being pegged as The Musical Adapter?

LEHMAN: Not for that reason. I have turned down some musicals I felt I didn't know how to do, or didn't think had a chance to be successful. I don't want to name this one in particular, but they told me that they wanted to do it very cheaply. And I said, forget it, because you can't do it *right* and do it cheaply. You just can't. And they did it cheaply. And it was terrible. I don't turn things down just to avoid being typecast. No, no, I don't care if two movies are similar. What I mean is, if another *North by Northwest* came along, I wouldn't turn it down because I had done that kind of picture once. I *like* films with intrigue.

BRADY: You've done both. But do you consider musicals as worthy a task as writing a drama?

LEHMAN: Worthy a task? I recognize the fact that other people don't consider musicals as a worthy task. But I'm aware of the fact that I seem to have the same creative worries and problems: How the hell are we going to make this a good and successful picture and what kind of reviews are we going to get? I go through the same miseries as with a *non*musical. If the screenplay isn't very good, you suffer. The picture suffers. The reviews aren't good. As a writer, you are associated with something that is not good artistically. But I know that as a screenwriter if I can pull off an entertaining, successful, highly acclaimed musical, I would say it's a pretty good feat. I *never* go around thinking, "Well, that's beneath me." I'm aware of the fact that if I had written *Midnight Cowboy* or *One Flew Over the Cuckoo's Nest* or *Network,* the admiration would be much greater, *including* self-admiration. I am aware of that. Musicals are a lesser achievement for a writer, but they're still an achievement, because I know how tough it is to make *anything* come out right on the screen. There aren't all that many good musicals. There never were all that many good musicals, really. Darn few, and lately fewer still. It's a tough game to do well.

BRADY: As an adapter, do you experience any creative surges, or do you view what you do as a craftsmanlike job?

LEHMAN: No, I don't regard it as only a craftsmanlike job. I definitely wind up feeling that I am involved in as much of a creative endeavor as though I were writing something totally original. It gets to be the same kind of writing experience to me. Whether it is or isn't, that's the way it feels. In other words, if there happens to be a ten-page scene in a novel and I am writing it as a two-page scene for a script and I like only two lines of dialogue in the entire novel scene, I don't stop to say, "Oh, yeah, that line I'm putting down was written by John O'Hara." In fact, one of the tricks is to be able to use things from the source material and create new material and not show the seams—so that you don't know where the novelist ends and the screenwriter begins.

BRADY: Do you write fast?

LEHMAN: I used to write painfully slowly. Of late, I have been gathering speed.

BRADY: What are the mechanics of writing for you? Do you have to be at a typewriter? Do you use longhand?

LEHMAN: I used to work at a typewriter almost exclusively, but over the years I've gradually evolved into following a fairly standard pattern. I work with a pen or pencil on yellow legal-sized pads first; then sit at the typewriter, and, in the process of putting it through the typewriter, rewrite it; then take the typed version and go over that with a pen, doing what's called the final version. Then I give that to a typist, and that in effect becomes a first draft of that particular scene. It is by no means final. But by then it has been gone over two or three times in the process.

BRADY: Do you ever dictate?

LEHMAN: No. That doesn't work for me at all. Not at all. I've tried it. And I find it's very soft writing.

BRADY: How many drafts do you generally go through before you have something that is close to a shooting script?

LEHMAN: I would say anywhere from three to five. Somewhere like that. It seems to me never less than three. And only rarely more than five.

BRADY: When you are adapting a book, play, whatever, do you adapt it to meet a certain rating? Are you told in advance, "We want this to be a PG," or, "We want this to be an R"?

LEHMAN: I have never been told that, but in the case of *Portnoy's Complaint,* I myself wrote it to be shot in such a way as to avoid, if possible, an X rating. The studio definitely didn't want an X rating. Now, that's a director's decision as well as a screenwriter's decision, because a director can shoot a scene in such a way that the film can get an X rating, or he can shoot it in such a way that it can get an R rating. So I made certain in the writing of the film that I was writing it for me, the director, to shoot in such a way as to be, at worst, an R-rated film. Most people didn't know how I could possibly do a film based on *Portnoy's Complaint* without getting an X rating. So, at the very least, if I achieved nothing else, I managed to do an R-rated *Portnoy's Complaint*.

BRADY: In bringing *Virginia Woolf* to the screen you accomplished a similar feat.

LEHMAN: That was before the ratings system. In fact, that picture was instrumental in bringing *in* the ratings system.

BRADY: Wasn't the commonplace observation about that play "No way they can make that into a movie"?

LEHMAN: That's what they used to say.

BRADY: And you made it into a movie. What were your methods there? How did you approach that task?

LEHMAN: First of all, I think they were wrong in assuming that it could never be made as a movie. It certainly had nothing visually objectionable. The language was what convinced them it could never be made as a movie. Our picture was a breakthrough in a way. In order for it to get the Production Code Seal or whatever they had in those days, Jack Warner had to make a contract with all the exhibitors under which *they* agreed not to let anyone under the age of eighteen into their theaters. In return for Warner Bros. making that kind of a deal with everyone who got the film, the Legion of Decency permitted the film to go out with a Production Code Seal. Did you see the television version? It's remarkable how CBS put it on with practically no elisions whatsoever. It's amazing.

BRADY: It tells you how far we've come since *Virginia Woolf* was a groundbreaker.

LEHMAN: Yeah. I never thought I would hear "Hump the Hostess" on television. Incredible. They took out the first syllable of all the "goddamn"'s in the soundtrack. And they took out a few lines which were authored by me and not by Mr. Albee. One of them I knew would never, never make it to television. I never even thought it would make it onto the screen.

BRADY: What was that?

LEHMAN: I don't remember specifically, but it was during the scene at the swing between Nick and George, and they are talking about how to get to faculty wives. I remember George Segal saying to Richard Burton in the picture that Martha (Elizabeth Taylor), who is the daughter of the college president, "probably had the widest avenue of all." It was very suggestive and very obvious, and it somehow wound up in the movie—but not in the television version.

BRADY: The casting for that film was much discussed, too. How did you go about that? What sort of decision went into casting beautiful Elizabeth Taylor as a frumpy middle-aged faculty wife?

LEHMAN: The only arguments *against* casting Elizabeth Taylor in that role were: One, the thought that maybe she wasn't a terrific actress; two, she was far too young and beautiful; and three, how could anyone take Elizabeth Taylor seriously in this very serious role? Well, I think she always was a tremendous screen actress. She's done many good things to prove that. But now we're talking about my decisions as a producer, right?

BRADY: Yes.

LEHMAN: I realized that in the play there were allusions to Martha being somewhere in her early fifties, I believe. And I decided that the drama was just as valid for two people who have been married five or seven years *less* than they had been married in the play. I realized that with makeup, a wig and added weight, she could look like she was in her beat-up forties, which was old enough for this drama to be valid. You don't have to be fifty-two; you can be forty-six. Everything that's valid about their relationship is valid at that age.

I felt that of all the actresses I knew, no one in her public life and her public behavior was closer to Martha than Elizabeth Taylor, *the actress,* not the private woman. There was so much of Martha in Elizabeth Taylor, *the actress*—the ballbreaking and the profanity and the deeply feminine vulnerability among a lot of other things. So I started getting very, very excited about the idea, which I kept a deep, dark secret, because everyone in town was playing the game of casting this picture. Everyone wanted to play the role. And everyone wondered who was going to get it. I went to Jack Warner and said, "I finally have made up my mind, and I am here to ask for your approval of the decision." He said, "Who?" And I said, "Elizabeth Taylor." He said, "Elizabeth Taylor? But she's young! A young girl." I said, "I know. We can fix that. We can make her look older. And I can eliminate all references to age. We can do it." And I must give Jack Warner credit for saying yes within five minutes. I said, "I have no idea whether she's ever heard of the play or whether she'd be inter- ested, but I think she would be *fantastic* in the role." And he said, "You know it's going to cost no less than a million dollars to have her. What do you want me to say?" I said, "I want you to say yes." He said, "OK. Yes." So that started my attempts to get Elizabeth Taylor.

My first meeting with her was at the Beverly Hills Hotel, and it was "Why do you want me for the role?" and "Richard, you shut up. I want to hear it from Ernie, not from you." I told her my reasons. After that there was a lot of negotiating. Finally we got her. Then I had to meet with her again to discuss an actor to play George. I had my list and wanted to see who I could keep on the list to think about, because she had approval. And she kept saying, "What about him?" And she'd point to Richard Burton sitting across the room. It was *very* embarrassing for me, because at the time I felt that Richard Burton was too strong to play George, and he was on my list, but by no means near the top. I got her to approve a few, including Arthur Hill, who played George on the stage. But it was a rough meeting because she kept saying, "What about him?" I kept saying, "Well, uh . . . ." Finally Burton said, "Look, Ernie, I just want you to know that if you don't get who you want, I'm there in the bullpen waiting to come in." And I said, "Why don't you figure out whether you think you can really play the role, because I feel you are so powerful on the screen, and this man has such obvious weaknesses." They were going back to Paris, and I was going back to the studio, and I said, "Let's both think about it. You let me know what you decide, and meanwhile I will think about it." And I really started thinking about it. I did not want it to sound like another Dick & Elizabeth picture. It was an important venture.

But somehow the more I thought about it, the more it became evident to me that I had been foolish, that *no one* was better for this role than Richard Burton, despite the fact that he had a slight Welsh accent. There was nobody better. And finally I wrote to Jack Warner and said I have made my decision about George. And I still have a copy of the letter giving all the reasons why, because I knew I was going to get resistance. He said, "We'll have to discuss this." We met, and he said, "Can we afford to pay this kind of money? Is there nobody who could be better?" And Burton's agent, the late Hugh French, did a very good job of making us think that somehow we would do all right, and I am very grateful to him. He was very instrumental in the whole thing working out. He steered it very well, even though it cost us an arm and a leg. Jack Warner could have said no simply on the basis of the cost. But we *got* Richard Burton, and I thought he gave the best non-Oscar-winning performance that I've ever seen on the screen. The best.

BRADY: What about the other two roles, though? Sandy Dennis . . .

LEHMAN: Sandy Dennis won an Oscar for her role.

BRADY: I understand that Robert Redford turned down the role George Segal got.

LEHMAN: He did. He was my choice, and he was Mike Nichols' choice to play that role, and he just turned it down. He wouldn't do it.

BRADY: Any reason?

LEHMAN: He didn't give a reason. Maybe he felt it would be bad for his image. He wasn't a big star yet. He didn't want to do it. Zero. He would not do it. Mike called him *personally* in Berlin, because Mike knew him. He had directed him in a play. So we got George Segal. Irv Kirschner, as a friendly gesture, shot a screen test of Sandy Dennis for me, and I was immediately sold on her. When Mike Nichols came on the picture, we showed him the test and he was reluctant at first; so Jack Warner said to him, "OK, you find somebody you like and *you* shoot a test of her." Within an hour Mike said OK to Sandy Dennis.

BRADY: How did you arrive at Mike Nichols? That was a dramatic decision, too.

LEHMAN: I was about to leave for Paris to confer with Elizabeth Taylor and Richard Burton to get their approval of a list of directors so that we could see who was available, who was interested, who we could make a deal with, which we couldn't do until we knew whom they would approve of. Just before I left for Paris I got a phone call from New York from a good friend, producer Larry Turman, who had already signed a contract with film-neophyte Mike Nichols to do *The Graduate* sometime in the future. Mike had *never* directed a film. Larry said to me, "I am calling you at the urging of a friend of mine who is right here with me who wants you to know that he would love to direct *Who's Afraid of Virginia Woolf?*" I said, "Who's that?" He said, "Mike Nichols." And I said (this is how bright I'm *not*), "Who's friend *are* you, Larry, his or mine?" That was my first response. And he said, "Well, I just wanted you to know."

Nichols had just done *Luv, The Knack* and *Barefoot in the Park* on stage. Hadn't done *The Odd Couple* yet, but he was the toast of New York. But his directorial efforts were in the theater; he'd never done a film. And I was flying over to Paris to sell the Burtons on another director, who must go nameless, or else get up a list for their approval. And I must say, flying over the ocean I kept thinking to myself, gosh, if this picture had Mike Nichols' cachet, and if he's as brilliant as they say he is, this could be something special. But I was on a mission to sell them another director or get an approval of a list of directors. I screened the director's film for them in Paris. They disliked it *and* the director. We got into a long, sodden brawl at a Paris restaurant. Burton wanted *me* to direct the picture, and Elizabeth Taylor kept telling him he knew nothing. And I kept saying, "Don't worry. I would never *dream* of directing this picture. Do you think I would do that to you or to Edward Albee?'' This went on all night. It got kind of boisterous. The next day Elizabeth made Richard come down and apologize to me (we were all in the same hotel) for his behavior the night before. ''What behavior?'' I said.

We had a very friendly time of it after that. I ran down a list of directors with them, and finally we got to talking about Mike Nichols, whom they had met when *An Evening With Nichols and May* was playing in a theater next door to Burton's *Hamlet* in New York. They had great respect for Nichols, seemed in awe of his genius, which I kept thinking would be good—someone to intimidate the Burtons. Finally we agreed on a list of six different directors. (At Elizabeth's insistence I had called California and verified what we had heard: that Fred Zinnemann did *not* want to do *Who's Afraid of Virginia Woolf?*). We all agreed that I would sound out Mike Nichols first. Mind you, Jack Warner didn't know any of what was going on. So I called Mike Nichols, whom I'd never talked to in my life. He was in Jamaica on vacation.

BRADY: You didn't talk with Nichols the day that he was with Larry Turman on the phone?

LEHMAN: No. I didn't talk to him then. I called Nichols in Jamaica from Paris. *Very* expensive phone call, I remember. It cost two hundred and forty dollars. We talked a long time. He said, ''You've got to get a first-draft screenplay to me. Let me see it before I make a decision.'' And he understood that Jack Warner knew nothing about this. This was all preliminary. It was too difficult to mail the script to Jamaica from Paris, so I flew it personally to New York and found in the waiting room of some airline a young couple who were going to Jamaica on their honeymoon. I gave them this envelope and asked them if they would leave it at the counter at the Jamaica airport for Mike Nichols. ''You've heard of Mike Nichols, haven't you?'' ''Yes, of course.'' Mike Nichols got it a few hours later. I waited in New York for his phone call. He said, ''Guess who's spending the weekend with me? The couple who flew the script down.'' He had invited them over to his place. We discussed the first draft, and he said yes, he wanted to do the picture but he had many reservations about it, which he would have to discuss with me. On the basis of that, I called his agent while I was in New York. He told me Mike's time requirements and all that stuff, and then I called Jack Warner in California and said I wanted to make a deal for Mike Nichols to direct the picture. His initial reaction was "Mike Nichols? I'm sorry. You'll have to come out here to California and we'll have to talk about this." He knew that Elizabeth Taylor had approved, among others, the man who had directed the play, Alan Schneider. (But who had not directed a movie.)

So I flew to California, confronted Jack Warner, and convinced him that the picture needed Mike Nichols. We needed somebody for whom the Burtons had great respect and a certain amount of awe. I said, "We need that or else they'll eat our director alive." And I said I thought he would enhance the project. It would take a bit of the Hollywood Curse off the project (in view of its Broadway genesis). And I said Mike was something of a genius, and maybe this was what we needed. Finally, Warner said yes. Very surprisingly. He said yes, even though Mike would get three or four times as much money as we could have gotten some other director for, and even though he had never directed a film, ever. Well, it was a good decision—and a gutsy one.

I think being the producer for the first time in my life made it a tremendous ordeal, because I had never dealt with people like this, ever. Imagine producing your first picture and who's in it? —Elizabeth Taylor and Richard Burton. Who's your director? —Mike Nichols, who's never directed a picture. Who's behind your back?—Jack Warner, who can be very formidable, too. It's a very scary, volatile situation. Somehow I survived it. I *handled* all these people. It was dreadful at times, humiliating, embarrassing. And there were a lot of creative conflicts between Mike and me. A lot of give-and-take. He gave and I took.

BRADY: You once said that good pictures occur when the people involved are fortunate enough to know which battles to win and which to lose. Can you elaborate on what you mean by that in relation to *Virginia Woolf?*

LEHMAN: I can think of two examples on both sides. My first draft, my big, big change in the play, was that the fantasized, nonexistent son had really existed, but had committed suicide at the age of sixteen. This is what comes out in *my* big denouement. He had hanged himself in the closet, and Martha couldn't face that fact, so she carried on this fantasy of her son, their son, coming home as though he were still alive. And Mike Nichols would have none of that. It *was* one aspect of the play that had been severely criticized by the critics. They had quarreled with the device of the nonexistent son. Funny, it worked powerfully in the play; yet there was always something about it that was bothersome. Anyway, I lost that battle, and I think it's lucky that I did. There would have been a furor if that picture had come out and there was that radical a change in *Who's Afraid of Virginia Woolf?* Then Mike became hung up on the idea of having all the events of that night take place while something else was going on at the college—not panty raids, but some kind of thing with a big bonfire and students dancing around the bonfire. I kept saying no, this drama only works if the whole world is asleep. All this horror goes on while people are asleep. It's just these four people, and this is all something like *night thoughts*. A couple of screenplay drafts actually had the bonfire in. But I finally won that one. So there's an example of being lucky enough to win one battle, and lucky enough to lose another battle where you were fighting for something that would have hurt the picture.

BRADY: Have you made a lot of enemies in this business, or nonfriends? Some of these creative battles would seem to leave scars, even if you walk away with a great film.

LEHMAN: Quite often you don't know. There are a lot of quarrels and anger and bad feelings. Sometimes it's serious and sometimes it isn't. Given my years on the battlefield, there's not much of a casualty list, though there may be some that I don't know about. Hell, you can be *sure* there are. I just don't like to think about them.

BRADY: When you knew the Burtons would be in *Virginia Woolf,* how did that affect your writing?

LEHMAN: I made a few changes to take care of Elizabeth's age and the fact that Richard might have been thought not to be an American.

BRADY: When an actor or actress wants to change their lines, what's your attitude as a screenwriter?

LEHMAN: I used to be very contentious and uptight about it. We were rehearsing *From the Terrace,* I remember, and word would be sent that they wanted me down in the rehearsal hall where Paul Newman had a speech he couldn't say. I remember coming down there and saying, "What's the trouble, Paul?" And he said, "I can't say this speech." And I'd look at the speech and I'd say, "Really? You can't say it? You want to hear me say it?" And I'd *say* it, then look at him: "Now, what is there about it that you can't say?" Which was pretty pugnacious, and unnecessarily disrespectful. He used to call me the razor blade personality of Hollywood. (We did three pictures together.) I used to have little patience with actors who would say, "I can't say that line. I'm sorry. I just can't say it." I always felt, "Bullshit. What do you mean, you can't say it? *Say* the damn line!" Cary Grant and I had a few fierce battles in the back seat of a limousine on location at Bakersfield during the crop-duster sequence in *North by Northwest.* He would sit there and go over some of his scenes with me. "This is ridiculous," he'd say. "You think you are writing a Cary Grant picture? This is a David Niven picture." I'd say, "Cary, I saw the rushes yesterday. What were you trying to portray in that scene?" Stuff like that. I used to get very annoyed and frustrated with actors. I think I have mellowed.

BRADY: Is it mellowing or do actors no longer get tough with you?

LEHMAN: Well, the last time I got into a real fight it was with Lee Grant in *Portnoy's Complaint.* Don't forget, I was the director. I can't remember what it was, but she wouldn't say something or do something the way I wanted her to do it. She just insisted on fighting me, probably because she knew a hell of a lot more about acting than I did. Finally, I said to her, "Oh, fuck off." And she said, "*You* fuck off!" And I walked off the set and started for the exit. Then I thought to myself, "What am I doing? How can *I* walk away? I'm the *director*." So I picked up a handy talkie radio and directed the scene remotely through my assistant director, who also had one.

BRADY: That sounds like a pretty thorough conflict. And yet you've written lines for lots of biggies. In general, is it the bigger they are, the harder they bawl?

LEHMAN: No. I don't know what it is. Some of them are a pain in the ass and some aren't. I mean it. Some of them want to have an hour's discussion about every damn little thing they do. I don't mean that a thoughtful actor is not desirable, but some of it used to just annoy the hell out of me. I would think for hours about a certain speech and hear an actor reading it *his* way, sort of doing an approximation of what I had written. I used to demand that the script clerk notify me if anybody was changing a *word*. And I used to drive people crazy. I once went down on the set of *Somebody Up There Likes Me* for a scene in which Paul Newman tries to explain to the boxing commissioner why he missed a fight. You know, he's pretty illiterate, Rocky Graziano, and he was in love with this girl and she ran away from him and he couldn't find her, and the line concluded, "I forgot what time is it." Paul didn't *say*, "I forgot what time is it," he said, "What time it is." And I *wanted* him to say "I forgot what time is it." It was supposed to be illiterate talk. So I go down on the set and Bob Wise is shooting the scene and I hear Paul say, "Your Honor, I forgot what time it is." I walked over to Bob Wise and said, "Bob, he's not saying that speech right." And it's a *long* speech. Very long speech. I said, "Bob, it's supposed to be 'what time *is* it,' not 'what time *it is*.' " He said, "Let me see the script. You're right." And he said, "Paul, it's what time *is* it. Not what time *it is*. OK, let's go again." And they do this whole scene, which ends with this long Newman speech, and I am standing there, and fifty-five other people are standing there, and they go through the whole scene. Paul gets through his long speech and finally gets to the end of the speech, and finally, "Your Honor, I forgot what time . . . is it?" And he bursts out laughing, because you know he was thrown. He couldn't remember which way to say it. He had to be deliberately incorrect, and he broke up in laughter and Bob was upset. He said, "OK, let's go again." And they go again. And Paul doesn't even *get* to the line this time—he bursts into uproarious laughter. So I turned up my coat collar and just slunk off that sound stage, and they never saw me again on that set, because I had cost them a lot of money just by getting "what time it is" to come out "what time is it." I don't even remember whether he even *said* "what time is it" finally. That's what I used to do, anyway. Take Hitchcock. He wouldn't allow a *word* to be changed. Billy Wilder, you can't change an *inflection*. I was very, very tough on actors changing lines or words. Or leaving one word out. Now I don't even think about it. It's too damned much trouble, and not all that crucial. In *Family Plot* I wasn't even on the set, and certainly on *Black Sunday* I wasn't.

BRADY: Do you find life easier this way?

LEHMAN: Oh, it's much easier. The pictures aren't better or worse, but it's much easier. The easiest thing is not to write pictures at all. Writing books, I tell you, can spoil you, writing without having to listen to a director or actors or a producer or eight million people telling you how to do it better, because *everybody* knows about writing.

BRADY: As a writer then are you heading away from pictures altogether? Did your first novel, *The French Atlantic Affair,* represent some sort of breakaway attitude?

LEHMAN: Not really. I still like to do both. I just can say in all honesty that it seems to be a little harder now for me to get enthusiastic about some of the film projects that come my way. A *little* harder than it used to be. Maybe the projects are lousier, or maybe I'm getting less excited about the idea of going through those battles again. I don't know. But I certainly can't say, "That's it. From now on, I just write books and go to the movies as an audience." But for me to take on a film project, it means maybe six or eight months just to write it. It's a year or two of commitment if you are going to produce it, too. I hardly think I could go through all those producing headaches again. I would keep saying, "What am I doing this for? For what? Who needs it?"

Producers usually have to hang around until the bitter end, until the release print is ready. If I am writing a picture and want to leave after I have done my work, I can. But the producer is on that picture *forever*. If I am the producer as well as the writer, I have to be there while the director is shooting the film. I have to be there while the director and the film editor are doing a director's cut. I have to be there while the director is getting his first preview. I have to be there when we take it out again to another preview. We are talking about months and months and months and months and months. I have to be there for the scoring, the dubbing, the looping. I have to be there for working out the balancing of the print before the release print is made. I have to be there to review the prints. I have to be there during all the press planning and publicity. I have to be there for the premiere. I have to be there *forever,* for a fee which is marginal compared to the screenwriter's fee, and, unless the picture is a great success, for what? I get a percentage of the profits as a writer anyway, so what's the big deal about hanging on as a producer? To protect my script? That has turned out to be a lot of baloney anyway. And what kind of true respect do producers get from the media, the reviewers, the audiences? Not what they deserve. It's *Thankless City.*

BRADY: Well, you took on *Virginia Woolf* because you said it gave you a certain measure of creative control.

LEHMAN: Yes, control over deciding who my executioners were going to be. A producer acquires the right to pick his own adversaries, to pick the man who's going to direct it, the stars who are going to control *everybody*. And the stronger the director, which is what you want, the less you are going to have to say as a producer. Really. It's like you own the airline and now you are in a 747 at thirty-nine thousand feet. You own the airline. How much do *you* have to say about how that plane is flown compared to the pilot? What are you going to do, say, "Look, I don't want to fly at this level. I want you to go down ten thousand feet. I *own* this airline," or some nonsense like that? I'm being ridiculous here, but the director is the pilot who can just tell you to go to hell. What are you going to do, shoot the picture yourself, crash the plane? He's the director, he's the pilot.

BRADY: You have been a writer-producer-director. Which is the easiest? The toughest?

LEHMAN: None of them is easy. Certainly writing isn't the easiest. There's nothing *easy* about writing. And being a screenwriter, there are many emotional hardships that make it anything but easy: The constant knowledge that somebody can say, "I don't like this. Screw it. We're getting another writer." Or, "I don't like this. You've got to rewrite this." That kind of nonsense. You have to have a charmed life. I had a charmed life for most of my career.

BRADY: How so?

LEHMAN: I seem to have had a lot of influence over the people I worked with. They *listened* when I talked, like "Hey, this guy knows something. If he says that's the way it should be done, let's listen." It isn't quite that way anymore for *any* writer.

BRADY: Has your work in these different capacities—writer-producer-director—altered your view of yourself in any of these capacities?

LEHMAN: I've never given it any serious thought. I've lived through a variety of experiences, and I will say to you sitting here now that I can't believe that I lived through it all. I don't know how I survived it. But I did. Still, I don't go around thinking to myself, You have far greater ability to handle yourself with formidable, powerful, frightening, contentious people than you tend to give yourself credit for. I just don't say that to myself. But if I could get objective, maybe I would see myself that way. But I don't get objective enough. I live in present time, and I don't think of myself as being permanently changed by an experience. I lived through working with some of the most humiliating personalities in show business. I've lived through a totally lousy relationship with a director—but am I any stronger as a result? No way.

I was much more capable in the old days of telling a Paul Newman, "What do you *mean,* you can't read that line? Do you want to hear me read it? Listen." You know, just like that. In that tone of voice. Today I would probably behave better, because I've learned a few things. I used to be guilty of not granting the other person his or her Beingness; it was a form of *withheld respect*. I guess I was a little afraid of these people, and felt that they were up there and I was down here. I couldn't bring myself up *there*, so I used to bring *them* down *here* by treating them in a way that they weren't used to being treated, and it was wrong. Bad behavior. I used to do that with Elizabeth Taylor. I mean it. With Mike Nichols, that was one of his serious complaints—that he was used to being treated with more respect. On a location trip he suddenly turned to me in an airport and said, "Why do you make me carry my own bags?" And I said, "Well, I'm carrying *my* bags. Haven't you noticed?" He said, "But you're the producer of this picture. I'm the director. You're supposed to see that I'm taken care of." And I said, "I've been a writer for a long time, and the studio has always taken care of *me*. I'm not *used* to taking care of other people. I'm just not well versed in that art."

Elizabeth Taylor would come storming into my office and say, "How dare you order me onto the set at nine o'clock when it says in my contract that I don't have to be on until ten!" And I would start *laughing* at her because of the size of her rage. And I said, "It's the first *I* knew about it. How do *I* know about these things? Let's find out who did it." She said, "You're the producer, and I'm the star!" I always treated people like, "Look, you and I are the same. I'm not going to treat you with kid gloves." And it got a lot of people mad. They felt they had earned the right to be treated with deference. I had a lot of trouble treating people with deserved deference. Some people had *earned* deference, you know—but I never learned to give it. Now, I think I am a little saner about that. I believe that you don't have to treat people as though they are *not* who they are, merely to protect yourself from feeling less important than they are. It's OK to treat them as who they are.

BRADY: Why did you do *Virginia Woolf* in black and white? Was that a popular decision?

LEHMAN: No, it was very unpopular with Jack Warner, though Mike Nichols and I were in total accord that the picture had to be in black and white or else it wouldn't work.

BRADY: Why?

LEHMAN: First of all, the words. The dialogue would have played differently in color. The film wouldn't have had that harsh nighttime look. We felt Elizabeth Taylor's makeup and aging wouldn't work in color. Somehow if you saw her wearing a red blouse and red patent leather shoes and lipstick, it wouldn't have been as harsh. And Jack Warner was equally harsh about having it done in color. It was a tremendous battle. I don't know how we ever won it. He claimed it would hurt the picture, it would hurt the sale to television because black and white pictures don't sell like color films do. We had a chance to see what the picture would look like in color because ABC was doing a documentary on Mike Nichols during shooting, and *they* shot in color while he was shooting the picture in black and white. So we saw some of our picture in color. And it looked terrible. Anyway, we won, and who knows whether the picture would have been better or worse, or would have been more critically acclaimed or less? I don't know. Thirteen Academy nominations have to mean *something*. And the film had *big* sales to TV, no-color notwithstanding.

BRADY: There's a big unknown in films, isn't there?

LEHMAN: You just never know. But the audience always does. You can be so damned sure that your film is going to be a smash hit, it's that good in the projection room. And then suddenly the audience tells you what you never knew. Almost immediately you find out to your dismay: Hey, they're not going to go *see* this picture. You can tell the first day or the first week. Sometimes, the first hour. And always, much to your amazement.

BRADY: What's your attitude toward the use of violence in films? Did you have much to do with it in *Black Sunday?*

LEHMAN: The novel on which the screenplay was based had all the violence that was in the movie; there wasn't very much *invented*. I think in fact that the book was probably even more violent. I noticed that when seeing the movie, I turned away at certain bloody moments. I don't know why I was all that interested in working on that film if even *I* have to look away during its moments of great violence. Sometimes I wonder why writers write such violence. I am not even sure why I wrote a novel like *The French Atlantic Affair.* God knows, it had enough violence in it. I guess a lot of writers get rid of fantasies and aggressions in their writing. Why did Paul Schrader write *Taxi Driver?* I believe he admitted in an interview that it was better than going to a shrink at the time he wrote it. I don't know if he would write that film today.

BRADY: Your movies have such dignity and intelligence for the most part. Do you ever feel you might be at a loss to write the hard stuff that goes into scripts today, given the age of spoken candor that seems to be about us?

LEHMAN: Unfortunately (or fortunately, who knows?), it would not be at all difficult for me to write with candor or violence or sex or vulgarity. I can't honestly say that that would present any problem at all. It certainly didn't when I wrote my first novel, or the one I'm writing now. It's quite obvious that I was straining at the leash even as far back as *North by Northwest,* always trying to slip things in, you know. I used to have running battles with the censorship board even before there was a rating system, even on *Somebody Up There Likes Me.* I always had that tendency. I got something into *Somebody Up There Likes Me* that was kind of ridiculous for me to fight for. In the script, Rocky has never fought professionally, and he's making believe he's a fighter. He goes into Stillman's Gym, and some manager says, "Rocky, go into the locker room and get yourself a pair of boxing gloves and a pair of trunks, and don't forget to get a cup." And Rocky says, "That's all right. I'll drink out of the bottle." And Geoffrey Shurlock, head of the Production Code Board, called me and said, "You can't have *that* in the picture. Are you kidding? You can't have that in the movie." I said, "Why not?" He said, "Because you can't, and that's it." So the producer said to me, "I'm sorry, Ernie. We just can't do it." I said, "Well, that's ridiculous. We're going to do it!" And I said, "Do you mind if I speak to the head of the studio?" So I went up to Dore Schary and said, "Can I take on the censorship board myself?" He said, "If you insist, but you're just wasting your time." I said, "OK, thanks for the permission." And I called Geoffrey Shurlock back and said, "Geoffrey, are you going to tell me that there is something *dirty* about the fact that fighters wear an aluminum cup to protect their genital area? Are you going to tell me that's *dirty?* Everybody knows that athletes wear aluminum cups. What's dirty about that?" And he said, "Who do you think you're kidding, Ernie? Come on! You know that women in the audience are going to nudge their boyfriends or their husbands and say, 'What does that mean? Why is everyone laughing?' " And I said, "Yeah, of course they're laughing. That's why I want it in. Because it's a laugh and it's in character. And there are a lot of women who go to fights, you know. I mean, what do you think women are, dummies? They know about aluminum cups." He said, "Yes, but what about the women who *don't?*" I said, "Men are going to *explain* it to them: 'Oh, that's because fighters wear an aluminum cup.' They're going to *explain* it to them, Geoffrey. What's dirty about that?" I went on and on and on. Finally, I could almost hear him throw up his hands at the other end of the telephone. He said, "Look, if *you* want a thing like that in a movie with *your* name on it, you're welcome to it." Boom, just like that, I had *won.* I had saved a big laugh in the picture, against hopeless odds. So, you see, I was slipping lines considered candid and daring into films long before the world became free. I remember in *North by Northwest* I had Eva Marie Saint say to Cary Grant, "I never make love on an empty stomach." Unfortunately, "make" was changed to "discuss" on the soundtrack . . . but I was for candor in screenwriting long before it became the fashion. Maybe "candor" isn't the right word. You might spell it "vulgarity."

BRADY: Increasingly, writers seem to be headed toward directing. You've been there. What are your theories on the topic?

LEHMAN: I don't know what the urge is. Maybe each one has a different reason—like they want part of that *auteur* acclaim for themselves. It's partly an ego trip, partly not wanting to see the director get all the glory for *their* film, partly the Peter Principle at work. Definitely the latter. And part of it is just wanting to play a more exciting game. Life consists of various games that we play to live and keep things seemingly exciting, you know? And after you do one game for a while, there aren't enough challenges. You want a *new* game, so you become a director, whether you know anything about directing or not.

BRADY: Keep the ball bouncing higher and higher.

LEHMAN: Yeah. It's just a striving of human beings to go farther than they have ever gone.

BRADY: You said once that you could always spot a poorly directed scene on the screen, particularly if it was something you had written. You said, "I know that the director didn't get the point, or that he went past the point and missed it." Can you give me an example of such a poorly directed scene in something you had written?

LEHMAN: No, I can't do that, because it would publicly criticize a director of a film of mine. But every writer has those feelings. Every producer, every writer. Anyone who knows the values and dramatic moments that are inherent in a particular scene and realizes that some of them are not there on the screen knows that the director simply didn't get them.

BRADY: You once said, "No director has ever tampered with my work. I've been lucky."

LEHMAN: I must have said that a very long time ago.

BRADY: You've worked most often with Robert Wise as director. What holds a screenwriter and a director together on repeat projects?

LEHMAN: Bob, for me, has always been a *very* good person to work with. And he's a good friend, too. He is intelligent, highly professional, skilled as a director, and I think he has the right amount of wary respect for a writer. I mean, he has no illusions about the writer always doing the correct thing. But he doesn't have this innate anxiety about the script. And when the script is kind of set, he has no desire to get somebody in to make it better. He thinks it's good, and that's it. I can't speak for his other films with other writers or anything like that. I just know that for me, working with him has always been a very exciting experience, and I've done four pictures with him, which is something I cannot say about any other director. And I have a feeling that he thinks his best pictures are the ones that I wrote, although he's had plenty of superb ones without me.

BRADY: You have spoken earlier about reviews and reading them and how sometimes they can be painful.

LEHMAN: They can hurt. Isn't that obvious?

BRADY: Do you think there is a certain amount of critical hostility toward artists living in Southern California?

LEHMAN: I don't think there is as much as there used to be. In the fifties and sixties I used to feel that there was an eastern literary establishment with unconscious contempt for everything that went on in Southern California, with special emphasis on "Hollywood" and Los Angeles. I think there is less of that today because the country has tilted decidedly toward the West, and in many ways California is looked upon as a kind of style leader. Television moved to the West Coast. The movie studios moved their New York offices to the West Coast. There are many highly respected novelists on the West Coast. Certainly, many respected painters on the West Coast. The music industry is big here. Our legitimate theater now is much more widespread and much more original than it used to be. We have some great theaters out here now, so you can no longer sneer with ease at California. The attitude is almost old-fashioned and a cliché, to be that New Yorker who comes in and stays at the Chateau Marmont and can't wait to get back to New York. That just doesn't seem to prevail anymore. And I think it has eliminated some of the hostility on the part of the critics. *Rocky, One Flew Over the Cuckoo's Nest, Network, Close Encounters, Being There,* Coppola's films, George Lucas's work—aren't we talking about California-based projects? Don't write off California, please.

BRADY: Is the treatment still a screenwriter's tool?

LEHMAN: I don't think it's used as much as it used to be. I'm not sure. You'd have to ask other writers. Hitchcock asked me to do a treatment for *Family Plot.* I wouldn't have done it if he hadn't wanted me to. I used to do treatments before I went into screenplays, but I just don't feel the need for it anymore. But there's no *harm* in doing a treatment first. They can be quite helpful.

BRADY: Are your first drafts concerned with camera angles and such?

LEHMAN: Yes. I find it hard to write a film without visualizing it all, and it would be difficult to express it in any way other than as a *movie*.

BRADY: Do you specify props?

LEHMAN: No, only if it's a very significant prop. If the gun mounted on the wall is going to figure in the scene, obviously I would indicate it.

BRADY: You have an incredibly high batting average as a screenwriter. Your work is with the best people. You work on the best films consistently. How do you avoid the kiss of death in this business?

LEHMAN: Well, first of all, thanks for the compliment, but I have to add that I've had my share of kisses of death, you know. I think what you are saying is, I haven't had as many as I *might* have had, right? How do I avoid disaster *some* of the time? First, simply by viewing a projected film venture, something that is offered to me to write, in terms of how I think it will do on the screen. Do people want to see this? Is it good material for a movie? That's one thing I do. I act as if I were a studio head, making a decision whether to buy a certain property and authorize the making of the film with all its millions in expenditure. It's *one* of the ways I try to avoid the kiss of death.

Second, I try not to get mixed up in any film venture which I feel I don't know how to do, where I feel I'm *wrong* for it. Maybe there *is* some writer who is bright enough to know how to lick this thing, but not me. A prime example of making that mistake was *Portnoy's Complaint*. I obviously didn't know how to do it. Ordinarily, if I have a project like *Portnoy's Complaint* thrown at me, I say, "Forget it." Now the truth just occurred to me as I am answering this question. Listen to this. The first group that sent me *Portnoy's Complaint* (they owned the soft-cover publishing company that was going to publish the novel) sent me the manuscript telling me that if I would agree to do the picture, *they* would buy the film rights because they had first option on it, and they would make it as a film. They were also filmmakers, as well as owners of a publishing house. I believe it was National General Picture Corporation. They sent me the manuscript of the novel. I read it, thought it was terrific, and turned it down. I didn't know how to do it, and I felt somehow it would never work as a movie. On the basis of *my* turning it down, *me,* just one writer, because they respected my judgment, they passed on the film rights. They passed. *They* turned it down.

Someone else purchased the film rights a few months later and called me on the telephone and said, "You don't know it, but I just bought the property that's going to be your next picture." And I said, "What's that?" And he said, "*Portnoy's Complaint.* It's still just a manuscript. I mean, it isn't a published novel. It isn't a best-seller." And I said, "I don't think so. I already passed." He said, "I don't care. This is your next picture." I said, "Oh, Christ, am I going to have to read that *again?*" So I read it again. I don't know what my state of mind was, but all I know is that I was once again hugely impressed on reading it, but still didn't know how to make it as a movie. But word somehow got out to the studio heads where I then had a contract that I seemed to be interested in *Portnoy's Complaint,* and one of them called me on the phone and said, "We hear you'd like to do *Portnoy's Complaint.*" I said, "Well, I'm just reading it, that's all, just reading it." And this gentleman said, "Look, we'll buy it for you if you want to do it. We'll make it your next picture here at the studio if you say so." And now my head is shifting a little bit in a slightly unexplainable direction, you know—*Forget whether you know how to do it or not, it's such an exciting project, how can you say no?* That sort of stuff. The attraction of the brilliant, still-unpublished novel was tampering with my judgment. Anyway, to make a long story short, my agent got into the act, and a lot of negotiations started, and I didn't like the way they were going for various reasons that I won't go into because they involve personalities. And finally I wrote a letter to my agent and said, I want all this to end. I have changed my mind. *I am not going to do* Portnoy's Complaint. *Forget the whole thing.* He acceded to my wishes. And that was the end of it for a *second* time.

Now several months go by, and the person who owned the film rights to *Portnoy's Complaint* shopped it around and couldn't find anybody willing to do it. Nobody would go near it, for all the same reasons, I suppose. ("You've got to be kidding. There's no way of doing *Portnoy's Complaint* as a movie. Are you kidding?") More calls from the studio executives where I am located at the time, saying, "We have information that things are getting a little difficult for the gentleman who owns the film rights, and we believe he would now be willing to accede to some of your wishes. Do you want us to pursue this again?" I forget where my head was at the time, but I do know that I said, "Yes, see what you can do." In other words, *twice* I had said, "Forget it, I'm not going to do it," and considered myself fortunate for having finally said goodbye to it. But finally, almost without knowing what had happened to me, I found myself easing myself into being committed to doing it. The deal was finally made, and I charged ahead with it. But after I wrote the screenplay—several versions of it, in fact—the studio read it and refused to make it. *Refused to make it.* How smart can you get? Within one day after that, the head of Warners was reading the script and was saying, "We want the project over here." And it was shifted immediately over to Burbank. Everybody over there was thrilled to get it. I'm telling you that damn screenplay fooled a lot of people, including me. You read that script and think you've got a hell of a movie.

So that's the second way I avoid the kiss of death, except in that particular case my avoiding it was only temporary. The *other* way is, I look at a potential film project and ask myself, "Does it interest me? Is it the kind of thing that really interests me?" It has to appeal to something in my psyche that makes me say, "I've gotta do it"—know what I mean?

BRADY: Has there been any anonymity in your career, work that you've done as a script doctor?

LEHMAN: No . . . you mean like Bob Towne in the old days?

BRADY: Yeah.

LEHMAN: No. Bob may *think* he was anonymous then, but he wasn't. No. What a tremendous reputation he had while he was doing it. Everybody knew about Bob, everyone. He had a tremendous reputation. It was almost as though by not having his name on it, they thought more of his effort than if he had had his name on it. If the picture was terrific, it was obvious that Bob had made it terrific. Now, if the picture was no good, nobody was going to blame Bob, because, first of all, he's such a good writer; secondly, his name wasn't on it. There's certainly nothing *wrong* with what he did. Nothing at all. It was relief pitching. It was terrific. With certain exceptions, he got saves, never the wins. He was the Sparky Lyle of Hollywood. Now he's Robert Towne, which is even better.

BRADY: Are your instincts pretty good at sizing up a property, or have there been some big films and some successful films that you have said no to that have gone on without you?

LEHMAN: I wonder. Let's think about it for a moment. Oh yeah. I said no to *Cat on a Hot Tin Roof,* but not because I felt, "Oh, nobody's going to want to see this." The only reason I said no to *Cat on a Hot Tin Roof* was that I had no desire to be writing Tennessee Williams for the screen with one of my hands tied behind the censor's back. Also, I had a feeling of wanting to do something on my own. I got into a big fight with MGM because I kept turning down projects, and I was under contract to them at the time. And when you were not working on a film, you were on what was known as layoff, meaning go home and sulk and break open your piggy bank if you have to. They had the right to do that to you. You never got paid for *not* writing a picture, contract or no contract.

Those days are over anyway for theatrical films. They don't have weekly contract writers anymore. We work on flat deal arrangements. Much better that way. Suppose you were working on a weekly salary and one day you couldn't come up with a *word?* You literally didn't write a word. You went home that night feeling you'd stolen money. But on a flat deal, you can have bad days, you can go as slowly as you want, and it doesn't cost the other guy anything. It just costs *you*—time. So you don't have to feel guilty about it. The meter isn't ticking. I *hated* that kind of pressure. I think I turned down twelve projects in a row at MGM after coming back from Tahiti while *Sweet Smell of Success* was shooting. I kept saying, "No, I don't want to do this picture." I remember turning down a picture that an eminent producer wanted me to do, and the head of the studio called me. I am not naming him, deliberately. The head of the studio called me up to his office, and he said, "Now look, this studio is bigger than you are, Ernie. And we've got more money than you have, Ernie. And we can hold out longer than you while you sit at home. Now, how many more pictures are you going to turn down?" And I said, "I am going to turn down every picture until there's something I think is worth doing." He said, "Well, why won't you do this one? So-and-So thinks it's worth doing" (naming the producer), and I said, "Well, I sure would like to know why he wants to do it." So the head of the studio pressed a button and said, "Send So-and-So up here to my office right away." We waited, and in came the producer, and the head of the studio said to him, "Ernie wants to know why you want to make this picture." And the producer said, "It's very simple. I want to make it because I have a seven-picture deal here." The head of the studio frowned and said, "Thank you very much." And the producer left. So did I. A few hours later I got a phone call from the producer. "Jesus, you sure did get me in a hell of a lot of trouble, Ernie." I said, "Why?" He said, "Because the head of the studio called me back up to his office and said, 'What kind of answer is *that* to give to a writer?' " *That* producer never made the picture. The property sat on the studio shelf and gathered dust, and years later someone else made it—and lost a bundle with it.

What the hell was the question you asked me? Oh, have I ever turned down pictures that were successful? I don't really think so. But I've pleaded with studios not to buy certain properties. I used to get insulted when I'd pick up the trade papers and read of literary purchases a couple of weeks later, after I'd not only turned those properties down, but had said, "Listen to me. *Don't buy these*." I remember that so definitely. And I'd pick up the trade papers and read that they'd bought something, and they'd make the movie and it would bomb. Which doesn't mean I am a genius. It just means that when I am *really* down on it, I think the odds are against it. But that doesn't necessarily mean that every time I say yes, it's automatically a hit.

BRADY: You tend to quit projects a lot, don't you?

LEHMAN: I used to quit every other picture.

BRADY: You quit *The Wreck of the Mary Deare* with Hitchcock. You even *wanted* to quit *North by Northwest,* didn't you?

LEHMAN: Every other week, but I never did. When the going gets tough, the tough want to get going. I was working on a movie called *The Labor Story* with John Houseman, who had even gotten rid of another writer to get *me* to work on it. I worked on it for about ten weeks, and I finally felt, this isn't going to work. I said, "Here's the only way I think we can do it," and John Houseman, who is brilliant, said, "Oh, that sounds like a gangster picture. I don't want to make that kind of picture." And I said, "Well, that's the only kind of picture that will work," and I left. And he wasn't all that happy, because that was the end of that project. It was never made. *Wanting* to quit is one thing. Actually quitting is another. I was once an expert at both.

The first thing I ever worked on, I quit. I was brought out to Hollywood by Paramount, and assigned to a producer, now dead, who had some idea for a little original. I had just arrived in Hollywood and certainly had no weight to throw around, and after a few weeks I felt this man didn't know what the hell he was talking about. There's no movie in this. This is no good. And I didn't even known enough to tell *him.* I went to the head of the studio instead and said, "I quit. I don't know how to write this picture." Some Hollywood debut, huh?

BRADY: As a writer then you seem to be a fussy man.

LEHMAN: If I don't believe in a project, or if I think it's a sinking ship and isn't going to work—I see no sense in staying aboard. A lot of times you don't know until you really have been at it and really tried to lick it; then you have a better fix on your ability to make it come off.

BRADY: On balance, would you say that screenwriting becomes easier or more difficult as you grow older?

LEHMAN: That's very hard to say. It *seems* easier, but maybe it isn't. It *seems* that there is more facility. But maybe that facility is the very thing which is dangerous to have. I don't know. It's quite possible. Show me a writer who is struggling to get the words out, and I always feel there's more of a possibility of something good coming out of that writer than out of someone who breezes through. But for all I know, some of the most admired screenwriting there is was done with great facility. I don't know. I'd have to talk to Bill Goldman, to Bob Towne, Paul Schrader, Bob Benton, Waldo Salt and all the others and say, "Did you breeze through? Did you write with great facility? Was it easy? Or did it come hard? Is your best work done easily, or is your best work done with great struggle?"

BRADY: If you were to answer that yourself, how would you reply?

LEHMAN: I would say the more the struggle, the better it probably is. The struggle indicates that you are not accepting the first or the second or the third thing that comes to mind at any given moment when you are writing. You are constantly rejecting and trying harder. Once you put words on paper . . . even though they are going to be rewritten, the die is cast. It's better if you can hold out, saying to yourself, "This isn't good enough. No, *that* isn't good enough"—keep rejecting, even before you hit the typewriter key or before you write on a yellow pad. Once you start putting words down, that means you think the words are almost good enough. The greater the struggle, the higher the level of critical faculties at work. That's what I believe, anyway.

In the old days, there were times when I would go crazy in my office, realizing, God, I have written only a page and a half today, or two pages, or one page, or no pages. Today, once I know what the scene ought to be, I have the feeling that I can write it. Fifteen years ago I might have said, "No, that isn't good enough. I can't write that." Today I don't think I would like the anxiety of nothing coming out. Not for too long, anyway. I would probably make something come.

BRADY: Do you see today's stress on original scripts as a turn-around period or a fad or what?

LEHMAN: I see it just for what it is. I have no idea what direction it will go in. It all depends on what the playwrights and the novelists are writing or not writing. If playwrights and novelists write things which would make terrific movies, filmmakers will buy them. They won't turn their backs on works from another medium simply because they're looking for originals. They know that audiences don't say, "I don't want to go to that movie. It's based on a novel." You know what I mean? People don't go to a movie because it's an *original* screenplay. They go to the movie because they want to see *that movie*. It can be an adaptation of something else, or it can be an original. More original screenplays are being written now because there is an open market for them. Therefore, more are being written. Therefore, more pictures are based on original screenplays; therefore, more writers are writing original screenplays. It's almost a cycle that feeds on itself. The market for them is there, which is why people are writing them.

BRADY: What changes or shifts have you observed in the lot of the screenwriter in the last twenty-five years?

LEHMAN: Marginal improvements at best, mostly in the area of financial rewards, and mostly through the bargaining power of the Writers Guild of America. Screenwriters still have as many beefs about their scripts being tampered with as they always did. Screenwriters complain about the critics not noticing them, just as they did twenty-five years ago. Screenwriters complain about other writers following them on their literary efforts and rewriting them, just as they always did. The biggest change is in size, in quantity. There's just so much *less* of everything today. We don't have studios the way we used to. We don't have stables of contract writers like we used to. We don't have writers with *big bodies of work* like we used to. You can get to be one of the top screenwriters in the land with maybe two or three films today.

When I first arrived in this town, the writers who were well known had maybe twenty or thirty or forty pictures to their credit. There just is no such thing anymore, and there never will be, because not that many pictures are being made. Writers used to do two or three pictures a *year.* They were under contract, and they would work on one for thirteen weeks, and on another for twenty weeks, and on another for nineteen weeks. The pictures were sort of ground out in a sense. Well, that has all changed. Today, you really are as good as your last picture— even if it's the only one you ever wrote.

BRADY: What is your attitude toward the Academy Awards for writers?

LEHMAN: In my opinion, they invariably go to the best scripts. I just wish more attention would be paid. The Oscars to screenwriters are major major awards. You'd never know it reading the newspapers the next day.

BRADY: What have you been working on lately?

LEHMAN: I had fun doing *my* screenplay version of *Brenda Starr, Reporter,* a movie-movie with equal portions of romance, comedy and suspense. However, I doubt if the screenplay is anywhere near as entertaining as the reasons why it will probably never reach the screen. I hope I'm wrong, and it does.

Also, I'm almost through with my second novel, a rather tense and tricky affair that has a Hollywood studio, a Malibu Beach pad and a Bel Air manse as its major locales. Thinking about it, I'm a bit alarmed at the fact that I seem to see nothing but lowlifes in high places. Can this *be?* I think maybe I need a new pair of glasses.

Lastly, and by no means least, because it was a major source of pleasure in my life, was the monthly column I had been doing the last three of years for *American Film* magazine. It forced me to look at the ever-changing Hollywood scene every month, and to try to figure out what I thought about it, and what I thought about my part in it, past and present; and somehow it always seemed to come out rather wry and jocular and tongue in cheek, but I haven't yet been able to decide whether or not I wasn't secretly damned serious about everything I said all along. To get on to other challenges, I recently gave the column up.

BRADY: Wearing your screenwriter's hat now, do you think courses of any sort are really helpful to aspiring young hopefuls?

LEHMAN: Yes, I think they are in a way. I used to think you can't learn how to write movies in a classroom. Well, obviously if you *see* a lot of movies, that to me is the best classroom of all: the theater where you are seeing films. And I realize that in screenwriting class you are going to discuss many pictures and analyze them. I think it would be foolish of me to think that that can't help. How much it can help is simply an individual matter with each particular student and with a particular class or instructor. You can't generalize too much. In general, I think cinema schools are helpful provided that the student doesn't think he's going to learn it *all* there. He won't. A lot of it has to come out of his or her own instincts and elusive talents as a writer.

BRADY: What advice would you give to a young screenwriter trying to break into the business today?

LEHMAN: Write something which is not only terrific esthetically, artistically and dramatically, but also something that deals with subject matter which would appeal to a broad, fairly young audience. In other words, the budding screenwriter has got to wear the hats of audiences, studio heads, distributors, producers, directors. First and foremost, everybody wants a hit, so try to give them one. That doesn't mean that it has to be artistically dismal or cheap or vulgar or crass. It does mean that it has to take into account whether or not audiences will care for it, and that means you have to have some knowledge of who movie audiences are. For example, I don't think if I were a beginning screenwriter I would sit down and write an original screenplay which takes place in a home for the aged. I think I would be crass enough to say, it could be beautiful, but not what *they* want. *Do Not Go Gentle Into That Good Night* was magnificent for television. I question whether young movie audiences would have paid to see it. All those movies which a lot of good writers are dying to write *are* being written and work wonderfully on television, whether as specials or as movies of the week, and they work wonderfully well because they've got a built-in audience. But when you have to sell tickets, when you have to get young people standing in lines, it becomes a slightly different matter. Sometimes it's much better to be Woody Allen than Hamlet. If this be treason, make the most of it.

BRADY: And ultimately, how would you like to be remembered?

LEHMAN: I don't know. I hadn't thought about it. It's not one of my favorite subjects to think about, I guess. I don't have an answer for you. We'll have to see what's waiting for me in the files of *The New York Times*. Filed under Ernest Who.

PAUL SCHRADER

Movies were forbidden in the Dutch Calvinist community in Grand Rapids, Michigan, where Paul Schrader was raised—ostensibly to become a minister. At seventeen, though, Schrader took a bus downtown and slipped into a theater, quickly paid for a ticket, and hurried up to the balcony for his first movie, Walt Disney's *The Absent-Minded Professor*. He was disappointed. "After all, movies were forbidden, and this one hardly seemed to qualify," he told a writer for the Los Angeles *Times* many years later. "But it was the beginning of a legitimate form of rebellion, and one with an artistic mantle to boot."

Though he saw his first movie at seventeen, Paul Schrader caught up fast by seeing several a day for four years. After graduating from Calvin College in Grand Rapids, he headed west to UCLA, where he became an intense student of great filmmakers. His master's thesis, a study of three of his film gods (Transcendental Style in Film: Ozu, Bresson, Dreyer), was published in book form, and the young author soon became editor of Cinema magazine. At twenty-four, by his own evaluation, Paul Schrader had become "an overly serious critic." Now he became a serious screenwriter. By the time he was thirty, Schrader had written a dozen scripts, most of which have been made into memorable movies: The Yakuza, Taxi Driver, Obsession, Rolling Thunder, Blue Collar, Hardcore, Old Boyfriends and American Gigolo. More recently, he worked on the screenplay for Raging Bull.

In addition to writing the screenplays, Schrader directed Blue Collar, Hardcore and American Gigolo. Today he is on the top rungs of the "film brat" generation that has emerged from university film schools rather than from Broadway and the theater, or from the world of fiction, or from cubbyhole offices on the studio back lot. His films often pay homage to his heroes. "I think the two best American films are The Searchers and Vertigo," says Schrader, whose Hardcore is The Searchers in pornland, and whose Obsession is Vertigo with incest. Even American Gigolo has elements of Bresson's Pickpocket, including the same closing line: "It's taken me so long to come to you."

In person, Paul Schrader is serious and somewhat scholarly, but not at all stuffy. He wears a custom-tailored overcoat over sweatshirt, jeans and sneakers. He is open, down-to earth, determinedly midwestern in a business where participants usually go Hollywood fast. Schrader has used his Michigan background as the backdrop for several films. Blue Collar takes place on the auto lines. Hardcore begins in Grand Rapids and includes scenes at

Schrader's family church and at a factory where the writer used to work. Even Schrader's parents appear in the movie briefly. *Old Boyfriends,* too, has a Michigan connection: About half of the script takes place in Ludington, just north of Grand Rapids. I asked Schrader if he considered himself part of that midwestern literary tradition typified by Scott Fitzgerald writing about St. Paul, Minnesota; or Sherwood Anderson reporting on Clyde, Ohio—authors who left their hometowns, but whose hometowns never left them. "It feels good to comment on things that are close to you," he replied. "There's no sense of getting back with vengeance or anything like that. It just feels natural. You feel at ease about it. You know you can do it, and you know you can do it well."

For this interview we met a few times initially at Schrader's Hollywood home, a plainly furnished place with a study punctuated by a photo of Robert De Niro and Martin Scorsese on the wall. In the picture the actor and director are sitting next to each other, relaxed, and De Niro has his arm around Scorsese. *To Paul, till the next one, Bob,* the actor has written; and beneath the director: *To Paul, for "Taxi Driver" and hopefully others—together. Thanks, Martin Scorsese.*

Taxi Driver remains Paul Schrader's most perfectly realized film as a writer. His growth as a director has been slower, and when we met for our final session he was doing research on "a working-class picture in a rock and roll environment in east Ohio" with the current title *Born in the USA.* Our conversation took place at a downtown-Cleveland hotel called Swingo's, heavily populated by rock music performers. Schrader had been listening to a lot of loud music lately, and his customary conversational intensity was now giving way to laughter and amusement at the crazier aspects of the movie business, including the need to be commercial as well as cerebral in a serious film. "You are very bright, very intellectual, yet working in a medium that depends on a popular audience," I observed. "Do you think your intelligence is a liability at times?"

"Andy Sarris does," he laughed. "He says I'm too

smart. Sometimes I think I'm too lukewarm—not smart enough, and not dumb enough. But I'm working on both of them." He laughed again and lit a cigarette in the top-floor Celebrity Suite that would be filled with musicians and roadies and hangers-on at the party later that evening. "Right now I'm listening to a lot of loud music and blowing out synapses in my brain."

BRADY: Is directing as creative a high as writing?

SCHRADER: No. Writing is more exciting because everything is possible. Things can look exactly as you want. People can do and feel and say whatever you want. The only limits are the limits of your imagination. As a director, the limits are quite real and immediate. Every idea goes through a series of diminutions. From the moment an idea is conceived, every step of the process diminishes it. By the time the movie is released it is a tattered shadow of what you had imagined it would be. Directing is more exciting in some ways because it brings you closer to the real thing, that is, there are actual actors out there, and sets; but it is less exciting in creative ways—just as print pornography is more erotic than visual pornography because it exists in the mind. When you are writing, it is all in the mind.

BRADY: As a writer-director, then, do you ever feel as though you are whittling your own ideas down to size?

SCHRADER: Yes. The ideas become flesh, and you deal with their limitations. You want your character to be handsome, sensitive, sexy, intelligent, and you quickly start to realize that there is no actor who is quite all of those things. You set your priorities and begin a series of compromises which stretches all the way through to editing, where you try to salvage the compromises you've made the day you weren't able to get enough setups, the day the sun wasn't right, the day a certain actor was off, the day you were shooting with a hundred-and-four-degree fever. You salvage as much as you can.

Being a director is not nearly as rewarding as I thought it would be. Far more tedious. You never get a sense of artistic completion as a director—at least I haven't yet. As a writer you really get a sense of the whole. That's very, very difficult to do as a director, because you are just dealing with pieces, repeated over and over again. Then, in the context of ten weeks, you're supposed to see the whole. As a writer you can see the whole very quickly.

BRADY: What is the disillusionment in directing?

SCHRADER: Hand holding and logistics. The difficulty of putting anything in the camera almost overwhelms you, much less putting anything of *quality* in the camera. It's difficult to shoot even a *bad* scene. You get swamped by logistics.

BRADY: I understand that your first few weeks as a director on *Blue Collar* were nightmarish.

SCHRADER: It was very bad. I would not put myself back in that situation knowingly again, where one invites three bulls into his china shop. Sometimes this can happen quite unwittingly; in that case, it happened quite wittingly. I knew what I was doing by casting Richard Pryor, Harvey Keitel and Yaphet Kotto—I knew that that was the only way I was going to get the movie financed—but it was very difficult. The *Gigolo* directing experience was the most gratifying, the easiest, the most confident, the most assured—and it shows up in the film, which has a very fluid, imaginative and confident style. Whether or not you agree with the style is a different point, but it clearly has a strong stylistic hand—a film under control rather than in the hands of the elements.

BRADY: What did you learn about the realities of directing that first time out?

SCHRADER: I learned that you are dealing with a huge piece of machinery. It's like a mega-combine that costs about forty thousand dollars a day to run. It has about a hundred people in it, and six of those people have serious ego problems. It is subject to all of the vagaries of weather and acts of God. You just try to keep the machine going, to survive and get the crop harvested. As you become more familiar with how the combine runs, what the roles of the components and personnel are, you start to use it with some finesse and subtlety. You can use the filmmaking machine to express personal feelings with precision rather than with broad strokes. When I began, I was in service to the narrative—the simplest, most obvious element of the filmmaking apparatus. Now I'm trying to make the narrative in service to the style—to learn to think visually. The interesting thing about my career is that while I've been growing as a director the last few years, I've not grown as a writer. I wrote all the scripts in 1976, and directed them in 1977, 1978 and 1979, and I think those three films—*Blue Collar, Hardcore, American Gigolo*—clearly show a progression, a development of my talent as a director, but not as a writer. The scripts are essentially the same writing mentality—products of my twenties, still not fully mature scripts. Good, but still the scripts of a young man. I haven't written anything original in four years, and now I'm going to write again. Now it's my obligation to find how I've grown as a writer rather than just as a director. I also intend to learn how much narrative a movie actually needs, and what audiences actually go to movies for. You learn these things when you see what you've done translated into an audience experience. You learn how to learn.

My training as a screenwriter has made me lean too much on narrative. I've used narrative as a stern taskmaster to whip my characters like galley slaves into action. I don't think I need quite as much narrative. It's allowable to let fewer things happen, to give a fuller sense of character and small truths rather than the Big Truth. That's my feeling now. It may change.

BRADY: What's a small truth in a script?

SCHRADER: Let me give you an example of what audiences really like. In *Kramer vs. Kramer,* you know the scene where Dustin Hoffman is talking to the kid about the ice cream? "You're in real trouble if you get the ice cream. OK, you open that ice cream and you're in *real* trouble. You put the *spoon* in that ice cream and it's real *trouble!*" Audiences love that, because it's close to things they've experienced. My scripts that I've directed, though, are a bit more dogmatic, didactic and intellectual—the scripts of a young man with a mission who wants to proselytize. I felt at the time I had to go out and teach the world something. But you get into your thirties—I'll be thirty-four shortly—and you start to realize that there ain't much to teach the world that it hasn't already heard, and that immortality and true art aren't what they're cracked up to be. It's probably better to be true to yourself and the small insights you've had, to live a reasonably decent, good life and forswear these adolescent dreams of artistic grandeur.

BRADY: How have your films done at the box office?

SCHRADER: *Blue Collar* was made inexpensively, but it still didn't do very well. The release was bungled: It was promoted as a Richard Pryor comedy. So that got screwed up. *Hardcore* did OK. It wasn't an embarrassment to the studio financially, but it wasn't a hit. It took in five or six million in rentals, but didn't make money for participants. *Gigolo* is a hit. They project it to be a twenty-five-million-dollar gross.

BRADY: Is that a good flight pattern for a writer-director in his early thirties?

SCHRADER: All in all, of the eight or nine films I've had my hand in as a writer or writer-director, three have become commercial hits: *Taxi Driver, Obsession* and *American Gigolo.* You can't ask too much more of me.

BRADY: Your directed films have a midwestern tinge—lots of Michigan in the first two, at least.

SCHRADER: It's where I come from. It's what I know. I know Los Angeles a little bit now—that sort of tony world of *Gigolo* is one that I aspired to and one that I coveted. In *Gigolo* I tried to make it look like Northern Italy—in the sets, the clothes, a feeling of narcissistic righteousness pervades the film. As a midwesterner from the wrong side of the tracks of Grand Rapids, Michigan, I come to Hollywood as an outsider. When you come to Hollywood you want to be part of the high life—and out of that yearning for physical things and superficial values comes this film.

BRADY: You did something similar in *Hardcore,* reporting on a world and life-style you could only be curious about back in Grand Rapids.

SCHRADER: That's one of the nice things about being a filmmaker—playing in everybody's sandbox. You get to be a black auto worker for a while; then a midwestern businessman, or a porno hustler, or a gigolo, a boxer. You get to hang around different kinds of people.

BRADY: I like the prostitutes in your writing. How do you do research on prostitutes, pornography and such?

SCHRADER: Hookers are both more *and* less interesting than what one would expect. A lot of the time hookers get paid to talk. A man can say anything he wants because he paid somebody for the talk, he knows that the listener will never repeat it, and that she doesn't really care. It's a very proletarian form of therapy. It's an occasion for truth to come out. An average American would never dream of paying fifty dollars to a shrink, but he will pay fifty dollars to a hooker and after he gets a fifteen-minute blow job or fuck, he'll sit and tell her his problems for forty-five minutes. Those make some very good moments to explore dramatically.

BRADY: The underside of life, the seamy nightlife, seems to be a strong card in the film world of Paul Schrader.

SCHRADER: I feel comfortable with it. I generally feel more relaxed in bars than in restaurants. But that has to do with hiding and the freedom that comes from being hidden, being anonymous.

BRADY: The late Alex Jacobs once observed in *New Times* that in the so-called New Hollywood "most of the young writers one meets are straight out of universities. They've never worked, they come from middle-class homes. They have been in film school, which seems to me the worst possible training, given the sort of film schools one sees in America." This would seem to include writers very much like yourself. Jacobs concluded that writers of the thirties and forties "had a vast variety of other jobs and experiences before they came to make films," and that because of these experiences "they were great raconteurs, and this was one of the gifts they brought along with them." Do you ever feel somewhat shortchanged in raw work and living experiences for the job?

SCHRADER: I knew Alex Jacobs rather well. And I agree with

him. Going from film school to films is a liability—something is lost. When I spoke earlier of the dogmatic, dialectical quality of my writing—that's what I was referring to. Screenwriting should be part of the oral tradition—good storytelling—and it hasn't been sufficiently realized in what I've been doing. I'm still washing this question out in my own mind. I find that on the one hand it's nice to be Damon Runyon, and on the other it's nice to be an intellectual stylist. I'm on both sides right now, and I don't know what the answer is for myself.

BRADY: Thomas Wolfe said a writer can't go home again; yet you return to Grand Rapids regularly. How's the going back there?

SCHRADER: I don't go back too much anymore. I went back recently to speak at my college because they asked me. But I don't have any people back there since my mother died in 1979. In fact, after her funeral I realized that there was no reason to go back anymore. It's history now. I had very little feeling when I went back to talk at my college. I remembered it, but the feelings were all gone.

BRADY: *Hardcore* has a rich slice of Grand Rapids in it. In fact, you used some townspeople you knew as extras when filming there. Can you tell me about the genesis of that script?

SCHRADER: Well, George C. Scott ended up doing it, but there was a whole series of drafts before it got that far. I sold a first draft to Warner Bros. Then I did a rewrite for Warners. Then Warren Beatty was going to produce and star in it, so I did a rewrite for him. Then Beatty dropped out and it turned around to Columbia. Then I did a draft for them. Then when Scott became involved, I did a draft for George. Throughout all of this John Milius was the producer. I originally sold the idea with John as producer so I could get it financed as my first directed film (in which he would also act as backup director).

So I had the first draft, which I called The Milius; the second, which I called The MacElwain, because Guy MacElwain was then the executive at Warners who bought it; the third, which I called The Beatty; and finally, The Scott. It kept shifting, and once we cast the lead I had to hone in on it all over again. By the time this was worked out, I had already directed *Blue Collar,* and *Hardcore* was my second film.

BRADY: It may sound like an obvious question, but going from Warren Beatty to George C. Scott just visually is quite a shift. How did you handle it?

SCHRADER: Well, you don't have to worry so much about changing dialogue, because you write dialogue loose enough so that any actor can make it work for him. Obviously George can handle long speeches—but so can Warren. I've never had the problem, say, of rewriting for Charles Bronson—in which I'd have to go in and shorten up a lot of speeches. George can read huge hunks of dialogue and make them play. And strangely enough, the scene in the script that was quintessentially Beatty worked very well with Scott—a scene I added for Warren that I took right out of a discussion with him. There's a short scene where Jake is talking with an art designer for his furniture company about changing the color of a set for a furniture display. He wants her to change the tone of the blue, and she doesn't want to. And he slowly gets her to change her mind, wheedles her around to his position. That's exactly the way Beatty works and thinks, and it's almost word for word the conversation I had with Warren. But with Scott, it worked very well, too.

When I rewrote the script for Warren, I changed the daughter to a wife, and I added a number of elements that were roughly related to Warren's life. I took all those out for Scott. The composite version, which is *after* The Beatty, kept the good parts of the Beatty version, but reinstated much material from the original script, and was pretty close to the one that was sold to Guy MacElwain.

BRADY: Why did Beatty change his mind?

SCHRADER: A better question is, Why did he *want* to do it?, because it certainly was not suited to him. I think he was intrigued by the idea of playing a role that would capitalize on his own backlash. But after we had the script in the shape that was acceptable to him, he gave it to a number of directors, and I think that they convinced him that it really was not suited to him. And so he dropped out of it.

BRADY: You said Beatty's "backlash." What sort of things would be incorporated in the script to account for that?

SCHRADER: Well, he loved the idea of playing the continent man instead of a man of the continent. Just taking his reputation and turning it on its ear, playing directly against his reputation. It tickled him enormously. But he finally decided not to.

BRADY: What was the story with *Rolling Thunder?*

SCHRADER: I can tell you what *I* had in mind, but that's not the film you saw.

BRADY: What did you have in mind? The script was much discussed.

SCHRADER: I had in mind a script about a man, a POW who was shot down on one of his first missions in Vietnam. He comes back a hero, but he feels guilty about being a hero because he never killed anybody. He gets a chance to become a hero in that he is very much a racist and his hatred of the Vietcong is displaced by racism against Mexican Americans. He's from the Texas border area, and so his DMZ becomes the border; he crosses over it, and he kills a lot of people with different color skins. Now the filmmakers, and particularly the actor, I am told, were very queasy and unwilling to play a racist character.

BRADY: William Devane?

SCHRADER: Devane. And in making the character more normal, they no longer had a movie about a racist, but a racist movie. There's a distinction. What they did would have been equivalent to giving Travis Bickle in *Taxi Driver* a dog. You take away his sickness, you take away the meaning from the movie. You then had a sick movie about a normal person rather than a sane movie about a sick person.

BRADY: A story that's often repeated is that Twentieth couldn't release it because of a violent scene featuring a hand in a garbage disposal.

SCHRADER: Well, not that Twentieth couldn't—Twentieth *wouldn't*. Twentieth had problems with its image releasing this picture. They sold it to AIP. Twentieth got every dime out of the picture they had in it. They didn't take a loss at all. They just preferred to have someone else release it. That garbage disposal scene stayed in the picture. It's just that Twentieth Century-Fox didn't care to take the rap that the film was probably going to get. But AIP didn't give a fuck. You can't rap AIP.

BRADY: The story I heard is that some preview audiences reacted negatively to the violence.

SCHRADER: They had preview audiences that just about beat everybody up from what I hear. But they also showed in that preview a very graphic version of the film, to see what the reaction was. Well, they got the reaction. They subsequently previewed it in the released version and got a more favorable reaction.

BRADY: How far did you go with that film?

SCHRADER: I met the director once for about five minutes and never met Devane. Do you mean how far *would* I have gone with it?

BRADY: Yes.

SCHRADER: I was going to direct *Rolling Thunder* at one point. I had cast it, scouted locations, budgeted it. I was all set to go at Columbia. Well, I sold it originally to AIP. Larry Gordon was at AIP, and he wanted to do it. He moved over to Columbia. AIP decided not to do it. Gordon bought it from AIP. The head of Columbia had given me permission to make a first film as a director, and I was going to star Richard Jordan. Larry, strangely enough, backed out of it as producer because it was cross-collateralized with a film he had just finished called *Hard Times,* which he thought he was going to make a lot of money on. He didn't want any potential loss on *Rolling Thunder* to eat into the profits of *Hard Times.* He went to Columbia and asked that they be uncrossed. Columbia says, "Why do we make a deal with you to cross your pictures if you want to uncross the first one?" He subsequently fell out with the people at Columbia and moved his whole deal over to Twentieth. (*Hard Times,* by the way, did *not* make the money that he had anticipated.) Well, then Twentieth decided to make *Rolling Thunder,* but without me. And with Devane. They made it, they financed it, and then they decided not to release it—they ended up selling it back to AIP to release it, which is who I sold the script to in the first place.

BRADY: It sounds like an Abbott and Costello routine.

SCHRADER: Every film has a similar story—but not all are as pristine in their circularity. Every film has a serpentine progress. Nothing is simple or direct. It falls in and out of many hands.

BRADY: Did you run into much of this when you had your own company at Columbia producing and developing scripts for other writers?

SCHRADER: Yes. It was a lot of work that I didn't care for, and they wanted me to continue, but it was hard to concentrate on promoting my own scripts when I was also promoting half a dozen other writers. It was tiring, but also very educational— learning how to function as an executive. I left that and made an agreement at Paramount instead.

BRADY: And what happened to the scripts that you were shepherding along at Columbia?

SCHRADER: A couple of close misses, but nothing came of them. One of them Bo Derek wanted to do, but Orion Productions didn't think she would be hot. They thought *"10"* was going to go in the toilet. Sometimes you guess wrong.

BRADY: You once did four screenplays in a year. What writing pace are you maintaining these days?

SCHRADER: I've directed a film every year since then—since 1976—and I wrote *Raging Bull* in the middle of all that. Now I'm researching and getting ready to write another script, a working-class picture in a rock and roll environment in east Ohio.

BRADY: What sort of work did you do on *Raging Bull?*

SCHRADER: First it was a book, and then there was a script by another writer, Mardik Martin. But Marty Scorsese, De Niro and UA didn't want to go forward with it. They asked me to come in and give it another try. I went in in 1978, researched it, interviewed the people, studied the materials, started from the beginning and wrote another script. Subsequently, it got made and I was listed in the first position.

BRADY: That inscribed photo from Scorsese and De Niro on your wall back in L.A. speaks optimistically of working on "the next one" after your collaboration on *Taxi Driver*. Were you satisfied with the way your screenplay was handled on the screen in *Raging Bull?*

SCHRADER: Well, I reworked something that was already there, but I think a lot of what I wrote is in the movie. The Mardik Martin script began as a street picture, a *Mean Streets* kind of thing, but it didn't have a clear enough theme. After Marty and Bobby came to me, I was able to give the script a strong sense of character in Jake and a clear sense of what the movie was about by using Jake's brother Joey, who wasn't in the script before, as an echo board for LaMotta.

BRADY: What prompted you to bring Joey into the script? That would seem to be a major addition.

SCHRADER: There was no Joey in the first script, nor was he in Jake's biography—because of the family problems that are now detailed in the movie. The falling out that occurs in the movie occurred in real life though, and I also found out that they were *both* good boxers. Joey, though, had a different way with people —he was sociable, good-looking, could talk and had a line of gab. Jake couldn't. Joey got out of the fight game and managed his brother. The only thing Jake was any good at was taking punishment. That was his hallmark as a boxer. I thought that was an interesting tool for a director to work with—each brother acting as a surrogate for the other—so that's where I took the screenplay, and I wrote it into a monocular theme film.

After I left, it took on a slightly different bent. The two scripts got merged by De Niro and Scorsese so that now, when you see *Raging Bull,* you see both of those elements very strongly: It is a sociological film about the Little Italy neighborhood, and it is also a psychological study of Jake LaMotta. It bounces back and forth between those two. In that sense, it is a very shared credit, for both the *Mean Streets* and the *Taxi Driver* elements are mixed up in a bewildering jumble. The movie is very good, that's for sure; but that's all I really want to say about the film.

BRADY: When projects get changed or, worse, get nowhere, doesn't this part of the business leave you a bit dispirited?

SCHRADER: Not at all. It's interesting, this business and how to get things financed. If I wanted to be *just* a writer, I could be just a writer very easily. I am not a writer. I am a *screen*writer, which is half a filmmaker. I can't *be* a writer because words are not my code—words and sentences and punctuation. My code is far more elaborate. It has to deal with images, montage, cinematography, editing, sound, music. You have to think in far different terms than a writer does. My words are not up there on the screen. What is up there is a collection of talents, and if you want to get in movies you can't think like a writer. If I wanted to be a writer I would not be writing screenplays, that's for sure.

I want to be a filmmaker; therefore, I *can* write screenplays. If you want to make a good *living,* you *can* be that bastardized thing called the screenwriter. But it is *not* an art form, because screenplays are not works of art. They are invitations to others to collaborate on a work of art, but they are not in themselves works of art.

BRADY: You've had this goal to be much more than a screen-writer, even when you were just writing screenplays.

SCHRADER: I was never just writing screenplays for very long. In fact, I spent a year trying to finance myself as a director on my first screenplay, *Pipeliner,* which never got made. From there I did *The Yakuza, Taxi Driver* and *Déjà Vu (Obsession).* Then in *Rolling Thunder* I started trying to direct again. So it was only about a year there where I was writing scripts I wasn't trying to direct.

BRADY: The road has been short and quick, hasn't it?

SCHRADER: I have not had a hard time. I've taken lumps in losing the directing of *Rolling Thunder.* I lost *Hardcore* for a while, for about a year when Beatty took over. And though I've had one script that is everything I wanted it to be—*Taxi Driver* —I've also had scripts become less than what I'd hoped they would become.

As a director I now know that when you are putting a film together, all you can see are things you didn't do: the shots you weren't able to get, the problems with actors which inhibited certain performances, the lack of creativity you expressed on certain days. It all comes right back on the Movieola to haunt you. You've long dispensed with what is good with the scene. You don't even *see* what is good in the scene anymore.

I hope I make the quantum leaps in writing that I feel I have made in directing. In *Blue Collar* I taught myself how to direct a movie. *Now* I think I know how to direct a movie. But *Blue Collar* is really a *coordinated* movie: I got the money, I got everybody there, I got the actors, I got the scenes, I managed it *all*. But my work as a director was not extraordinary. I just *directed* it, set up the scenes in an interesting way, and hopefully the performances and the story made up for any lack of imagination on the director's part. I have a few interesting shots, but it's not exceptional. It's as well directed, say, as The Movie of the Week, you know. It was a very interesting script with rich characters in good performances, and it didn't need to be a tour de force of directing.

BRADY: You sound a little harsh on yourself.

SCHRADER: I hope the day never comes in which I am not. You can't afford *not* to be harsh on yourself, because there are too many people who are willing to let you get off easy in this business. Especially if you meet with some success. You are very soon surrounded by people who tell you that you are intuitively and irrevocably talented, and it's very easy to believe them. And that's when your work starts to decline in quality.

BRADY: You strike me as being a fighter. Someone who's had self-confidence in his work from Go. Can you fight the fights that you've fought and succeed in this business?

SCHRADER: Yes. One of the problems in the motion picture business is that the survivors are not necessarily the artists. It's very much like politics in that way. And the things which make one survive as a politician, the qualities that make one win elections, are not necessarily qualities that make one a good politician; therefore, many of our finest politicians don't have the stamina, the backroom sensibility to become politicians. They end up as college presidents or teachers or whatever.

Same thing in the movie business. Many guys are able to push and elbow their way up to the top, scrounge out financing, put together difficult arcane packages—and make very banal, mediocre, uninteresting films. Because *that's* not what they're really good at. What they are good at is *getting* to that point where they *can* make a film. And the rare film artist is a man like, to my mind, Francis Coppola, who is equally good at the infighting and at the filmmaking. I mean, there aren't any Emily Dickinsons in filmmaking. The retiring types simply don't get a start today.

BRADY: When did you first realize that? Or has it always been a part of you?

SCHRADER: It's a fact of life when you have to be a writer. It doesn't take very long to realize that.

BRADY: And yet your background is rather uncalloused. Non-Hollywood certainly. You saw your first movie at seventeen, and had a rather Calvinist upbringing in Michigan. Did you undergo a sea change?

SCHRADER: I think everything in my background is advantageous for me. I am very happy with it. The first twenty or so pages of *Hardcore* are essentially autobiographical. That is, I did go to Twelfth Street Christian Reformed Church. And those really are my uncles. And that Christmas reunion—all those scenes really did happen. Our church believes in the "TULIP," you know—all those doctrines that Jake spells out to Niki the prostitute in *Hardcore*. TULIP is an anagram that comes from the Canons of Dort. Every letter stands for a different belief.

T stands for Total Depravity—that is, all men, through original sin, are totally evil and incapable of good. "All my works are like flighty rags in the sight of the Lord."

U is for Unconditional Election. God has chosen a certain number of people to be saved, the Elect, and He has chosen them from the beginning of time.

L is for Limited Atonement. Only a limited number will be atoned, will go to heaven.

I is for Irresistible Grace. God's grace cannot be resisted or denied.

And P is for the Perseverance of the Saints. Once you are in Grace you cannot fall from the number of the Elect. That's the "TULIP."

That whole side of it's true. What is beneficial about my up-bringing is that it was hard knocks in terms of the traditional disciplines. At Calvin College they were great believers in education, so in order to graduate you had to take a lot of theology, a lot of philosophy. You got a classical education in that sense, which I am very happy with. But, more importantly, going to Calvin College gave you a real sense of who *you* are because you know who *they* are. *They* is very clear. They are the church society structure. They tell you not only how to live—they tell you how to think. In order to fight that, you find out who you are very quickly. And you find you are who you are because you are not *them*. It is a rare treat to have a firm definition of *them*—that is, to live in a place where you know who the bad guys are. I think one of the fears that Russian dissidents have about leaving Russia is that you lose a sense of who the bad guys are. It's very hard to redefine one's life when that's taken away. All through college I was able to define what I had to do in terms of what they *wanted* me to do. Now, for me, the gospel's changed, but the zealotry hasn't; the need to promote, to preach.

Therefore, I have a firm notion of who I am because I know what I was. What that background gave me is invaluable. It gave me a sense of place and a sense of mission. I'd wish it on anyone. If I had a child, I would want my child to go through the very same thing. On the other hand, it did squash some people. Some friends of mine got sort of crushed by the notion that they couldn't beat the system. But the system is always beatable. You just have to learn to outwit it. Make it think it wants what *you* want.

People have asked me, isn't it hard to wheel and deal in the movie business? And I say I've never felt that at all, because if you have lived twenty-one years, as I did, with mind-control people—who want to establish the way you *think,* much less act —it's very *easy* to deal with people in Hollywood who just want you to do certain things to help them make money. They don't want to change the way you think. They don't want to change the way you live. They just want to change the way you write.

You can work and deal and twist and negotiate with *these* people. That's easy in comparison to having been raised by people who want to determine what your private thoughts are.

BRADY: You said the gospel has changed. Zealotry goes on. What has it changed to?

SCHRADER: Certainly I was raised to be a minister, though I am not preaching orthodox Christianity. What I am preaching is a certain moral vision which has roots in that. And everything that I do is sort of intertwined with the notion of sin, guilt, blood, redemption, grace. (Grace has been getting a short shrift in the last several years, but eventually the notion of grace will get its due place.)

BRADY: So you feel that your work as a writer, director, filmmaker is still structured along theological and Calvinistic lines?

SCHRADER: Yeah. *Taxi Driver* is the script I am most proud of. It is waist-deep in Calvinistic notions of worthlessness, purging, blood, redemption. It's all tied up in that script.

BRADY: There are many parallels between *Taxi Driver* and *Hardcore*. The protagonist Jake in *Hardcore* has a sense of powerful mission. Although his broodings are not as subliminal as Travis Bickle's are in *Taxi Driver*, Jake also has an explosion at the end. There are young prostitutes in both films, too. Their names are even similar.

SCHRADER: Jake is a man of great moral strength. He has at the beginning of the picture solved his problems, he thinks. But as he opens doors that he was told not to open, things come rattling out of closets. The character in *Taxi Driver* is a terrified little mouse of a man. And nothing is resolved in his brain. His brain is being torn apart by contradictions. He uses a purging of blood to give his life definition—whereas the character in *Hardcore* has a life with a great deal of definition and purpose, and the violence is a reaction against the forces which threaten that definition. *Taxi Driver* is more twisted and complex but less instructive; *Hardcore* is more straightforward and far more instructive.

Blue Collar is also an extremely instructive film. It's almost like a lesson.

BRADY: Where did the idea of *Blue Collar* come from? That has some Michigan to it, too.

SCHRADER: Because the car companies are there. I was talking with an aspiring screenwriter who was having some trouble—a black guy—and he started talking about his father, who used to work in one of the auto plants. It struck me as a very interesting notion—a film that needed to be written about blacks in auto plants. I sort of dwelled on that subject, and a rather basic thought started to form: a story about friendship and three guys. It needed some sort of action to define it, to define their lives. What better thing to define their lives than to have them rob their own union? It is symbolic self-negation. And then you proceed with the consequences there.

BRADY: How did you go about casting it?

SCHRADER: Well, I went to Richard Pryor even before I wrote it. I knew him through a mutual friend. I told him what I had in mind and asked him if he would be interested, and he said he would be. And I knew Harvey Keitel. So I wrote it with Richard and Harvey in mind. I went back to Richard, and he said that the script was everything I had promised and that he would commit to it. He did it for about one-third of what he was getting otherwise. Harvey agreed to do it. And then I went to Norman Lear's T.A.T. Productions and got them to bankroll the three of us and got Universal to pick up the film. It took a while. It obviously was not the kind of film that anyone would jump at.

BRADY: How do you research a film like that, which has a certain amount of technology as a backdrop?

SCHRADER: You go talk to people who work in the plants. Research is not a big thing with me. I don't think it should be with any screenwriter because it's very hard to make errors in research if you are doing a contemporary piece. You can set a scene in L.A. and write: "A red and white police car pulls up," and you know damn well when they go to shoot that scene they aren't going to paint that police car red and white just because you wrote it. They are going to say, "Well, police cars are black and white." So you can't really make that kind of mistake, because it will get corrected.

In *Obsession* I set a scene in a church in Florence which was subsequently torn down. I set it in that church because I read an old tour guide book. The director called me up from Florence and said, "The church has been torn down." And I said, "Well, what are you going to do, rebuild it? Let's find another one!" Research is not as important as you think it is to a writer. What you need to give is a sense of feel and texture. But when they start locations, *that's* where the research really has to come in.

BRADY: Is your writing then usually a creative burst? *Taxi Driver* was written fast, I know.

SCHRADER: Yes. I had all the streets wrong in *Taxi Driver*. The script was full of mistakes when I sold it. It had blue cabs and red cabs when all the cabs in New York were yellow. And the hotels were on the wrong streets. Everything was all screwed up factually. Of course, when you come to making a film you fix all that up. You do the research then. Research can often become an excuse for a writer not to write. You keep doing research until all the desire to write the material is passed. It's the difference between those who want to write and those who want to *be* writers, as Faulkner once said.

BRADY: When you were studying to be a minister, when did you realize that was not you?

SCHRADER: Obviously, I was sort of chafing under the bit. And movies became a logical way to revolt because they were both art *and* forbidden. It was better than setting off firecrackers in the dorm. I got interested in movies mostly as a method of revolt rather than as movies per se. I started a film group up there. And the films that I screened at Calvin were films not intended to enlighten but to disrupt. Films that I knew would just really shake the hell out of everybody.

The film group was a *sub rosa* outfit. After I was a senior, they legitimized it because I had been robbing them blind. The film group was technically illegal; therefore I could pocket the profits. Finally, since they couldn't *stop* the film group, they decided to make it legal—with the provision that I not be involved in it. Then I moved on to the school newspaper and got into journalism. They threw me out from there, too.

BRADY: Why did they throw you out?

SCHRADER: We did a couple of things they didn't approve of. We used school funds to march on the Pentagon in October of 1967. Connived school funds to send off three or four buses. They didn't like that. And we were relentlessly attacking the administration. Finally it became more than they could handle, and they shut down the paper.

BRADY: What was the attitude of your parents through these years?

SCHRADER: Not one of approval. My parents would have preferred that I be an obscure deacon in a church in Frostbite Falls than a screenwriter in Hollywood. Better to be a fly on the walls of heaven than a prince in hell. So they weren't that happy. I think they did derive some satisfaction in that I became financially successful. "So he has made a mess of his life. At least he's making money. At least he's not a junkie."

BRADY: The Calvinistic success ethic?

SCHRADER: "Granted, it's nothing to be proud of, but at least he makes money out of it."

BRADY: What was the first movie that you saw? Surely you must have seen TV movies when you were young.

SCHRADER: Well, TV was a problem. As I was growing up, there was a debate in the church: They were trying to keep TV out. They weren't able to do it, and when TV *did* come in, it undermined the church position. *Hardcore* is full of that. TV bringing down the church values. There are three or four references to TV eating away the fabric of the community. The value system of the outside world shot straight into the homes. After TV there was no way to keep the outside out. If you didn't let your kids watch it, your kids went to the neighbor's house and watched it.

BRADY: And when did you make your quantum leap as a filmgoer?

SCHRADER: I think I saw one or two films in high school. I was brainwashed by watching the "Mickey Mouse Club" as a kid, so I went out and saw *The Absent-Minded Professor*. Snuck in. Not snuck in, but tried to get in so nobody could see me going in.

With a couple of friends. We were all quite disappointed. There was nothing nearly as sinful as we had been led to believe.

BRADY: Does the *lack* of moviegoing in your background give you problems, or is it an advantage as a screenwriter?

SCHRADER: Absolutely an advantage, because I don't see movies as anything special. They're just another medium to communicate in. If I didn't get involved in movies, I would find some other way to communicate. I think kids who are *raised* on movies have a special mystical sense of what movies are, which is a lot of baloney. Somehow young kids sort of *believe* in movies. How can you believe in movies any more than you *believe* in the telephone? It's a *tool* that you can use. Also, when other kids were sitting in darkened theaters being fed pablum, I was reading and engaged in more stimulating pursuits.

BRADY: You have brought an element to screenwriting that is highly original. Do you see yourself as part of a continuum? Are there influences, literary or otherwise, in lieu of film predecessors?

SCHRADER: No, no. Not really. Except for *Raging Bull,* I've not done any rewrites or adaptations—and you can make a lot of money that way. And it's easy money. And, with one exception, I have written all my scripts on spec, which is hard to do, too, because sometimes when you write scripts on spec nothing happens to them. You can write a script that someone else wants you to write for a hundred and twenty-five thousand dollars for a first draft, or you write something original you want, and you end up selling it for thirty thousand dollars because nobody will pay any more for it—or not sell it at all. You have to learn to live with that, especially if you have written a couple of scripts on spec and not sold them. You get scared, and you start taking the money.

But I am still writing on spec, and I am very happy that I have been able to continue that. I just find that the reason I am writing scripts is undermined by the Hollywood screenwriting tradition of adaptations, rewrites and assignments. I don't know anybody else who works the way I do, except for one or two first scripts —and then they quit. But my reasons for writing are greatly damaged by that system, and I am afraid that if I get into that system I'd lose my originality. Because I am not that great a writer per se. My *writing* is not that much better than anyone else's writing. If I had to live as a stylist or as a rewriter, I would be one of one hundred guys. But as an *idea* man, as a creator of original screen stories, I'm relatively unique. And I'm smart enough to stay at what I'm unique at. There's less competition.

BRADY: You had a rather publicized three-hundred-thousand-dollar sale the first time out with *Yakuza*.

SCHRADER: That was a lucky thing, and I milked the publicity out of it as hard as I could because it enabled me to create the momentum which has put me where I am now. Because money and power are interchangeable commodities in this business. I think of money as an extension of power. I love to get huge salaries, not because I need the money, or want to own a lot of shit. But I love to make money, because that's power. And every time your name and picture appear in the national media, the cash register rings. And the more money you make, the more power you have.

People are going to respect a writer they pay two hundred and fifty thousand dollars to for a script a lot more than a writer they pay fifty thousand. They are going to take your opinion a lot more seriously if they pay you more money, because they can't think of themselves as having made a mistake. If you establish a reputation as being a six-figure writer, you can also come in and say, "Well, I will write this, and I will sell this to you for much less provided I can direct it." The reason I was able to get *Blue Collar* on was that we did it cheaply. People thought they were getting a bargain. You can only use that lever if you keep your price up to a certain level—so every year or two you have to make a killing. It's just like movie stars and athletes. You have to come through every once in a while to keep your price up. I sold *American Gigolo* to Paramount for two hundred and fifty thousand. That's good. It keeps the value up of what I am doing, so that I can sell things cheaper—and make them more valuable to myself.

As it turned out, I was later hired, in a separate agreement, to direct *Gigolo,* which is the flip side of *Taxi Driver.* It's about a man who's compulsively sexual. The difference is that at the end of *Taxi Driver* you have an explosion. At the end of *American Gigolo* you have an *im*plosion. The *non*sexual man bursts out. The sexual man bursts in. It's a different thing.

BRADY: You once spoke of Travis Bickle and the lack of sophistication in an American society that has people opening a window and firing out when perhaps they should be firing into themselves.

SCHRADER: It's just my feeling that Travis is a familiar character in international literature. But if he were French he would, like the character in *Le Feu Follet,* put the gun to his head and shoot himself. But in America he acts out his personal drama on the stage of *other* people's lives and forces other people to go through what *he* is going through, which is a very selfish and aggressive and frontiersmanlike thing to do. Not very mature. It's a reflection of the immaturity of the national personality.

BRADY: And *American Gigolo* is a portrait of someone who has Don Juan characteristics? How are they destructive?

SCHRADER: Well, Julian is a servicer of sexual needs, and he's a drifter. He has to fight the emptiness in himself the same as Travis in *Taxi Driver* does. But he fights it by actually dealing with someone. And his problem is he is unable to accept pleasure or love. He can only *give* it. The final sacrifice he can make is to accept someone else's love, which he does. There are no fireworks at the end. There is something equally shattering, which is the *acceptance* of someone else.

BRADY: Your use of the camera in *American Gigolo* is often quite cerebral. Anyone seeing the film is aware of its lingering quality, and its angular use in scenes. I am thinking of that moment when the camera pauses on the Parke-Bernet Gallery, for instance, after Julian and the woman he is escorting have left the scene. They move off to the left, but the camera stays there—momentary, but deliberate.

SCHRADER: It's a track and a back-pan. They are coming out the door, and you're tracking toward them; then they move to the left, and you're back-panning—that is, panning against the track, away from your subjects. Then they leave and you just hold the frame. Then we cut to the shot of three white chairs on brickwork—another static frame. Then that moves out and Julian is sitting at the pool. We use two frozen frames—one from the previous scene, then one from the next scene. One comes from movement, and one goes into movement.

BRADY: There is also a stationary shot of the car going across a bridge when Julian travels from L.A. to Palm Springs. It's almost like a painted surface on which the car alone is moving.

SCHRADER: With *Gigolo* I was really trying to think visually a lot, trying to say things with images more than with words. Fernando Scarfiotti, the production designer, had a lot to do with this, too, as you can see from his work in Visconti's and Bertolucci's films. We wanted to make Los Angeles look like some place it's never looked like before.

BRADY: Why did you pay so much attention to the trip to Palm Springs?

SCHRADER: Primarily because it came immediately after a long dialogue scene in the Polo Lounge. That's why I used the helicopter shot. It was just time to lay back, play some music, and give you a sense of this guy again on the move in his car in his precision world. There's a five- or six-minute scene ahead of it, two people sitting, not moving, in the Polo Lounge. After it's over, you want some movement.

BRADY: Toward the end of *Gigolo,* there are several long takes with fade-out/fade-ins separating them—quite a change in tempo for the film. What was your thinking here?

SCHRADER: Yes, this device upset a lot of viewers, and some people at the studio. It was a very intentional device to stop the movie. To stop it cold. Boom. To knock you out of the movie, and to create this other little spacy movie that occurs at the end —in blue rooms, and prison, and it's fade out, fade in. It's taken from the end of Bresson's *Pickpocket,* which operates that way. It's a very intentional device to distance the viewer from what he has just seen. The reason a lot of people don't like it is exactly the reason it was put in there: to knock them out of the movie. They didn't know if the movie was over, they didn't know what was going on, they got confused. But that's what was intended —to sort of take the movie into space. I loved it.

BRADY: The first credit after the movie ends is Fernando Scarfiotti, Visual Consultant. How does a visual consultant work with you on a picture?

SCHRADER: Nando is a foreigner, and the union wouldn't let him in. Thus, the credit at the end. Scarfiotti was production designer for *Last Tango in Paris, The Conformist, Death in Venice,* three of Visconti's operas, *Daisy Miller*—I think he's the best in the world. He's doing a film with John Schlesinger now, and he won't get a credit on that one either because the unions don't want him.

BRADY: What decisions does he help you with? Camera setups?

SCHRADER: Not so much camera setups, but everything else that contributes to the look of things: locales, building of sets, color schemes, clothing schemes, lighting schemes—everything. Most of the rooms for *Gigolo* were built: Julian's apartment; the house in Palm Springs—I mean, no one could *live* in a place like that, it was so bizarre; the house at the beach; the lineup room for the police scenes; the visiting area in jail; the Polo Lounge— all of these sets, these spaces were built by Scarfiotti for an overall look and feeling. If he were to do the room that we are in now, he would do the shape of the room, the furnishings, the lighting, the clothing we are wearing—everything. And if he comes to the set and something has been moved, he will get very upset.

BRADY: When Julian writes his phone number on the forehead of the guy who is following him, it's a palindrome, the same frontward and backward: 636-1636. Is there any significance to that?

SCHRADER: I didn't realize that. We got the number from the studio legal department; they have to clear all such numbers.

BRADY: Were you mindful of Jay Gatsby's shirts, which he tossed on his bed for Daisy, in the scene where Julian dresses and packs for the trip to Palm Springs? It seems to be shot very much in that spirit.

SCHRADER: Someone else mentioned that to me. *Gatsby* is a book that I read way back in high school, and I don't know it too well. The more influential text, I would say, is *The Red and the Black*. That's why he is named Julian, and why there is a restaurant called Sorel—after the character in *Red and Black*, Julian Sorel. As for the dressing scene—the shirts and ties on the bed —Julian is an artist, and that is his palette, and he is his own object. He is looking over the colors of his palette, creating his object of art: himself.

BRADY: How did you decide to use Julian's interest in various languages as a characteristic in the film?

SCHRADER: Julian is an *American* gigolo, sort of the Horatio Alger of sex. He is not your conventional gigolo, the layabout type who waits for people to pay his bills. No, he's the American gigolo who goes out, works hard, studies and improves himself. He's the All-American Boy, pride of the new land—a character who longs to be more than what he is at present. And part of his self-improvement—to be a companion, guide, chauffeur, translator, confidant—is the study of languages.

BRADY: Julian seems a little dim-witted to me, despite the attempts at language.

SCHRADER: I didn't ever think of him that way. I think of him as someone who is pliable, who plays many roles. So when he's in the hotel room and opening the champagne for the woman, he's playing the pool boy—"Aw, gee!," talking like a kid. Somewhere else he plays a different role. He is these many things. He often plays the innocent as well. But those are all roles.

BRADY: And we don't see his true self until the very end?

SCHRADER: I don't know if you see it even then. His "true self" is probably some vague sense of wanting to go somewhere, be somebody. He has a feeling that he'd like to be somebody, that he can be important; but he doesn't know quite how. As he says, "All my life I've been looking for something." But he doesn't know what it is.

BRADY: When John Travolta withdrew from the role of Julian

in *American Gigolo,* you told the press it was "an act of emotional and physical self-preservation." What happened when you were casting your screenplay?

SCHRADER: When I sold the script, there was no director. Someone suggested that Richard Gere be the star. I met with him and thought it was a good idea, but nothing came of it. Later, Travolta got involved, and I came in as director about the same time. When John dropped out, I went back to Gere.

BRADY: Why did Travolta drop out?

SCHRADER: He was terrified. Things were coming much too fast. His mother had just died; he was trying to deal with the *Moment by Moment* debacle; he had qualms about this role in *Gigolo*—he just wasn't ready to work.

BRADY: I understand that Travolta's contract called for approval of the movie's final cut.

SCHRADER: We had worked out some sort of weird mutual final cut, which was a lot of hooey. One of the nice things about John dropping out is I didn't have to deal with that.

BRADY: Was Julian's frontal nudity in the original screenplay? Was this a stumbling block in the casting?

SCHRADER: No, that decision was made on the spot. It's a longish scene, just too boring to do in bed, and somebody had to get up and walk around. So as we were blocking it out, I said something's got to happen here. Somebody's got to get out of bed, and it's going to look kind of dumb if you get out with your drawers on. It didn't bother Richard at all, so I had him walk from the bed to the window. I thought that was a good idea because the film is about a male sex object, and you should show his body at one time or another. For the sake of the film, it was something we had to do and get out of the way. So it was a director-writer's decision, with the actor's consent.

BRADY: Where do your titles come from? They are often striking.

SCHRADER: I try to find something that has a salesmanlike quality. I'm not happy with all of them. I'm not happy with *Blue Collar.* I just was unable to find anything I liked better. I find it very hard to sit down to write unless I have a title, because if you have the title, the image goes back and forth in your mind when you write.

BRADY: Why was the title *Déjà Vu* changed to *Obsession?*

SCHRADER: The money people didn't think anybody would understand what it meant. I thought they were wrong, but they changed it.

BRADY: You've been rewritten a *few* times. Robert Towne did some rewriting on *Yakuza.*

SCHRADER: Yeah, and *Rolling Thunder* was rewritten.

BRADY: And *Obsession.*

SCHRADER: Yeah, but not my writing. It was rewritten by the director, which is a different thing. I mean there was no credit to another writer.

BRADY: But didn't Brian De Palma take part in the screenwriting credit?

SCHRADER: He took part of the *story* credit.

BRADY: What are the rules of war in something like that?

SCHRADER: It's all the director's decision. *Sometimes* producers decide to bring in another writer. Obviously if Marty Scorsese had wanted another writer on *Taxi Driver* he would have gotten it. Now, in *American Gigolo,* before I became director, I had a very unique clause in my contract that said another writer could not be brought into the project as long as I was able to perform that service. I was going to waive that, however, though it was nice to get a groundbreaking clause. It's not a very practical clause.

BRADY: It can tie you up while you are on other things, I assume.

SCHRADER: No, it's just not good for the picture. If the director wants another writer, let him have it. Better to have it be a *successful* film, even at a less ambitious level. Let's say, hypothetically, you have an A script, and a B director comes and says, "I need this rewritten." He brings a little B writer, who rewrites it to a B level, and he makes it a successful B film. That's better than if he had tried to attack the A material and made an unsuccessful film because he was only a B director. You have to think of collaboration. You can't protect the integrity of your work at the expense of the film. You may be getting a sense of satisfaction saying, "I didn't let them screw up my script," but the satisfaction is rather short-lived if you realize that they screwed up the movie instead.

BRADY: Has your becoming a director tempered any of your earlier attitudes toward rewriting?

SCHRADER: Absolutely. If there is no sympathy between the director and the writer, you have to bring in another writer. All you can ask is that the other people are interested in making the same movie you are. And that's actually quite rare, because often a director sees a different movie than the one you have written. And he needs a writer to write the movie he wants to direct. The rare case is one like *Taxi Driver,* where the director wants to make the movie that he has read. That's quite rare.

BRADY: Your films are noted for their violence. Are you obsessed by violence?

SCHRADER: Well, there are a couple of things to consider. One is that at the time I wrote those scripts violence was more commercially viable. Today it is not. You can't get a violent film made at the moment because of the backlash. So my violence was part of the commercial instinct. Second, it was part of the expression of the hunger, frustration, resentment of an unsuccessful artist. And thirdly, it remains tied to the whole notion of blood and redemption.

I don't feel the need to slaughter people on the screen the way I used to. I don't say that to denigrate violence on the screen, because I think violence in movies is very proper, very purgative. It *is* possible to have a gratuitously violent film. I think *Rolling Thunder* is probably a gratuitously violent film. If I had done it the way I had chosen, many people would have been killed, but it would have seemed—at least to me—less gratuitous.

BRADY: What are your notions of blood and redemption?

SCHRADER: Just that in order for guilt or sin to be purged there *has* to be some blood. Pain is a part of the process. It doesn't come through intellectual enlightenment or thought or meditation or contemplation. Somebody's got to pay. And you have to see

blood on the hands. And thorns on the forehead. Movies often
are involved with these symbolic acts. They serve the same function as the scapegoat, the Christ or other mythic figures—they
create symbols who suffer and purge your guilt.

BRADY: Do you still read the Bible?

SCHRADER: It's hard to forget it. As a child I spent the better
part of a year recopying Genesis. Part of my upbringing was to
systematically memorize as much of the Bible as you could. So
it's a little hard to forget.

BRADY: Do you still consider yourself basically religious?

SCHRADER: I would think so. Not churchgoing. I am still a
confessing member, but some years ago I asked my church to
drop me from the rolls—not because of any lack of faith; it's just
that I abhor clubs, societies and organizations of any sort. I dislike the church in the same way I dislike the Writers Guild. I hate
any kind of group that's got to tell you how to act.

BRADY: And you don't like unions?

SCHRADER: Don't like unions. But then I ain't so crazy about
management either.

BRADY: You wrote *Transcendental Style in Film,* which dwells
on how transcendental style may be used to approach The
Wholly Other. Can your violent films—*Taxi Driver, The Yakuza,
Rolling Thunder*—in any way be considered spiritual expressions?

SCHRADER: No.

BRADY: You mentioned earlier that in your early scripts you
included a certain amount of violence because it was a salable
commodity. . . .

SCHRADER: Sex and violence. When you write movies you
write for mass audiences, and the two fantasies which permeate
all levels of society are sex and violence. You know that if you
address a movie to the fantasy of sex and violence that it will
appeal to everyone of every social strata in the entire world,
whereas other fantasies tend to limit your market.

BRADY: Such as?

SCHRADER: *Blue Collar,* for example, is about the working
class, and a lot of people don't respond to that. If you make a

wonderful film like *My Night at Maud's,* about middle-class morality and religion, you know that it's a limited market. You make a film like *Death Wish,* about revenge, you can play it everywhere.

We who write for the mass media have to take these things into account because in order for your work to be valid—that is, in order for it to exist—it has to appeal to a minimum of three million people. Otherwise the screenplay will not be made into a film and therefore will not exist. So you have to ask yourself: What do you have that at *least* three million (hopefully five or ten million) people will respond to? Well, a novelist only needs a base of about fifteen to twenty thousand readers; a musician needs fifty to a hundred thousand album buyers; a painter needs several hundred. You have to judge your work by the demands of the marketplace. If you have a good idea but you don't think it is going to appeal to several million people, then you shouldn't even waste your time writing it. You have chosen the wrong medium.

Over and over again I have ideas that I have not written as screenplays because I did not feel that they would appeal to a mass market, whereas if I were a playwright I *would* have written them because I feel they would be successful on the stage. Sex and violence are all-encompassing fantasies that permeate every possible market. Screenwriting needs them more than the other forms of media—because the numbers have to be bigger.

BRADY: What about the backlash? How do you explain that?

SCHRADER: The backlash is against violence as violence. A well-made movie full of violence will make as much money now as it did in the past. It's just that there *was* a market for mediocre violence and that market is gone.

BRADY: What would you consider mediocre violence?

SCHRADER: *Black Sunday.* At one point the audience just wanted to see violent movies. Now they have turned against them. They feel a little guilty, and they want to see "upbeat" fantasies at the moment. But this will all pass too. The pendulum swings continually.

BRADY: How do you keep ahead of it?

SCHRADER: You try to tell genuine stories and create your own trends. *Taxi Driver* was not ahead or behind anything. A film like that creates its own market. I don't write scripts that capitalize on trends. On the other hand, you can't ignore trends either. You can't fly in the face of convention. I would not write a western. No western has made money since 1969 and there is a reason for that. The metaphor of the West is inappropriate at the moment; therefore, a mediocre western or even a good western will fail to make money, whereas a mediocre or good science fiction film *will* make money, because the metaphor of science fiction is more appropriate today. However, an *excellent* western will make a fortune.

As an artist, your goal is quality; trends don't mean a damn. But as a businessman, your goal is trends. Every executive, when he contemplates a script or project, never says, "If this is good, it will make money." He knows *anything,* if it is good, will make money. But he has to look at the project and say, "If this is done in a very ordinary way by very mediocre people, will it make money?" And if he feels it will, then his decision is to go forward. He's betting on a *trend.* He can never plan on a project being excellent. If he does, he will be out of a job.

BRADY: How mindful are you of ratings when making the final cut?

SCHRADER: The studios demand an R. You can't release an X. Neither *Hardcore* nor *Gigolo* are about sex, really. I've never made a movie about sex. Sex is just a device for getting to other things.

BRADY: You were once quoted as saying that you are the only one who could make *Hardcore* because you are "the last person in Hollywood who still thinks sex is dirty."

SCHRADER: I was being facetious. That's a "good quote." There's an element of truth to it, but only a small element. It's a puritanical film, a film about a puritan; yet a lot of it took place in sexual arenas. For it to be cohesive, it should have a puritanical view from the director, too. That's the small element of truth beneath the facetiousness of that answer.

BRADY: Were you being facetious, too, when you once made

some disparaging remarks about screenwriting classes? You have recently taught screenwriting yourself at UCLA, Sherwood Oaks, and Columbia.

SCHRADER: I have certain lectures worked out, and they cover my method of screenwriting: one is devoted to exposition; one to metaphor; one to plot; one to the marketplace; et cetera.

BRADY: What sort of ear do you have for dialogue? Do you find yourself listening more closely to people and blending things into your scripts?

SCHRADER: Occasionally you hear something, some conversation, that you steal. But very rarely. The way I write dialogue is, I have an idea of how long the dialogue should be—a page, two pages, three pages—how much the scene will support, and how many points I have to make in that dialogue, either expository points or character development points. Then I just start working it out, the conversation—using what seems natural to get from one point to another. If you gave me a situation with certain points that would have to be made in a scene, I would sit here and give you the dialogue. Within five, ten minutes, you would have the dialogue. All paced out. Dialogue is the easiest thing in the world.

BRADY: What's the tough part when you're writing?

SCHRADER: Getting an idea. A metaphor. Having one or two lines that describe a film—that's the hardest part. Once you get that, if you have any common sense, you can execute it. That's very cavalier of me to say, because I've run across people who have had very good ideas but who just cannot execute them for reasons that I can't understand. It seems to me that if people are given a scene, it's the easiest thing in the world to pull off the scene. But they'll write it, and it won't work. They'll rewrite it, and it won't work. I don't understand. Because to me it seems the most obvious thing in the world. How to cross the street. How do you get from here to there? It's like moving furniture. Certainly I'm being cavalier in saying it's easy. For some people, it's not that easy.

BRADY: Do you know where you're going when you sit down to write word number one in your script?

SCHRADER: Do I know where I'm going? I know *exactly*. I know to the half page if I'm on or off target. I draw up charts before I do a script. I endlessly chart and rechart a movie. Before I sit down to write, I have all the scenes listed, what happens in each scene, how many pages I anticipate each scene will take. I have a running log on the film. I can look down and see what happens by page thirty, what happens by page forty, fifty, sixty, and so forth. I have the whole thing timed out to a hundred and five, a hundred and ten pages, to what I *think* it will play, so that as I write I can tell if I'm a page ahead or behind. You may go two, three pages ahead or behind, you may add or drop dialogue or scenes; but if you're two pages ahead or behind, you have to work that into the timing. Especially if you get five pages ahead, or, worse, five pages *behind,* then something you had planned to work on page forty may not work the same way on page forty-five. Because what the audience sees as an intriguing development on page forty may be a predictable development on page forty-five. And if you start slowing down your script, you have to accommodate the fact that you're getting there five minutes later.

BRADY: So it's stopwatch writing.

SCHRADER: Completely timed out. Then on your charts you can see how the characters interplay. Like in *American Gigolo* I have the characters meet eight times in the movie, and I can see what pages they would meet on those eight times, and the different things that happen between the times they meet, so that there's always something to talk about when they meet, something to pick up, something they had discussed previously, something to develop. They don't just meet and talk. The viewer wants them to meet because things have *happened,* and the viewer wants to see how they will deal with them.

BRADY: You always have a character on the ascent.

SCHRADER: You try to time these things out. It's like running the mile. You start to recognize signposts peripherally, and you know as you're running past this house, this corner, whether you're ahead or behind your time. And if you're pushing too hard, you back off; if you're not pushing hard enough, you speed up—because you have to reach that point at the end of the mile where you are *totally* spent. If you have any energy left, you have failed; and if you run out of energy *before* the end, you have failed. You have to calculate while you're running how much reserve you have, and how much farther you have to go.

The same thing applies to writing a script. You have to calculate how much juice is left in the story and how much you've used up. If you're behind, you have to speed up; and if you're ahead, you have to go back and cut. When I block out a scene and I say three and one half pages on a scene, I'm very shocked if I write the scene and it's four, four and a half pages. It means that something new has come in. Because if I say A meets B in a restaurant, they discuss C and D, X walks in, another bit of exposition, and another event happens . . . boom, boom. I will list these things and calculate how long that will take. Then I figure out in the structure of the script how long I can support that scene. Often you'll come across a scene that you feel has enough interesting material to support four or five pages. But the structure will support only two or three. So you have to find *other* places in the movie to put that dialogue. Because the audience only wants to sit and watch that scene for about two minutes; then it wants to get on to something else. If you make them sit for five, you slow them down, and you hurt yourself. Better to cut out the good stuff, find another place for it, and keep the pace going. A viewer cannot set a movie down. He can set a book down. He can stop, take a break, pick it up later. But when a viewer is bored for three or four minutes, the movie slows down. If he's bored for *more* than three or four minutes, the movie is irreparably harmed. The flow is broken. He will never be able to accept the movie as innocently as he could before. Whereas you can bore the reader of a book, because he'll stop, or he may even skim a section if he's not interested. If you're not interested in whaling in *Moby Dick,* you can skim that section. You can't skim anything in a movie; you have to sit through it. Although I've learned to skim movies now by going out and making phone calls.

BRADY: During movies?

SCHRADER: Oh, yeah. Five, six, ten phone calls. Do all my business during bad movies.

BRADY: How visual are you as a screenwriter? Do you think of scenes expressed in terms of props and positioning?

SCHRADER: Yes, but I don't write that out in the script. I don't write "close-up" or any of that. There are code words you can use in writing that indicate shots, visual things. If you say, "He fingers the glass," that indicates a shot that would show him fingering the glass. You don't write, "He fingers the glass" unless you have that shot in mind. You can write, "From a distance he is only a figure among the cars, but seen up close, anxiety covers his face." Well, that's one sentence, but to a director it's a long shot and a close-up. Without having to say "long shot," "close-up," one can put those suggestions in the director's mind. There's nothing a director hates more than to read a script that tells him how to shoot a movie. That's his job. He isn't going to have some writer tell him when to use a close-up and when to use a long shot. What you do as a writer is *suggest* images which he will react to.

BRADY: Your scripts are very rich in characterization. But the plots are somewhat meandering; they seem to be casual.

SCHRADER: They *seem* to be casual. That "seem" is very hard to achieve. Look at *Taxi Driver*. Joan Tewkesbury, who did *Nashville*, came to me and said that *Taxi Driver* knocked her out because every scene moved the story forward, yet *seemed* to be episodic. That was the whole goal—to create a series of episodes which *look* episodic; yet every single one deals with the movie thus far, then moves the movie forward. You can't point out anything that happened in the movie that isn't tied into everything else. It *appears* to be episodic, but that appearance is not artless.

You have to try—in the structure of an hour-and-a-half movie —to arrange scenes that appear to follow each other in what *seems* to be a natural way, but is anything but natural. Because you can choose only forty, forty-five, fifty scenes to tell a story. You have to pick those fifty scenes very carefully if you're going to get a rich story.

BRADY: How do you start with an idea and build it up to forty or fifty scenes? Is there an intermediate process?

SCHRADER: You *tell* it, and you keep telling it to people at five, ten, fifteen minutes. As the story grows, you gather from their reactions whether you really have something. If you're enthused and can't seem to get somebody else enthused, you're on the wrong track. So you keep telling, and you keep feeding and working with their reactions. If during the telling of the story, the story starts to lag for a couple of minutes, you change it extemporaneously to juice it up; that is often where important story points come from. If I say, "X and Y go to Z, and Z says *Yes*," and you don't seem to be that interested—and I don't just mean in your immediate expression, I'm watching how you're sitting, how expressive your eyes are—I can tell whether you have been hooked or not. If you're not hooked, you'll reveal it nonverbally. You can't trust what everybody says. And if you see they're not hooked, you have to throw out something in order to get that hook in. You tell and retell a story till it gets to be forty-five minutes long. Then you know you have a script. Then you draw an outline of scenes.

BRADY: So you see this screenwriter initially as a raconteur rather than someone at a typewriter in an attic.

SCHRADER: Without doubt it's part of the oral tradition because it's a form of storytelling; it's not a form of literature at all. Your writing counts for nothing.

BRADY: I don't follow you on that.

SCHRADER: Counts for *nothing*. In the end it doesn't really matter whether you're a good stylist or not. A lot of very good screenwriters have been bad stylists. And a lot of extraordinary stylists have been bad screenwriters. In fact, a script in some cases need not be written down *at all*. It can exist in a *purely* oral state. So I don't know how you can call it a form of writing. The only reason it *needs* to be written down is so that it can be remembered, memorized, rewritten, sold . . . things like that.

BRADY: Well, then, do you view the screenplay as a blueprint? —a term that makes some screenwriters bristle.

SCHRADER: *At best.* I think that a blueprint is even too confining a term, because one doesn't usually change a blueprint for a house, and it's possible to change a script *in medias res*. A director can add things right in the middle of it. You can't do that to a blueprint. Can't throw in another room once you've laid out the foundation. You can lay out the foundation of a script, though, and still throw in another scene.

BRADY: You said you prefer writing short scripts. Do you think you could ever write something with the wide scope of, say, *Nashville?*

SCHRADER: I wouldn't want to, to tell you the truth. I think *Nashville* is the largest wading pool constructed by mankind. I mean, just because you cover twenty-five characters superficially doesn't mean that it's a greater accomplishment than covering *one* character superficially. It's like multiplying by zero.

BRADY: One of the current laments is the lack of "good" female roles in scripts today. Certainly your male roles are strong, but your female roles are negligible.

SCHRADER: I did write *Old Boyfriends,* about a woman. It is obsessively female as the other scripts are obsessively male. *Taxi Driver,* of course, is extremely masculine. There's no room for a female point of view in the whole film at all. *None.* Women are never seen objectively. Of course, *nothing* is seen objectively in the whole film. The film is far from realistic. Extremely distorted view of human life.

BRADY: You come from a large family?

SCHRADER: I just have a brother, Leonard, three years older.

BRADY: You collaborate with him on occasion?

SCHRADER: I did *Old Boyfriends* with him; I did *Blue Collar* with him.

BRADY: Didn't you do *Yakuza* with him in part?

SCHRADER: On the story, not the writing. The two scripts I've written with Leonard were what I call "nighttime scripts." Because if I'm doing a script during the day and I have an idea for another script I want to do, I'll do it with my brother. I'll outline the picture, and then we'll go over the script, and I'll describe each scene to him, how many pages it should be. Then he'll go write it a couple of times. He'll hand it back to me, and I'll rewrite it. I can do that at night. That way I can keep doing the daytime scripts. I do the nighttime script in collaboration. *Blue Collar* was a nighttime script. And *Old Boyfriends* was.

BRADY: You can turn your attentions on and off two scripts that deliberately?

SCHRADER: Only if I have a collaborator to force me.

BRADY: If the team shows up, you gotta play the game.

SCHRADER: Yeah. I count on my brother to force me to do things I wouldn't do otherwise.

BRADY: That system says something about your need for someone to prod, but there's also emotional economy in it as well. You draw out of others instead of drawing out of yourself altogether. When you collaborate, I assume it's not sitting in a room, one guy at the typewriter, one guy at the couch. That sort of stuff.

SCHRADER: No. I tell Len *exactly* what I want. If he were sitting here right now, I'd say, "I want a four-page scene, So-and-So walks in. . . ." He goes off and maybe he writes an eight-page scene. He hands the pages back to me, which include things that I didn't tell him. And I cut it back down to four pages and rewrite it. So that we get both inputs. The four pages and all the things that I needed are still there. Plus some other interesting things he has added.

BRADY: You have turned out an incredible amount of product for someone thirty-four. Is there some need to do this? What sort of decision making goes into doing four scripts a year?

SCHRADER: If you ever read a book by Philip Slater called *The Pursuit of Loneliness,* you'll understand me. Obsessive pursuit of product as an avoidance mechanism.

BRADY: What does it mean in terms of your life?

SCHRADER: I think it means a lot. *Transcendental Style in Film* was a book that I felt qualified to write at one point because I understood both theology and movies. I looked around, and I didn't see anybody else who really did. I knew I was too young to write the book; I also knew if I didn't write it now, I would never write it. I didn't see anybody else coming along to write it. I figured, better to have me write it prematurely than not to have it written at all. So I wrote it. That's why it's so defensive in its philosophical posture. It moves very slowly and states a conclusion after all the premises have been proven. I'll quote Susanne Langer on A premise; quote Coomaraswamy on B premise; John Dewey on C premise—before I reach D conclusion. Very, very slow and very plodding; very academic. But that was simply because I wasn't confident or accomplished enough to state a conclusion without stating the premises.

Well, in terms of my life I have written scripts of which I would not have approved as a critic. My whole thrust as a critic was antithetical to my thrust as a writer. As a critic, I was interested in the common and the universal. As a writer, I'm interested in the individual and the idiosyncratic. As a critic, I was always interested in the styles and sociological realities that unite films. As a writer, I'm trying to find what is unique about me as a screenwriter. Someday I expect these forks to merge and I will write and direct a film that I would have been proud of as a critic. I don't expect this to happen for about twenty years.

BRADY: Between your days as a critic and your days as a screenwriter, you experienced some changes in your personal life-style—there was a divorce, and you underwent analysis. Could this account for your change in direction, for your going down alleyways as a screenwriter you might not have traveled earlier as a critic?

SCHRADER: It's just a change in media. Being a critic has certain demands. When you're a critic, you're dealing with a cadaver. You are taking apart a cadaver trying to see what made it live, why it lived, the meaning its life had, how the life of this cadaver is related to other cadavers. As a writer you're dealing with an unborn, inchoate force. *Totally different things*. And that's why I think it is very hard to be a critic and a writer at the same time. Why *I* can't be. I've tried. I've *tried* to go back and write criticism. I can't do it.

BRADY: It's Jekyll and Hyde.

SCHRADER: Jekyll, then Hyde. There are many famous filmmaker-directors who began as critics, all of whom are unable to go back.

BRADY: There are many critics today who would like to be filmmakers. Many are running around with scripts pulled from their desk drawers.

SCHRADER: The best aren't. They have committed themselves to their discipline. Certainly a good critic is as rare as, or I think rarer than, a good filmmaker. The people I read and respect are more often than not more intelligent than the work they review. They're trying to understand and put inferior works in perspective.

BRADY: Can even a *good* critic really separate a film's parts? Whenever a critic mentions a screenwriter in a review, I can't help but wonder if the critic isn't engaging in guesswork.

SCHRADER: There is absolutely no way to individuate the elements of a film. The people *involved* can't separate the work of the director and the writer and the art director and the cinematographer and the actors and the producer—even the propman. You may see a wonderful bit of business in a film involving a prop and you think, "Gee, that was clever of the writer." It may end up that the propman was very imaginative and before the scene suggested to the director that he use this. Much of what goes as directorial skill is in fact cinematography: the laying out of shots, composition.

BRADY: You once wrote that Americans created the western to codify the morality of the frontier. And we created the gangster film to cope with the new social form of the city. Do you see your films as a metaphor to deal with some problems of *our* time?

SCHRADER: To answer in a roundabout way, films should not address themselves to what people want to see, because no one *knows* what they want to see. They only know what they want to see after they've seen it. Instead, films should try to address themselves to what people *need* to see. Movies work with an eighteen- to twenty-four-month lead time, and if you go by what people want to see today you're fucked. Needs last a bit longer; if you can figure out what people *need* to see, they will *want* to see it. One of the best ways to figure out what people need to see is to look around you. Read the newspaper, watch people on the street, listen to conversations; you can see the problems people are trying to deal with. If you can confront those needs with film metaphors, the want will be there.

If you find a rip in the social fabric and create a film metaphor which deals with that tear, that is as good a way as any to be commercial. For example, people *need* to see a movie about pornography. Pornography greatly confuses and upsets Americans. They don't know what to think about it. They don't know whether to damn it or not. And if you can make a film which helps them explore this problem, they'll want to see it. Likewise the future is something that scares a lot of people—and the most important thing about *Star Wars* was not its quality; the important thing about it was it's benevolent view of the future. The reason the film was so successful is that it told people that you don't have to be afraid of the future. Practically every other science fiction is based on a fear of the future. People need to embrace the future because the future is coming so quickly; it's become almost impossible to resist it.

BRADY: Several of your films are job-oriented: driving a cab, the automobile assembly line, the pornography business. Does this say something about your view of screenwriting and film-making?

SCHRADER: I think it's fair to define people by what they do. It's fair to define me as a screenwriter. It's fair to define you as a writer-interviewer. Those are starting points. Then you can explore character from there. For that reason all scripts—not just the ones I write—use what a character *does* as a starting point.

BRADY: A man is the job that he does? And he acquires individuality from there?

SCHRADER: He becomes less or more. Because in movies you're often not privy to a character's private thoughts, whereas in fiction you are. In fiction you can take a character who works almost anywhere and get into his mind. His job becomes secondary. In films you have to *see* him at work or whatever he does, so his occupation is far more important.

BRADY: Is there any particular difficulty in writing lines for a black actor cast as a black automobile worker in a film such as *Blue Collar?*

SCHRADER: There's no difficulty writing lines for Pryor, because if he doesn't like them he changes them. You can write anything you want. He'll only say what he wants.

BRADY: Is that a plus or a minus?

SCHRADER: It's a definite plus when it comes to Richard.

BRADY: But you take those attitudes one at a time.

SCHRADER: There's no way I'm going to tell Richard how to be funny. If I write a comedy line, nine out of ten times he'll have another line for that line. Even if his line isn't funnier than mine, he'll have one anyway. Because he's the comic, and very reluctant to have anybody else write comedy for him. And if a line has to do with black identity—with one exception in the film—he changed it, because he's just not about to read any line a white man has written about being black. Even if my line is right. One or two times he read my lines, but most of the time he had to put it his own way. I don't begrudge that at all.

BRADY: I found myself laughing aloud at some of the lines in the *Blue Collar* script. The lines in the bowling alley, which I thought was a great scene—where all this serious talk is interwoven with the score-card talk, the wife talk, and so forth. It reads as though you could have played that for laughs.

SCHRADER: Oh, no. All the comedy in the film comes out from underneath. For me, though, Richard is funnier in this film, which is very serious, than he is in any of his other films. Because the competition was strong, and the making of the film was so unpleasant, he used comedy to fight back.

BRADY: Casting and directing a film is, I assume, nearly always dealing with mixed marriages. Do you ever really know what you're going to get when you draw all the parts together?

SCHRADER: No. You just hope your exposition gets across.

BRADY: Why the Mohawk haircut on Travis in *Taxi?*

SCHRADER: That was a Vietnam thing. Marty Scorsese and Bobby De Niro interviewed an ex-Green Beret who told them if a Special Force member felt he was going to die, he would shave his head into a Mohawk as a warning to his fellow soldiers. What he meant was "Don't fuck with me. I'm going over the hill." It's part of the private Vietnam language of the film. The film never mentions Vietnam, but it's full of Vietnam language.

BRADY: That's quite revealing.

SCHRADER: Some people pick up on it.

BRADY: I think, though, in terms of the film, it's obscure. Is that intentional?

SCHRADER: Yes. There should be things in films that only five percent of the audience picks up on. You put things in a film that not everybody gets. Some things seventy-five percent get; some fifty percent; some ten percent. You can't make everything obvious. Sometimes I say to the cinematographer, "If we hold a little longer, this will be clear." But we don't do it. I say, if twenty-five percent of the people who watch this movie understand this bit of action, I will be happy. Because if I had to show it long enough for everybody to see, it would become noticeable and wouldn't work. I love to throw things away. Let each viewer pick up what he wants.

BRADY: But if a film gets too internal, it becomes like some contemporary poetry. Unreadable.

SCHRADER: No. You have to have a strong center line. You throw away from there. You keep your center line strong. You don't fuck with that. But you throw away a hundred things out of that so that people can go to the same movie and come out with entirely different experiences because they pick up on the things that mean something to them. They miss the things that don't. But they're all valid. Like *Blue Collar* is full of black code language that whites won't understand. It's full of worker code language that non-autoworkers won't understand. And that's good. The moment you explain it, you've hurt it.

BRADY: In *Taxi Driver* Travis says, "I think I've got stomach cancer." And in *Blue Collar* Jerry says, "I think I've got brain cancer." Is there an echo chamber in your writing?

SCHRADER: There's an unconscious one, I'm sure. But the line in *Taxi Driver* is a tribute to Bresson. The one in *Blue Collar* is a character trait; the character is a hypochondriac. That's how I built the character—as a man who doesn't know whether to shit or go blind. There's no conscious tie.

BRADY: I see a lot of parallels, though, between *Taxi Driver* and *Hardcore,* as I said earlier; and when lines begin to echo each other, I wonder if the critics aren't going to be saying, "Ol' Schrader's going to the well once too often" after turning out three, four, five screenplays in close order.

SCHRADER: I don't think there's anything wrong with that.

BRADY: It's certainly a novelist's tradition—working out of familiar territory—but I wonder if for a screenwriter there isn't a certain risk? Other screenwriters seem to keep moving, trying to do different things.

SCHRADER: I keep the themes, but change the subject, the tableaux. You can't fuck with the internalization. You can't say, "I'm going to become another person." You say, "I'm going to put myself in another environment and see what happens." You grow the same root problems in a different environment. That environment may be New York or pornography or auto plants. You force yourself into different slots, and, as you turn and modify, that friction creates, hopefully, enlightenment for you and the viewer. You can burn yourself out very quickly. You can be Tennessee Williams. You write four or five great plays on the same theme, and all of a sudden you've expended your theme.

BRADY: And you are Tennessee Williams the rest of your life.

SCHRADER: Then you're through. You've had your creative lifetime. Most artists have very short creative lifetimes. It's just reality. Every artist is afraid he'll wake up and that peculiar little bit of juice will be gone.

BRADY: Are you ever afraid of running out of ideas?

SCHRADER: After I finished *Gigolo,* I found myself blocked as a writer. I had been working almost nonstop for ten years and for the past three years had been working on scripts written by myself in the mid-seventies. I was just sinking in my own depression, and since I wasn't able to write, I thought the best therapy possible would be to direct—so I agreed to direct a remake of *Cat People* for Universal, and once I did that, the writing broke

through and I was able to work on the *Born in the USA* script.
When *Gigolo* was over, though, the well was finally dry. I had no
more scripts piled up. I needed to start over again and I needed
some time for introspection.

BRADY: Evelyn Waugh once said that screenwriters are
"highly paid and incompatible" as a lot. True or false?

SCHRADER: Certainly it's true. But who *is* compatible? I think
it's because screenwriters are highly paid that they *seem* incompatible. They're probably no more or less incompatible than anybody else. It's just that you don't pay any attention to everybody
else because they aren't so highly paid. Or let's say, the people
who are *not* as highly paid can't afford to be incompatible. They
have to get along. Screenwriters have the luxury of being arbitrary, idiosyncratic.

BRADY: How do you write? Longhand? Typewriter?

SCHRADER: Never longhand. The only thing I use a pen for is
to write my name.

BRADY: Do you dictate?

SCHRADER: No. Always type. I have to see it.

BRADY: Do you do much rewriting in the early stages?

SCHRADER: No. Once you commit yourself to moving forward,
you can't stop. It goes back to the metaphor of the miler going
back to rerun a last quarter mile because he didn't do his best
job. You can't do it! To understand the rhythm of writing a
hundred pages you have to write it right through. Feel the pages
under you the same way a runner feels the gravel under his feet.
He can tell how fast that gravel is moving under his feet as he's
going a mile, the same way you can tell how fast the pages are,
how fast the scenes are moving. You need that intuitive drive
and force. You fuck with that, you lose pacing, because I believe
the script should read and feel *fast*.

You have to feel space. If the run is a mile and the script is a
hundred and five, a hundred and ten pages, you have to feel that
space is tangible. Understand that space. Feel comfortable in
that space. Page twenty, page forty, sixty, seventy-five, eighty.
My favorite pages are eighty-five to ninety-five. I love those
pages. If I don't feel good from eighty-five to ninety-five, there's

something wrong. If I don't feel good after page ninety, ninety to ninety-five, the script was a mistake.

BRADY: Your scripts build exactly that way: interesting at the beginning, a little bit technical and then, once you settle into the characters, I find I can read the last half of a script in almost half the time it took me to read the first half.

SCHRADER: The last twenty pages are always exciting, because you can see the ribbon. And you know you're going to make it.

BRADY: Well, given all that excitement, what does it do to a writer's psyche when the director has another idea? Or when you have all that emotional investment in draft number three, and then draft number four is required?

SCHRADER: Well, usually there's enough time involved so that you repress the original excitement. What you do is you modify, try to create the same build within the context that the actor and director demand. If you're not able to do that, then you walk away. You concentrate on something else.

BRADY: How many drafts of a screenplay are you usually good for?

SCHRADER: Before I put it on the market?

BRADY: Initially, yes.

SCHRADER: Two. And a technical rewrite, which means going over the whole script line by line, changing but not retyping. When you start retyping from page one, you get a lot of freedom because you don't really have to obey the other stack of papers; you just type. So I usually do two drafts from page one, and the third draft I do as a mark-in, which limits you a lot because you accept the script. You may cross out a bit of dialogue, delete, add, stuff like that. Page changes. But you don't really add or subtract more than one or two scenes at that point.

BRADY: And once it's to market, what are you good for on a script?

SCHRADER: Well, I'm good as long as my enthusiasm and the enthusiasm of those I respect is there. I've let rewrites go by because I didn't think it would serve any purpose for me to rewrite the script.

BRADY: Such as?

SCHRADER: I didn't get involved in *Rolling Thunder*. I didn't think that they'd be receptive to what I would have done. Better to move on and do something else.

BRADY: What does *Rolling Thunder* mean?

SCHRADER: It's the code name for air operations over North Vietnam.

BRADY: Is there any Vietnam connection in your life? Do you have some special interest in that?

SCHRADER: It's the definitive event for people my age. You measure things in terms of where you were if you weren't there. John Milius' great regret is that he wasn't allowed to fight. He felt he should have been there, if only to see what was happening. I didn't want to be there, but I couldn't let those days go by without actively protesting. It became part of defining myself, to go to the street at that point.

BRADY: Do you ever write for a specific actor or actress, or do you write for your characters?

SCHRADER: I've never written with an actor in mind, except for *Blue Collar,* which I wrote for Richard Pryor and Harvey Keitel.

BRADY: As a writer do you stay around the set a lot, or do you write and run?

SCHRADER: Your job is pretty well finished by the time they start shooting. If you've done your job well, you should be finished by the time they start shooting, because by that time the movie will belong to the director and the actors, the cinematographer; and they will almost know the movie better than you at that point. If a writer needs to be on the set, it's usually an indicator that something is going wrong. On *Taxi,* occasionally I got a call from De Niro saying this and that, but for the most part he knew the movie as well as I did and his instincts were more likely to be right than mine.

BRADY: Are you ever surprised by what an actor or an actress does with a line?

SCHRADER: Rarely am I *un*surprised.

BRADY: For better or for worse?

SCHRADER: By and large for better. Simply because it's more immediate. Most lines are better when said by professional actors, because they can put a punch in almost anything. There are a few lines that you write that are beautiful in the abstract—until you discover that they really can't be said, or read.

BRADY: Are there any particular scenes that you recall that were better in performance than they were on paper?

SCHRADER: In *Taxi* the best scene on paper was the scene in which Scorsese plays the guy in the back seat. That was the best scene on paper, and it turned out to be good in the film, too. For the most part, *Taxi was* better on the screen, scene by scene. There are scenes that you wonder why they failed because you thought they had been written right. You hear them, and you try to figure out why they failed. Was it the actor, was it the director, or was it you? Did you write the scene wrong?

BRADY: Now that you're on both sides of the camera as writer and director, what do you think of the Writers Guild argument against the director's use of the possessive in front of the title?

SCHRADER: As a rule I think that anything the guild does is wrong. They are the most nefarious bunch of nincompoops ever assembled under one roof. However, I think a possessive credit in most cases is rather preposterous. In this specific case, I think the guild is right. You can get away with, say, Woody Allen's *Annie Hall,* Mel Brooks' *Young Frankenstein,* Alfred Hitchcock's *Family Plot.* But there's no way to take John Gellerman's *King Kong,* John Huston's *The Bible* seriously.

I think it should be reserved for people who have solo credit on at least two of the three major functions: actor-director, writer-director, writer-producer.

BRADY: How much thought do you give to the names of your characters?

SCHRADER: It depends on how important the characters are. Like in *Blue Collar,* I have three main characters, and I use their first names mostly, so it was very easy. Just picked three names that are interesting to hear together: Zeke, Smokey and Jerry. But when you only have one character, it's more difficult. I was very happy with Travis Bickle in *Taxi Driver.*

BRADY: How did Travis's name occur to you?

SCHRADER: It has to be euphonious, because you want people

to repeat the name: to use it in reviews, to use it in copy, a name people want to repeat. And Travis Bickle was successful in that way; people remembered the name and it appeared in a lot of reviews. It's like Bobby DuPea in *Five Easy Pieces*. A memorable name. Beyond that, you want to have at least one component which is evocative and/or symbolic. Travis is evocative rather than symbolic, Travis/travel. The sense of traveling, never stopping. Then Bickle. Travis is romantic, evocative and soft—and Bickle is hard, an unpleasant name. And it fits the character. The character's name in *American Gigolo* was originally Julian Cole. Julian, which is reminiscent of Julian Sorel, Julian English, Julian Hadrian. Julian is a poetic and royal name. Cole is like *cold* and is like coal from the earth. Thus, Julian Cole. Julian Cold. That's how I named him. Unfortunately, we couldn't get legal clearance on Julian Cole so I mixed Stendhal with Kafka and changed it to Julian Kay. And there's the character in *Hardcore* called Jake Van Dorn. Dorn means *thorn*.

He used to be called Jake Zondervall. Zondervall is Dutch for "the fall of man." It was an instance when I chose a name that meant something, but which was *not* memorable. Jake Zondervall—too hard to say. Jake Van Dorn is easier to say, easier to remember. So I had to move away from something symbolic to something easier said. Jake, of course, is a Biblical name, from Jacob, who wrestled with God.

BRADY: That's an interesting approach to names. There are no accidents in your naming characters, then.

SCHRADER: Not principal characters. Secondary characters you can have a lot of fun naming. In my first draft of *Obsession,* all the cops were named after cheeses. Edam, Gouda, Camembert, and the fourth guy was named Brie. (And Brie stayed in the movie.)

BRADY: Why would you do that?

SCHRADER: Just for the hell of it. I thought it would be funny to name all the police after cheeses.

BRADY: There seems to be similarity in your naming prostitutes: Iris, with two *i*'s in *Taxi;* and Niki—again, four letters, two *i*'s—in *Hardcore*.

SCHRADER: I try to make their names a little strange and a little memorable. Iris, of course, suggests an innocence, an opening up. You think of a camera iris, and you think of a flower. And I thought Niki was a little interesting.

BRADY: You depict New York City as a villain in *Taxi Driver*. What was your own introduction to New York?

SCHRADER: The film is not about New York. And I'm not that interested in New York. The main character goes to New York because he has to find an externalization of an evil he sees in himself. If it wasn't New York, he'd search the world over till he found that sewer he was looking for. It reminds me of a story about Picasso. He had an abstract painting titled *Fish*. And a woman came up to him and said, "But it doesn't look like a fish." He said, "Madam, it isn't a fish, it's a painting." So it isn't New York; it's a film.

BRADY: In the film Travis is not too smart, and yet his diary has a rather literate tone.

SCHRADER: I think that's common. The diaries of psychopaths often have a convoluted vocabulary that suggests aspirations toward importance. They have learned a number of words one would think they wouldn't know. I wrote the script before Bremer's diary came out, but Bremer's diary is full of those sorts of things.

BRADY: The script was written in June of 1972, one month after Bremer shot Wallace. Did the Wallace shooting help the screenplay's chances of selling?

SCHRADER: No. It had nothing to do with the sale.

BRADY: Was there any connection?

SCHRADER: Oh, yeah, it was one of the triggers to writing it, obviously. But I didn't set out to write about Bremer. He didn't particularly interest me.

BRADY: How did the idea for a taxi driver as assassin come to you?

SCHRADER: Well, the first thing that came, the most important thing, was the metaphor with a taxi, the cab. And then in order to create a world that represented the thinking of Travis Bickle, you had to have a girl he desired but couldn't have and another girl he could have but didn't desire. The film is riddled with the mechanisms of self-destruction. Therefore, these are the two kinds of girls who appeal to him. You create those two characters, and then you start building the tension up, and you find that he has to do a kind of bold act to resolve that artificial tension which he has created—and so the assassination thing becomes a *thing*. It's not *that* imaginative. It's just building blocks.

BRADY: He fails at that assassination attempt and his attack on Betsy's world. So he regroups and attacks Iris's world.

SCHRADER: It doesn't really matter to him. He had reached the point where he needs a stage on which to act out his personal drama. He moves to attack one father figure, and when that fails he goes after the other one.

BRADY: Is it legally plausible that he would come out of all that as a hero still on the streets?

SCHRADER: No. It is sociologically plausible to the extent that our society does reward those who do outrageous acts. Squeaky Fromme does get on the cover of *Newsweek*. There's something in our society that says, "It doesn't matter how you got there as long as you got there. If you're on the cover of *Newsweek,* you must be important." Publicity is a reward in this society. And you do get attention when you walk in a room with a gun.

BRADY: How realistic do you endeavor to be as a moviemaker?

SCHRADER: Aristotle makes a distinction between what is possible and what is plausible. A movie does not have to be possible; it has to be plausible. It's not quite possible that the whole story of Oedipus would ever happen; it's only remotely possible. But it is plausible—that is, it satisfies some psychological need in response to a personal notion of what is true. So therefore Oedipus is plausible because it *should* be true or needs to be true, not because it *could* be true. And in the same way any fiction should be plausible, though it need not be possible. The world of the gigolo, I would say, is plausible but not very possible.

BRADY: Did you do much research for *Gigolo?*

SCHRADER: Not too much. Mostly it's based on things I've seen or heard over the last ten years in L.A. I know the moneyed world of Beverly Hills a bit. I wasn't that interested in gigolos realistically. I had a conversation with Richard Gere similar to one I had with De Niro in *Taxi Driver*. Bobby wanted to meet some taxi drivers, and he did. Gere wanted to meet some gigolos, and he did. But I said in both cases: You can meet these people, but you are not to copy them, because you are first of all my taxi driver, and my gigolo—and you are not like anyone else. You owe your allegiance to the script, not to life. You can steal little things from them—ways of talking, mannerisms—but your *raison d'être,* your soul, belongs to the script, not to these people. Therefore, research is good for the finishing touches and the sense of reality and credibility, but it can never give you the soul of a character. That's in the writer and in what caused him to write it.

BRADY: How close do you become to your actors? Robert De Niro wore your boots, your belt and I think your shirt in *Taxi Driver.*

SCHRADER: That's De Niro. That's not me. In *Blue Collar* I didn't become that close at all to Richard Pryor, because there was a gap between us we both had to appreciate. I had no real idea what it was like to have lived his life. I could sympathize, but his instincts were better than mine at that level.

BRADY: In the final draft of *Taxi* you note, "The screenplay has been moving at a reasonably realistic level until this prolonged slaughter. The slaughter itself is a gory extension of violence more surreal than real." Does the movie satisfy your prescription?

SCHRADER: Absolutely. The movie goes out of whack at that point. The color goes crazy. You no longer hear the sounds of the street. You get into that weird slow motion. *Intentionally* out of whack.

BRADY: Did you collaborate on that?

SCHRADER: Oh, yeah. That was very much our intention, Marty and I.

BRADY: Travis is rather more of a monster in the final draft of *Taxi Driver* than he is in the first. In the first, for instance, he stops short of killing the old man; in the final draft, though, after

Iris and the man plead with him not to kill him, he blows the back of his head off. Why that change?

SCHRADER: Well, I began to realize how much of a monster he was. In the first draft I was writing a picture about what I thought to be loneliness. After the first draft I realized that I wasn't writing about loneliness at all, but instead I was writing about *self-imposed* loneliness, which is a different thing in that no one was *making* Travis what he was. He was *choosing* to be a misfit. Society had not wronged or harmed him. He was *manufacturing* a society in which he could feel a victim. And therefore I began to have less sympathy for him.

BRADY: The greatest difference between the first and the final drafts of *Taxi Driver* is the ending. In the first draft Travis visits Iris in a girl's academy, has a brotherly talk with her, even agrees to let her read his diary. In the final draft, of course, he never sees Iris again; her parents write, thanking him. And that's it. In the first draft, too, he asks Betsy to look in on Iris: "She's just a little girl, and she's trying hard to grow up into a big one."

SCHRADER: Be sure you use the word "rough" draft because that is *not* the first draft. That rough draft was never shown to anyone. You're the first person who has read it since it was written. It was a rough draft. I wrote it, and three days later I started rewriting it.

BRADY: OK. To continue from the rough draft: "She needs a grown-up girl friend," he tells Betsy. And Travis will apparently call Betsy again. In the final draft, he leaves her mooning as he drives away. In the rough draft Travis seems to rejoin society after his slaughter. In the final draft he remains a loner, although a somewhat respected loner.

SCHRADER: Absolutely. Because as soon as I realized the depth of the sickness of the character, any kind of assimilation into society is not plausible. He would remain as he was. Nothing has changed for him. And I could not write anything which indicated an improvement.

BRADY: How would you rate Scorsese's direction of *Taxi Driver*?

SCHRADER: It was extraordinary. It's far better than I would have done myself. The quality of the script was multiplied twice —once by De Niro, once by Scorsese.

BRADY: In the script version of *Taxi Driver,* Travis knocks over the TV by accident and places his head in his hands, despairing of himself. But in the movie he seems to knock it over more deliberately.

SCHRADER: It is pretty deliberate when you rock something until it falls. A self-destruct mechanism. You start something in motion, the ending of which will be a destructive act.

BRADY: Do actors improvise with your scripts?

SCHRADER: Good ones do—so do bad ones. But the good ones you respect.

BRADY: In the rough draft of *Taxi Driver,* Travis's first kill in the city comes when a black man tries to rob him in the cab. Travis blows him away after telling him, "I got no more reason to live than you got to kill me." In the movie, of course, the kill is in a delicatessen.

SCHRADER: You're kidding. That was so long ago, and that draft was so temporary, I don't even remember it. Like I say, I wrote that draft years ago in a day and a half, and I haven't looked at it since. So I don't even know what's in that draft anymore. I know what's in the draft *after* that, which took about eight days to write. I showed that to you so you could see me throwing out ideas, just throwing them on the paper to see what they look like. You can see the tons of junk I threw away—a scene like that, which was a bad scene.

BRADY: That was a pretty good line.

SCHRADER: *That's* what was wrong with it. That line was much too much on the nose. I mean, that line would have died in a movie. The scene is much better now in the deli, where you don't have a line.

BRADY: In the movie Betsy attends a dirty film with Travis, then walks out. In the first draft she doesn't go into the movie house at all.

SCHRADER: Yeah. I added that because it's interesting to see her inside there.

BRADY: That *is* an interesting scene. It overcomes a certain amount of implausibility, in fact. I remember saying to myself, "She won't go in that movie house; I mean, what is she doing with this guy?" And yet she's curious about a world she doesn't know.

SCHRADER: There's also a certain amount of comic relief. If I could get her inside there, I could show what was on the screen, and I could get into that comic relief, which I needed to break the build of the film.

BRADY: In the revised draft Travis tells Betsy of a woman who spreads her legs in the back seat of his cab. And Betsy says, "Maybe you should have helped her out." But Travis doesn't understand. He says, "What do you mean?" This seems revealing, but it's cut from the final version.

SCHRADER: Yeah, I remember writing that. With Cybill we shot a lot of film. That scene where Travis talks to Cybill? Scorsese shot three hours of film on that and cut it down to what it is now. A lot of lines were read in that scene. It was very long; it could have been fifteen minutes long. It was just a matter of which ones Cybill played best. That's how it was cut.

BRADY: Why did you add to the shooting script that scene where Betsy explains to Tom that pushing a politician is like selling cars?

SCHRADER: We built up Tom's character. Marty's very smart about this. To me a character like Tom could be a flat, uninteresting backboard. But I learned from Marty—and I did it in *Blue Collar,* too—you take those flat, uninteresting characters, and you cast very interesting actors (*i.e.,* comedians), and then they jump out. Then you start giving them lines. Marty had two suggestions when he shot *Taxi.* He wanted two new scenes. He wanted one new one for Harvey Keitel and wanted a new one for Albert Brooks. I was opposed to both scenes because they didn't take place from Travis's point of view; but I wrote them both and he shot them both. In the final version he only used the one for Harvey, which is the one where he and Iris dance around in the room.

BRADY: Although it's clear why Travis wants to kill the pimps around Iris, it's never clear why he wants to kill Palantine, the politician.

SCHRADER: Because Palantine represents a man who is at ease, and the one thing that Travis is not is at ease. He's the most uncomfortable man alive, and he hates and fears relaxation. That's why he hates Palantine. The same reason he hates the pimp. The very same reason. He hates men who are relaxed with women. Because they are the one thing he can't be. So it doesn't have anything to do with politics. It has to do with sexuality.

BRADY: In the first draft the movie opens in the spring, but in the final draft it opens in the winter with Travis looking for a job and then shifts to the spring by the time the credits are rolling. Why the shift in seasons there?

SCHRADER: I had originally hoped to do it starting out in winter, but of course that's very difficult to do when you're filming a movie. It costs too much money.

BRADY: *The Yakuza* would seemingly have a built-in audience from two sources. That is, fans of gangster films and fans of kung fu or Asian martial arts type of films. But it didn't do well at the box office. Why not?

SCHRADER: I think it sort of fell between two stools. It wasn't really a gangster picture, and it wasn't an international romance.

BRADY: What interested you in doing a script such as *The Yakuza* in the first place?

SCHRADER: It was just a sort of coincidence. My brother had been living in Japan, and it was an interesting subject. I was interested in Japanese films and the whole notion of sacrifice, blood, giving up something of oneself to assuage guilt.

BRADY: Why did you write *Obsession?*

SCHRADER: *Déjà Vu?* It was an idea that Brian De Palma and I had. We were sitting around talking. I was talking about *Autumn Afternoon,* by Ozu; and we were talking about *Vertigo,* and we just got a notion for a movie.

BRADY: Would it be accurate to say *Obsession* is an *hommage* to Hitchcock?

SCHRADER: Well, not really an *hommage,* though it does work in that genre. It's like, how can you shoot a western in Monument

Valley without it being some kind of *hommage* to John Ford? It's just not possible to work in certain areas without acknowledging what's been done before.

BRADY: Why did you choose New Orleans as a setting?

SCHRADER: American Gothic. It's a kind of Gothic American city. And it's sort of rich in elements of the foreign and the mysterious. It makes a good bookend for Florence.

BRADY: In the film when Courtland meets Sandra, she's restoring an altarpiece of the Madonna and Child, and under it is an earlier draft of the Madonna. The point is clear and arresting. What was the genesis of that scene?

SCHRADER: Well, it's a scene which defines the movie—whether you preserve the beauty of the present and ignore the past, or go into the past at the risk of losing the present.

BRADY: That sort of writing is lush.

SCHRADER: I made a mistake. I got florid—and got caught. You have to watch that kind of writing. It kills screenplays.

BRADY: They do get through, though; and sometimes they play well.

SCHRADER: They can hurt you just as bad. Especially if you start piling them on top of each other. You can put one or two in a film, at most. You put in any more than that, your whole film sinks like a rock.

BRADY: Obviously, you took a few out of the script as it moved along. For example, in the first draft of *Obsession,* Courtland and Sandra sit by a reflecting pool in Audubon Park in New Orleans to discuss their marriage. The pool is a reminder that Sandra is but a reflection of someone else. In the shooting script they merely sit on a bench in a square. Is this the sort of streamlining that you do?

SCHRADER: Well, that somebody does. Of course, the biggest difference in *Obsession* is the whole third section is dropped.

BRADY: Yes. What happened?

SCHRADER: That's really where I dropped out of it—when that third section was dropped. Because I happened to like that. The thing that intrigued me most about that script was the notion of creating a love story so strong that you could transgress the boundaries of time without jarring the audience. The notion that you can move from that past to the future without it becoming science fiction. The love story could be so strong that the audience would allow you to go into the future to tell it. Creates a sense of "This story is so strong that we can't stop just because we've run out of present time." That intrigued me *most* of all. So when that element was dropped, I sort of dropped out myself.

BRADY: You did none of the rewrites, then? The ending is the "De Palma Version."

SCHRADER: Brian wrote that. He asked me to write it, but I couldn't. I wanted just to move on to something else.

BRADY: There's a lovemaking scene in the first draft of *Obsession* between Courtland and Sandra.

SCHRADER: It was cut from the film. The actors wouldn't do it. That's what Brian told me.

BRADY: It pins down *vividly* the point that the price of Courtland's obsession is incest.

SCHRADER: Well, it also rather vividly scared the producer. I can't imagine why. Maybe because he thought he would lose his PG or something. So only the *hint* of incest remains. But the smoking pistol is gone.

BRADY: Well, having your incest and wanting to see it too is a tough battle to win.

SCHRADER: Yeah, I felt it had to be spelled out; but it didn't get spelled out.

BRADY: There's an eerie scene in the original draft of *Obsession*. After Sandra tells Courtland that she's really Beth, he visits Beth's tomb, opens the vault with a crowbar, and turns the urn upside down. It's empty. And then we hear Sandra: "I'm no longer there; Michael, I'm no longer in that cold marble; I am here; I am Beth."

SCHRADER: That's a nice scene. I think that's just money, again. They made the film very cheaply. They had to cut a lot of scenes. They had to take dialogue from scenes and put it into other scenes to make it cheaper. The budget was only like one million four hundred thousand.

BRADY: Is that all it was? It did pretty well.

SCHRADER: Yeah, I've gotten a profit check from it.

BRADY: In the first draft of *Obsession,* a jealous boyfriend, Franco, shadows Sandra and Courtland—

SCHRADER: That is another thing—there's a tripleganger in the original script. There's a character who's in all three levels of the story, and I wanted the same actor to play all three roles: one of the kidnappers, Sandra's boyfriend, and the doctor in the future section. It was my intention that the same actor play all three roles. As a kind of Peter Sellers-like turn from *Lolita.* I wanted a kind of Quilty character to take the script away from direct realism and make it a little more relative.

BRADY: It sounds in general as though you were going for a more artistic film and the director, maybe others, were going for a hard, commercial reading of things.

SCHRADER: Well, I'm sure *they* wouldn't agree with you.

BRADY: I thought he had some good lines, this boyfriend who never showed up in the shooting script.

SCHRADER: I loved it.

BRADY: Jane's role, too, is cut drastically in the shooting script of *Obsession.*

SCHRADER: That was really unfortunate; she's an important character because she humanizes Courtland. She represents normal sexuality. And you needed that balance to make the abnormal work. But—money again. Scenes like that, you're not even talking about writer-director disagreement; you're talking about money. When you have to make a film that cheaply, a lot of things go. That's why the future thing went. Money.

BRADY: Yeah. In the original draft of *Obsession* Courtland's wife dies when the death car fails to cross the gap in a drawbridge ramp, and in the shooting script, the car just crashes after an oil truck explosion. The first version seems more spectacular; the second one we've seen in every "Mannix" TV script. Money?

SCHRADER: It's cheaper. There are *big* concessions you make for money, and there are *small* concessions you make for money. That's a small one. Some of the others are so big that they cannot be overcome.

BRADY: In the original draft of *Obsession* Courtland dances first with his daughter at the party and then with his wife. In the shooting script he continues to dance with Amy. Is this to reinforce the end of the movie where Courtland dances with his daughter years later?

SCHRADER: Those dance scenes were lost. The money thing that hurt me most in the movie was that I lost the Patti Page song, because that to me was just everything that the movie was about: "Changing Partners." *I'll keep changing partners till you're in my arms again.* If *I* had directed it, I would have taken the money out of my own pocket to buy the Patti Page song.

BRADY: What would it have cost?

SCHRADER: Probably about fifteen grand. Songs are very expensive. In *Taxi Driver* we bought one song—Jackson Browne, "Too Late for the Sky," as Travis watches TV. We got it for five grand. And we also wanted a Barry White song for when Sport dances with Iris. It was fifteen grand, and we just couldn't afford it.

BRADY: *Hardcore* has a lot of music, including hymns like "Precious Memories." How careful were you in selecting songs there?

SCHRADER: That song, and that version by Susan Ray, is just a song I've always loved. It has a line—*Precious memories haunt my soul*—that just seemed to fit into the film.

BRADY: The theme in *Blue Collar* is underscored at the end of the movie. We hear part of Smokey's speech again in voice-over. Why so much emphasis?

SCHRADER: I wanted the film to appeal to an uneducated audience. I think that a college audience will understand this theme completely, but there's a very large segment of the moviegoing public that you have to say to directly: *This is what the movie is about.* There's a point at which subtlety is useless. It's all right to be subtle in *Taxi Driver,* not to have a shrink come out at the end and explain that Travis is disturbed. But I think because *Blue Collar* is a political and socially involved film, you have to spell it out. The kind of ambiguity which surrounded the ending of *Taxi Driver* I don't think can surround the ending of *Blue Collar.*

BRADY: While the credits roll in *Blue Collar* we see a man in a plant pound a soft drink machine and then run back to the line. Later in the film he finally gets fed up with the machine and demolishes it. You do something similar in *Obsession*.

SCHRADER: Yeah. That's a screenwriting trick in which you get your comic relief in while you're reiterating the message of the film, which is: "This is the last time you're going to fuck me, you goddamn machine."

BRADY: OK. In *Obsession* you begin with Courtland showing home movies of the Italian church where he met his wife, and then he revisits the church and meets his second wife. This echoing effect—is it characteristic of you?

SCHRADER: Yeah, I am unfortunately addicted a bit to parallel structure in films. I'm a great one for bookends.

BRADY: And ultimately, how would you like to be remembered?

SCHRADER: At the moment, as the writer of *Taxi Driver*.

NEIL
SIMON

In an interview with himself for the Los Angeles *Times* a few seasons ago, Neil Simon asked Neil Simon, "Are writers born or made?" "Most of them are born," replied Simon. "The ones that are made generally break down after a few years and their arms fall off." Good answer. Neil Simon, a writer born fifty-four years and a few thousand rewrites ago, still has his arms attached and poised over a typewriter turning out script after script.

Some critics regard Simon as an American Molière, or as a writer in the tradition of Balzac sketching the human comedy of his time. Moviegoers just consider him funny as hell, and most of his seventeen films (usually based upon his own Broadway plays) have been notable successes. Among them: *The Odd Couple, Come Blow Your Horn, The Goodbye Girl, Murder by Death, The Cheap Detective, The Sunshine Boys, Plaza Suite, Barefoot in the Park, California Suite* and his most dramatic work, *Chapter Two.*

Anyone who has seen *Chapter Two* knows how Neil Simon and Marsha Mason met and married. They met on October 3, 1973, at a Broadway rehearsal for Simon's play *The Good Doctor*, less than three months after Joan, Neil's wife of twenty years, had died of cancer. Nineteen days later Neil and Marsha were married. Then came a period of guilt and remorse for the writer—one that jeopardized his marriage, his new life, his emotional stability —which led in turn to the purgative writing of *Chapter Two.* By the time the play became a movie in 1979, Neil Simon and Marsha Mason were enjoying the second chapter of their lives in full, and Marsha Mason was playing Marsha Mason in the film version. Thus it is no surprise that when Neil Simon asked Neil Simon in that Los Angeles *Times* interview if most of his work was autobiographical, Neil Simon replied, "No. Generally, I write about myself and my experiences."

Neil Simon began writing about himself and his experiences at the age of fifteen while still in high school in New York City. His older brother Danny needed a writing partner, and he knew that young "Doc"—so nicknamed because of his ability to mug the family doctor—could do funny things on paper. Neil had written some short stories and pieces in high school, and he was an admirer of Kaufman and Hart on Broadway. He read Benchley, Twain and Stephen Leacock, and now he began to develop his own sense of humor professionally—and to sell it. Doc and Danny wrote a show for the employees at Abraham and Straus, where Danny worked at the time. Then they began to sell lines to stand-up comics and special material to radio shows.

During World War II, Neil served in the Army and was editor of the base newspaper at Lowry Field in Denver.

After the war he worked as a messenger in the mailroom at Warner Bros. in New York, where Danny had a job in the publicity department. The brothers started writing again and sent scripts around to comics and radio shows. When a press agent at Warners sent them over to meet Goodman Ace at CBS, the Simons became part of a stable of young comedy writers for a year, feeding lines and sketches to network shows. They did spot work for television as well, working for Jackie Gleason, Tallulah Bankhead and others. "We got quite a good reputation as special-material writers," recalls Neil Simon today. "This went on for a number of years until 1952, when Danny and I met Max Liebman, the mentor and producer of 'Your Show of Shows,' starring Sid Caesar."

Liebman hired the team for a six-week period, extended it to a full season, and eventually two years. Then Danny decided to try the West Coast, and Doc stayed in New York to work with Liebman for another two years, adapting old Broadway shows for a series of TV specials: *Best Foot Forward, Dearest Enemy, Connecticut Yankee* and others. "It was my first experience writing books for musicals—although, in effect, I was *rewriting* books— and it was an education for me," says Simon. "I started to have aspirations toward playwriting."

With his aspirations on hold, Neil Simon continued to write some of the funniest TV comedy material of the fifties. He worked with Sid Caesar again on "Caesar's Hour"; did scripts for "You'll Never Get Rich" (aka the "Sergeant Bilko" show); and by twenty-nine was earning $1,500 a week, but growing restless. "I decided to move on," he recalls. "I did not want to end up doing situation comedy for the rest of my life." He took a job writing sketches for "The Garry Moore Show," but began to write his first play during spare hours. Despite his speed of delivery today, that first one came slow and hard for Neil Simon. Not until three years and many rewrites later was *Come Blow Your Horn* finished and on Broadway; but since that 1961 premiere, life has been different for the most successful comedy writer in America.

Our conversations took place at one of Simon's favorite hangouts, the Beverly Hills Tennis Club; and at Simon's nearby office, which overlooks the club's courts. He had just returned from a three-week vacation in Europe to a schedule filled with work, meetings, phone calls. But all of this stops when it is time to play tennis, which Simon does three times a week, no matter what. I had been told that he was rather serious in person, that comedy was no laughing matter in conversation. Not true. There is a tranquility about the writer that puts anyone at ease and open to gentle laughter. Simon comes across as an amalgam of that odd couple, Oscar and Felix—wearing a floppy hat and slouching in a chair down by the court, yet organized, neat and methodical back at his office. In both demeanors he seemed relaxed, and on this particular day, reflective. "When Danny and I started out, our aspirations were not very high," he said, leaning back into a chair and into the past. "We just wanted to write gags for stand-up comics and make a living. Playwriting and screenwriting seemed a long, long way off to us."

———————————

BRADY: What was your family's attitude toward you and your brother?—two writers in a crazy business.

SIMON: There were a lot of problems. We came from those Depression years, and my father, who never made much money, always looked for security in his life and hoped that his sons would do the same. My father was a salesman; rather, he sold the piece goods to dress manufacturers. He didn't necessarily want us to go into that business, but to find something that was secure: The post office or civil service would have been perfect for him because we would have gotten a hundred dollars per week every single week. They don't lay off at the post office. I had an uncle who worked there almost fifty years. Never made much more money than that, but he never made less.

So my father was pretty much against the writing, more against my brother Danny doing it than against me because Danny, eight years older, had a really good job—first at Abraham and Straus selling boys' clothing; then he became the buyer for boys' clothing at that department store. Later he had another good job at Warner Bros. So Danny had a lot to give up. Since I was eighteen, nineteen years old, any job was fine with me. My father, though, was leery of it all. My mother wanted peace in the house, and whatever was going to make us happy would make her happy. She was happy that we found something we wanted to do. And my father, later, took great pride when I started to become successful, principally with *Come Blow Your Horn,* which was about him and my mother, and *Barefoot in the Park.* He died right after *Barefoot,* but at least he got to see the fruition of some of that. Though there were problems in the beginning and not an awful lot of encouragement, gradually he saw that we could make a living and that we were pretty good. He accepted it.

BRADY: Your family life when you were growing up wasn't always the most stable, from what I've read.

SIMON: Try "terrible." It wasn't a broken home; it was a *repeatedly* broken home. My father would go, then come back, go, then come back. This went on for years and years. I was so young and so caught up in it all that to this day I don't have a clear perspective on why it all happened, why my parents broke up so much. For the most part, I only heard my mother's version because I was with her all the time. I don't know what drove my father away, what devils were bothering him. It's odd, talking with you and thinking about it. I wrote a play called *I Ought to Be in Pictures,* which is the story of a reunion of a father and daughter after eighteen years apart, but I know it's really about myself and my father. I mean, it has nothing literally to do with the same incidents, but the emotional life between two people trying to rediscover each other is, I guess, what I'm doing now in my own life. And it's odd because it's close to eighteen years since my father died.

BRADY: Do you consciously cultivate the past? It sounds as

though the themes you strike and the relationships you write about are based upon a lot of Neil Simon's subliminal past.

SIMON: I think that most writers do that. Obviously, my mother, father and brother are dominant roles in my life and play various dominant roles in all my plays under different disguises.

BRADY: *Chapter Two* is probably your most overtly autobiographical work. When you did the film, did you return to the actual places you experienced in real life?

SIMON: No, that wasn't important. We didn't go where I went on my honeymoon, because it doesn't make any difference to the audience whether I went there or didn't. It's just the feeling one gets. As a matter of fact, few of the incidents really happened in my life. The only thing that really happened is what I felt about the passing of my wife, and the starting of a new life. But I'm not trying to be a photographer of the past and track down the exact places and locations. I am not doing a documentary. I am doing a fictionalized piece based upon an incident that happened.

BRADY: Isn't it risky using your wife, brother, other friends and relatives in your characterizations? Do your sources know that they are being so employed?

SIMON: Everyone does this, and—I'm not giving myself any position in history—if you read the biographies of all the great writers, they were always writing about themselves, about their families. Tolstoy was writing about everyone he knew, always worrying about what society, what the public, was going to think. Sometimes I'm very specific about my characterizations; sometimes I disguise them; and sometimes my subconscious disguises them and they become other people. But who else am I supposed to write about? Is it better to write about two people in Des Moines that I've never met so there is no risk involved that I am betraying who they really are? Of course, I don't have the faintest idea of what their lives are like—so I'll write something inferior.

I write about myself, my brother, my parents, my wife, my children, my friends, my coworkers, the people I meet all the time. I try always to write about them with some affection, but mostly with some honesty. And I have never ever once had anybody come up to me and say, "How dare you put me down that way." Never.

BRADY: Is writing out of personal history ever a cathartic experience on a movie?

SIMON: Depends on the movie, and on the need for a catharsis. *Murder by Death* is certainly not a cathartic experience; I just felt like having some fun with it. But interviewers, reviewers, journalists sometimes look for meanings that do not exist. A British journalist interviewed me during the making of that movie, for example, and he said, "This is really dealing with the passing of your wife, isn't it?" I said certainly not. (This was before I wrote *Chapter Two*.) He said, "Yes, but your wife died, and you're writing a comedy, so in a way it is murdering death." I think my answer was "Leave me alone, please."

BRADY: What does that title mean, *Murder by Death?*

SIMON: It's just a play on all of those titles. Murder by poison. Murder by assassination. Murder by the noose. So I said I know a funny way to murder somebody. It's by death. There was a line I once made up that has become very famous: "Death is nature's way of telling you to slow down."

BRADY: That's your line?

SIMON: Yes, I wrote it on "The Garry Moore Show." I don't know if it's apropros of this discussion, but it's just a play on words. So is *Murder by Death. The Cheap Detective*—I don't even know what that means. Again, sometimes when looking for a fun title, you're looking for something that's going to grab them. In the titles to my plays that really mean something to me, I try to tell the audience what the play is about, what the character is about. I try to tell a little story in the title.

BRADY: Does the title usually come to you early in the writing?

SIMON: It helps if it does, and generally it does. When I don't have it, I'll work very hard because it's as important to me as writing the first scene, getting the title. I feel comfortable if it sounds right.

BRADY: How do you decide on the names for your characters?

SIMON: Sometimes I do it well; sometimes not. An image

comes to mind. Felix Ungar sounded like a very prissy name to me. A guy who is very fastidious shouldn't have a strong, earthy name.

BRADY: How did you come upon Gwendolyn and Cecily Pigeon for *The Odd Couple?*

SIMON: That was subconscious. I just wrote Gwendolyn and Cecily, brought it in, and Mike Nichols said, "Oh, that's very clever." I said, "What do you mean?" He said, *"The Importance of Being Earnest,"* and I said, "It didn't occur to me." But obviously Oscar Wilde's characters were in my subconscious, because you don't come up with a coincidence like that.

One of the great coincidences for me occurred in *Come Blow Your Horn* when I needed the name of a fictitious producer because the older brother is going to fix up the younger brother with a girl who is an aspiring actress. "We'll say you're a producer from Hollywood," he says, "and you're sure to make it with this girl, because she's going to go nuts over the chance to meet a producer from Hollywood." And the younger brother says, "What's my name?"

"Paul Mannheim."

"OK, where do I work?"

"You work at MGM studios."

I was just writing this. I needed a name. Fine. We open the play, and I get a letter from Paul Mannheim from MGM studios saying, Hey, don't do this to me, OK? Take it out. What must have happened is again the subconscious—in reading through *Variety,* the name Paul Mannheim at MGM must have entered my mind.

BRADY: *The Odd Couple* is about your brother Danny. Why didn't he write it?

SIMON: Danny tried, then he told me he gave up on it. "I really can't write by myself," he said. He had written about ten or fifteen pages, infinitely different from what I wrote, from a different perspective. He had written it at my request. I was with Danny a lot during that period, and I saw the story being lived out. I said, "Danny, what's going on between you and Roy Gerber—it's a play. Two guys living alone, and the two of you are fighting like husband and wife. You've got to write it as a play.''

But at the time I think he was a little afraid of it. Danny writes alone now; he's working on a play. But back then, after ten or fifteen pages, he said, "I can't. I've got to give up on it." So I said, "Well then, I think I would like to write it because I think it will make a great play." I did. I made a financial arrangement with Danny so that he received a good percentage of it in perpetuity. On reflection, though, I think it would have been more generous of me had I put Danny's name on the credit: "Based on a story by . . ." I didn't, because I thought at the time that it was my own personal point of view. There was no necessity to do it, but I regret not having done it.

BRADY: What were your early screenwriting days like after all that early success on Broadway?

SIMON: Well, I made my reputation as a playwright, so it wasn't a matter of life or death to me with the movies, whether I made it or not, in the beginning. It was another outlet for me. I had already done *Barefoot in the Park* and *The Odd Couple* as plays, so I was established. Still, I went through some depression. I was depressed when I saw *Come Blow Your Horn* as a movie, even though I didn't write it, because it was still part of my output. And I was depressed about some movies I did in the early days that I learned a great deal from.

I learned that I had better speak up and not turn over so much power to the director, which is a very difficult thing because in this town if you don't have any personal clout, that's what's going to happen to you. Writers are treated really as the low men on the totem pole. Not me, because I had a reputation that preceded me—but in the beginning it was still difficult. The studios had a lot more to say about the casting and the interpretation of a property, and I was also disappointed in my own work as a screenwriter. So I had to go through some apprenticeship years writing movies that I wasn't very happy with until I learned to do it right, just as I had spent all those years writing special material in nightclubs, working in television—making a living, but still learning my craft—so that by the time I got to Broadway, I knew a lot about writing for the stage. Not so with the movies.

I just sort of plunged in, and when I wrote that first movie, *After the Fox,* I thought I had a very funny, satirical, contemporary script. It got in the hands of Vittorio De Sica, though—whom I idolized and was so in awe of that I wouldn't dare say a word about what he was doing to the script—and I didn't understand what he was doing. It just seemed all wrong to me. I watched it and said, "This is a fiasco. This picture is never going to work." I used the experience as a learning device, and one of the things I learned is never do a movie with a man who doesn't speak English very well.

BRADY: I should think that some of the humor would be lost in translation.

SIMON: All of it. All of it.

BRADY: What happened?

SIMON: Well, I just rewrote the script completely. I rewrote it with De Sica's writer Cesare Zavattini, who wrote *The Bicycle Thief, Miracle in Milan* and many other brilliant films. Zavattini is a great social writer, a great social commentator. But I was not writing great social commentary. I was writing a contemporary farce with some satirical overtones about the making of foreign movies at the time. Zavattini and I literally collaborated on the screenplay, but neither of us spoke the other's language—so we had an interpreter in the room. The interpreter was a writer himself, so he didn't really interpret what we said; he just put down what he felt like writing.

The script became a mishmash, and Peter Sellers and I both wanted to get out in the middle of it. We both asked United Artists to let us out, and we would give them a movie free; but they said, "No, we think that between De Sica and you all, you can pull it out." Well, none of us did. But I learned from that one, and I learned from some of the others.

I learned from *Plaza Suite,* for example. I was very obstinate —because I consider myself essentially a playwright, I think. I thought I could take my plays and translate them to the screen with very few changes. What I got with *Plaza Suite* was a film version of the play, which is not as good as the play and not as good as most movies. I did that pretty much with *Last of the Red Hot Lovers,* too—left it so you're spending an hour and a half virtually in one room, and it becomes claustrophobic. I didn't open it up, and I was not being fair to myself about learning the craft of screenwriting. I think it's only been in the last six or seven years that I learned how to write a good screenplay.

BRADY: Are you now reevaluating some of your early work? When you were doing *Plaza Suite,* you must have had a pretty good measure of confidence.

SIMON: Well, obviously you don't sit down and write something and say, "I know this is bad, and I will learn from it years later." At the time I thought, "Yes, this is the right way to do it." What I disagreed with the studio on was having Walter Matthau play all three roles in that film. I said that won't work. You need three separate actors to give it some new input at least every thirty-five minutes. But Walter was adamant. That's the only way he would do the film, and the studio said Walter was the star. So they did it.

That's why I like the theater a lot better. One never has to make those kinds of compromises. I could do a play starring an unknown actor, unknown actresses, and have a big hit. That's almost impossible to do in films; at least it was in those days. One can do it a little bit today; audiences are willing to accept it more.

BRADY: Yet *Plaza Suite* had the same actor in all three segments on stage. Why doesn't it work in film?

SIMON: As consummate an actor as Walter is, I don't think his judgment is always accurate. I think he cannot play the part that George C. Scott played on stage in the first act. I think that George is just better at it, whereas I think Walter is wonderful at farce. When I gave him *The Odd Couple,* Walter wanted to play the role of Felix (which Jack Lemmon eventually played). He said, "Oscar is too easy for me." I said, "If you want to act, act in somebody else's movie. I just want you to do what I think is the right character for you."

I think that the idea of one person playing six or seven roles in a film really went out years ago with Alec Guinness and Peter Sellers, too. It's just a gimmick that doesn't work and doesn't interest me. For example, in the play *California Suite* we used four actors to play all the various roles—four separate roles apiece in that play. But in the movie we used all new actors, and it was the right thing to do. I didn't keep it in one room. I opened it up all over Los Angeles, all over the Beverly Hills Hotel and its environs. It was an infinitely more successful movie.

BRADY: Did your personal involvement in *Chapter Two* make it difficult to "open up" the script for the movie version? Isn't that a bit like tampering with a precious memory?

SIMON: I no longer say, as I did earlier on, "How do I film this play?" I say, "I'm going to write a film. Now, what material from this play can I use to help tell the story of the movie that I am about to write?" I think of it in cinematic terms completely —going to various places and following the story. It was a lot easier with *Chapter Two,* actually, than with, say, *Plaza Suite,* because all the action in *Plaza Suite* takes place in one apartment. Same for *Red Hot Lovers*. The action in *Chapter Two,* though, occurs in various places offstage as a play: They come home from their honeymoon; he just gets picked up at the airport; they were playing softball in the park. These things are mentioned on the stage, so it was infinitely easier to do the screenplay because I could just go to those places. And it's strange, because the movie is forty minutes shorter than the play; yet I think there is more material in it. I was able to get more information in it because the stage often creates obligations you have to fulfill. For example, while two actors are off changing costumes for the next scene, you've got to do a scene waiting for them. I can't have a bare stage. Well, I don't have that problem in the movies. There were sections of material that I did not need from the play, so I just got rid of them. Many scenes with the secondary couple in *Chapter Two,* for example, were tossed. I just used them for key moments and for pushing the story and the main point ahead.

In the play, of course, the actual honeymoon occurs between acts. It's not seen on stage; yet it's a peak of interest. In the movie the honeymoon is one of the vital parts. I think it takes about twelve minutes of screen time in various stages, from the time they arrive for the honeymoon, then how well it's all going, then George's first encounter with someone who reminds him of the past, the haunting feeling of the past—to his first bit of antagonism and his guilt feelings about starting a new life while his wife is now deceased. All of this is graphically shown in the movie, which I couldn't do in the play. The play worked despite it, but I wish I'd had that opportunity.

BRADY: Why didn't you write it as a movie from the start?

SIMON: There is no way I would write that movie as an original script. I have to write the play first to get deeply into the characters. It's like making a big sketch of this canvas you are about to paint on later—and I don't mean that the play is really a test for a movie; to me the play is an entity in its own, and it's still what I prefer to do more than anything, because a play is so verbal. I can spend a lot of time learning about the characters. It's very hard to do that in a movie. That's why I've done few original screenplays: *The Goodbye Girl, The Heartbreak Kid, After the Fox, The Out-of-Towners, Murder by Death, The Cheap Detective;* and those last two are different—I almost had a form to copy. They were satires of other forms of moviemaking, and that's not as difficult. And *The Out-of-Towners* was really elongating an episode, though it was partly successful, I think.

BRADY: You went from a period of low involvement to one of high interest in your films. What accounts for the shift in attitude and commitment?

SIMON: Well, in the beginning I was in New York. I'd write the screenplay, send it out here; they would say, "OK, fine," and I would come out for a week's rehearsal. I hated Los Angeles and Hollywood, went back and let them shoot the picture. After four or five pictures, though, I said, "These are lousy. I'd better really learn the medium. I'd better stay on the set and see how it's done."

I would never do a play the way I was letting them do my movie scripts. I would never give them a play and not show up for rehearsals, only coming to opening night. No. And that's what I did with some of the movies. So I decided to learn my craft. I think that movies are just as important a medium as the theater, and I want to do good work.

BRADY: Paddy Chayefsky and William Goldman have done time in Hollywood, and they hate it. They write in New York City and deal with the elements from there, as you once did. How are you and L.A. getting along these days?

SIMON: Well, to each his own. I don't hate it. I like it. I don't think I could take it twelve months a year. We took an apartment in New York a few years ago, and we go back and forth. I do a play every year, I have business and friends, and I love New York. I'm there about four months of the year all told. But weather is very important to me, and when you come back here the temperate climate makes my writing easier at this point in my life. When I'm either too cold or too hot, I don't feel like working. I get bogged down, I get depressed by weather. Hollywood is a company town; it's mostly business.

BRADY: It seems to have been good business for you. You've been extremely prolific the last four or five years here.

SIMON: Mike Nichols told me that Lillian Hellman told him the years between fifty and fifty-five are the peak writing years for a writer, because all your powers are under control; you've had a great deal of experience in life and see things from a different perspective. And, at least for me, I've found it to be true. One is aware—without getting maudlin—that time is running out. And I'm just not the kind of person who can take two years off and think about things, then write something. Writing must be very, very important to me because it is my main outlet for expressing all my pent-up emotions. As I think on it, almost everything I write *is* in a sense cathartic for me. Without realizing it, my writing *I Ought to Be in Pictures,* which deals with the relationship of this girl and her father, gives me the opportunity to deal in some measure with my own relationship with my father, even though he's gone. I find I wrote about the past a lot in that play. That's why writing is important for me.

Even writing something as inconsequential as, say, *Murder by*

Death is a way of having a good time, of being a little boy again. I loved those horror movies when you came into the haunted castle and somebody's eyes peered out. . . . It gives me a chance to relive being eight or nine years old, using whatever craftsmanship I now have to tell those stories. My favorite classic of all time is *The Maltese Falcon.* And I loved all the adventure pictures as a kid—*Gunga Din, Mutiny on the Bounty* . . . everything. I find today that principally very young kids loved *Murder by Death,* because I think they see it the way I did back then. When I was eight I laughed at those things and was scared by those things.

BRADY: Were you a good student in school?

SIMON: Half and half. I was in the rapids, and I graduated from high school when I was sixteen, so I guess I was fairly bright. But certain subjects eluded me, and still do. I was very good in English, very good at history. Creative subjects. Languages, forget it. Math, forget it.

BRADY: I'll say. Your success has been smooth, steady and spectacular; yet I understand that you've not made a penny from *The Odd Couple* television series, and that you are not seeing performance royalties from *Barefoot in the Park.*

SIMON: True, which is no big loss. I mean, it's a lot of money, but what you lose in the beginning of your career, you make up later on. It might have been a tragedy if that were my only play, my only hit, and I didn't make that money. But nobody knew. The people who were my financial advisers back in those days (some of them have changed since then) suggested that I sell my company for a capital gains at that time, so I would be getting more money immediately, but I would be giving up money in the long run for those other projects. All of the royalties of *Barefoot in the Park* were included, and the television rights to *The Odd Couple.*

I just didn't think that *The Odd Couple* would be a television show. I was not very farsighted about that, so I said, "OK, fine," and I received no royalties. That thing has been going on reruns for five years or more. I could have made millions of dollars from that; but I haven't spent a single day's regret, because I've made so much money on other projects that I thought were really lousy —like *Star Spangled Girl,* I made a ton of money from that. So I guess those things even out. I don't spend a lot of time on the business end of it anyway. I am concerned with the making of deals, but I would rather use that time at the typewriter.

BRADY: Your personality is somewhat mild-mannered. Mel Brooks says you are shy. Producers gobble people like you up and spit you out in little pieces during deal making, don't they?

SIMON: No. Not me. I am shy and mild-mannered, but I think I am rather strong. I know exactly what I want, and I don't think I would have gotten as far as I am without being obstinate, and without being able to say no to making movies in the beginning and staying in New York to do plays. I opted for what I knew was right for me.

Before I was making lots of money, I was offered a million dollars by Bing Crosby and Bob Hope to do *The Sunshine Boys* as a film. I said no, they're wrong for it. It was a guaranteed million dollars. I wanted to do the movie with Sam Levine and Jack Albertson, who had done the play. I was later talked out of that casting because it would have been hard to get movie audiences in to see Jack Albertson and Sam Levine starring in a film that's going to cost, say, three, four million dollars to make, and has to do nine, ten million dollars to break even. So we went with Walter Matthau and George Burns, and they happened to be perfect casting.

BRADY: Wasn't Jack Benny originally cast for it?

SIMON: Jack Benny and Red Skelton were both supposed to do it. Jack died, then Red Skelton pulled out of it for whatever reasons of his own, and George Burns inherited the part.

BRADY: Do you ever have creative battles in story conferences or on a project?

SIMON: I don't have story conferences. Who would I have them with? I don't bring the producer or director a story; I bring them a finished product. I would never go to a studio and say, "Listen, I have an idea, and I would like to do a movie about such and such; and they would say, 'Fine, let's put that on contract now, and we'll pay you x-number of dollars up front.' "

No. I don't want that. I don't want anybody's money. I don't want to be obligated or tied down to anybody. I write everything on speculation. I have enough confidence in myself that if it's good, I'll sell it anywhere; and if it's no good, I don't want to sell it to anybody. I don't want my name on it. They're all after me, always: "Let's make a deal now. We'll give you all this money, and write this play for us, write this movie for us." I always write it on my own. I learned that a long, long time ago.

Consequently, I don't have creative battles. In plays I don't have them with anybody, because the playwright is the king in the theater. It's the director's job to interpret his play. If the director feels that the play is really all wrong, it is his prerogative to quit. I have had conferences and discussions with directors in the theater, but generally it is up to me to write the play. With screenplays, when I have conferences with a director like Herb Ross, his major contribution is in showing me how to make what I have written more cinematic. If he says, "I think this scene would be better if you put it in another locale," it doesn't mean just changing where the locale is; it means a rewrite. But Herb has a wonderful visual imagination. I am still a little stagebound; that's why the two of us work well together.

I write it first, then show it to a director. It's what makes my approach and my life with all of these people different than some other writers out here. I've never been a studio writer. I didn't come up as a screenwriter—and screenwriters suffer that. I came in with a reputation as a playwright, and it's important for me to keep myself in the driver's seat so that I can more or less control what I want to do. It's what Woody does, too.

Woody Allen gets carte blanche from United Artists because he doesn't take enormous amounts of money up front. He says, "If a picture is going to make it, it'll make it later on." But in order to keep his own freedom, his own independence, he asks for no studio interference. Not a lot of people can get that. Some people can, if you're willing to work on small budgets. Paul Mazursky, I think, gets that—has a great deal of freedom, but he doesn't ask for an enormous outlay of money. But if you were to say, "I want five million dollars up front," or whatever it is, then the studios demand a lot more control.

BRADY: You are a writer whose name is above the title. What sort of contractual clout does this signify, and how did it come about?

SIMON: It came about through success. In my plays my name just grew over the years. In *Come Blow Your Horn,* of course, my name was down there where it said: *Opening September Seven at Seven P.M.* But as the plays became more successful, my name moved up because people wanted to see my plays. In movies it didn't mean as much, because I was not that successful as a screenwriter; but in the last five or six years my name seemed to become more prominent—though I never asked for it. Ray Stark gave me above-the-title billing. He and Columbia Pictures did a survey throughout the country. They gave a list of names (including mine with many stars), and they asked, "Whose picture would you go to see?" Well, a lot of people said they would like to see mine. Ray and Columbia concluded that Neil Simon's name as a writer was as valuable to them as some stars'. I never put it in my contract; I just know that it's going to be up there.

BRADY: What does your contract say about script control?

SIMON: I don't think it said anything on the seven pictures I made with Ray Stark as producer. If I worked with some other producer or some other studio, I would put it in the contract. I did have it in my contract in certain places, as a matter of fact— when I did *The Heartbreak Kid* for Twentieth Century-Fox. Ed Scherick was the producer, and Elaine May directed it. My contract specified that nothing could be rewritten without my approval; neither Elaine nor any other writer could be brought in to redo my work.

BRADY: Didn't Elaine May try some end runs around that line?

SIMON: She did, and I could have really screamed about it; but some of the changes I liked. Some of them I *didn't* like, but it was not worth it to go through what she herself did, taking her name off *A New Leaf* when they were going to open because

Paramount had reedited the picture . . . and the day she was going to get an injunction to stop the picture from opening, it opened and got brilliant reviews. So it looked kind of foolish to get an injunction to stop this very successful picture. I was for the most part very happy with *Heartbreak Kid,* so I said OK. So I lost a few battles here and there.

I thought the ending of the picture that I wrote was infinitely better than what Elaine had. It was the one thing that I really regretted. I was so angry at the producer for the way he behaved in that situation, I wouldn't work with him again. The original story by Bruce J. Friedman is about this young man whose life is a constant search for somebody else. He marries, leaves his wife for a beautiful girl, and as they are walking off in a garden he gets very interested in the girl's mother. That is an interesting and provocative character, and that's what I wanted to capture, though I wrote it somewhat differently. In my ending he starts to behave with his new wife the same way he behaved with his first wife: He started to see all the faults . . . and what was interesting was that she was gorgeous. But it wasn't the physical things that were bothering him. It was the way she talked, the little things that she would repeat in her sentences. He was tired of her, and he wanted to move on to the next one.

I thought my ending was better. They shot it. They filmed it and never showed it to anybody. I begged the producer to at least screen it in front of twenty people. He said, "No. I won't even do that." I was really furious at that. I'm *still* furious at him for doing that. I'm not furious at Elaine for wanting to try it, because she did it both ways; but it was the obligation of the producer—and it just makes sense—to screen it and see how others feel about it. Ray Stark would never do that. Ray would say, "Let's try everything and find out how it works."

BRADY: That's interesting, because the ending is everything. *The Heartbreak Kid* comes off as a simple beauty contest to the average viewer today.

SIMON: That was another thing that I did not agree to: the casting. I wanted Diane Keaton to play the first wife, and Diane is a very attractive girl. I never wanted it to be the story of a guy who meets a homely girl, then meets the most gorgeous girl in America and wants to leave one for the other. That's too simple.

That's another very complicated interplay between Elaine May and myself; and while I would still ask Elaine to direct the film —because I think I could reason with her more now—those were very special circumstances. The girl, Jeannie Berlin, was Elaine's daughter; and she obviously gave a very good performance. She got nominated for the Academy Award, won the New York Film Critics Award; but it was *not* the picture that I had in my mind. I was very upset about that.

BRADY: You recently decided to go it alone as producer on your films. Why break up with Ray Stark after seven successful movies together?

SIMON: The pictures I did with Ray were successful, but that's a relative term. One wants to move on in the world. When I first started doing the plays, I did not have as much to say about them as I do now; and when I first started doing the movies, I did not have as much to say about making them as I do now. Doing a film with a producer is like collaborating. The producer gives his interpretation of how the material should be done and what it should say. I could never collaborate on a play, and I feel that a screenplay is as personal as a play—it reflects your own thoughts. Therefore, I want it all to come from the same person.

A producer is the man who puts all the component parts together. I have learned from the business end and from the practicalities of film making about casting, releasing, advertising and promoting pictures. I have learned, too, that there is no one better than Ray Stark. He is as good as anyone, particularly when it comes to bottom-line thinking. But that is not what I am concerned with. I am concerned mostly with the creative element of a film, and in *Only When I Laugh* I picked the director, the set designer, the costume designer, the editor and others right down the line because they in turn would reflect my attitude toward the picture. That is not to say that Ray and I haven't been successful in the past when he was doing the producer's job; but it's time for me to do that for myself now, and at this point I am happier with *Only When I Laugh* than with any film I've done.

BRADY: There was a report in *The New York Times* that your displeasure with Stark crystallized over the casting of James Caan in *Chapter Two*. Was that accurate?

SIMON: It is in part accurate, but not specifically about *Chapter Two*. Jimmy Caan keeps getting the brunt of the blame, such as in the *Times* story, and that's not true. It was an overall thing. I felt that at times Ray, who had his eye on the box office (which is exactly where it should be), tended to look for a star where I might have looked for the actor who best suited the part. Sometimes he was right. When I wanted to do *The Sunshine Boys*, for example, I wanted Jack Albertson and Sam Levene. Ray insisted on bigger stars, and he was right; we would not have done business with the other people. So I can't blame Ray for that attitude, but I prefer to take the chance and make the film the way I want it, rather than listen to someone else in terms of casting. I have very good, strong instincts about casting because I know what the dialogue sounds like in my mind, and I know what the character looks like in my mind. Ray Stark (or whomever the producer might be) could only get it from the written work. I'll admit that Ray has been right more often than he's been wrong; I don't want to shift the blame to him. It's really just a matter of taking my product in my own hands.

BRADY: According to another report, there was a disagreement between you and Stark about whether *I Ought to Be in Pictures* should be made into a movie. Is that accurate?

SIMON: No, there was never any problem over that. Ray didn't buy the property, but it was understood that he was going to do so. Then, when I decided to do pictures on my own, I took the project elsewhere. Ray always wanted *I Ought to Be in Pictures*. There was never any disagreement about that. That story may have come out of Ray's office, but believe me, Ray Stark was very anxious to do *I Ought to Be in Pictures*.

BRADY: You are the writer and producer of your films, and your wife is the star of one production thus far. That sounds like quite a powerful combination on the set. Does it create any problems when working with others?

SIMON: I don't see why it should. First of all, Marsha is treated like any other actress of her calibre; it has nothing to do with me. Secondly, the director really takes over once the picture is in progress. On *Only When I Laugh,* Glen Jordan was director, and I think he was terrific. My relationship with a movie director now is the same as the one I have on the stage: The director interprets the meaning of my work, and he can open things for discussion —perhaps we can strengthen the work here, or delete something here, or come up with a new idea there. There is a much closer relationship between writer and director on a movie because we are dealing with the work on a creative level. In fact, *Only When I Laugh* turned out to have one of the best groups I've ever worked with. For one thing, we were all friends, with the exception of Kristy McNichol, who was new to a group that pretty much knew each other—Jimmy Coco, Joan Hackett, Glen Jordan. But Kristy is the most professional young actress I've ever worked with, so it was an extremely happy company. As a matter of fact, there was less "power," as you might put it, on this picture than on any other picture, because if anybody is powerful, it is Ray Stark. When Ray Stark comes onto a picture, one feels the power of a man like that, and one wants to accede to his wishes. Maybe there is that same power with me now, but since I'm walking around with it I don't feel it. I feel it's just me doing the same work I always do.

BRADY: Bill Goldman says it is unfair to compare a movie to a novel it's based upon, and he's written many novels that have become films. Is there likewise some unfairness in comparing a film to a play upon which it is based?

SIMON: Yes. I don't think a film should even be compared to another film. Comparisons are useless. I don't know why people play those games: Is the film better than the play? Is the play better than the film? Either you like the film or you don't like the film. Either you like the play or you don't like the play.

BRADY: You've said yourself, though, in discussing your work that some of the plays had become better as movies, whereas others had been merely adapted and didn't become such good movies.

SIMON: Yes, but those are emotional responses made just as

the thing comes out. When *Chapter Two* opened on Broadway, I had an enormous emotional response. I said, "Gee, that's good. It says what I wanted to say. In places it's courageous. It delved deeply into areas where I had not gone before." And now it's past. It's on the shelf now, and I did the movie *Chapter Two,* and suddenly it's this new love in my life, and I say, "Gee. I like it better than I like the play."

Ask me five years from now, and I may change my mind. I may say, "Gee, the play *is* better than the movie." I have no idea. But those are all emotional responses, depending on the frame of one's mind at the time, and many different reasons. It has nothing to do with whether the film medium lends itself to making plays work. Maybe the film director wasn't as good as the stage director on this one, or the screenwriter, myself, was not as good as I was in writing the play on that one. Or the actors were not as good. Many different reasons.

BRADY: You once spoke of poor writing and how to recognize it. You said, "The minute you see the sweat on a word you're aware of it being a joke."

SIMON: It doesn't have to be a joke. You can almost hear the typewriter on certain lines. I can't be specific, because I'd have to give you a whole play, but when a line seems to come out of the mouth of somebody else and not the character, it's written. And you know it right away. You see bad movies, bad television things, and you say, "God, this is awful." The reason it's awful is that it doesn't come out of any truth; it comes out of the imagination of some not-very-talented writer who is more likely imitating something he saw in the movies or on television rather than something he saw in life.

I'm not saying that *all* writing should come out of complete reality. You make special rules for television sitcoms, for instance, because no one expects to believe them. You don't say, "Gee, 'Happy Days' is very true to life." You say, "It's a silly little comedy, so forget reality for thirty minutes, and some of them can be amusing." I never thought that people watching "You'll Never Get Rich," the "Bilko" show, thought it was really happening—but there was a certain style and craftsmanship to a show like that . . . or like "M*A*S*H" today . . . that is, the quality is so good and there's such an intelligence behind it that you accept it, reality notwithstanding.

BRADY: You are unique for your accomplishments in three areas of comedy writing—television, Broadway, and the movies. Is it a matter of flexing different muscles as a writer?

SIMON: Well, you have to go in the order in which I did my work. I was successful in television in the fifties, but I'm not so sure I could do it today. I could sit down and write a play today, and if the quality is really good, I have a chance of having a hit. The same thing applies with a movie; if the movie has some real quality, it has a chance of being a hit. But that does not apply at all in television.

I could write something with great quality and television is not interested. If you look at some of the hit shows—"Three's Company," "Eight Is Enough"—I mean, if you can find any quality there, you ought to go mining for gold. And those are the hits. "Charlie's Angels," number one. Or "Fantasy Island." How low can you sink? I cannot sit down and write that. I cannot. I don't known how anybody does it. Do you lower your standards? I think a lot of people do. Or is that as good as someone can write, or as good as someone can produce?

When I worked in television, I worked on rather esoteric shows like "Your Show of Shows," which really appealed mostly to urban areas, the college crowd. "Bilko." "Bilko," I think, is on a par with something like "M*A*S*H," though I think "M*A*S*H" is even better, more cerebral than "Bilko" was. Those are the kinds of shows that I used to like to work with, but I would find it very, very difficult to make a living in television today.

BRADY: You once told some students at the American Film Institute, "TV is a great place to begin and learn, and a good place to get out of."

SIMON: Absolutely—though not everybody has my aspirations. A lot of people are quite content to spend their lives in television. Some of them make more money than I do. People with the Mary Tyler Moore organization or with Garry Marshall, people who have had four or five major hit shows that run for years and years—they have become multimillionaires, and I think they have all the gratification they want. If they have aspirations to write films or plays, though, they should sit down and do it.

BRADY: What happened to the TV pilot for *The Sunshine Boys,* which I understand you wrote?

SIMON: When I wrote *The Sunshine Boys* as a play, I said to myself that even if it's a wonderful play it will not make a bundle of money—because it is for the most part dealing with the elderly. It's about show business—yes. It's about relationships—uncles, fathers, grandfathers—yes. But mostly it is about dealing with the aging process, and that is not something that people line up to see.

The movie was very successful—George Burns won an Academy Award—but it was not a box office bonanza. It just made its money back and a profit. So there was no way that I thought *The Sunshine Boys* was ever going to become a hit TV series in which people are going to tune in every week to see these two old men yelling at each other. They want to see Suzanne Somers or some other sexy girl.

Television is really for the young; that's mostly who watches it. There are shows about older people, of course—like Archie Bunker—but even they have younger people in them. So I never thought that *The Sunshine Boys* would be a successful show. But it was in the contract that they were going to make it into a TV series, and I said I might as well write the pilot. I won't do that again. The pilot was an hour; the series was to be a half hour. But it just wasn't as good as the movie. Red Buttons and Lionel Stander starred, and they were good; but they're not George Burns and Walter Matthau.

They're supposed to do *The Goodbye Girl* as a TV series, too. I will get a royalty this time—not like *The Odd Couple.* But it would amaze me if *The Goodbye Girl* is a terrific series. It takes a minor miracle, like having someone as talented and knowledgeable in television as Garry Marshall was to take *The Odd Couple,* a really solid idea anyway, then get two terrific talents like Tony

Randall and Jack Klugman to do it. Then you've got a big shot at it. You're dealing there with major talents. So it depends on who they get to write *The Goodbye Girl*, who's going to direct it, and who those two actors are, plus the kid. You've got a lot to contend with to come up with a Richard Dreyfuss and a Marsha Mason and a Quinn Cummings. Yeah, I don't hold much hope for it. But who knows? They're liable to surprise me. I would like it if they did.

BRADY: They will probably write Dreyfuss out and have another safe mother-daughter show with a laugh track.

SIMON: No, I don't think they'll do that. But it just doesn't interest me.

BRADY: You and Woody Allen are both veterans who worked on the old Garry Moore TV show. Yet you recently concluded that *Annie Hall* and *Goodbye Girl* were easier to write than a funny lead-in to a song by Jo Stafford.

SIMON: I didn't mean to single out poor Jo Stafford, who is a wonderful singer; but that's tough writing. They would say, "OK, we're introducing the singer, and Garry's got to come out." There's no situation, there's nothing. It's just direct writing. I don't know what one does. What was fun on that show was writing sketches for Carol Burnett. That was really good. But as for the so-called golden age of television—I don't know. One always looks back on the past with such fondness, and it's not always a very accurate picture.

BRADY: When you are working on a movie script today, is there a range in the humor scale? Do you find yourself going for a laugh here but only a smile there?

SIMON: It depends. If I'm writing *Murder by Death*, then yes, I'm going for laughs. I'll say, "I need a joke here; I need a piece of business here." If we are talking about *The Goodbye Girl* or *Chapter Two*, projects like that, I never think of the laughter; I think of how a character speaks and expresses himself; and I never know what we are going to get. I write what the moment requires from a character's point of view.

In most of the things I write, you will find that if you take what the character says out of context, it's not funny. It is not a gag.

The Odd Couple: Felix is blowing his nose, and he's making these terrible mooselike sounds trying to clear his sinuses. Oscar looks at him in disdain and says, "Hey, Felix, don't do that. You'll hurt yourself." That's not a joke. If you tell that to somebody, he'd say, "What's funny about that?" You do it in a play, and the house comes down, because it's truth. It's what the characters feel. So my writing is not this calculated business about what is a joke, what is a gag, and where do you put them in.

BRADY: Is there progression to the humor, however innate? Does the scene build as you write and rewrite it?

SIMON: It's the same as a dramatic scene, or building to a musical crescendo. Writing music, writing drama, or writing comedy—all have their own rhythms, their own emotional beats that build. It's also very much like the sexual act. In a play or movie, the emotional impact is this pulsating, beating thing that has a climax. Then after the climax is the emotional release.

BRADY: Then it builds again . . . and again?

SIMON: If one has that kind of staying power, yes.

BRADY: In a multiple-story work like *Plaza Suite,* what determines the sequence of events? How do you decide which comes first, which comes last?

SIMON: Again, it's music, it's orchestration. You listen to Beethoven: *Da-da-da-dum!* So you start with your heavy piece first. *Plaza* was designed as three separate styles of comedy or drama: the first was realistic; the second, satire; the third, farce. I thought of those three words before I thought of the pieces. I knew I had to have the realistic piece first—with the husband and wife breaking up after twenty-three years. Then came satire: a Hollywood producer, or at least the popular image of what a Hollywood producer is like, trying to seduce a girl. And finally, farce: the father trying to get his daughter out of the locked bathroom on her wedding day. I start serious and build toward a happy ending.

BRADY: When you build toward a line that has comedic value, do you know its impact?

SIMON: I don't build toward the line, because I never know what the next line is going to be when I write. I am trying to tell the story moment by moment. I know what the situation is, and I just try to follow it. Let's say the Sunshine Boys come in, sit down. The two old men haven't seen each other in eleven years, so I've got a very taut, tense situation. I have to follow the natural progression of conversation that would happen to two people who are antagonistic toward each other, but who know each other very well.

"Sit down." One sits. (I don't remember all of this in detail.)

"Would you like some tea?"

"Tea would be nice."

"Would you like a cracker?"

"What kind of crackers you got?"

"I've got everything. I've got chocolate, I've got graham, I've got vanilla."

"I'll have a plain cracker."

"I don't have a plain cracker. I have chocolate, I have graham, I have vanilla."

"I'll have chocolate."

"It's in the kitchen. Go get it yourself."

I don't say that to get a laugh. It's character. "Go get it yourself" means: "I'm not going to do you any favors. You walked out on me eleven years ago. I don't like you. I'm not going to try to be sociable to you. I told my nephew I would try to work things out with you. You want to try to do the old sketch, I will do that. But that's as far as I'm going to go." And when he offers him sugar, he *pushes* the sugar bowl over to him. He won't be very generous with him. I don't sit there and think, "What would be a funny line or gesture here?" It is just the next moment, and they fall in place naturally. It becomes as instinctive as fielding a ground ball when you're at shortstop. You don't say, "Well, let's see, that ball is coming over here. I think it would be a good idea to move to my left." You damn well better move to your left, and move fast. Maybe not the best analogy in the world, but that's the kind of instinct I feel in doing this. It's something that

I hate discussing, hate talking about—writing, especially comedy writing—because it's something that I don't think you can pass on to anybody.

BRADY: It's innate. It's a creative act, better experienced than explained?

SIMON: Absolutely. I have seen really good writers say, "Jesus, these comedy writers are making all this money. I think I'm going to write a comedy." And these really good writers fall flat on their faces. You either have this oblique, unusual way of seeing life, or you don't. Go ask Mel Brooks, "How do you plan that joke?" or, "What do you think of as you're doing that?" It just comes out of Mel. It is born into him. I don't think he calculates it; it's the way he thinks. He's one of the funniest men I've ever met in my life. You sit at a table for half an hour with Mel, and thirty-five things he says are hysterical. He doesn't sit and think of them and wonder, "What can I say?" There is no hard work at it, though yes, there is hard work in writing a screenplay, because one has to think of beginnings, middles, ends, motivations, characters, where it is all going and all that. But the business about writing particular lines, I don't think can be explained. It's just there.

BRADY: Is there much laughter at the typewriter when you are working, or is the comedy business a pretty serious one?

SIMON: It's both. It's serious, but sometimes if it's funny, if the person is really in trouble and I think of a moment, an expression, the way he's saying something, it'll break me up. I'll laugh at it because I'm hearing it for the first time, too.

BRADY: Do you talk aloud when you're writing to hear how the lines might be delivered?

SIMON: Yes, barely aloud. Nobody three inches away could hear it, but I do. I have to say the lines because I'm saying what the actors are eventually going to say, and I want to hear if the words will be confusing, if it's a mouthful, if the syllables are right. It's like writing music lyrics; you want to test it before you demonstrate it for others.

BRADY: Is movie laughter different from stage laughter?

SIMON: How would that be?

BRADY: Well, do you have to leave space in a screenplay for laughter?

SIMON: Well, you can't really. First of all, you don't know when it's going to come. If you have ten people in the movie theater that day—as opposed to a thousand—and if you leave the space, that gap is going to seem like an hour because you won't get that kind of laughter. What I try to do is cover it with some sort of business. If you think something is a really big funny moment, it's always safe to cover it with something visual and not come in with another line right on top of it. On the stage, of course, you don't have that problem, because the actors just wait it out.

BRADY: What is your attitude toward slapstick as a comedic device?

SIMON: It's terrific if it's good, though the connotation of slapstick is almost very low-level humor. It's a very old expression, going back to vaudeville and beyond that. Chaplin did slapstick and it was art. W. C. Fields did it and it was art. Some guy in television does it and it's crappy. It depends who does it.

I personally don't think in terms of "Gee, that's slapstick." I think, "That's a wonderful piece of physical business," as opposed to lines. My use of it depends on what kind of thing I'm doing. If it's a farce, a very broad farce, certain kinds of physical business are funny and effective—such as that scene in *California Suite* where Walter Matthau is trying to get the girl out of his bed and into the closet before his wife comes into the hotel room. Whether one wants to call it slapstick, with that low-level connotation, depends on one's point of view.

BRADY: *California Suite* and *Goodbye Girl* are a bit grittier in terms of language than some of your earlier scripts. What is your view of four-letter words as a writer's tool?

SIMON: If it fits, I use it. I never use it to shock people because how much shock can you get from somebody saying "Shit"? I had the kid in *Goodbye Girl* using it because her mother was on her own a lot, hanging out with a lot of show business characters; thus, the language was a lot looser in that apartment than it might have been if she grew up in the home of a banker, say . . . though the mother was trying to curb it. When the kid said "Shit," the mother punished her. The kid said it again, and the mother said, "Don't you speak that way," and she put her into the other room or something. But if you go through the script, the kid didn't say an awful lot. She said "Shit," "Jesus Christ," and that was about it. It was not an awful lot, if you go back and see it again. It amazed me that anybody would make a fuss over it. A lot of critics said, Wow, salty language from a nine-year-old girl. I used it, too, in *California Suite* where I thought the fit was right. The English couple swear a lot, but when she says, "You asshole," it was funny, and I mean they were *really* angry with each other.

BRADY: Does a screenplay have acts one, two and three for you, similar to a Broadway play?

SIMON: Not literally, of course, because the curtain doesn't come down; and there are no particular breaks—but it does have a rhythm of its own. You set up the problem, which is the first act; the second act is the complication of the problem; and the third act is the working out of the problem. So it has to have a certain harmony to it, like a piece of music; but I don't have to look for a curtain line in a screenplay as I would with a play.

BRADY: After going through all of the rewrites for a play, is it tough to get up the motivation to write and rewrite the various drafts of a screenplay? Don't you ever get a bit tired of the subject matter?

SIMON: Sometimes I say, "I don't feel like doing it right now." But there is nothing worse for me than seeing something *not working* in front of an audience; so when I see my work in trouble, if I have the opportunity to go home and rewrite, I can't wait. The car can't go fast enough to get me back to the typewriter—because I don't want anyone to see what's embarrassing me. So I don't have to get myself up to rewrite. I enjoy it. I love bringing in something new that is going to work better than something I already have up there.

In fact, I feel more confident when writing a play than I do with a screenplay because I can't do *enough* rewrites on a screenplay, can't enrich it as much. You write it once, do a rewrite or two in spots, and it's been shot. I am always more confident writing a play because I'm going to be rehearsing it for four solid weeks, eight hours a day. Then I am going to see it in front of tryout audiences for at least four to eight weeks, night after night . . . forty, fifty performances or so. I get to change it every single day, make it better. I don't get the chance to do that detail work on a screenplay. It's harder for me to write an original screenplay—though none of it is easy. It's all hard. Writing quality is hard no matter what you do.

BRADY: What writers do you read with personal pleasure and admiration?

SIMON: I read ninety percent nonfiction; no, I'd say ninety-eight percent nonfiction. Lots of biographies, and good nonfiction as it comes out. I'll read books on the building of the Panama Canal and the building of the Brooklyn Bridge—two wonderful books, I think, by the same author, David McCullough. The biography of Tolstoy. Nonfiction interests me because it's real life. Even the best of fiction I have a difficult time with, because somebody can write prose beautifully, and you're reading along saying, "God, this is good, these descriptive sentences." Then comes the dialogue—and the dialogue sounds like the prose, and you're saying, "When did you ever hear anybody speak for seven pages?" Not that it isn't possible, because then I'd have to say James Joyce is a lunatic. But fiction is just not for me. I have a better time reading nonfiction.

BRADY: What is the percentage of change in a play script as you are doing all these rewrites—from first version to final performance?

SIMON: It depends on the specific play. I have changed anywhere from ten percent to sixty or seventy percent. For *Come Blow Your Horn* I went through twenty drafts, word for word; things were thrown out the window. Others I've had not an awful lot to do . . . three or four drafts, then rehearsal changes.

BRADY: Are start-up problems similar for writing a stage script and a screenplay?

SIMON: You have the same problems. You have to have a beginning, middle and end. The blueprint is always in my mind. It's a feeling. It's instinct. You just get a glimpse of something that's almost subliminal. It flashes by in your mind somewhere. I hear one sentence in my mind: *The Sunshine Boys*—the story of two old men who get into terrible battles trying to have a reunion to do their old act, and they eventually end up in the Old Actors Home. That's about as much as I know, and I start to write it. I know vaguely where I'm going, but I let the incidents unfold for themselves.

The only good piece of advice that I ever read about playwriting was from John Van Druten, who said, "Don't outline everything, because it makes the writing of the play a chore." In other words, the fun and discovery are already gone . . . and now you've just got to write it out. Some writers *must* blueprint, but I would find it a chore to do that and then just try to dialogue it. I'm in the middle of a new play now—got about two-thirds of it done—and I don't know *exactly* how it's going to end, but I know I'll get it, and if one ending doesn't work, I'll just keep writing until I get it. They're all like big jigsaw puzzles, and that's what the fun of it is. You just keep looking around for the pieces. And I am not afraid of the innumerable amounts of rewriting that one has to do. It's the process I grew up on. It's the only way I know how to do it.

I don't like working with other writers. I could not collaborate. I don't even like collaborating with the director. If a director says to me, "I really don't think this scene works," and if I see his point, I don't need any more discussion with him. I'll say, "I'll see you next week," and come back with another version. Sometimes that version is the right one, or the fifth version is the right one; but I don't like to collaborate with a director, because then it means seeing the play from his point of view, and I don't want it from his point of view. Almost all of my works are highly personal, and I want them from *my* point of view. What I want him to do is to tell me whether he believes it or not. If he says to me, "I don't believe this. It doesn't smack of the truth. It sounds like something you wrote rather than really experienced"—and I don't mean *lived,* but something that comes from the place inside us that is a common truth, which is what we all respond to when we see something good—then I say, "That's OK with me," and I have to go back and work on it. It's like getting to a funny line. If he says, "This is not funny to me," I can't keep knocking him over the head, saying, "I'm telling you it's funny." That's petty, because you find out soon enough when you get in front of an audience with a play. They tell you if it's funny or not.

The advantage of all of this for my screenplays is that I will often be able to explore a character much more in depth for the movie version. By being able to rework the play script, by evaluating all of what I've seen on the stage over, say, a two-year period, I can often say more with fewer words for the screenplay. And a camera going up close can reveal something in a character's face infinitely more than seven lines of stage dialogue, too. So you change the approach.

BRADY: What does your office look like when you are writing?

SIMON: Neat. I like to be able to find things. I used to type exclusively, but now I find it boring to just sit over the typewriter. I'll write out two pages or so and then I type it up. I won't go further than that. I don't want to write fifteen pages, then type it up, because the typing is such a chore.

BRADY: Does anyone help you clerically?

SIMON: No. I don't want anybody in the room with me when I'm working. That's my private time. So I'll write two pages and then type it and rewrite it as I type it. Then I'll write two more pages, then put it down and type it and rewrite again.

BRADY: It all sounds just a bit fastidious.

SIMON: When I was starting out, I once visited Herman Shumlin, the famous old director who directed many of Lillian Hellman's great early plays—*The Children's Hour* and others. I had this filthy manuscript called *Come Blow Your Horn* with all of my little personal notations on it, handwritten, blacked-out things . . . a line with an arrow saying this line goes here and everything. He read the script and said, "I really like it. I think it's good."

"What do you think I ought to do?" I asked.

"Have it retyped," he said.

"Why?" I said. "You were able to read it."

"But I want *you* to read it."

"Well, it's going to be the same script."

"Just listen to me," he said.

So I had it typed again, then read it and said, "Oh." I saw the difference. Things that are not right suddenly come out at you. It's like doing a painting, a little sketch, and then you put a frame on it and hang it up on the wall. Only then can you say, "Wait a minute, this isn't good enough. It was good enough on my drawing board, but it's not for keeps yet." So when I type my pages out and see everything clean, I get a fresh view of my work. Those are little idiosyncrasies, I guess, but a lot of them have value.

I have to see the words clean. It's the material I'm dealing with. If I were a sculptor, I wouldn't dictate the sculpture, saying to my secretary, "Put a nose over there." I've got to feel the putty in my hands. My words are the putty, the clay, and I want to see them in front of my eyes, and I want to say them aloud to hear the rhythm, to see if there are too many words on that page, in that speech. Is there a way to make it more succinct? Is there something that stands out clearly?

BRADY: Do you pay much attention to the length of a script as you move along?

SIMON: I'm aware of it. I would never write a three-hundred-page screenplay. I've heard about that: "We've got a great screenplay. The only trouble is it's three hundred and twenty pages." The writer must be crazy to write three hundred and twenty pages, or even to write two hundred pages. When I write a screenplay, the first draft may come in at a hundred and fifty pages. I know I have to cut twenty pages from that, so I don't write much more than that. The second draft will get down to about a hundred and thirty-five. In the shooting of it, you will lose five, six pages, but not much more.

BRADY: How much of your material doesn't make it out of your office at all?

SIMON: There are lots of beginnings of plays, but I can't answer that question yet. I'll tell you in twenty years how much makes it out, because sometimes I go way back and say, "Gee, that idea was really good," and I want to write it. There are only a couple of things that I wrote completely that have never been done, for various reasons. One was the film script of *Promises, Promises*, which I still think was a super script; but David Merrick owned it, and he was having problems with Twentieth Century-Fox, and we couldn't go elsewhere with it because they had bought the rights, I think. They were having problems with Merrick, I think; so once they turned it down, that was the end of it. I could resurrect it if I wanted to. I could really push it now and say, "Let's get it done." But it's past. I'd rather go on to something else. I wrote two other movies that never got made. One was *Bogart Slept Here*, which we shot seven days of; the other was *Mr. Famous*, a sequel to *The Goodbye Girl*.

BRADY: I thought they were, at least in part, the same.

SIMON: They are. That's why neither got made—because I found out that the story really doesn't work. It was basically the story of a young actor who gets discovered by this director, makes a picture, and suddenly becomes this major star. Well, the audience was not interested. Just listening to the script being read, I felt the audience is not interested in the plight of a guy who has made it real big and can't deal with all of the success and how everybody else around him is affected by his success. It becomes a self-serving, self-pitying story. So Mike Nichols called it quits on *Bogart Slept Here* after seven days of shooting, and I called it quits on *Mr. Famous*. I just stuck it in a drawer, took no pay, and said forget it.

BRADY: *Bogart Slept Here* was originally called *Gable Slept Here*, wasn't it?

SIMON: Yeah, but then *Gable and Lombard* was coming out, and I always liked Bogart, so I made the title change.

BRADY: Is there a Neil Simon formula for success?

SIMON: I'll answer quickly: No. Someone else would have to answer that one. I mean, if there were a formula, I would never have had a flop; and I've had flops. *God's Favorite* was a flop. It ran three months on Broadway. Not all the movies have been successful. *After the Fox* was a flop. *Last of the Red Hot Lovers* was a flop as a film.

BRADY: Aren't most Neil Simon comedies about two characters at odds with each other, yet trapped in a situation—usually marriage or an apartment—that throws them together?

SIMON: I will say that is a fairly common theme in a lot of the works. But if you go through the plays and movies, I'll show you at least half, maybe more, that do not have that "formula," though some of the more famous ones do—like *Barefoot, The Odd Couple, The Sunshine Boys*. But *God's Favorite* does not. *The Good Doctor* does not. *Chapter Two* does not. Many of the movies do not. *Heartbreak Kid* does not have two people confined in one situation. I think people like to pigeonhole and categorize you and say everything you do is in that vein, and it's not the truth at all.

BRADY: How would you categorize yourself as a writer?

SIMON: I wouldn't. The only generalization I might agree to is that I'm extremely optimistic in my writing. I don't like unhappy endings. I don't necessarily always write happy endings, though; people have a misconception about that. For example, they think that at the end of a play, if a couple gets married, it's a happy ending. If you look at the percentages of how many marriages end in divorce, who says it's a happy ending? I mean, your life can be miserable in marriage. I just said that's where this particular story happens to end. But my viewpoint is that I like to think positively about things.

My mother used to say things like, "Don't worry, everything always works out for the best." It all depends how you look at events, including the tragedies. Things work out for the best—if you conceive of them as being that way. I feel different now than when I wrote, say, *Prisoner of Second Avenue,* when I literally felt like a prisoner in New York—imprisoned by my life, by success, by obligations, by the responsibilities to continue it . . . all of that. And I felt—I've got to break away from all of that. I've got to change my life. I have always tried to change the pattern of my life, but it was an enormous step to marry Marsha after twenty years of marriage to Joan, not knowing who this girl was. An enormous step to leave New York, which I vowed I would never leave—but I knew I had to get away, because I couldn't live the same life with Marsha as I did with Joan. There were just too many ghosts then. So we moved here, and it did change things for me.

I have always tried for change in my writing pattern, too. I can write a romantic comedy, or a sort of downbeat comedy like *The Gingerbread Lady;* then suddenly I've got to do something that's completely different, even though the chances are it won't work. So I'll do things like *The Good Doctor* or *God's Favorite,* knowing they are not the kinds of shows that automatically get a line around the block the next day at the box office. They are not those kinds of smash-hit shows. I say I don't care—I want to experiment with new kinds of writing.

There are certain things that audiences really respond to. If you do a romantic comedy really, really well, you've got a chance of having a big hit. It's very affirmative—again, you've got to do it *really* well. There are millions of romantic comedies just sitting in drawers somewhere, or already folded. But those kinds of affirmative statements are more easily acceptable to audiences, just as musicals are. But once in a while I like to write something completely different and take a chance. Shake things up for myself.

BRADY: Do you consider your work on musicals as worthy a task as writing your other scripts?

SIMON: Not really, although I think that the work I did in *Promises* and *Little Me* and, particularly, *They're Playing Our Song* is good work. I don't put it on a par with *Chapter Two* or *The Odd Couple,* because you don't have as much time. You have, say, seventy pages of dialogue as opposed to a hundred and twenty pages; so, missing fifty pages, I'm not going to really tell the story as I want to. It's a craft more than anything else, and it's one of the hardest crafts. It is *much* harder than any play, *much* harder than any movie. I spent a year and a half writing a musical, and it was complete collaboration—numerous conferences with the songwriters, the director, the choreographer. It goes on and on. That's why I don't do them very often; and I will probably never do another one again. *They're Playing Our Song* was very gratifying, great fun. I enjoyed it. But it was a break between doing what I consider more personal projects.

BRADY: You once wrote a film for Marsha Mason and Burt Reynolds that was scratched, didn't you?

SIMON: That became *Seems Like Old Times,* with Chevy Chase, Goldie Hawn and Charles Grodin.

BRADY: When the casting changes, does that mean a heavy rewrite?

SIMON: I did a rewrite. Marsha wasn't right for it, in my opinion. I didn't think Marsha had the qualities that were needed for this girl. I think Marsha is best at things that require complete honesty of character. This was a farce. It needed somebody immediately identifiable with something that's funny. That's why I think Goldie Hawn was righter for it than Marsha.

BRADY: Is it true that you check your film casts with prerehearsal script readings?

SIMON: Yeah, it's been the case since I've been personally involved in my movies—about five years. I'm a great fan of Billy Wilder. We had lunch one day, and I mentioned to him that I was going to have a reading for this movie that I was about to go into rehearsal with. It was unheard of to Billy—to have a reading prior to the first day of rehearsal. I said it's something I discovered in playwriting about ten years ago. Why wait until the very first day of rehearsal to find out I'm going to be in trouble?

All I do is get the actors together and say, "You want to come over to my house Sunday? Let's just sit around and read it." This occurs three months before rehearsal, if I can get them that soon. We just sit around and read the script, and I say, "Thank you very much," and then I rewrite it. I did that with *Goodbye Girl* three times before we ever started the movie, and by the time we got to rehearsal I was no longer in major trouble; most of the rewriting was done. But if we went into rehearsal or started to shoot the picture with the first script of *Goodbye Girl,* no way could I have saved it—because I did a month's rewriting on that film before it even began.

BRADY: What goes on during a reading? Do you sit there scribbling notes?

SIMON: I don't take a note. I just hear it. It's like I have a tape-recording machine in my head. I will be able to go over every single line of the script and tell you what works for me and what doesn't. Not only the lines, but entire sections—if they seem wrong, I throw them out, don't even listen to the lines there. A reading is like the first night with an audience when I do a play. I sit down with a pad and pencil and say I'm going to take notes on all the things that I like and don't, and I end up without a single note—because I've recorded it in my mind, and generally I can jump on it next day and improve the script.

I think that's a block a lot of writers have: They get no help from hearing their work read. They listen to it and say, "Well, we'll see when it gets in front of an audience." As for me, I like to anticipate all of that stuff. I rewrite a lot sooner.

BRADY: Do you base your rewrite upon the personality of the actors and actresses?

SIMON: No, never the actor or actress. Always the character they are playing. Well, in a movie, maybe. Because in a movie, only one person is going to play that character. It's going to be, say, Chevy Chase. No one will ever play that role again. So maybe I will use some of the facets of his personality to make the character stronger.

When I decided I was going to write a movie for Marsha and Richard Dreyfuss, I wanted to use as much of Richard's personality that I knew about, too. I knew he had great aspirations to do Shakespeare, because whenever we met and talked, he'd say, "God, I want to do *Julius Caesar*," and "I want to do *Othello*," which he has done since. It's the dream of every young actor who is serious about his craft to want to do really good work like that, I think. So to show him in trouble in *Goodbye Girl*, with his career really on the line in a devastatingly terrible production—I decided on *Richard the Third*, in which the lead is gay. I once happened to see a production of that play in which the lead played it rather fay, and Richard was such a strong, dominating character—it's the last way you want to approach that project. So I wrote it, Dreyfuss tried it, and it was very funny.

BRADY: Where did you get the idea for that tender Bogart scene on the roof in that film?

SIMON: From my fantasies. It's funny—I spoke at the Ninety-second Street Y in New York recently, and a woman raised her hand and said, "I just want to thank you for letting me live out my fantasy. I've always wanted to be asked up on a roof and have somebody do that for me." It's the most romantic thing that anybody could do for a girl; it's really putting yourself to a lot of trouble, being very open and laying yourself on the line. That's where the real fun in writing occurs, in being able to express yourself that way. It's as though I *did* it. I really don't have to go up on the roof now, put out the champagne, the music, get the pizza, wear the white jacket and talk like Bogart. I've done it up there for everybody.

BRADY: Herb Ross directed *Goodbye Girl,* and your collaborations with him have been productive and positive. You have called him "the best director today in terms of the writer." Is it a blend of personalities that accounts for that?

SIMON: *Very much* a blend of personalities. Herb understands my writing as much as anyone else; but I would have to include Robert Moore in that category as well, because Bob and I have done, I think, four shows and three movies *(Murder by Death, The Cheap Detective* and *Chapter Two),* and all of them have been to some degree successful. None have been flops. Bob understands the rhythms, what it is I'm trying to say, as does Herb. I would include Mike Nichols in there, too, but I've never worked with Mike in movies except that one abortive attempt on *Bogart Slept Here.*

BRADY: After a few drinks, do you ever think of directing?

SIMON: I can't drink, and I almost never think of directing. I *re*direct. I annoy a director once in a while, saying, "Gee, I wish you would do this and do that," but I don't want to spend my time directing.

BRADY: Do you ever have problems with writer's block?

SIMON: It's a different kind of writer's block than one commonly thinks of. I have occasionally written myself into a corner I can't get out of with a script, but I don't have writer's block in which ideas don't pour out. My block means I set it up wrong, put things in the wrong places, and found that it's not going to work, so I have to reassemble it. But I can always think of something; with me it's a matter of coming up with something that I consider *good* enough. What I am afraid of mostly is a loss of enthusiasm, a feeling of "I don't want to do anything now." I am unlike a great many writers who have to spend a day sharpening pencils, reading all the newspapers . . . anything to avoid sitting down at the typewriter. Thus far, sitting down at the typewriter does not bother me; sometimes I look forward to it. Sometimes I'm not that eager, but I give myself a little push, and once I am into about five minutes' work, I am hooked. Then I'm OK.

BRADY: The dime-store generalization from some critics is "When is Neil Simon going to write something serious?" Then, of course, when you've done some serious things . . .

SIMON: . . . they say, "Give us the other stuff." I know, you live with that.

BRADY: But seriousness is very much within the Simon strike zone, don't you think? The episode in *California Suite* with Maggie Smith and Michael Caine, for example, consists of some of the strongest writing one can imagine for the screen—and one can envision a full-length feature of similar intensity. Which leads to the overwhelming question: When is Neil Simon going to write something serious?

SIMON: I never knew what quality that segment of *California Suite* would have when I was writing the original play. I knew as I was writing, it was good. It was like magic. I wrote that thing in about four days, the original draft; then I went over it and over it and over it. But I knew it was a terrific subject. I didn't know if I could write a full-length play based on that, because I didn't know how much material was there; and I don't necessarily think that because it's a one-act play it's not as important or as good. It's like somebody writing a concerto. A concerto can be as important as a symphony if it is a beautiful concerto. *The Gingerbread Lady* is that kind of play to me. So is *Chapter Two*.

If I had done *Chapter Two,* let us say, as a one-act play, you might well be saying the same thing: "Gee, that was a wonderful piece. Did you ever think of expanding that?" Well, that one lent itself. I found the form for making it a full-length play by adding the other couple, by showing the other side of the coin of a good, happy, meaningful relationship—two people who are never going to be able to find it. I think I did it with *Gingerbread Lady,* and when we do *Gingerbread Lady* as a film called *Only When I Laugh,* I'm going to try it again. Now, ten years after the play— and knowing a lot more about moviemaking, about writing, about life in general—I think I can make that work. I think. And I know I will lose a segment of the audience because it's a story about a woman who is self-destructive. That, to me, was the story; never a story about alcoholism. People always like to pigeonhole things and say, "Oh, it's a story about a drunk." I say no, it's a story about a self-destructive person. You don't need alcoholism to self-destruct. You can do anything. But in this particular case, she drank a lot, and it was detrimental to her life.

BRADY: Someone told me that's the story of Judy Garland.

SIMON: It's the story of about twenty actresses that I've worked with. And as many actors.

BRADY: Why did you change the title from *Gingerbread Lady* to *Only When I Laugh?*

SIMON: The original title of the play was *Only When I Laugh,* but previous to this play I had only done comedies; I had not gotten into a really serious play. I was afraid if I used *Only When I Laugh,* the audience would expect some big raucous comedy and be disappointed. I thought *Gingerbread Lady* was a title that would neutralize the audience and make them more open to something else when they came to the theater. Now, with the film, I've done quite the opposite, because I'm afraid the audience will think the subject—about a woman who is an alcoholic —is downbeat, so I looked for an upbeat title. My feeling is that once I've got the audience there, they might be willing to accept the seriousness of the story. So it's back to the original title, though the script is practically new.

BRADY: Most of your plays are collected in two volumes now,

published seven years apart. In your introduction to volume two (1979), there is quite a noticeable change of mind or attitude toward things. You go from being sort of a happy schizo in volume one to "a daily struggle to keep the deadly radiation of neurosis from melting down and destroying this prolificity plant and all that live in a radius of its emotional and co-working environs" in volume two. Has success been emotionally expensive for you along the way?

SIMON: In some ways. The last couple of years, everything has gotten better for me because I've gotten older. I'm in my fifties now, and you start to drop things. You drop a lot of the baggage as you go along. You pick up some things—I don't mean just in reference to one's work or career, but in regard to one's life. You change. You are no longer struggling. You don't have the same sort of aspirations you had in the beginning. You mellow. At least it's true for me. I can't speak for everybody, but I do find I am beginning to accept things that I did not accept four years ago.

When I came out here, for example, I used to play tennis four and five times a week. I tried doing it until last year, and it was taking a physical toll out of me. I decided to play only three times a week instead, and I find that I do not get tired; I am very strong and have enough strength left to do the rest of the work. So you make some of these compromises, physically. I have not had to make them as much in terms of the work, because the work has been flowing very well—but I realize I must take vacations or breaks.

Not long ago I took a three-week vacation in Europe with Marsha. In years gone by I would have taken the pad with me, and generally I would get up early and use that time to work on something. Well, I didn't write a word on this vacation. We spent nine and a half hours flying back on a plane, and I used to sit and write ten, twenty pages in that time. This trip I didn't write a word. I bought books, I read, and I was able to drop all of those old work habits. I'm able to do that now, relax more. But the minute I'm back here, of course, I'm at the typewriter.

As for the emotional price that you pay for all of it, I think what prompted my writing those remarks in the introduction to volume two was exactly what I said there. I went back to see *Chapter Two* and *They're Playing Our Song* both on the same night. *They're Playing Our Song* was playing to a packed house, the audience was screaming with delight, and suddenly I became aware of my body. It had gotten rigid. I was putting body English on the actors and I thought, "Gee, it doesn't change." You just don't go in there and forget about it. I realized that my tightness, my fears were practically the same as on opening night. Not as much is at stake, but you always want it to be good. That's why I stay away a lot now. I don't want to police my shows constantly; there are directors and stage managers to do that. It's like a movie. I've written it, I see it a lot in the beginning, and then I don't see it anymore. If it comes on television four years later, I may watch it, wince a little; but it's old news to me. And one of the really good things that I've done as the years have gone on is to drop the past.

When I wrote *Come Blow Your Horn* I went to see it three times a week because I thought it would be the only play I would have on Broadway. I wanted to savor the joy of my one and only play, because it took me three years to write that play and get it on. I wanted to savor every moment. The rest of the plays, I wouldn't go to quite *that* often, but I went often. *Barefoot in the Park* I would go see every time I was feeling down. The play would pick me up because there was something positive and affirmative about it. But the years go by, and I've now seen *They're Playing Our Song* only once since the first week it played in New York. And I enjoy it, but there is no point in spending a night there. The producer will be after me, saying, "I wish you would go see the play. Go back and speak to the actors and tell them where they're falling, where they're good." Which is what the director generally does, but he's not in town; so they'll ask me to do it, and I really don't have the patience, because my mind is no longer there. My mind is on the project I am working on.

BRADY: And you go back at your own emotional expense.

SIMON: Well, like the night I wrote about in my introduction,

I get annoyed with some of the audiences, when they cough, when somebody comes in late. It's like dating. This is probably a poor analogy, but seeing an old play is like going out to dinner with an old girl friend that you no longer have an interest in. The romance is over as far as I am concerned. All of those plays that I have done—the seventeen that are now published—I don't have any emotional interest in them.

BRADY: That sounds creatively healthy.

SIMON: Oh, it's enormously healthy. I know so many writers who spend years just dealing with the past. That's why I don't even keep my rewrites. They're of no interest to me. I'm not looking to build up a stockpile in some library somewhere of every scrap of paper that I've written. If I threw it out, then it's not worthwhile to me. There may be some good material in it, but I'm not going to use it somewhere else. I don't want to save all the scraps of my past. I just throw them out. The published plays are certainly not scraps, but I know I could do better now —so why read something that I feel is inferior?

BRADY: Bill Goldman doesn't look back either, but he drops everything earlier. After being mauled a couple of times by re-writes and problems on the set, his attitude now is: Write it, give them your best shot, then take the money, and run.

SIMON: Oh no, I couldn't do that. I do not have that attitude. That's different. You're talking about work in progress, and with work in progress I am vicious, I am a killer then. To protect my material I am there as much as I possibly can be. I want it to be terrific, and until the very last moment, until that film or play is opened, it is work in progress. I'm talking about once it's gone and out of my hands. Then I have no interest. But I would hate to have the attitude of take the money and run. I don't believe in it. I think you suffer for it. Your projects suffer for it.

BRADY: You are so prolific, are there periods of overlap to your various projects?

SIMON: More so now than there used to be, but it still does not detract from the amount of energy and emotional investment in each of the projects. I don't dismiss one and say, Well, this one isn't important and that one is. Some need more care because the details are infinitely greater. For example, in the film *Chapter Two* every single moment, every nuance was important to me because the project was vitally important and I wanted it to be exactly the way I saw it. When it comes to doing a farce, a comedy—let's say *Murder by Death* or *The Cheap Detective* or even *Seems Like Old Times*—it's up for grabs. Chevy Chase, on the set of *Seems Like Old Times* would do some wacky, crazy thing that might be terribly good for the picture, and I'd say fine, leave it in. I don't care about that. Everything doesn't have to be mine. But in a thing like *Chapter Two,* since it is an absolutely personal point of view, then I want it to be exactly that up there on the screen. Another important project to me is *Only When I Laugh.* I had strong feelings that it would work, because I'd already done it as a play.

I have started three or four other plays, too—thirty pages of one, fifteen pages of another—but I just let them sit there. There's plenty of time to go back and do them. It is important for me to write a play every year. These are my productive years. I won't be able to do it forever. I enjoy doing it, and I think they're all good ideas. If, when I get to one of them, I am stuck on it as I have been in the past, I'll just let it sit and go on to another play. So there are all of these projects in my mind, but somehow they don't get cluttered.

BRADY: How do you do it?

SIMON: I'm very organized. I even have time to go across the street and play tennis. Life is very simple when there are no distractions like having to go someplace to speak, do interviews, do other things. I come to my office in the morning, write three pages before noon, go play tennis, have lunch, come back and do another few pages. If I stick to a schedule like that, doing three pages a day, at the end of a five-day week that's fifteen pages. In ten weeks I have a screenplay.

I don't keep to that schedule rigidly, because there are other distractions—I must travel, I must do other things—but still, if you just keep going at it, the discipline is as valuable and as important as the talent. You can't have one without the other.

BRADY: Yes, but not long ago you had two hits on Broadway, a new play ready for tryouts, a film ready to be shot in California —and an ulcer in your stomach screaming "slow down." What happened?

SIMON: Well, I did get an ulcer, the first one in my life, in March of 1979. So I stopped everything for three or four months. I did some work, but I didn't do a lot of writing. I think most of my writing, fortunately, was already done. But it was a period of some reevaluation. I had to stop and think things out. I found an analyst, went to see him three times a week, and the ulcer went away—through discussing it with him, and through introspection, which I do a great deal.

I am always putting myself under the microscope and trying to examine why I sometimes get into trouble in my life and why things work out for me, just as I do with my characters. I don't do it all for the purpose of eventually putting things down on paper. I do it because it fascinates me, human behavior. And the conclusion I came to, basically, was that the ulcer came on because my mother died six months before that, and obviously my relationship with my mother was even more complex than I imagined it would be; and, having lost my wife, then losing my mother, with my daughters both growing up . . . I think I have a very strong pull toward women in my life. I've constantly been surrounded by them, and my mother was really my champion all my life. My father was somewhat negative about my going into show business, as I said earlier, but my mother wasn't: I was the perfect son.

So I think losing my mother at that time was the key, although I dealt with it well. She was eighty, had lived a good life, and died a relatively peaceful death; so I thought I was dealing with it very well. We put her to rest, and I went about my life. There was no great emotional breakdown like there was when Joan died at thirty-nine. But I think psychologically something was going on, and that's what caused the ulcer, because I have been under the gun too much in my life in terms of work and deadline pressure not to have had this come up before. That's not to say that the ulcer will not reappear, or that I have solved all of *those* problems; but I do think there was some connection between the ulcer and the passing of my mother.

BRADY: Did analysis displace the handful of pills you were taking during this period?

SIMON: Well, I've always been something of a hypochondriac, but I also have a fairly delicate system. I mean, I travel and I get sick. I'm famous for it. I once spent eight days in bed at the Connaught Hotel in London while my wife and children were out seeing all the shows. I got sick in Italy, ended up in the hospital there. I don't travel well. You can look that up in Freud. I forget what the name of it is—when you have to make a connection to home, something that is safe, where you know you are protected. But I do travel anyway. I go. I never let it stop me, because I never know when it's all going to be terrific. This recent trip to Europe was one of the great exceptions, and I think the fact that it was all terrific this time was because I had let go of the past again. I remarked to Marsha, "I have never felt as comfortable on a trip as I have this last time." I didn't rush to get back, which I always used to do. I used to go and buy *Variety* in Paris to see how things were going. No desire to do that. No phone calls back to the office to see how the plays were going. They called me, but I had no desire to call them. I was having a good time.

But about the pills, yes, when Joan first got ill, my blood pressure elevated enormously. I've had it for the last seven or eight years now, so I have to take pills for the rest of my life to control it. It has certain side effects, and you have to watch all the little breakdowns in parts of the body. But it has been in check, my blood pressure is normal now, and I lead a normal life. We talked about this earlier—how I felt that night when I went back to see two of my plays on Broadway. For a while there I was tense, but you shouldn't think that I am always looking in the mirror with seventeen pills in my hand, saying, "My God, why am I so worried about the play?" I'm not.

But I live under great pressures, self-induced pressures, because I don't have the attitude of take the money and run. My work means a great deal to me. I have terrific *simpatico* with

Woody Allen, who I saw sitting in Elaine's looking morose one
night just after *Manhattan* had opened. I had never seen reviews
like that. People went nuts over it. I loved the picture myself. I
love Woody. I went over to him and said, "How are you,
Woody?" and he said, "Oh, OK." It surprised me—and it didn't
surprise me. It surprised me because I thought he would be feeling a lot better, because I have experienced that. When I have
something that's a really big hit, like when *The Goodbye Girl*
opened, I was delighted. People came up and said, "It's terrific!
I'm so glad!" I said, "Yeah, I'm really happy about it." Woody
doesn't seem to react that way overtly. Though he may be enjoying it, you don't see that. But I have done the other thing, too.
I've had a big hit and people say, "Congratulations!" and I say
to myself, "Yeah, so what." I was not happy about some aspect
of it. So you can never tell.

BRADY: Happiness doesn't necessarily come with success,
does it? Success can go merrily along, but happiness is at a
different level.

SIMON: For me, happiness is having control over yourself, not
being at the whim of the outside environment, of letting other
people control your happiness. If you want to get upset over a
John Simon review, you've got to be crazy. You really have to
be masochistic, and I was that way for many, many years. I don't
just mean John Simon either. Anybody. I got very upset when I
first read Richard Eder's review of *Chapter Two* in *The New
York Times*. I didn't even read his review of *They're Playing Our
Song*. I knew it was not good, but it didn't bother me, because I
knew the show was a great entertainment. I knew that people
were going to like it, and I knew that it would run a long time. I
would only read the review if I respected the reviewer and I
wanted to learn something. But even those I do respect, a lot of
them sometimes are so off base in understanding what I was
trying to achieve that I don't bother reading or absorbing them
. . . whereas others can really get to me.

There's one critic that I find always seems to hit at the truth
with me: Ted Kalem of *Time* magazine. He has a very clear
picture of where I am emotionally, intellectually, without even

knowing me. I think we met once, said hello briefly at some function or other; but we've never spent any time together. But I remember his review of *The Gingerbread Lady* said that Neil Simon is too morally responsible to really understand what is going on inside the head of this alcoholic woman. At the time I agreed with him. Now eight or nine years later, I think I know more about life to be able to go back and write about that character from a much greater perspective. I think I understand her now. I've had a lot more ups and downs in my life. I don't think one has to be morally *ir*responsible to understand the workings of an alcoholic, but I have seen enough self-destructive people in my life. I've seen my own self-destructiveness in periods to understand that character more.

BRADY: You seem more at ease with yourself as a writer today as opposed to a few years back. Would you say your writing isn't getting older, it's getting better?

SIMON: Oh, I think it's infinitely better now—though I think, too, that if I were to write *The Odd Couple* today I might screw it up, because *The Odd Couple* was all of a fabric; it stayed in a certain level, in a certain vein, and I didn't mess with it. I kept it a certain kind of comedy. Today I might try to make it a little deeper, and I might upset that fabric. I just read a recent review of *Come Blow Your Horn* that said it would be interesting to see how Neil Simon would write that play today. The reviewer thought I would get more things out of it. Some things I would have improved on, but some things, I think, I would hurt.

Since I'm more comfortable with myself, I'm more comfortable with the work, and I know that I can just put it aside. I am not fighting for attention anymore, which I used to be after—my place in the sun. I cannot ascertain how I am perceived by our culture. Am I a great playwright? Am I a poor playwright? Am I just a popular playwright? Am I an important playwright? Am I an inferior playwright? Those opinions are completely up to the person who is perceiving me. They have nothing to do with my own viewpoint, and that changes from day to day. That's why I don't go back and read the old plays, because I start to pull myself down, saying, Jesus, you could have done better.

Woody was telling me about how he felt after he had finished both *Annie Hall* and *Manhattan* and was putting the films together. Then came these terrible fears: What have I done? Is this any good? You don't know. You've lost all perspective at that point. Very often I will write something—a movie or a play—and people will see it and say to me, "Gee, it just doesn't work. That's too bad," and I will agree with them; or they could see the very same thing and say, "It's wonderful. It's just terrific," and I will say, yes, I think so, too. I am ready to accept either answer, and I think Woody feels the same way. But we both agreed that we enjoy doing the work, though it's only the inspiration that's the fun—sitting there and thinking of that idea for that moment.

BRADY: Despite the success, you sound a little insecure.

SIMON: Some days you look at the stuff and say, God, this is really good. Other days, you say it's just garbage. And it is not a very clear picture at all. All during the making of *The Goodbye Girl* I kept saying to Herb Ross, "Is this any good?" I never said, "This is no good." I never had a positive/negative attitude about it. I just kept wondering, saying, "I don't know, it just seems so easy. They come in and they talk. They don't seem to be doing anything exceptional." And Herb would say, "I think that's why it's good. It's so real, it's so effortless." But he would say, "Sometimes I wonder, too." The only other experience I had similar to this was with *Barefoot in the Park,* because the story was so fragile and light. It was all in the characterization, the details, what they said, when they said it, and how they said it. In *Goodbye Girl* it's not like you're working on this monumental story and you've got this big thing to deal with—like *Chapter Two.*

With *Chapter Two* I knew I was dealing with major issues. I had my doubts about that, too, but never the same kinds of doubts as with *The Goodbye Girl.* The *Goodbye Girl* doubts are "Is this any good at all?" *Chapter Two* is, "Did I do this well enough? This is important, and I've really got to do this well." *The Goodbye Girl*—I don't know what it is. It's a soufflé. Did I make it properly? As I showed it to people and people saw the dailies in all of the studios, the word started to come back: "God, it's wonderful, it's wonderful!" The same thing happened with *Chapter Two,* though I really couldn't be positive that we were doing it well enough until I saw it all put together. A movie and a Broadway musical are the same thing: You don't know what you have until you put it together. With a play, I generally know how it feels; but a musical, you don't know. They're doing the numbers in the other room, and you're doing the book here, and you've got to put them together—and that doesn't happen until four weeks later.

It's the same with a movie. You don't know until they put it together. After you've done those ten days of rehearsal, which are really kind of meaningless—they just kind of block things out, and it's mostly for the actors to get to know each other—you shoot page twenty-eight, then page seventy-six, then page three, then page ninety-eight. Then you see dailies and you say, "Yeah, ten seconds looked good to me." I don't know what it means. It's like going into rehearsal with a play in the theater and you say, "We're just going to do act two, pages seventeen and eighteen." So you look and you say, "So? Looks OK. What do I know?" I want to see the whole thing, the whole fabric. A play is not that way, because a play you always see put together. You read it from beginning to end. You could even get up there holding the books and act it out without the actors knowing it, and you can tell if it's something.

On some movies they'll put a scene together, a five-minute scene, and you might say, "Ah, I have an inkling that that looks good to me. That scene seems to come together." But you're never sure. I have done films like *After the Fox* where they start to put things together, and I saw them and thought, "Oh, boy, are we in trouble." And I saw those people over there deluding themselves, saying, "It's a masterpiece! It's a classic!" Meantime I am saying to myself, "I think it's a piece of junk." But I was afraid to speak up.

BRADY: Have any of your films been shot in chronological sequence? I should think that would give you a better perspective than the out-of-sync method you describe.

SIMON: *The Goodbye Girl* was shot fairly much in continuity. I liked what I saw every day. I just thought we were making this tiny little movie.

BRADY: The characters are incredibly rich, though.

SIMON: Yes, but as you do just little bits and pieces, you don't see that richness. It takes development. I watch it now, and I say to myself, "That's really good," and even get a little awed by it. "That's hard work," I say to myself. "I don't think I could do that again." That's when you get scared—when you sit back at the typewriter and say, "My God, all of those *details* that I've got to try to get into something again."

Nobody—the best—Woody, anybody, ever really knows, ever is that positive. I am speaking for all of the good writers, all of the good directors, all of the good actors. You *should* have great self-doubt, because if you don't you become pompous, rigid, and you do not improve on the work. I know people like that. There was a writer friend of mine many, many years ago whose one piece of advice was, "Don't let the producer or the director change anything. You just tell them to go screw themselves. They don't know what they're talking about." It seemed a very rigid way of working. I said to myself, "It seems wrong to me. I want the input of everybody. I don't have to accept it, but I want to hear it." His attitude was no, his was the final authority and he was going to control everything. Well, that guy barely works today, and he was once extremely talented.

BRADY: You have to be a team player.

SIMON: Because it is a collaborative medium—both films and plays, as opposed to doing novels.

BRADY: And ultimately, how would you like to be remembered?

SIMON: As a good playwright.

ROBERT TOWNE

For years Robert Towne was one of the busiest, most successful unknown screenwriters in Hollywood. He was the script doctor, arriving late at night, after all attempts had failed, and saving the project from certain death before the cameras. The next day he was gone, and only insiders knew how valuable his talents truly were. "He's legendary," says William Goldman. "I first heard of him on *Bonnie and Clyde*." Says producer Robert Evans, who saw Towne do rewrites on *The Godfather* and write the original screenplay for *Chinatown*, "I would rather have the next five commitments from Robert Towne than the next five commitments from Robert Redford."

Robert Towne, forty-five, always thought he was going to be a writer. A native of Los Angeles, he was raised in the San Pedro fishing port area and wrote his first short story when he was six. He worked as a tuna fisherman, attended Pomona College in Claremont, studied philosophy, and wrote more stories. He left school in the early fifties, went into the Army, and in 1958 attended an acting workshop in Hollywood taught by Jeff Corey. Here he met a struggling twenty-year-old actor named Jack Nicholson, who became Towne's roommate for two years, and a low-budget film producer, Roger Corman. "Anything that anybody wanted to do was fine with Roger," recalls Towne. " 'You want to write a movie, kid? Sure. OK.' "

Towne worked with Corman on several quickie projects, including *The Last Woman on Earth,* "a grim science fiction thing" that the writer would rather forget; and *The Tomb of Ligeia,* an Edgar Allan Poe adaptation that is one of Corman's better films (with Vincent Price) and can still be seen making the late-movie rounds on TV.

Towne himself worked in television, writing briefly in the early sixties, was unhappy, and got back to movie work by doing a rewrite on a western for Columbia. Warren Beatty read the script, liked it, and remembered Towne's work when he and director Arthur Penn encountered difficulties with the script that David Newman and Robert Benton had done for *Bonnie and Clyde.* Towne was hired to do a rewrite. His work, which included structural changes as well as line and scene rewrites, went uncredited, but it got him tagged as a master rewrite man and led to other jobs. Thus, when Francis Ford Coppola (also a Corman alumnus) was so immersed in directing *The Godfather* that he had no time for rewrites on the script, he put in a call to Bob Towne. The writer came to the set, conferred with Coppola, Marlon Brando and Al Pacino, then wrote until four in the morning—forging the brilliant scene just before Don Corleone's death in which the old man passes the torch of Mafia power to his son. Towne was so helpful that Coppola acknowledged the script doctor's work when he accepted the Academy Award for the screenplay.

Since then Robert Towne has been getting credit where credit is due. After *The Godfather,* he did a revision of Paul Schrader's *The Yakuza,* for which he shared screen credit. Then, in quick sequence, three movies written solely by Towne were released: *The Last Detail* (adapted from Darryl Ponicsan's novel) and *Chinatown,* both starring Jack Nicholson, and *Shampoo,* starring Warren Beatty. When *Chinatown* earned Towne an Academy Award for best original screenplay of 1974, *Newsweek* reported that "right now there's no hotter screenwriter than Robert Towne."

Since *Shampoo,* Towne has slowed his writing pace. In fact, at the peak of his demand as a writer, he took a year off and spent the time trying to negotiate a settlement between the tuna industry and environmentalists so as to ensure safer fishing practices and fewer porpoise deaths in tuna nets. Though he did some rewriting on *Marathon Man* and a few other scripts for which he was not credited, he sees script doctoring as "a limited role" in his writing future. Instead, he has devoted his energies to a new adaptation of the original *Tarzan of the Apes* novel, by Edgar Rice Burroughs, for the screen; and to *Personal Best,* an original screenplay about women track athletes and Olympic competition. *Personal Best* will also be Towne's debut as a director.

For almost ten years Towne and his wife, Julie (daughter of actor John Payne), lived in a stucco bungalow perched on a hillside surrounded by oak trees and scrub brush in the Santa Monica mountains. In recent years, though, they moved to the Malibu beach to live full time in the area's oldest house on the ocean. It is a comfortable, thick-walled home with tile roof and a small interior courtyard; it is a home redolent of an earlier California. Here, as the ocean waves roll in, they are broken by some jutting rock formations, and they are punctured on this particular day by the bobbing head of a sea otter who comes in to feed on clams and to swim with Robert Towne as he does his daily three thousand yards. Towne, once chronically ill with allergies, is now a tautly muscled health nut.

The house is also populated by three huge Hungarian sheepdogs, weighing a hundred pounds apiece and resembling giant white mops; and by Katharine Towne, age three and perhaps thirty-five pounds, who sits on her father's lap as he reflects on *Personal Best* and the changes in his life since late fatherhood. In *Personal Best* he cast Mariel Hemingway as "the more central of the two central characters," and working with the teenage star on this particular day had left him moved by her mixture of youth and maturity. "Now that I have a daughter of my own," he says, lighting a cigar, "the temptation is to fantasize and escalate Katharine up to age eighteen and to see her as Mariel, who is what anyone would want a daughter to be. In some ways she is so young, and in some ways she is so old; a little baby, and a contemporary."

———————————

BRADY: Has your life as a writer changed much since you've become a father?

TOWNE: Well, the business hasn't changed, but I was terrified at the idea of becoming a father. I'm rather old as fathers go, and I always thought that fatherhood meant shouldering a confining sort of responsibility. I associated it with conservatism, with decay, with growing old and dying—and actually I have found it the single most liberating experience in my life. It's altered my sense of how one should work.

What it comes down to, I guess, is, because of my daughter, I'm less frightened even about work. That's one reason why I wrote *Personal Best* very quickly. As a writer I've always been frightened: "I'll screw up here," "This won't be good"—that sort of attitude. *Personal Best* was just as much work, but a lot less strain; it flowed a lot better, and in terms of directing and whatever I want to do now, I'm less frightened than I was before, because of this little creature.

BRADY: How did *Personal Best* get started?

TOWNE: It began with my acquaintance with lady athletes I met when I was working out at UCLA, in particular Jane Fredericks, one of the leading pentathletes in the world. I was working out in the men's weight room just before going over to the pool, straining and grunting at one of the bench-press machines . . . and out of the corner of my eye I saw somebody at the next station repeating at one hundred and fifty, with total ease, and I thought, "God, that guy is really strong." That guy got up, and it was Jane. A real impressive creature—quite feminine in body, but amazing in strength. I just stared at her and couldn't believe it. I was stunned. It was a revelation to me. That was the beginning of an idea to do something on women athletes.

I think, too, that writers generally tend to identify with women, or even to identify themselves as women—particularly movie writers. I do. You are always the one at home sweating over the hot typewriter while the authority figure is out on the set telling people what to do. A writer is always trying to be the supportive one. If I am on the set, it's to say, "What about . . . ?" or, "That's great." I think that writers have tended to be the niggers of the industry, so to speak; and I think that women in track and field have tended to be that in their sport. So there are those parallels—plus greater strength than one is likely to think there might be in someone with such sensitivity. And so as I got to know women athletes and their way of life, I was moved to write about them.

I see a kind of purity in women athletes in their desire to jump higher and leap farther and run faster than any other kid on the block. It's not unlike the purity of my child's desire to get up and be able to walk, to make her hands move in a new way—and the joy that accompanies physical progress. I started writing *Personal Best* about four months after Katharine was born, and I finished it in a month, which is very fast for me.

BRADY: It sounds as though the idea overtook you.

TOWNE: It's an idea that was simmering for a while. I had

known these girls for a couple of years by the time I was ready to write; then it did in fact overtake me. But who knows all of the elements involved? I just wanted to do it, and I did it. I had known the girls for so long, talked to them—I had to do no research on their lives and that particular combination of elements that goes into a woman athlete.

BRADY: Is the story line based upon real events?

TOWNE: Not really, though there are elements that *could* have happened to some of the athletes I know. Two women meet under one set of circumstances: one is victorious, going to the Olympics in 1976; the other fails to qualify. During the next four years they become intimate with one another—but they also begin to compete against one another. Ultimately they face each other as competitors at the 1980 Olympic trials.

BRADY: Has the U.S. boycott of the 1980 Olympic games caused any story difficulties or alterations?

TOWNE: Only to the extent that the title *Personal Best* has added significance: These people do well, and they are only testing themselves against themselves. For the athletes as athletes —well, that is another story.

BRADY: What has the work on *Personal Best* done to *Tarzan?*

TOWNE: Nothing. One of the reasons for doing *Personal Best* first is the realization that it would take months to train the *Tarzan* apes to do the kinds of things I felt they would have to do. Right now that is occurring in Oklahoma. When *Personal Best* is finished and released, I expect to do a script I've been working on called *Tequila Sunrise,* fast; then move into full production on *Tarzan.*

BRADY: You now call it *Tarzan,* but at one time it was called *Lord Greystoke.* Why the change?

TOWNE: I was always going to change it. I used the title *Greystoke* at one time because it's Tarzan's family name and because I felt that it was a disadvantage to the project to be called *Tarzan.* I was worried that people would think, "Christ, a Tarzan movie. Who wants to see that?" I'm hopeful now that people will want to see it *because* it's a Tarzan movie. But the film will be very much about a child who is raised by animals, done as realistically as possible while still remaining fundamentally a romance. Tarzan may not mean that to everyone—being raised by a troop of apes; an alien culture; dealing with that culture's effect on a human child, and the subsequent events when he does encounter human beings. So I hope those people who go to *see* Tarzan movies will not be disappointed, because it's something a little bit different than what they've been normally led to expect.

BRADY: How has the writing on that script been going?

TOWNE: I never ever have done so much research. Reading personal journals about nineteenth-century Africa, nineteenth-century England, reading about animal behavior, meeting Jane Goodall. I did all kinds of things to satisfy myself that, in the words of Plato at the beginning of *Timaeus*, his dialogue on the creation of the world, "I do not say that this is exactly how it happened, but it's a likely story."

BRADY: How does such intense research show up in the script?

TOWNE: In Jane Goodall's book *In the Shadow of Man*, David Graybeard, who was one of her favorite apes, and another ape, maybe Mike (I can't remember who it was), were so overcome with joy at seeing fresh fruit and bananas that they actually groaned and hugged one another with joy. I found that charming and stimulating. In the script, Tarzan kills a bush pig, and it's one of the relatively few times when the troop of apes gets to eat meat, and in this scene two of the apes, with whom you are familiar, hear the kill, see him bringing in the meat, and groan and hug each other with joy over the fact that the food is coming.

BRADY: From just browsing through the script thus far, I can see there are long stretches where there is no dialogue. What keeps the story moving here?

TOWNE: Decent direction, I hope. Apes don't talk, and there's no narrator, and the story takes Tarzan through seventeen to eighteen years of life.

BRADY: The Burroughs story is make-believe; yet the approach you are taking here is quite realistic.

TOWNE: In comparison with the Burroughs approach, I suppose it is. In comparison with what actually would happen, I don't think so. Many feral children either are or were retarded to begin with, and that's why they were abandoned.

BRADY: What sort of language goes on in this child's first eighteen years?

TOWNE: Well, just the range of vocalization that the apes have. I'm using as a range the sounds that Jane Goodall and others have recorded.

BRADY: So it is to be a script, then, without much spoken English?

TOWNE: Half of it is without any English at all.

BRADY: How are you preparing to direct it?

TOWNE: By trying not to think about directing. When you write a movie, particularly a movie that has taken this long, you're geared to think that "Ah, this has been a punishing experience, but I will be rewarded with relief and relaxation when this writing job is over." But in fact my work will just *begin* when this is over. And that's a hard thing to get into your head—that after all this work, your work begins.

BRADY: Did you have any apprehensions about becoming a director?

TOWNE: Yeah, I had some. I never directed a movie before, although I was never off the set of *Shampoo,* and Warren and Hal Ashby allowed me to participate in that process. But I will always consider myself a writer. I don't know. I think, having been on many sets, that directing is the most demanding work you can do—except for facing blank paper.

When you are writing you are alone and can confine your foolishness to a room; but when you work with people, when you're directing, it's quite possible to feel like the biggest idiot on earth. Here is this elaborate machine, this infernal machine—it's out of Rube Goldberg—and you're there. Trucks. Maniacs carrying things running all over the place. Lunch wagon. Everything. Suddenly you are this guy that everybody is *looking* at, and it's intimidating too. Directors all have to feel like idiots and assholes. I know I do.

One feeling I'm experiencing as a director is that it's like rewriting standing up. The actors do the scene, you are looking at the take, and then real fast you've got to figure out how to rewrite that take before the next one. You've got to watch it as though the writing had nothing to do with you—as though *they* are the writers. Forget that you are watching your own stuff. You are watching this Thing coming out from the actors, the screenwriter, and everybody else, and you've either got to figure how to rewrite the scene immediately, or be able to tell that it's good enough and doesn't have to be rewritten. Doing that as a writer in your own room—"This doesn't look quite right; I'll go out and think about it for half an hour"—is one thing; on the set, you've got to do it right away, or not do it at all, or run the risk of going up to a producer and saying, "Jeez, I've been looking at that scene, and I think we should reshoot that." And you get a very unhappy producer. The necessity of having to do it *fast* under that special kind of pressure is a different kind of discipline than what I've known as the discipline of writing.

Writing is creating something out of nothing. Rewriting is creating something out of what is there—but doing it with fifty-five thousand people and trucks and equipment standing around, staring at you, wondering what you are going to do next, or if you know what the hell you're doing, and somebody asking you, "Do we break for lunch at twelve-thirty or at one?" and, "When do you want to look at dailies?" and, "We can't get this actor for that. Do you want to see So-and-So?" and, "Do we this?" and, "Do we that?" and trying to clear your head and think: *Did I really like that take or didn't I?* It's a fucking gaggle of noise.

I lost consciousness once in Madrid. I was in an elevator with Sal Mineo. I was real tired, and I had eaten something that didn't feel right, and I passed out. It was a tiny elevator, and Sal was much shorter than I, but he draped me over his shoulder and, with a couple of other people, pulled me out of the elevator. As they were walking me, I slowly regained consciousness, and it was the weirdest sensation in the world. Things were totally silent when I was unconscious, and as I came around the voices slowly began to grow—and it was like I was surfacing through water into sound that seemed incredibly loud. Going from writing to directing is like going from that incredible silence under water to the surface and that gaggle of sound where it's very fucking noisy—a very different sensation indeed.

Another difference between directing and writing is political —how you are perceived. As a writer you are somebody who can be occasionally irritating, but who can also be a great help to other people. As a director you are something very different— not necessarily helpful to anyone but yourself. And I'm afraid that when people want something from you, they don't *like* the fact that they want something from you . . . and you can get an unhappy admixture of flattery and contempt: people saying you are better than you are or worse than you are. It is a medieval hierarchy, nineteenth-century Japan, where people wore clothing that had something like the back of a sailor's suit—the more aristocratic you were, the longer that flap was. When you bowed, if it was real long, you hardly had to bow at all. Of course, as you dropped down toward the working class, your flap went up and up and up until it was almost at your neck—and you practically had to grovel and do a somersault if you were a peasant. It's that Mikado kind of ritual that I find scary as a director. You want somebody to say, "Hey, I don't like that" or, "I like that" or, "That's a lot of shit." You want people who are there to work, not to bend the way they think you want them to bend.

As a writer, I was often working with friends—but that generally consisted of the director, the cameraman and the actor. I didn't have to deal with the guy somewhere on the set who has a studied indifference toward making movies and who would rather be practicing his golf swing on the back nine of some golf course when this job is done for the day. But as director, I have to put up with that guy, and it isn't easy.

It affects other friendships, too. I'm so busy now, it's not easy for a friend to call me up and say, "Hey, will you look at this scene for me?" or, "Can you read this script and let me know what you think?" I can't be as available as I used to be—though that's a slightly different matter.

BRADY: You've been on the sidelines watching so many directors over the years, surely you must have said on occasion, "I can do this, and I can do it better."

TOWNE: Everybody says that, but the director is there getting shouted at by fifty people, and the guy on the sidelines is shrouded in his own particular silence. Second-guessers usually don't have to answer to anybody. The director has to answer to *every*body for everything from costume changes to actor difficulties. You don't have the luxury of that silence, and I suspect that what happens with really good directors is that they just learn to tune those noises out. That's why some of them obviously turn into major pricks. It's the only way they can discourage people from talking to them when they are trying to think about what's going on. Then you realize why these guys turn mean. When you are directing, everybody unavoidably wants to talk to you; they want to please you, they want to help you—and they can kill you with their help and not allow you to stand there and try to figure if the thing you are looking at is good or bad. And I think that's the only thing you should be there to do.

BRADY: It sounds as though there is some emotional crossfire going on within you. Why have you become a director?

TOWNE: I guess it started with *Tarzan* and with the realization that an hour and a half of that script is silent, and it would be the ultimate dishonesty to give that to a director with a bunch of camera directions and say, "Go shoot it." How could you ever feel the guy screwed it up? No matter what he did, it wouldn't be fair; you pretty much have to mess that one up yourself. And despite the disagreeable things I spoke of, I do love actors—they are more fun, more pleasurable, more exciting to work with than people in other lines of work. You discover things in your writing that you didn't even know you were writing about when they do something you didn't realize was in them or in the material. It's an extension of the creative process that I think is thrilling. And the rest of it—the kind of embarrassment at being this guy that everybody has to show up for so he can say "Action!" and all the trucks lined up in the street for two people in a room, and all of the money being spent, which somehow seems corrupt—is stuff that you can put aside when the actors work, when they give you those things that only they can give. A movie, I think, is really only four or five moments between two people; the rest of it exists to give those moments their impact and resonance. The script exists for that. Everything does. And when actors are really into it, giving you those moments—nobody is more re-markable than they are. Over the years, my closest friends have been actors—and so in that sense, working with actors, it's not as much a stretch for me as you might think.

BRADY: You are a pretty sensitive guy, and you speak of some well-known directors becoming "major pricks" out of necessity on the job, just to get their work done. Do you see that necessity for Bob Towne?

TOWNE: Well, there is that pitfall; it's a job with a short sensi-tivity span. And it's sort of easy to say, "Oh, I'm too sensitive for this business." But there are some directors I've loved work-ing with, too—Arthur Penn, Hal Ashby, and others. I have al-ways resented authority, and I suppose I hate turning around and *being* authority. And I have hated directors very often in my life (aside from the ones I've been crazy about), so it is tough to turn around and be the person that everyone else has to deal with now.

Not long ago, however, I ran into Roger Vadim, and I told him how tough and alien it was for me to be this male authority figure, this tough guy on the set. Vadim smiled and said, "Of course, it is always possible to be the mother." And so there's that side of it, too. You can be protective. I fantasize that Renoir must have been like that, and I do feel protective toward the actors I am working with—like I do toward my child. Actors are like chil-dren, which is in no way to demean them or to suggest that their intelligence is in any way limited. I mean it in the sense that they are very much in touch with themselves, and they are willing to give you their responses in a very trusting manner. They are the people with the most to lose in a movie. It's their faces on the screen, and when you ask an actor to laugh, shout, cry—he is going to be up there on the screen, and he is entrusting you with his image not to make a fool of him, not to fuck him up. Then he gives you everything he can. That is an act of faith, and when an actor does that, you cannot help but love and even revere him.

BRADY: Did directing *Personal Best* change you in any way?

TOWNE: Directing this movie was one of the most important experiences in my life, and it has made an irrevocable change in me—more than I ever imagined. It's a change that is good in some ways, bad in others. I also produced the picture, and I think the real corrupting job is producing, which I did because nobody else could do what had to be done. You rewrite a scene twenty-five times in the privacy of your room because you want to get it right, and nobody sees the rewrites; they only see the scene that is shot. But as a producer, if you are going to be that exacting with a film, you also have to rewrite people. Let's say that somebody—say, the production designer—is not good enough. You know him, you like him, he's got children, but he's not good enough. You know him, you like him, he's got children, but he's not good enough. I can say to myself as a writer that my scene is not good enough and rewrite it again, but who am I as producer to say to another human being that he is not good enough? Yet, that's the job. If you have a passionately cold-assed vision of what must be on a film, and if you know that he cannot deliver, you need someone else. And yet who are you to say he's not good enough for—what?—a movie? That gives you an idea of what I mean.

A writer doesn't want to be told what to do, and he doesn't want to tell people what to do; so he tells it to a piece of paper. To make the choice of telling people what to do has real theological implications, and (if you are me) you must wrestle with that choice and never stop wrestling with it. There is pain. I got a dim but real glimpse of what it must be like to send men into war in order to be killed—that feeling of judgment that can really affect the life of a human being. It's terrible. Moreover, you must accept the worst of all things: the fact that everyone is dependent upon you. So if you can't see the need to replace the production designer, you'll destroy them because they are hoping that somebody sees it for the sake of their jobs, their pride in performance. Thus, in a very real sense, you cannot violate your own vision, because you will be violating those people you work with and depend upon, those people whose work you respect and admire. Producing is a job filled with hard, hard choices.

There are distinctions between writing and directing that have changed me, too. You are always discovering yourself as a writer, but over a period of time—days or even weeks at a time. As a director, I've found I can discover who I am minute to minute, and that immediacy is exciting and scary and humbling. You are a performer for everyone, whether you like it or not; you've got to keep their interest in what is going on, and oh God are there demands. I say this as a writer: There is no more important person on a set than a director. I wrote the screenplay, but I also put the whole thing together. I hired myself, for better or worse, as director. I had to become the producer. I hired every actor in the movie. I fired the ones who didn't work. I worshiped the ones who did. Same is true of my crew. I know them and I miss them to this day. I loved them. I was considered a nut because I fired people in almost every job, I kept trying till I got it right—and I don't think I'll ever want a better crew. I'll die a happy man if my future crews are as good as the one on *Personal Best*.

BRADY: How did you approach the job of directing for the first time?

TOWNE: In a systematic way, but with a good deal of eccentricity. I was, after all, a first-time producer and director working with people who had never acted in major roles before, and I didn't want to yield to any protocol. I remember a production manager coming up to me shortly after the project was on go, saying, "Now that this is a Warner Brothers picture, we are going to go by the book." I said no. Expertise doesn't mean going by the book. "The book is here only for us to know what we must go around," I told him. I told the crew at the very beginning, "I don't know what's going to happen to this movie, but I do know this: I am not here to duplicate, I am here to discover." They went along with me, and it was a voyage of discovery for everyone.

I remember one of the first days of shooting, when the shots and the speeds I was calling for were very unusual, and I was working with guys who had been behind the cameras for a long time. You always feel like an idiot and a sissy when you're doing such things. At the end of the day, Eric Anderson, the camera operator, came up to me and said, "I want to thank you for the day." I thought, "Oh my God, I am really being given the red-ass here." I said, "What do you mean, you want to thank me?" He said, "Because I've never done things that way before, and it was exciting." I looked at him and I thought, holy shit, this guy actually means it.

One thing I remember from *Bonnie and Clyde* is Arthur Penn saying to Warren Beatty, during a fight, "You just wait till you have to worry about where to put the camera." For fifteen years I worried about that question: Where do you put the camera? Then I walked onto the set and realized I didn't know where *not* to put the fucking thing. In fact, I had the opposite problem: Talk me *out* of putting the camera here. After all, I had dreamt the movie, and thought it through, and I was actually confined or disciplined or liberated (or all of the above) by having written the screenplay. I had no choices to make; I had already seen the movie in my mind. We did a lot of unusual things photographically. At one point in this movie, I used eight cameras. Mariel Hemingway worked out for a year and a half for her role, and we used an industrial camera that goes into 360 frames for a shot that has Mariel over a hurdle for five seconds.

BRADY: Did you do much rewriting on the set?

TOWNE: Yes, especially when the script didn't fit an actor comfortably. There's a scene, for instance, where the two heroines are running, and they are being watched by two big men who are shot-putters. Originally, I had one shot-putter saying to the other, "We should say something."

The other guy says, "What?"

"Something friendly."

The second guy hollers, "Hey, girls! Come on over here and sit on my face and let me see how much you weigh!"

His friend says, "Jesus, that was gross."

And the guy says, "Well, it was friendly."

Brian Oldfield was originally supposed to play the gross shot-putter, and Brian has that rare ability to turn something that is grossly crude into something that is inane, goofy and funny. For him the lines were perfect. But Brian, as it turned out, couldn't do the film, and at the last moment we had to fly in Al Feurbach, a beautiful shot-putter from Germany, and a sensitive man in an entirely different way. Well, the minute he said those lines, they were dead. It sounded like chalk screeching across a blackboard: hideous. I told Richard Prince, the assistant director, that we were all going to go off for a little talk, and we went to my trailer.

"Al, what do you think of that line?" I said.

"Well, I can say it."

"Forget the script. What do you *think* of that line?"

"It's nothing *I* would say," he said. "I wouldn't dream of saying it."

"Then why say it?" I asked.

"It's the script."

"Forget it. If you have to choose between violating yourself and the script, it's best to violate the script."

"I can act it out," he said.

"Don't act it," I said. "Tell me what you would say in that situation." He then explained that while he was a giant of a man, a body of brute force, he was also sensitive. "I wouldn't talk to a girl that way," he said. "I think of girls as people, and perhaps at the end of a day—after you've engaged in conversation and have gotten to know them—if something develops between us, that's all well and good."

"Fine, Al," I said. "You'll say that in the movie, or something like it."

"But—" he started to say, and I held up my hand. "You're covered," I said. We went back and shot the scene with three cameras.

One camera is on the two shot-putters watching the girls. One camera is on the shotput in Al's hand, and he's turning it. And the other camera is on the girls. The exchange now goes:

"We should say something."

"Who to?" says Al.

"What do you mean, 'Who to?' "

"I don't talk to people I don't know."

"People?!"

"Girls are people," says Al.

"Shit."

"Listen, I've been all around the world and I think of girls as people just like you and me. If you have a conversation and get to know them, and if something develops at the end of the day . . . all well and good." Meanwhile, as he goes through this sensitive little speech, mingled with androgynous equality—the third camera is focusing progressively tighter on these girls running, and focusing on one thing and one thing only: their little terry-cloth-covered crotches, which get bigger and bigger as they get closer, finally filling the screen as the girls go running by. Then Al says, "I must say, they do look like good conversationalists."

That's an example of changing a scene 180 degrees to accommodate an actor, and I think that it actually works better this way. That's also an instance that typifies the one big surprise on the job for a first-time director: I could do it the way I wanted to. I never got over that one. It was like a miracle, and a big part of that miracle was the discovery that there was a definite way I wanted to do the movie, and I did it. I can truly say that nobody kept me from doing what I wanted to do. It was a difficult movie, and there were some hairy times—two interruptions for strikes (one by actors, one by writers)—but we had fun doing it, too. At one point, I asked our sound man Bruce Bisenz to put earphones on the actors so I could talk to them during a take. He did, and I was able to talk to the actors, break them up ("You dumb cunt, what do you think you're doing?"), make them laugh, keep it spontaneous. It made a significant difference in performance. I was able to direct the way a silent director used to direct. Bruce made that possible. A genius. There is joy in working with a good crew.

BRADY: With *Shampoo* you shattered a common notion—that male hairdressers are generally gay . . .

TOWNE: I suppose so. However, I think other things about the movie as well.

BRADY: Oh, yes. I don't mean to be simplistic.

TOWNE: It's just that every now and then I feel a certain twinge, and I wonder if the movie was about what I wanted it to be about in my original draft. Movies are a collaborative effort, though, and finally it was about what all of us were trying to make it about.

BRADY: *Personal Best* is about women athletes, who—the common notion goes—are supposedly masculine, even Lesbians. Do you give thought to this issue in your script?

TOWNE: It's an issue that I would rather not talk about, other than to say that whatever their sexuality might be, I think it's an extension of their being children, of discovering in the simplest, most physical way what they are through elemental bodily functions. Again, like children: poo-poo, pee-pee, burping, farting, food, sex . . . everything you can put into a body, squeeze out of a body, make it move in certain ways, shape it, torture it, twist it, pleasure it, pain it . . . and in that process use the body itself as a mode of knowledge through which you learn about yourself, rather than more cerebral modes. In that sense they are truly like children, and anything to do with sex—whether masculine or feminine—it's just all on the way to their discovering what they are all about. Whatever they do—and they do some astonishing things, some shocking things—to me they remain quite feminine, quite beautiful, and quite desirable.

I never read it, but I was always told that Richardson's *Pamela* is a story of a girl who goes through all of these trials and tribulations and holds on to her purity, which in her case was her virginity. In *Personal Best* these girls go through a lot of trials, and they don't hold on to anything like that; but they do hold on to a form of purity. Maybe it's as simple as something from Kierkegaard, in his essay "Purity of Heart," where he says that purity of heart is to will one single thing.

BRADY: Some viewers are bound to think you are cashing in on the Billy Jean King headlines when your movie comes out.

TOWNE: If I did not know that Billy Jean King had that relationship with another woman, I have certainly been aware for some time of the more inventive physical lives these athletes have in every way, including sexually. They will try something, discard something, much in the manner that they might try an altered version of the flop in high-jumping. I admire that willingness to follow something out. To me the term is a shameful thing to even lay on Billie Jean King or any athlete like her—not that I think it's a shameful thing in itself; I just think the poverty of imagination that goes into labeling her as Lesbian is demented, sick, twisted, dumb and gross. In my script, one of the heroines ends up with a boyfriend, and the other may or may not end up with a boyfriend. It's a phase that maybe you grow out of; or maybe not. But let's be honest about it, not accusatory. Women athletes are the niggers of the profession, surrounded by monsters and a pecking order that has them being hit on, by guys, with the overwhelming threat that they are dykes if they don't fuck them. Like penguins on an ice floe surrounded by sharks in the water, they are really thrown back on themselves. It's an outrage, the way they are treated. It's one of the reasons why I wrote the screenplay.

BRADY: You sound very mellow in your approach to things— your touchstones are babies, being a father, actors as children, and now the purity of women athletes.

TOWNE: I suppose a lot of it has its beginning in the birth of a child. *Tarzan* is about innocence, too . . . the innocence of animals and the innocence of a wild boy. I guess I'm more affected by this than I realize.

BRADY: Isn't there an old truism in movies about not working with animals and kids? Isn't that unpredictable, not to mention expensive?

TOWNE: Yes, that's true. But Warners is really being pretty good about the project. They have spent a lot of money on research, and they trust me with it. I have nothing to complain about.

BRADY: I should think that with *Tarzan,* which has been in the planning and preparation stages for years, boredom must be something of an enemy by now. Don't you get tired of the same project after a while?

TOWNE: I'm very lucky in that when I like something I like it for a long time—whether food, people or movie projects. Boredom? I don't understand it. Maybe it's that I'm fundamentally lazy, able to sit back and be rather interested in just about anything. I get bored.

BRADY: On *Shampoo*, you were involved to some extent in the promotion of that film. As I recall, you went to several openings. Is it unique for a screenwriter to undertake such promotional trips? What was the thinking there?

TOWNE: The reason for it? Just another person who would be sensitive to problems that might arise at openings. In fact, to give you an illustration, the opening in Detroit (and this is where it was to be reviewed) was at twin theaters where they put the film on computers or something and the projectionist just locks the booth up and goes to the other one, goes back and forth. *Shampoo* came on and it looked very milky. As you know, the film opens in the dark, and I'm there thinking, "This is weird. Why is it so white? It's supposed to be in the dark." And then the lights were turned on in the opening scene and Warren's face was distorted—suddenly he looked like he was in a fun house. And I realized the projectionist had an anamorphic lens on the projector. He had a Panavision lens. And the film was not in Panavision. It was one eighty-five. I almost had a heart attack. All the critics are there. I get up and grab the guy, saying, "This is the wrong lens! What do we do!" He says, "We can't find the projectionist." And I go pounding on the projectionist's door, and I finally grabbed him, made him stop the film and start it over again. Otherwise they would have sat through that entire movie with the actors' faces looking like balloons, and God know what the reviews would have been like. And you never would have known why it was bad in Detroit.

That's just one example of why it's important, particularly when a film opens, to have somebody there who's intimately familiar with the film. It was opening in several places at once; that was one reason why I did it. To talk to people about it. Also, we wanted *Shampoo* not to be taken as a totally frivolous exercise, as just a sexual escapade of a Beverly Hills hairdresser. It was that, but it was also an attempt to give a fairly realistic account of life at a certain time and place, the way it was. Only a slight exaggeration of reality. It was a little bit like *Our Town 1968,* only in this case it was not Grovers Corners but Beverly Hills. So we just wanted to make sure that—whether it was liked or disliked—it was taken seriously, that *we* took it seriously.

BRADY: Are you related to Gene Towne, the screenwriter of the thirties?

TOWNE: Billy Wilder asked me that once. No, I'm not at all. I know who he is, but I don't know what he wrote. That's about it.

BRADY: He did *You Only Live Once,* the Fritz Lang film. I thought perhaps there was a second generation of Townes about to move in.

TOWNE: I'm the first generation in my family to have this name. Although my brother was born with the name, I wasn't.

BRADY: Really? How does that work?

TOWNE: I was four years old when my parents changed their name. My brother was born a Towne, but I wasn't. So I'm very much *not* related to Gene Towne, who I assume was English, and I'm a Russian-Rumanian Jew. My father was in the dress business and had bought a ladies' apparel shop in San Pedro on Sixth Street called The Towne Smart Shop—with an *e*—and that's where the name came from.

BRADY: Did you do *Villa Rides,* the Mitchum-Brynner film?

TOWNE: I'm very sorry to hear you say that (laughter).

BRADY: I can be very discreet about this information.

TOWNE: Bob Evans, when he wants to *really* hurt me, brings that up. It was for Paramount. Actually, it was the first film I did for Paramount. I really hated it. It was weird, though it was one of the most interesting experiences I have ever had working on a film. And it was also one of the least successful. It was a textbook on How Not to Make a Movie. Though it was not singular. I've worked on a lot of films I've hated.

BRADY: How so?

TOWNE: I would have to be very insulting to a number of people in order to tell you the truth about that. A *lot* of movies don't turn out well. When studios put films together, or package them —it becomes a pay-or-play situation. In other words, in the case of *Villa Rides* they had to pay Yul Brynner and Robert Mitchum regardless of whether or not they made the movie. So you've got, say, over a million dollars tied up in salaries between the two guys, and they figure it will take maybe two million to make the movie, so they say, "What the hell, we might as well go ahead and get something for an extra million. We'll come out of it somehow."

What happens is you pay a lot of people a lot of money to make a movie that *nobody* particularly wants to make. The result is something that is lacking in cohesiveness, conviction, everything else. In a situation like that you are often involved with a producer who is more interested in making money on the *making* of the movie than he is on the releasing of the movie. There is a lot of money to be made on the production of a movie, not just in salary, but all sorts of ways that are just not altogether honest. So he's going to make his money on the *making,* which is really reprehensible. Movies are so difficult that you should really make movies that you feel you absolutely *have* to make. If you don't have that kind of conviction about it, along with the hope that a sufficient number of people are going to want to see the end result, it can be pretty tough.

BRADY: Could you name a few of the tougher ones?

TOWNE: *The New Centurions.* I took my name off that. I shared credit with Stirling Silliphant, but after seeing twenty minutes of the film, I disliked it so much I walked out a little bit dizzy and told my agent to take my name off the picture, which they did.

BRADY: Really?

TOWNE: Oh, yeah. I worked with Joe Wambaugh on that, and we almost invariably agreed on the approach to scenes. The arguments would come in when we had to deal with Other People. Afterward, he asked me to do *The Blue Knight* for television. I didn't do it, but we got along well. We still talk from time to time. I think he's terrific. And I think that *The New Centurions* could have been a terrific movie, but it turned out dogshit.

In order for it to be good, the movie had to end (as the book did) in the Watts riots. That's what was exciting about his book:

the progressive exacerbation between the Occupying Army, which was the blue suits, and the Occupied, which was the blacks. The whole situation forced them into conflict, then riot. Any time a cop had to deal with crime, the criminal had a black face. Any time a black was being harassed or bullied, the bully had a blue uniform. It just exploded. That was what was exciting about Wambaugh's book—and the protagonist's relationship with a black girl had an added meaning in terms of the Watts riots. And the corruption of the L.A.P.D. was not the corruption of, say, *Serpico*. It was the corruption of people who had a moral certitude. That's why *The New Centurions* was such a good title. The cop was so certain that he was above any kind of reproach that he couldn't understand that the riots were not simple law-breaking, but the results of social forces that finally exploded and were beyond anything he was aware of. It was beyond his comprehension completely.

BRADY: The movie was just a cops 'n' robbers thing.

TOWNE: Of course. The whole purpose of the book was lost in the movie.

I did another film I hated—at Columbia. I don't know what they ended up calling it. It was a western with George Hamilton and Glenn Ford. I did another film called *Cisco Pike,* which I didn't hate—with Gene Hackman, Karen Black and Kris Kristofferson—but I was so angry with the director, I said, "That's it." Actually, it turned out to be a pretty good movie—due in no small part to the editing of Bob Jones. In fact, I've worked with Jones more than with anyone, as I think of it. He did the editing on *Cisco Pike,* on *The New Centurions,* on *The Last Detail,* and on *Shampoo.* He's a terrific editor—tasteful, innovative. It's weird. The little things like that in a movie *do* make a difference. In fact, they're *not* so little, but unglamorized people who are truly gifted at what they do make an enormous difference in the success of a film.

BRADY: If you were to apportion things out—the writing, the acting, the directing, the editing—how would you weigh the part that each plays in the outcome of a film? Is the writing more important than the editing? Or what?

TOWNE: You can't cut what you don't have. The editor cannot create out of nothing. You have to give him something to edit. In that sense, the writing is more important. But it's easier for a director and an actor to be mediocre and get away with it than it is for a writer. Even a writer who happens to be mediocre has to work pretty hard to get through a script, because a writer is essentially self-generating, whereas a cameraman will say to the director, "Where do you think you want to put the camera? You want it here? All right, I'm going to put it here." In other words, a director can be carried along by the production if he's mediocre, to some extent; and that's true of an actor, too. But if he's really working hard and well, there's no tougher job on earth than the director's. It's the toughest. At that level, I would say that the director is the most important force in a film. But if everybody does what they do well, then there's a sense in which all the skills tend to merge. You call the writer the writer, the actor the actor, and the director the director. But they are really working together in a way that melds their respective jobs.

I'm on the set during the making of a movie, for instance, and I might be saying some things that would normally be the province of the director. Or a really good actor will say, "This line doesn't work," and he'll make suggestions about the writing. What you learn on a film is that no matter how much you worked on the script, no matter how well you know the characters as a writer— if an actor is really good he will know more about the character than you. He'll know more about the character moment-to-moment because he's interested in the guy every millisecond he's on the screen. He'll know what he's thinking, and what he's not thinking. If you have been sloppy and not filled a moment in which the actor thinks the character's behavior is less than honest, he's going to pick up on it and tell you. It's no longer your character exclusively. It's your character *through* Jack Warden or Warren Beatty or Jack Nicholson or whomever. And they know it, and bring themselves to it. That's what everyone who's good does. An actor brings all of his skills and sensibilities to the role, and you *want* him to.

BRADY: When did you start writing for movies?

TOWNE: About 1960. It was on and off. I started with Roger Corman doing horror and science fiction films—almost the same time that Jack Nicholson started acting. Nicholson and I were in the same acting class (run by Jeff Corey), but I always thought I was going to write. It was a class that included many directors, producers—Irv Kirschner was in the class, for instance. Roger Corman was in the class. That's how I got my first job. He was producing and directing. There were a lot of actors, too—Sally Kellerman was in there, Jimmy Coburn was in there . . . Dick Chamberlain. It was invaluable for me—for all kinds of reasons. I met a lot of people, who I thought were terrific at the time, and as it turns out most have done very well professionally. In some cases—Jack's, in particular—the acting influenced me as a writer. Watching Jack improvise really had an effect.

BRADY: In what way?

TOWNE: His improvisations were inventive. When he was given a situation, he would not improvise on the nose. He'd talk around the problem, and good writing is the same way: It's not explicit. Take a very banal situation—a guy trying to seduce a girl. He talks about everything *but* seduction, anything from a rubber duck he had as a child to the food on the table or whatever. But you know it's all oriented toward trying to fuck this girl. It's inventive, and it teaches you something about writing.

BRADY: You started writing for Corman. Can you tell me about the writing that goes into a horror movie?

TOWNE: It's the toughest kind. Really, it's a tough form. Roger and I were really a classic mismatch. It was very painstaking, the screenplay of *The Tomb of Ligeia*. In fact, I worked harder on the horror screenplay for him than on anything I think I have ever done. And I still like the screenplay. I think it's good.

BRADY: Roger works so fast, and you seem to have a slower sense of craftsmanship. How did you adapt?

TOWNE: Actually, I didn't. It just meant I practically starved to death while I was writing.

BRADY: Not even time for meals?

TOWNE: No, it just meant that Roger was not really lavish with the money he paid anybody. I think that *Ligeia* may have been made for about a hundred and fifty thousand dollars, and the amount of money on the script was negligible. So if you take a long time writing something like that, it works against you.

BRADY: How do you write a horror movie, particularly when you have a short story in front of you that must be expanded into some ninety minutes of screen time?

TOWNE: Well, *Ligeia* was a *very* short story. I remember reading all the body of Poe's work, and I felt the best thing to do would be to take Poe's themes and expand on them. There was a strong hint of mesmerism in the story. I decided to make it overt —with all that emphasis on Ligeia's eyes and how they held the beholder. Also in Poe there is a lot of necrophilia—implied if not expressed. So I took the combination of mesmerism, which was there, and necrophilia, which was sort of there (because the first wife was always in the background), and brought them together. It provided a natural explanation for this woman. She had hypnotized the protagonist, and he was making love to this body under posthypnotic suggestion, literally being controlled by someone who was dead—which is kind of a gruesome notion, but perfectly consistent with Poe. I was trying to use a theme consistent with him, even though it wasn't in the story.

American horror stories tend to provide natural explanations for events—like "Oh, well, she was hypnotized"—whereas the English tend to go for supernatural explanations. I tried to have my cake and eat it too in *Ligeia*. There was that natural explanation of posthypnotic suggestion, along with the supernatural explanation of a possession. That was also a theme in the story —this vaguely pantheistic notion of being able to come back from the dead in a blade of grass or an animal—and there was the cat and all that.

Some people liked the movie quite a bit. I think it was a little dull. I think it would have been better if it had been done with a man who didn't look like a necrophiliac to begin with.

BRADY: You disapprove of Vincent Price?

TOWNE: I love Vincent. He's very sweet. But, going in, you suspect that Vincent could bang cats, chickens, girls, dogs, everything. You just feel that necrophilia might be one of his

Basic Things. I'd felt the role called for an almost unnaturally handsome guy who the second wife could fall in love with. There should also be a sense of taboo about the really close tie he had with his first wife—as though it were something incestuous, two halves of the same person. The intensity of the relationship is a sacrilege in itself; just *being* together is almost an unnatural act.

At the outset, Corman told me he wouldn't cast Vincent Price in the film, but when it was done he called me in L.A. from London. He told me he had cast Vincent, and added: "It's OK, we've got Marlene Dietrich's makeup man." I've never been able to figure out what difference *that* made.

I did a couple of films for Roger Corman—*Ligeia*, and another horror film I'd rather not mention. Then I did some television work—"The Outer Limits," some "Man from U.N.C.L.E." work, a show called "Breaking Point," "The Richard Boone Show," an anthology. I also did "The Lloyd Bridges Show," an anthology he did after his "Sea Hunt" shows.

BRADY: Can you draw any comparisons between TV and movie work?

TOWNE: I think that dramatic writing for television is, if anything, almost harmful to the potential screenwriter. The only good thing about it is that it allows you to, theoretically anyway, make a living writing. Censorship is one problem. It was then, anyway. There is more permissiveness in television today, but a lot of it is still the same. I once did a script for "Outer Limits" which presented an interesting problem. These guys came to me and said, "We want to do a story on how adaptable man is, how chameleonlike human beings are. We want a story in which creatures come to earth from outer space, and, in order to study them, a man gets transformed into one of them to figure out what they are." Which is a wildly improbable story. I remember saying, "Fellas, did it ever occur to you what would happen if we went on a five-man space mission to Mars, and we're walking around and suddenly a sixth man shows up that none of us knew? Don't you think we'd be a little dubious about the new guy?" It's an impossible problem. But they said, "No, go ahead and do it."

Well, in those days I would try anything. I was just trying to work. So I came up with these creatures who were almost bear-like. I had them in these weird iron bars high up in the Rockies or the Sierras or someplace, and a forestman came across them. He was killed by them. People found his body, and they realized that his killers had taken him apart, literally, system by system. His vascular system, his muscular system . . . and so on. They had literally pulled him apart. Then they tried to put him back together, but they didn't do it quite right. People were appalled and frightened. They didn't know quite what to do with these creatures because they seemed so brilliant, yet erratic.

They got a piece of tissue from beneath the fingernails of the dead ranger and tried to program these creatures genetically to learn how they could transform a guy who goes there to find out how they can be so brilliant and so erratic. What he finds out is that they are children, and that they are literally in a playpen waiting for their mother, who has deposited them there temporarily. Which would explain why they could be precocious and bright but unpredictable.

Well, ABC Continuity read it and said, "No, we can't do this because we don't want to have anything to do with children." I said, they're not *children* children. They're these creatures from outer space. "No, can't have it." Well, that's insane. I don't know if it would happen today, but it was deeply demoralizing, and it was the only solution I could come up with for the partic-ular problem that these guys wanted to do. The script had to be entirely rewritten. I did the rewrite in one day—eight hours—and it was terrible. I just didn't care what I wrote. It was shot (I don't know who did it—Bobby Duvall, maybe), but it was no good at all.

That sort of thing would happen time after time after time. Censorship like that is so demoralizing. Also, you had to write so explicitly. If a story had a theme, you had to *state* the theme. Scenes had to really be kind of on the nose. In every way. It got you into the habit of writing too much. Too much dialogue. Be-cause they wanted it.

I think by and large it was not a terrific period for me, and I did not enjoy it in any way, shape or form. I should say one thing, though. I think that comedy writing on television is terrific —all those "Mary Tyler Moore" scripts, for instance, were very well written. But one of the things that is almost implicit in comedy is something that is repetitious, static—that is, you pretty much leave a character the way you find him. That's OK in *all* comedy. Repetitive or even compulsive behavior is what *makes* comedy. Archie Bunker is funny because he keeps repeating his prejudices in one form or another, and you expect these things. Jack Benny's repetitive behavior, his stinginess, was funny, and you came to appreciate him for it. Comedy in that sense lends itself better to television, where you have to have a running character the same every week, whereas in dramatic writing the very *essence* is character change. The character at the end is not the same as he was at the beginning. He's changed—psychologically, maybe even physically. He may be dead by the end of a show. Yet in a running dramatic series for television, you have to leave the characters the way that you find them—and that is basically antithetical to good writing.

BRADY: Do you think you came too late to television? Do you believe in the so-called golden age of television in the 1950s?

TOWNE: No. I believe that there was some good stuff written in the fifties, and there were some terrific writers. But who knows? I've seen some of the stuff. Some of it was dogshit— pretentious, silly and precious. But some of it was great. There's nobody better than Paddy Chayefsky. An incredible writer. But he would have been incredible anywhere. A talent like that is as responsible for the golden age as is the so-called climate that went into creating him.

BRADY: After working in TV, how did you get back into movies?

TOWNE: Corman again. He was doing a supposedly big-budget film at Columbia and needed a western script rewritten. He asked me to do it. I did, but there was a lot of subsequent difficulty between Roger and the studio over the movie. Roger left the picture, somebody else did it, and I took my name off it. But the script attracted attention from Warren Beatty. That's how I met Warren. At the time he and Arthur Penn were having trouble with the script for *Bonnie and Clyde*. They felt that they had reached a dead end with it, so I was asked to read it. I was brought together with Arthur, did the rewrites on the film, and that's how I got back into the movies.

BRADY: Arthur Penn has called you Warren's best friend.

TOWNE: We're as close as two people are likely to be, I suppose.

BRADY: The work on *Bonnie and Clyde* sounds like it must have been especially close.

TOWNE: It was. I was rewriting scenes time after time. The movie was impromptu in the sense that there was rewriting going on constantly, but once Arthur was satisfied with a scene, once the rewriting was done to everybody's satisfaction, there was no deviation whatsoever from those lines. That's the way it was shot. There was less improvising in *Bonnie and Clyde* than in any other movie I have worked on. Which speaks well for the acting and directing, I think, because the film was praised for its free-wheeling sense, as though the cameras just *happened* to be there to record real life.

BRADY: What were the rewrite problems on *Bonnie and Clyde*?

TOWNE: The original script, by David Newman and Robert Benton, was very talented, but it was written as a *ménage à trois* among Clyde, Bonnie and W.D. At that time the climate was not so permissive that it would be easy to do something like that, so, for several reasons (partly because of the studio), it had to be changed. Also, the script was kind of static. I mean, it was funny —Clyde and W.D., Bonnie and W.D., and so on—but ultimately it didn't go anywhere. If you're going to do a movie about shifting relationships, like Truffaut's *Jules and Jim*, it is tough to do a gangster movie at the same time.

Arthur Penn and Warren decided that they didn't want the *ménage à trois*, but instead a relationship between Bonnie and Clyde, and asked Benton and Newman to do it. But the script just didn't seem to work after that change was made. One of the problems was in making that relationship go somewhere. Arthur was very unhappy with it. That was when I was called in—things had reached an impasse. I remember the first suggestion I made.

It was obvious that everybody knew the people in the picture were going to get killed, so that was never an element of mystery, but rather one of suspense. *When* was it going to happen? The other element was: Would Bonnie and Clyde resolve some element in their relationship before it happened? Which is one of the first things I think I said—that we would have to heighten the fact that the particular roads they were traveling on led to one place.

In the original script the mortician episode came *after* Bonnie went to see her family. She went and saw her mother, had a nice time, then picked these people up along the road, after stealing their car and chasing them, had hamburgers with them, then learned that Gene Wilder was a mortician—and kicked him and his girl out of the car. I suggested that they take that scene and place it *before* Bonnie sees her mother so that the impetus of having a good time, only to find out that the guy is a mortician, strikes Bonnie, who is the most sensitive and open of the group, and makes her say, "I wanna go see my Mama." It scared her. Pacing like that gives the character a little drive, makes her want to *do* something as a result of it. And then, at her mother's, instead of having a happy scene, I suggested that the scene end up with Clyde saying to Bonnie's mother, "We're gonna end up living by you," and with the mother replying, "If you're gonna live three miles from here, you're not gonna live long." In effect, Bonnie can't go home anymore. All of these avenues are being closed off, and she is being thrown back on Clyde for a ride that is going one way. Then came a scene in a hotel room where Bonnie says, "I thought we were really going someplace," with disillusionment setting in. And Clyde says, "Well, I'm your family," heightening the intensity, the meaning and the need of that relationship for her, and hopefully something will be resolved about it before they are killed. Of course, they eventually end up sleeping together.

Then one had to be careful (we all worried about it) about Clyde. Suddenly, just because he could have a normal heterosexual relationship, it could not mean that he would put down his gun and stop robbing banks, which is a script problem to deal with. Those were the initial changes. I started working with it then, always under Arthur's guidance—he would have me rewrite something ten or fifteen times, until I felt I just couldn't write at all. He used to scare me. I used to think, "Gee, I must really be terrible if he keeps having me rewrite like this. God, I'm really bad." Then they asked me to come down to Texas, where I stayed all during the picture, working even in postproduction, writing wild lines for background.

From a writing point of view, the thing that was interesting was the number of times I rewrote scenes. But when you're rewriting, very often you're doing the scenes that *don't* work. The toughest scenes in a piece of material may not only have been the toughest for the writer who worked ahead of you, but may also be the most difficult scenes to solve, period. So they are the ones you have to keep redoing, whether it's you or somebody else. Tough scenes create problems. All other things being equal, some scenes are easy for seven out of ten writers to do— the actions of characters are clear, and it's simple to get through. But other scenes are more difficult. There may be more ways in which a scene can go. Maybe a scene reaches a point where you have to carry both plot information and character information, which makes it difficult. There are all these problems, which I didn't realize at the time.

But afterward I realized that was one of the reasons why I was rewriting scenes so many times. There were other reasons, too. It was very valuable for me. I was learning an awful lot from Arthur just by doing and redoing. From Warren, too. There was constant collaborative effort. Story conferences. Arthur, Warren and myself down there in Texas.

BRADY: When you come in to do rewrites on a script, do you ever work with the original writer?

TOWNE: I did work with Francis Ford Coppola when he called me in on *The Godfather.*

BRADY: Mario Puzo shared the credit on that. Did you work with him?

TOWNE: No, I didn't meet Mario until afterward.

BRADY: The reason I asked is that he wrote an article afterward which made it sound like that was a rather traumatic period for him.

TOWNE: It always is. Your first movie is terribly traumatic. But I'm sure he's gotten over it. He's survived, hands down. He's a terrific guy. But I didn't work with him.

BRADY: I wondered how far the rewrite man works from the guy he's replaced. It sounds as if they want a fresh opinion, and don't want any . . .

TOWNE: Usually *very* far removed. Invariably. But sometimes the person who does the rewrite can write a whole new script. Literally, a whole new script. It wasn't the case in *Bonnie and Clyde* or in *The Godfather,* but in other films I've done, it's been entirely new scripts. I mean, the rewrite in that western I did was virtually a new script. Rewrites at times can be entire.

BRADY: What were the rewrite problems on *The Godfather?*

TOWNE: Mainly, Francis was perplexed. In the book there wasn't any resolution between Vito Corleone and his son Michael—their relationship. He needed a scene between the two of them. Francis kept saying, "Well, I want the audience to know that they love each other." He put it that way. But you couldn't do a scene about two people loving each other. So I wrote a scene about the succession of power, and *through* that it was obvious that the two men had a great deal of affection for each other. Through Brando's anxiety about what would happen to his son, and his anxiety about giving up his power—his ambivalent feelings about, in effect, forcing his son to assume his role, and having to give up his role—that was the key to that scene.

If you want to use the "script doctor" analogy, it wasn't a major operation—just spot surgery in a highly specific area. That creates all sorts of problems by itself. I wasn't rewriting the script from beginning to end, which I've done most often. Instead, I was adding outside material and had to fit it in with what existed, make it consistent—and this meant knowing everything that had been shot, and everything that the director had in mind. An interesting problem. Usually you're rewriting right along with the director as you know where you're going. On *The Godfather* it was a case of someone saying, "This is where I think I'm going, but I don't know where to go anymore. You help me make up my mind where I want to go next." And yet I hadn't been in on any of the original process. They'd been shooting for five or six weeks before I even got there. So I had to look at the footage and say either, "This is terrific" or, "This is so bad, I can't possibly fix it." Which, of course, was the last thing in the world from the truth.

BRADY: You were called in under extreme pressure, weren't you?

TOWNE: That was the scariest situation I've ever been in, because I knew they were going to lose Brando within twenty-four hours. It was a tense situation at that particular point because no one figured that the film was going to be the big hit that it was. I saw about an hour of assembled footage, and I thought it was brilliant. Francis was troubled. There was a lot of backstabbing on the set, and he was constantly being undermined. So I couldn't get over it: The footage was so extraordinary. I felt that I was going to make a contribution to a film that was virtually assured of being a major hit, although that was not the prevailing opinion on the set.

I worked on a few minor scenes. I remember restructuring Michael's speech for the scene where he tells how he is going to kill the cop. I just did a simple thing there. The way that Francis had originally written the speech, Michael says at the beginning he's going to kill the cop, and then he tells about the newspaper story and other things to justify it. But it was much more dramatic for him to withhold what he was going to do until the end of the speech. I just reversed it. There were a few other little things like that.

But mainly Francis was concerned about having a scene between Michael and his father. So we sat down with Marlon and Al Pacino, got their feelings, and began writing about eight o'clock that night and did a scene about the transfer of power: Uneasy lies the head that wears the crown. I don't know if you remember the scene at all, but that's the gist of it. The don is saying, "We've got to see about this," and Michael is saying, "Dad, I told you I'd take care of it, and I'm taking care of it."

What seems to be a kind of absentmindedness on the part of Vito Corleone as far as protective measures are concerned is really his unwillingness to accept the position he's placed his youngest son in.

But the two men in the course of the scene really accept the dictates of fate. It's sort of a perverse *noblesse oblige:* Vito is obliged to pass the cup, and Michael is obliged to take it. He does, and through that you see that the two men love each other very much, rather than my writing a scene about love, which wouldn't have worked in that movie. It's illustrative in a way of writing in general. Most scenes are rarely about what the subject matter is.

BRADY: You mentioned this earlier in relation to Jack Nicholson improvising scenes at Jeff Corey's school—improvising off the point.

TOWNE: Corey had an exercise in which he would take a scene from, say, *Three Men on a Horse,* which is a farce, and he would say, "OK, you're a junkie, and you're trying to sell this guy some dope." In other words, the situation that he would give would be totally contrary to the text, and it was the task of the actors, through their interpretation of the various bits of business they could come up with, to suggest the real situation through lines that had no bearing on the situation. When you see that for three years running, when you are asked for improvisations in which you are given a situation and told that you must talk about everything *but* the situation to advance the action, you soon see the power of dealing obliquely or elliptically with situations, because most people rarely confront things head-on. They're afraid to. I think that most people try to be accommodating in life, but in back of their accommodation is suppressed fear or anger or both. What happens in a dramatic situation is that it surfaces. And it shouldn't surface too easily, or it's not realistic.

BRADY: How much do you take from your actors when you sit down and have to structure a scene with twenty-four-hour notice?

TOWNE: It depends on the actors. I took a lot from Marlon and Al. Particularly Marlon. He said, "Just once in this part I'd like *not* to be inarticulate.'' So I took the notion that he wanted to have this man try to express himself. I took the notion of Vito Corleone trying to talk, then, rather than having him give sage nods. Through most of the film it is the power of his silence that carries force. But in the situation I was asked to write, he actually talks. Most of the time the power of the character is conveyed through pregnant silence.

I took a lot of things from Jack Nicholson in life for the character of Gittes in *Chinatown,* too. Things that happened. I used his idiosyncrasies, but, more importantly, I tried to use his way of working. I've seen him work so much that I feel I know what he does well. In fact, I don't even think about it. I just do it. I saw Jack work and improvise two or three times a week for maybe five straight years. It's hard *not* to think about Jack even when I'm not writing for him. His work literally affected the way that I work, totally independent of doing a movie with Jack. He and other people in that class.

In the case of working with Warren on *Shampoo,* obviously there's an effect there. I definitely take him into account when I am writing scenes for him, because I feel that I know what he does well. I feel that Warren always has to be tougher than he thinks. He presents a peculiar problem as an actor because he is a man who is deeply embarrassed by acting. Unlike Jack. Warren is a very talented man, but he's so embarrassed by his acting that you have to constantly force him, one way or another, to use himself, whereas Jack doesn't have that reluctance. He doesn't mind using himself. Warren has the instincts of a character actor. He'd rather hobble around on one foot in *Bonnie and Clyde,* or wear a gold tooth in *McCabe and Mrs. Miller.* He's a little bit like another great actor who is embarrassed about using his own instrument—and that's Albert Finney. In *Murder on the Orient Express,* for instance, he plays Hercule Poirot and manages to cover himself up completely as a character actor. Both men have the instincts of character actors, and that's not really good for movies, because after a time if an actor is playing a ''leading man'' he has to be willing to use aspects of his own personality for a role. It won't look real if he doesn't. Film is just too sensitive. When you are dealing with someone like that, if you know him well, you are obliged as a writer to try to push situations where an actor must use aspects of himself, and you remind him of it in the way in which you write scenes. Or when you write scenes together, as Warren and I did in *Shampoo*, you've got to say, "Look, you've got to be tough with yourself here, and not be afraid of yourself."

Now I am talking about two cases in which I enjoy close personal relationships with actors whom I respect professionally. In many ways I'm as close to Jack and Warren as I am to anybody. When you work with people you don't know so well, the problems are much more complex. Then you've got to go through a lot of diplomatic crises. When you say you don't approve of something (whether it's with an actor, a director or whatever), then they assume that what you are saying is you don't approve of their talent or of them—the way they part their hair, whatever. That's very time-consuming and exhausting, and there is not that kind of time on a movie when it's being shot—which is one reason why, whenever possible, you should do movies with people whom you are intimate with at one level or another. You can cut through that shit. The disadvantage, of course, is that over a period of years you can get sloppy, I suppose. John Ford finally just got tired, got very old. But for years he was working with people he knew. All really good directors do it. Fellini does it. Bergman.

BRADY: He has a repertory company, I think.

TOWNE: Sure. And there's a reason for it; it's just too hard otherwise, too hard to keep working with strangers. It's like starting a marriage over and over and over again.

BRADY: I'm very interested in how you write with somebody else. On *Shampoo*, you and Beatty shared writing credits. Does it come down to two men sitting in a room, or is it a back-and-forth type of arrangement?

TOWNE: In the case of *Shampoo*, it goes so far back I can't tell you. I had done an early draft—about two hundred and twenty pages—of the thing that I was interested in having Warren do around the time of *Bonnie and Clyde*. It was very amorphous, though. Warren looked at it and said, "You really seem lost, though the writing is interesting." I still have that draft, as a matter of fact. We sat and we talked for about a month about a new shape it might take. Warren went to Europe for a couple of months while I rewrote the script. When he came back we had a big argument over the script because there were *two* strong female parts. He had wanted one part for Julie Christie, and a very secondary part for another female. As it happens, there were two major parts in the final script—for Julie and Goldie Hawn—but at this time it was very dicey, and Warren was very unhappy, and we didn't speak for about six months. I thought that was the end of that particular arrangement. He had given me option money, but I felt the script would never be made, and there was some mutual confusion as to who had the rights to it. So it was left in limbo for three years. I went on to do other things—*The Last Detail, Chinatown,* and so forth. I did *The Yakuza* during this period, too.

Finally, Warren sat down and took the script and did a draft with some new material, including a couple of party sequences. He was trying to restructure it in a more interesting way, particularly after a lapse of three years. One particular sequence in the old script which involved dope was bad. He did a draft that really just didn't work. It wasn't much related to what I had done. Then he did another in which he rearranged a lot of the original material. We talked, and I took that draft and in a seven-day period in December 1973 we sat down in the Beverly Wilshire Hotel with Hal Ashby, whom Warren had hired as director, and the real collaboration took place.

We thrashed out and rewrote entirely the rewrite of the draft I had done in 1970—if that makes any sense. It's a very convoluted history. Hal, Warren and I would sit in a room and thrash out the sequence of events in the picture. We had very little time to do this because they were going to try to shoot it in six weeks. In order to get Warren, Julie, Goldie, Lee Grant and Jack Warden together meant you had to be ready to *go* during these six weeks, or you'd end up costing yourself a lot of money. Warren had committed himself financially to people prior to finalizing the deal with the studio, which meant that he was personally on the hook for a *lot* of money. So there was enormous pressure to get it done immediately. We went through the draft then, and in many ways it ended up, at least in spirit, very close to the earliest version— that is, with two women, and with the guy more attached emotionally to the less naive of the two. The work on that final draft, though, was the most intensive I've been through in a long time. We'd start about nine in the morning and work until about eleven at night, then sleep and start again.

We would talk through the scenes, and I would go into another room and do the writing of the scenes themselves. Some writers can collaborate and write on the spot. I can't. Maybe comedy writers work that way: You say this line, and I'll say that line. But I prefer to talk through the scenes, reworking their structure, arguing back and forth about the party sequences, trying to make them an organic part of the whole script, and making relationships between characters come to a head during the parties, and not just having a party for a party's sake. It was completely rewritten in about seven days. Then I went to Japan to do the finishing touches on *The Yakuza,* then came back to do the rewriting on *Shampoo* as it was being shot.

In *Shampoo* the rewriting during shooting was less extensive than it has been in many other cases. It's a film that I like about as much as I like anything I've written in a while. Maybe other people don't, but I feel very positive about it. I was given an ongoing voice in the process of the making of the film. I was on the set every day, rewriting every day. At one point I even asked to have a scene reshot because I saw that there had been a crucial mistake. I rewrote the scene, and it was reshot.

BRADY: Which scene?

TOWNE: It's between Warren and Goldie—the climactic scene in their relationship. She has caught him with her best girl friend. She faces him and says, "There were others, too, weren't there?" And he says, "What do you want to know for?" "Well, there were, and I want to know," she says. Finally, he blows up, and tells her to grow up, everybody fucks everybody else, and he goes into this whole speech about why he went to beauty school.

I took a couple of my dogs for a walk, and it occurred to me that as the scene was shot, he advanced on her; but as it was written, she advanced on *him*. In order for the scene to work at all, he had to be the passive agent and have it forced out of him. Anger or fear, as I've said, can't come out of a person too easily. It has to be *forced* out of him to be realistic, to make him more of a person. I realized, too, that the speech itself wasn't working. It was didactic when it should have been personal. He should have said it's *me*, not that's what *people* do. The speech was changed. He sits down (so she's towering over him), and he fumbles, but he gets it out—and it's a speech that we worked out with Warren. The part that's most important to me occurs when he says, "Well, look, I don't know what I'm apologizing for. I go into an elevator or walk down the street and see a pretty girl, and that's it: It makes my day. I can't help it. I feel like I'm gonna live forever. Maybe it means I don't love them, and maybe it means I don't love you, but nobody's gonna tell me I don't *like* them very much."

What I was getting at with the last half of that speech—the notion of seeing pretty girls and feeling like he was going to live forever—was someone as far away as possible from compulsive Don Juanism, or latent homosexuality, or someone who is trying to prove his masculinity. None of these things interested me, nor did I believe in them in the case of this guy. Instead, I perceived him as sort of a crude Pygmalion—he makes women pretty, then falls in love with them, moment to moment. They're pretty, they're nice to touch, they smell great, they look great, they feel great—which is what he says in the speech. They are a life force for him in the classic Don Juan sense. The man just has more *life* in him. He is a rebel in the sense that he doesn't want to deny himself. The man sort of goes through a breakdown. He really is getting old in the course of the two days in the film. It's never quoted in the film, but that line from William Butler Yeats's "Sailing to Byzantium"—*That is no country for old men*—is never far from the back of my mind when I think of this film and of Southern California. And never far from the front of my mind.

Julie Christie has gone with George, the hairdresser, and at one point wanted to marry him. But he's always running around, having a hell of a good time, and she says, "You know why I always used to be so angry with you?" And he says, "Because I wouldn't settle down." And she says, "No, because you were always so happy about everything." And he says, "I was?" Because in the two days of the film he's kind of frenetic and occasionally very funny. But he's not happy. It's *that* element which it was necessary to deal with and carry through in the speech to Goldie, from a guy who really had a greater, more genuine appetite for certain kinds of enjoyment—particularly because the film is filled with people who *settle* for things. They settle for things because they *feel* they should, or because they are *told* they should, or because they're afraid not to. But the hairdresser is a guy who is dumber than the rest of them, in a way. He doesn't even *know* enough to settle for things, and he's lived his life in a certain sybaritic way. But there's nothing corrupt or crude about the guy at all. He's very sweet.

BRADY: You've been called an Abe Burrows of Hollywood because of the years you spent doctoring the scripts of others. What's your attitude toward that kind of reputation? Is it an exalted role, like that of a star relief pitcher? Or is it a minor role, like someone who plays only when the star pulls up with an injury?

TOWNE: I don't know if a relief pitcher is an exalted role, but I think it's more like that than the other. It's misleading, though, to talk about script doctoring or polishing as though it were a specialized art. *All* scripts are rewritten, whether they be yours or somebody else's. The only question is whether it is rewritten well or badly. But everything is and should be rewritten. Movies are not done under laboratory conditions. They are done over a period of time, under the gun of a budget—maybe a film will cost a hundred thousand dollars a day—and there are all sorts of problems: weather problems, people problems, lots of surprises. People may not know each other, and there may not be enough time to rehearse. You can lose locations. You can lose light. You can lose your fucking mind. So there are tremendous numbers of variables.

Also, when you are looking at something, and then it is blown up thirty-two times, just *that* can surprise you. You don't know what you've got. You see it on the set, and then you see it on the screen, and you say, "Hey, that's good!" or, "That's bad!" For example, at an early point in *Bonnie and Clyde*, everybody was worried about establishing their relationship in a particular scene. I must have written seven or eight little scenes. Then, one day, we were looking at dailies when they came in, and there they were in the same frame on the screen, and Warren was saying, "I'm Clyde Barrow, and we rob banks." It was obvious. Their relationship *was* established. It would be stupid to write any other scenes. You are always miscalculating in a movie, partially because of the disparity between what you see on the set and what you see on the screen. No matter how skilled you are in anticipating what the image is going to look like finally, you can still be fooled. So you have to rewrite, and be rewritten —not because the original is necessarily badly *written*, but because, ultimately, if it doesn't *work* for a film, it's bad.

Some people may think there's something pejorative about the term "script doctor." But on the whole it's better to have a reputation for fixing things up than for messing them up. I have enjoyed the role, and conceivably would and will do it again. If for no other reason than you force yourself into somebody else's world and you learn things at every level that you don't if you are doing original material. It's a way of revitalizing yourself. You learn things from other people. In rewriting someone or in adapting a work, you can come to feel it's your very own, too. Or you can feel that you are in the service of somebody else's material that you love very much, and you *want* to work. We all have rescue fantasies. Somebody may have a terrific idea, but they've screwed it up, and you'll fix it.

I was also chronically ill during all of this period. I suppose there's an irony there: someone who is ill, doctoring scripts. But I just didn't feel I had the energy level to start a script and follow it through to the end. Physically I just couldn't sustain it. Something was always coming up. I was ill all during *Bonnie and Clyde,* as a matter of fact. *Very* ill. I could hardly get out of the hotel room, and when I did I would either go to the set or to the doctor's office. I'm still not sure what it was—a complex of allergies. I hesitate to say I am cured, but I'm about five times healthier than I ever was. I thought, about 1969 or 1970, that I was not going to be able to work at all. Something would always seem to hit me physically. That seems to have changed.

BRADY: Is there much money in script doctoring?

TOWNE: You're making a separate category of it again, and it really isn't. Every good screenwriter that I know of spends an awful lot of time rewriting. Really top writers. Alvin Sargent. Nobody is better than Alvin, and most of his time is in rewriting. He's not known as a script doctor, as I seem to have become, but I think that's because I got involved in some projects that became rather prominent. Terry Malick. Charlie Eastman. All the writers I know are *re*writers. It's always been that way. Ben Hecht and Charlie MacArthur, they were rewriting themselves, rewriting each other. It's an interesting distinction to draw, but it's somewhat misleading.

There's a lot of money in it if you're in demand—in anything. And payment varies. You can be paid by the week, by the project. In some cases, you get a percentage. I've been paid all ways. You're paid what you're worth at the given moment. It can vary widely and wildly.

BRADY: You turned down an opportunity to do the screenplay for *The Great Gatsby,* I understand.

TOWNE: For a couple of reasons. I was writing *Chinatown* at the time, for one thing. And I think it would have been a disaster for me to do *Gatsby.* Here I was with this supposed reputation for doctoring scripts, doing rewrites, coming in and messing up a literary classic. I just didn't feel that I could risk that. It would not, and could not, come to good, as I saw it. *Gatsby* is very difficult to do in any case, and I felt that if it did not turn out well, the writer on it would suffer. Unless, oddly enough, it had been someone like Francis Ford Coppola, who had just directed *The Godfather*. Of all people, I think he could have afforded professionally to do *Gatsby* most easily—because he had a name and a reputation in his own right. I think it could have been very detrimental for someone who was an unknown to get in on that.

BRADY: That script had a lot of headaches even when Truman Capote worked on it at the outset, as I recall. And he certainly has a reputation in his own right.

TOWNE: Yes, I think he did do a version. I didn't see it, though. I don't know what happened. I wasn't that close to know. All I know is that it had not gone well, for whatever reasons. Jack Clayton approached me, we talked—and that's how I got involved with Bob Evans on *Chinatown*. "Well, why don't you want to do *Gatsby?*" he asked me. "I'm working on something else," I said. (I didn't want to say, "Look, if I did *Gatsby*, and it turned out badly, it might end my somewhat undistinguished career." Though that's what I felt.) Eventually, one night over dinner at Dominick's, Evans asked me what I was working on, and I told him about *Chinatown*, which was still in the early writing stage. He was very interested.

BRADY: He was married to Ali MacGraw at the time. I understand he was looking for a vehicle for her.

TOWNE: I think he probably was.

BRADY: Did you write the script with her in mind? Did it affect your conception of the female lead?

TOWNE: Not at all. I was writing it for only one person.

BRADY: Who?

TOWNE: Nicholson. I wasn't writing the girl for any actress in particular. I was just writing that one part for Jack.

BRADY: In the midst of all that work, did you ever get the god-awful fear that maybe it would never be filmed?

TOWNE: I had it. It was an abiding feeling. I was thousands of dollars in debt. I thought, "I'll just finish this because I said I would, and to hell with it." I thought it was a complete disaster.

BRADY: How do you live with that feeling?

TOWNE: You just do.

BRADY: Is good writing enough? Or does a screenwriter also have to be good at story conference strategies for dealing with producers, directors, and the like?

TOWNE: Well, it helps. But the best answer to that problem is to work with your friends, because no matter how much moxie you've got, if you're with a guy who is fundamentally not congenial to your point of view, or if he's worried about what somebody else is going to think, it just doesn't matter. So if you can sidestep such things, it's best to work with people you know and trust—and who know you and trust you—and to work from that vantage point. There are going to be disagreements, for sure. But there is also mutual respect, and work that is bound to be satisfying insofar as everyone on a movie *can* be satisfied with the outcome.

BRADY: I assume that you had some enemies on *Chinatown*. The early drafts of that script are completely different from the shooting script, especially at the end.

TOWNE: Yeah, there was some conflict there between Roman Polanski and me. We went over everything, and he said he didn't like the ending. In the original, I had Evelyn Mulwray going to jail and her daughter escaping to Mexico. Roman wanted Evelyn to die at the end. "You're kidding," I said. "Well, think of something else," he said. And I did. I came up with an alternative ending about four or five days before shooting. I brought it over to him, and he said, "Well, it's too late. We're going to shoot in a week and I can't change anything. I just can't do it." That was the last we spoke during the picture. It was very quiet, subdued, although we'd had several fights in which I'd blown up and yelled at him, and he at me. But I must also say that except for Arthur, Roman taught me more about screenwriting than anybody I've ever worked with, both in spite of and because of our conflicts. Roman is great at the elucidation of the narrative—to go from point A to B to C. In that sense, he is excellent.

BRADY: The shooting script of *Chinatown* is such a reversal of everything the first, second and third drafts build toward. Can you recall the compromise version that you came up with?

TOWNE: I never wanted Evelyn killed. I can't recall the specifics of the original scene because I've lost it—but in it she did kill her father in Chinatown.

I remember that the second draft was very clumsy, and I was forced to embark on a third draft. One of the things about the first and second drafts is that Gittes is told by Evelyn, when she feels backed up to the wall, that she is seeing somebody else, that she's seeing a married man and that's her reason for not wanting to go to the police. It was a little lame in the third draft, a little vague in the shooting script, but in the earlier drafts it was very clear. Gittes says, "OK, I'm going to the police unless you tell me what is going on." And she gives the most plausible reason to her mind that he would accept, because it involved a certain amount of culpability on her part: She's a married woman, and she's making it with somebody else. Because he thinks that she's being honest with him, and because he's been kind of a sucker, he decides to go along with her. Then he becomes slowly jealous of this mythical character. So when he goes to see who she's seeing—when he follows her—he thinks he's going to find her lover. Which I felt would have been much more interesting.

The postcoital love scene, in which Evelyn adores Gittes (in the shooting script), was improvised on the set. In the original scene, Evelyn was so upset after having sex that she was ignoring him completely. And he was misconstruing it as her being concerned about her other lover, whereas, as she'd indicated earlier, her reaction to sex was very neurotic. But, frankly, I don't think Roman Polanski could be interested in a woman who is involved with somebody else, or, in this case, a hero who would *worry* that his lover was fucking somebody else. And it was Roman's identification with the hero that was making the film work. It has to be unqualified involvement with him. As with the love scene. The woman has to approve wholeheartedly of the man's performance in bed.

Roman needs that kind of approbation from both women, men and everybody on the set. He's the little king. That's a case where that kind of attitude warped the mystery, the tension at a point in the film. Also, it prevented the film from dealing with what I thought was the most important missing thing of all—namely, that Gittes was getting progressively, insanely crazy about this woman. He was jealous, and really falling in love with her. Although she came to like him very much, her other problems were so overwhelming that she couldn't . . . she came to admire and like him and really find him enormously attractive. But he was falling in love with her.

That kind of passion I felt was very important for the film, in order for his betrayal of her to have any significance. He had to really love her.

At any rate, the script had to be turned into a shooting script. I was struggling through the first and second drafts simply trying to figure out the story for myself. The second draft was so complex that a shooting script based upon it would have run close to three hours. I would have had to do a radical rewrite in order to simplify it.

BRADY: There's incredible texture to it.

TOWNE: In the film I missed that kind of progressive jealousy by Gittes—his thinking that she was involved with someone else. And the ending, as shot, is very harsh.

BRADY: Didn't you want to direct *Chinatown* yourself?

TOWNE: Initially I did. That's why I wrote a detective script. I figured that no matter how badly it was directed, if I wrote a story that people wanted to know the outcome of, it would carry. That was one of the reasons for the genre. There were others that I discovered as I went along with it.

BRADY: I hope you do the novel. There's so much puzzlement in the film of *Chinatown*. I came away wondering, "What does this or that line mean? Why does Gittes repeat 'as little as possible' at the end?" The reference to Evelyn's flawed eye. There's so much going on in the film that is cerebral, that is just not visual enough—it's like a tease. I think the novel would answer many questions the film poses.

TOWNE: The novel would be very different, all right. What do you mean about the eye reference—are you referring to Evelyn's getting shot in the eye in the end?

BRADY: Yes, but earlier Gittes notices some flaw in her eye. It's a point of discussion. Then, at the end, she is shot in the eye.

TOWNE: That shot in the eye at the end *does* make you think of that earlier line, which is unfortunate. The flaw in her iris was intended for another purpose. You may remember an early speech in the script, and Gittes says, "Who does she think she is? She's no better than anybody else in this town." She was sort of a perfect, upper-class lady. So Gittes comes up against this woman who is infuriatingly correct, and everything about her is an insult to this lower-class guy who monograms everything and is made to feel like a crude, dumb asshole. And finally: He sees a flaw in the iris. It's emblematic at that moment of her vulnerability. If you've ever seen such eyes, you know they are very pretty. To me it was also emblematic of the fact that she is psychologically flawed. The fact that she was shot in the eye later is a coincidental echo.

BRADY: All the more reason for doing the novel.

TOWNE: Either I will do it, or it won't be done. It's a highly personal thing. In fact, most of the locations that Roman chose for the film were ones that I directed him to. I remembered them from my childhood.

BRADY: What sort of childhood did you have?

TOWNE: I grew up in California, around San Pedro. I grew up amidst fishermen, Mexicans, chief petty officers in the merchant marine with three-day growths of beard who would come up and *wheeeeze* on you. Sailors and guys with raspy voices. It was kind of a fun neighborhood, actually. Rather polyglot: Slavs, Italians, a total melting pot. I was the only Jew on the block, I think. It was terrific. I've never regretted it. I even worked as a fisherman for a while on a boat, and when I was in college I wrote maybe half a dozen short stories that were largely descriptions of my life on that boat. Even today, I don't think they're bad. Every writer has to use the world he lives in as source material, I think, though it shouldn't impose restrictions or limitations on what you write. You have to be able to get into the worlds, the fantasies of people outside yourself as well.

BRADY: Besides writing out of experience, how much research goes into a script like *Chinatown?*

TOWNE: I did a lot of research—mostly reading to get a feeling for the ambience of the time, the way people spoke, what their inhibitions were. For example, today it's perfectly proper to talk about all sorts of intimate sexual things, but people are rather chary of talking about how much money they make—whereas in the 1930s I think the reverse would have been true. People wouldn't have minded talking about how much money, but *boy,* would they not have talked about sex. To get attitudinal differences like that, you have to read, and I suppose that's research. You have to find out what people would say or would not say in a social situation. And the basic premise of the scandal was researched, too. I read about the Owens Valley, and became interested in it. But I didn't base a single character in *Chinatown* on any person I read about in the Owens Valley episode. My characters fulfilled roles that in some cases were analagous to roles in the original scandal but were wholly made up. Mulwray was perhaps somewhat like Mulholland of the Owens Valley deal, but in *Chinatown* Mulwray was depicted as a very decent guy, whereas I think that Mulholland was a corrupt man who allowed himself to be used by Chandler and everybody else. He was ambitious. The Mulwray of the film was intended to be a tough but decent man who was trying to avoid a scandal that would have ruined the public ownership of his department, which he had fought for, while at the same time trying to keep the thing from taking place which eventually took place.

BRADY: And yet you have a William Mulholland statement as a prefatory quote to the first and second drafts of your script.

TOWNE: Which I would use in the novel. Sure: "There it is, take it." That's what the attitude had always been out here about everything. L.A. has never been viewed as a city, but as a place where hustlers come. It's like a mine, and everyone's trying to hit the main vein and get it out, then leave the fucking place. It's never viewed as a city. Never has been. It's a place where you just Get Yours, then get out. It doesn't matter what happens to the land, the air or any of its natural beauty. That's the attitude.

So I felt that the Mulholland quote was apropos not only of Mulholland, but of everyone who was here to make a fast buck, to make it big and fast.

BRADY: I liked the Seabiscuit material in the early drafts. That shows research, too, I suppose.

TOWNE: Right. That was an interesting thing. Big argument over it. Remember the early draft of the barbershop scene?

BRADY: Yes.

TOWNE: Remember when he gets mad? Somebody says "Boy, did Seabiscuit fold in the stretch the other day," and Gittes gets furious. He threatens to get in a fight over it. And later, when he goes to see Noah Cross, Cross offers him, by way of payment, a horse. The point (and I would have smoothed it out in the final draft if I'd continued to use it) was that I wanted to show a venal, corrupt man in Gittes—well, pettily venal and crude, rather than corrupt, really—crass, crude, self-serving, social-climbing—who admired the character of this tiny horse named Seabiscuit. At one point in an early draft he is asked why he thinks so much of the animal. I don't know how much you know about Seabiscuit, but it was a horse that came back from a complete breakdown, and *won* the following year. The animal didn't look like it could win anything, but really was one of the classiest horses that ever lived. A small horse with tremendous character. And Gittes' admiration of that character was meant to be an early tip-off that the guy was susceptible to class in one form or another. Of course, he would be susceptible to class in a woman, too. Seabiscuit was meant to be the transfer. But Roman said, "That's folklore," although he ended up using the Seabiscuit thing in the paper. What he insisted on using in the barbershop scene as a means of getting Gittes mad was a story in the newspaper and some guy calling him a headline seeker. Gittes is then called upon to justify his work—which he had to do with Evelyn anyway, when he went to her house after being threatened with a suit. I disliked the self-serving moment there in the barbershop. I wanted to suggest at that point that the guy had the capacity to admire something, just for the sake of its beauty or its character. In one way or another, it was thoroughbred. Which is a tip-off that he could be in real trouble with a woman he admired. I missed that. I felt it was a mistake to get rid of it. It made that moment kind of petty and dumb, whereas if the Seabiscuit idea had been developed, I think it would have been more insightful to the guy.

BRADY: It's an angle on Gittes that is simply not fleshed out in the film at all.

TOWNE: That would have done it, really. Everything I was doing was driving toward Gittes falling in love with Evelyn. Everything that Roman was doing was blunting that.

BRADY: An influence that I see in the early writing is Dashiell Hammett. In the first draft, Gittes at one point says, "In my case, being respectable would be bad for business." Hammett's Sam Spade in *The Maltese Falcon* says, "Don't be too sure I'm as crooked as I'm supposed to be. That kind of reputation makes it easier to deal with the enemy."

TOWNE: I remember the line very well from *The Maltese Falcon*. It may be an unconscious echo there.

BRADY: Are there any parallels between Sam Spade and Brigid in *Falcon* and Jake Gittes and Evelyn in *Chinatown?*

TOWNE: The relationship in *Chinatown* is meant to be the opposite. In *Falcon,* Brigid is the villain. The woman is usually a femme fatale, and I was trying to suggest that that was the way I was going, but go against that convention and make her the only decent person in the story, which is what Evelyn is meant to be. She is acting from a pure, basic motive—mother love. That's generally conceded to be the most unselfish motive there is, and that was the basis for all her actions in the film. I was trying to make Evelyn the opposite of what someone like Brigid was.

Hammett's toughness of character was the main value in his work, I would say, at least for me. If you reread all of Hammett and Raymond Chandler, though, I don't think you can touch Chandler. Hammett ages badly in some of his short stories. Chandler doesn't. Both Hammett and Chandler, though, were so much better than anybody else. Chandler's prose about the city of Los Angeles at that time is really inspiring. I'm old enough to remember what the city was like then, and reading Chandler filled me with such a sense of loss that it was probably the main reason why I did the script. Just reading Chandler kept me going.

BRADY: Your background readings, then, were used more often to acquire a mood for your own writing than to acquire outside material, it would seem.

TOWNE: No question. That's what it was really all about.

BRADY: Who else did you read?

TOWNE: John Fante, who wrote one of the best books about L.A. ever—called *Ask the Dusk*. A terrible title, but a terrific book. I had read Nathanael West before. A very telling writer, but I'm not one of the unqualified admirers of *The Day of the Locust*. I don't think it's that good a book. West was brilliant, but *Locust* was not a great book in the manner that *Miss Lonelyhearts* was.

BRADY: How did you decide on the names in the film?

TOWNE: I picked my names on the basis of sounds. I thought Mulwray had a romantic sound, redolent of some heroines of the past. It had a ring to it. Hollis Mulwray sounded good for the husband. Julian was the original name for Noah Cross, but there was a Julian Cross living, so it had to be changed. For which I'm sorry, because Julian Cross is now actually dead. If I do the novel, I'll return his name to Julian. Gittes' name was chosen because I wanted an antiromantic name for him—a name that sounded like a hustler. Jack Nicholson and I have a friend called Harry Gittes, and I've always loved his name. Just pronouncing the name is vaguely insulting: Gittes. Jake is a good name from the time period, and it is also the name I have always called Nicholson. Jack's full name is actually John J.—so I took that, too, and it became J. J. Gittes, which seemed like a reasonable name, a real name. I tend to name characters that way, on the basis of their sound.

BRADY: How did you decide on the dirty joke that Gittes is telling when Evelyn comes into the room?

TOWNE: I was talking to a fellow who lived out here in L.A. in the thirties, when there was much antipathy toward the Chinese and when that joke had its origins out here. I asked him to tell me everything he could remember—what people called people, what they did when they went out, how they fucked, did they use rubbers, and so on. I went crazy with details like that. I talked to guys in their fifties and their sixties who were resilient, sharp. There was one writer in particular, and he told me this joke.

I thought, that's the perfect kind of joke for that time, because it was a time when people's prejudices were much more out front, and I wanted to make use of that throughout the movie. "Do you accept anyone of the Jewish persuasion?" Gittes asks at the old folks' home. "Sorry, we don't," he is told. Jake: "Well, that's good; neither does Dad."

I wanted to be consistent with that. I had some Mexican stuff that I wanted to use, too. People then were more ashamed of their origins. Prejudices were more open. They all wanted to be Americans, and were vaguely ashamed of being anything else. Society was more stratified at *every* level. People had principles. There were certain things they would do, and certain things they would not do. Fucking. Not fucking. Marriage. Adultery. Abortion. All these things were really major issues. Behavior was much more codified, and people were much more certain of the limits on their behavior—which is what Gittes learned. Gittes thinks he understands people's limitations, and then he comes up against a monster, Noah Cross, who will do *everything*. There is *nothing* he won't do. Man *has* no limits. That was the point of that confrontation scene, which Gittes didn't understand: Cross tells him that some people have *no* limitations. At a given place and a given time, people are capable of anything. Gittes' cynicism, by comparison, is petty, naive, and almost sweet.

BRADY: When and why did you decide to call it *Chinatown?*

TOWNE: The origin of that was the vice cop who sold me one of my dogs and who used to work in Chinatown. "Down there," he said, "we never do anything, because the tongs are still working. We don't know all the dialects, and they say don't do anything, because you could make a mistake. You don't know who's a crook and who isn't a crook. You don't know who you're helping and who you're hurting. So in Chinatown they say just don't do a goddamn thing.'' Which I found an intriguing notion, and when I started working on the script I tried to elaborate on that idea—turning it into a metaphor. Chinatown is the place where Gittes fucked up, and Evelyn is a *person* where he fucked up. That was the idea. But ultimately, I think Chinatown—where if you're smart you do nothing—suggests the futility of good intentions.

BRADY: Did you have trouble getting the name through?

TOWNE: Oh, yeah. That was why the last scene was set in Chinatown. These guys sat around like Harry Cohn saying, "How can you call a movie *Chinatown* when there's no Chinatown in it?" Roman led the way. One highly sensitive man whom I *love* went so far in this discussion—and things had gotten so out of hand—that he actually said, "Well, maybe if Gittes liked Chinese *food*." At which point I blew up. It was one of those story conferences with the best of men, I'm afraid, saying these crazy things.

BRADY: How did the idea for slitting Gittes' nose come about?

TOWNE: I didn't want to use a lot of overt violence in the film, because I felt that the only real way you could be scared for your hero is emotionally—that is, if he got hung up on somebody you were afraid he shouldn't have gotten hung up on. Or if he committed some act that destroyed him as a character, because your identification with him as a detective is probably the greatest instant identification an audience can have with any hero. You follow the guy, the mystery, and try to unravel it the way you follow yourself around in a dream. You know you're not going to die—in the dream, anyway. So the only fear you can threaten the viewer with is something suggestive of a deeper horror. So I just sat back and asked, "What is the most horrible thing I can think of that would really scare you?" And I just came up with that. I thought of slitting his ears and everything else, but he's a nosy guy, and a knife up his nose just seemed to work.

BRADY: I would think it takes a special actor to agree to a role requiring that he go around in half the film with a piece of gauze over his face.

TOWNE: That's Jack. A grand guy.

BRADY: Which is easier, adapting the material of others or creating your own?

TOWNE: I think that almost always it's easier to adapt. Your writing inhibitions are lower. In a sense, you might even be writing a little bit better when you're adapting somebody else's material because vanity, fear and all the things that inhibit you as a writer don't come into play. You tend to be a little looser, taking shots from different parts of the court that you wouldn't normally attempt—and making them—just because you are looser. Sometimes with your own material you get constipated, vain and stupid. For that reason it's somewhat easier to adapt. But not always.

BRADY: In *The Last Detail,* how did you approach the transformation from book to film?

TOWNE: My main decision was to do a story about *typical* people instead of atypical characters. Buddusky in the novel is sort of a closet intellectual who secretly reads Camus but tells the fellas he's reading skin books, and who has an amazingly sophisticated, attractive ex-wife in New York for a fellow who is a lifer in the Navy. I felt this was dangerous for the script because if he is running around in New York with this beautiful girl, and his shore patrol buddy, who is black, doesn't have any girl, it would be implausible. It was also unrealistic. I know from my own experience in the service that the uniform is enough to turn *any* girls off, so I used a Greenwich Village party in the movie instead.

BRADY: That's not in the book at all. They go to Buddusky's ex-wife's apartment, as I remember.

TOWNE: Right. In the movie, the girls are at this party, and Buddusky is trying to bullshit them, but the girls aren't having any of it. The only way that guys in the service get laid is with hookers, which is what happens in the film. I eliminated the kid's mother, too, because I wanted it to be a case of missing people, the way you do. And I wanted to stress the idea of these three guys just being thrown in on each other. They're really all that they have.

At the end, I didn't want Buddusky and Mulhall to feel overly guilty about transporting Meadows to jail. I didn't want them to ruin their lives over it. They were a little unhappy about it, but typical people are usually very decent, and will go out of their way a little bit to help someone as long as too much courage and too much thought aren't required. Without saying it, I wanted to imply that we're *all* lifers in the Navy, and everybody hides behind doing a job, whether it's massacring in My Lai, or taking a kid to jail, or chopping down all the trees on a block, making the residents miserable, because that's your job. Or shoving eight million Jews into ovens. People really hide behind doing their job. We're all cowards, really, when we're faced with doing something we sense is immoral or cruel. We rationalize it by saying, "That's my job." As if that makes it all OK.

In an earlier time, it might come under the notion of allegiance to the king or something. With Buddusky, in order to make his behavior typical in this fashion, he had to be a more *typical* lifer in the Navy. In the novel, though, he was a man of rather extraordinary sensibilities who deliberately talked like a sailor at times, but underneath it all had a sophisticated Whitmanesque appreciation of the sea, the joys of physical labor, and all that shit. From my point of view, that was wrong. That was the starting point for the changes I made for the script. I think the characterization may be a little harsher than the novel. But more realistic, too.

BRADY: You dropped the scene with Meadows' alcoholic mother and her lover in the book, but you insert a Port Authority washroom fight that is not in the book. What sort of thinking goes into such insertions? Is it a matter of pacing and tempo within the script?

TOWNE: I wasn't merely trying to create physical action. It was part of the education of this boy Meadows. What do they do? They get him in his first fight, they get him laid, they take him to places he hasn't been, they get him drunk. And getting in your first fight is really part of that. It's an exhilarating experience. From Buddusky's point of view, I wanted to show the tug-of-war between him and Mule Mulhall. In fact, I wanted *more* of the back-and-forth stuff between the two of them to come out in the screenplay, but it may have been vitiated by the fact that Rupert Cross, for whom the screenplay was written, died, and Otis Young is a different kind of actor than Rupert was.

BRADY: I wasn't aware of that.

TOWNE: The picture was actually written for Rupert and for Jack. Rupert tragically got lung cancer and was unable to do the picture, and died. There was a lot more overt hostility between Buddusky and Mule in the original screenplay than in the book, too. When they are between trains in the movie, for instance, Mule comes down hard on Buddusky in a scene that, again, is not in the book. "Listen," he says, "you ain't no simple shit bad ass; you're a dangerous motherfuckin' menace." He yells at him and says, "I'm not taking *any* more shit from you. From now on you're doing what I say."

Mule was asserting himself. He realized that things were getting out of hand. It was that tug-of-war. So the fight scene was Buddusky's way of breaking out of it. He was pissed off, unhappy. Mule had made a fool of him. He was generally angry and wanted to go out and fight anyone. It was his way of getting back on top of the pecking order. He brought it off, and how can you argue with success? It was fun, exhilarating, and Buddusky's way of having the final answer in the argument. That was the reason for the scene.

BRADY: One glaring distinction between the book and the movie, of course, is that in the book both Mule and Buddusky go AWOL after delivering Meadows to the brig, and Buddusky is eventually killed. In the movie, though, they deliver Meadows and walk away alive and well.

TOWNE: As I said, I don't think that *most* people in that situation would do anything but say, "That goddamn sergeant, he doesn't know what he's doing. He doesn't even know enough to pull copies. That's how stupid he is. At least I know my job better than anybody in the goddamn Navy." In other words, Buddusky felt guilty about what he had done, but he wasn't going to go AWOL or get killed over it. Both men know that they've done something wrong, but they can't face it. So all they can say to each other is, "Well, I'll see you later." They don't want to stay with each other. If he goes AWOL and is killed (as is done in the book), from my point of view the audience has been let off the hook. The audience doesn't have to feel guilty anymore for identifying with these two characters: These two guys felt so bad that they destroyed themselves in one way or another. A viewer is left to feel, "Well, I'm really a pretty decent person. I felt so bad that I destroyed myself." And I didn't want to let that happen. Like I said, I felt the film was about the fact that we are all in one way or another lifers in the Navy. We would help people to a point, but if they really threatened us we would throw them in the pokey no matter how horrible an act it was, just to save our jobs, our reputations, anything.

I don't necessarily think they were bad guys; in fact, I think they were *good*. Most people are decent. But given a situation like that, they took the path of least resistance.

BRADY: Is technique easily learned?

TOWNE: I think that it's never learned. I think you're always fooled—you write too much, you do too much. You're always learning.

BRADY: What sort of training did you have?

TOWNE: None.

BRADY: There is no Short Course in Screenwriting that you'd recommend then?

TOWNE: No. Movies are like wars. The guy who becomes an expert is the guy who doesn't get killed. Ah, here's Pancho Villa, the greatest expert on guerrilla warfare in history. It's because he didn't get killed. Everybody else got shot, and he survived, so he's an expert. How many wars are fought? How many movies are made? Not that many so that you can become this Great Expert. Let's say you work on ten movies. Well, that's not a lot of projects, relatively. I've worked on maybe a dozen films. But if you *survive* in any shape or order, then theoretically you've *learned* something. And I don't know what you've learned, except maybe that you've learned you can survive. But each project is so different, there's not very much carry-over from film to film.

I've learned certain things for myself, but you don't learn technique in the same sense that, say, an architect learns how to draw a rendering. It really isn't the same. The very technical aspects of screenwriting are just totally unimportant. About as unimportant as whether or not to write "FADE IN" at the beginning of a script. It's meaningless writing camera angles or any of that. Virtually meaningless. You've just got to get a sense of the movement of a piece, so that it's lucid, it's visualized well, there's rhythm and orchestration in it so that scenes are not choppy where you should take some time, or too long-winded where you shouldn't. I mean, you just come to sense these things from project to project. You learn the obvious pitfalls, of course. I think that any time a movie opens spectacularly, you run a risk.

One of the things that people say when they first start writing movies is, "Jeez, I have this idea for a movie. This is the way it opens. It's really a great opening." And of course they don't know where to go from there. That's true not only of people who are just *thinking* of writing movies, but very often of people who *write* them. They're anxious for a splashy beginning to hook an audience, but then you end up paying for it with an almost mathematical certainty. If you have a lot of action and excitement at the beginning of a picture, there's going to have to be some explanation, some character development somewhere along the line, and there will be a big sag about twenty minutes after you get into a film with a splashy opening. It's something you learn. I don't know if you'd call it technique. It's made me prefer soft openings for films. It's been my experience that an audience will forgive you almost anything at the *beginning* of a picture, but almost nothing at the end. If they're not satisfied with the end, nothing that led up to it is going to help. Unlike television, you don't have to keep people from turning the channel to another network when they're in a theater. They've paid three fifty or five dollars and if the opening ten or fifteen minutes of a film are a little slow, they are still going to sit a few minutes, as long as it eventually catches hold. I believe in soft openings.

BRADY: You've got a captive audience.

TOWNE: Right. So why bother to try to capture their interest at the expense of the whole film? They're there. They're not going to go anywhere.

I know there are places where they teach screenwriting, but there are no rules. The only way you can effectively learn about screenwriting is to write something and then see it done as you've written it. Then you can see where you went right, and where you went wrong. One of the virtues of working on *Bonnie and Clyde* was that despite the fact that I rewrote and rewrote, I had an idea in my mind of how it would play. Then I got the opportunity to see how that material played—which is a valuable learning experience. You are able to measure what you imagined against the reality of what the execution did. That's valuable. When you're working and imagining on some future project, your experience tells you: This will play, or this won't play.

BRADY: You never *really* know though, do you?

TOWNE: No. You can be fooled. Absolutely. No question about it. You may think that something is well written, and be disappointed in the outcome. Or the opposite may be true. You may write something, and think, "Jeez, if I get away with this I'll be so lucky, I won't believe it." I hated *The New Centurions*, but there was a scene that everybody objected to on paper because I wanted a black nurse to remember that she had been in a hospital when a cop had been brought in with a gunshot wound. She said, "Oh, yeah, I was on the floor." Everyone said that was an insane coincidence—meeting the same cop later and getting involved with him. But it was forty-five minutes later in the film, which is a *lifetime* later, and that's what L.A. is about: these weird coincidences. And I saw that scene, where he goes to her house and she's been robbed and they talk and she remembers who he is, and she says, "Are you all right now?" And he says, "No." It's one of the best scenes in the movie. In fact, it's one of the only scenes in the movie I liked. There was no indication at the time, however, that it would come off that well. From my point of view, anyway. So you can be fooled by a scene.

Also, you will sometimes write a good scene that under different circumstances would have played terrifically well, but you get unlucky: You lose the light, or they are in a hurry, or the actor isn't as good as you thought he would be. And it turns out shitty. Then you're stuck. You think, "Well, maybe it *was* a bad scene, though I thought it was good. Maybe they didn't do it well. Maybe they did their best." You don't know. And you'll never know about that scene for the rest of your life.

BRADY: If you were conducting a course in screenwriting, whose work would you study?

TOWNE: The greatest filmmaker that I know of, the one who moves me the most, is Jean Renoir. If I were ever to do a course in screenwriting, I would deal a lot with Renoir. *Grand Illusion*. He's the richest, the fullest artist, really. It's difficult to extract technique from a movie that large. In a great film, you're not even aware of it, I suppose. I recall a scene in *Grand Illusion* where Pierre Fresnay has been shot by Erich Von Stroheim. He's dying in the hospital, and the two aristocrats—who are emblematic of the fact that the old order is dying—play this incredible love scene. Fresnay is dying, and Von Stroheim has been instrumental in his destruction. The scene would be very sentimental if it were not tinged with the irony of the man who has done the shooting—with his aristocratic *noblesse oblige*—saying, "Forgive me," while the dying man is going to equal pains to reassure him that it was not his fault: "I would have done the same thing . . . duty is duty." "I was aiming at your leg." "More than fifty yards away, very bad light. . . . And then I was running. . . ."

The scene has an edge of humor that takes any of the melancholy away, and leaves reality and wit instead—which are even more moving. Individual instances like that can be pointed to in a film and can be instructive for a writer. But ultimately all I can say to a beginning writer is, "See these films, and enjoy them for what they say about life. Absorb them. Renoir got more of life into his art than anybody I've seen before or since. That's the way I feel about him, so I commend him to you. I'm sure you'll learn things from him that I haven't."

BRADY: What's your attitude toward the *auteur* theory?

TOWNE: That's like waving a red flag at a bull. You don't say that to *any* writer! But in some cases it's truer than in others. In the case of Bergman, who else is it going to be? To some extent Stanley Kubrick—or Coppola in his collaborations with Mario Puzo—is the overpowering force. But even then, a movie is always collaborative. I believe the *auteur* theory is merely one way it is easier for historians to assign credit or blame to individuals. It's a simplistic way of interpreting facts, and it often has very little to do with what actually happened. Unless you've worked on a film, it's literally impossible to know who did what. I've read reviews of films, for instance, in which I have not disagreed with a critic, but the reviewer will assign credit for the writing to the director, or credit for the writing to the *wrong* writer, or credit to the actor for something the director did, or something that a set designer may have done, or a cameraman may have done. It's impossible to know who did what unless you've worked on the film. It's like trying to describe what happened at an orgy when you weren't there.

Despite the *auteur* theory, you look around and you will find that certain directors have functioned better with certain collaborators than with others, and you know that it's had a great deal to do with the people *around* the director on a film. Take an extreme case from history. We are told that Napoleon directed every battle. Yet if you were there you would know that Marshal Ney really had a great deal to do with it all. And Marshal Ney probably had a lot of help. But you just talk about Napoleon, not because it is accurate but because it's easier. People in general, and *auteur* critics in particular, love heroes. But great directors are exploiters. They provoke. Certain directors can see what is going on on a set and not interfere with it. Which is very good. They don't inhibit their actors; they let them perform very naturally. I know a terrific director who almost considers it a *sin* to interfere with what's going on on the set. It would be the violation of an esthetic principle. You'd be interfering with an honesty that is going on. Other directors who have the ability *not* to inhibit their actors also have the ability to say, "That fucker is not giving me what I want," and to provoke the scene—which is a very unique talent. First of all, he must see what he needs.

Then he must be able to *get* it. Some directors can see what they need and not get it. All I am saying, I suppose, is that a director's authorship is limited, and the number of directors about whom you could seriously discuss authorship is very, very limited.

BRADY: Do screenwriters have individual styles?

TOWNE: I don't know. Some people maintain that they do. I remember Jeremy Larner once picking out lines that I had done in a film, but I think that's just because he knows me. And I remember seeing *The Way We Were*. There were three writers on that—David Raphael, Alvin Sargent and Arthur Laurents. Well, Raphael and Sargent are sensational writers. Two of the best, really. And I remember a moment in the film when they are making fun of Eleanor Roosevelt at a party, and Barbra Streisand is insisting to Robert Redford that they leave because she finds his WASP friends insulting. She wants to get him to go, and he turns to go after this ongoing argument, which they are to have for the rest of their lives, and she says, "Come on, let's get out of here. Let's go somewhere else." And he says, very abruptly, "And then what?" It was such a sensational line because it gave insight to a character who, up to that point, seemed rather superficial. It told that he understood his own limitations so beautifully that he could tell where their whole relationship was going. An unexpected line. It was economical, it was brilliant. I asked Sydney Pollack, and it so happened that David Raphael wrote that line. Otherwise I'm not sure I'd be able to guess. All you can tell is what's good. Certain screenwriters have identifiable styles, I suppose; but a script can be interpreted on the screen in so many ways, it's very difficult to tell. God knows Pinter has a style that is recognizable, because his attitude is so pervasive. His characters are indulging in this constant one-upsmanship, being cruel. Everything being said is the tip of an iceberg of malevolence. Constantly jabbing.

So I'd say yes, there are styles, but it isn't just writing style; it's really an attitude. And a certain body of work—or a close personal knowledge of the writer—is required to be able to pick out the attitudes that identify a screenwriter.

BRADY: Is there much fraternizing or camaraderie among Hollywood screenwriters today?

TOWNE: Not that I know of. I have three close friends—Ed Taylor, Dick Collins and Curtis Hansen—who one way or another have helped me through scripts and through my life over the years, but there's no commissary klatch or group of writers periodically getting together over drinks at the contemporary equivalent of the Garden of Allah. At least I don't know about it. One close friend I have who is a writer is Buck Henry, but we *never* discuss writing. He's just somebody whose company I enjoy almost more than anybody's. I don't *know* any other writers, really.

BRADY: John Gregory Dunne once said that writing for films is like writing for *Time* magazine except the pay is better. Here's the quote: "The film writer is first of all *hired,* and as an employee, no matter how grandiose his salary, he must tailor his ideas to those of his employer. He can wheedle, cajole, or even scream, but if he fails to persuade his employer, he either goes along or gets out. If he gets out, he is easily replaced."

TOWNE: I've never written for *Time* magazine, but I think there's a good deal of truth in what John says. I think it's sad. I hate to keep harping on this, but that does not have to happen if you work with your friends, or with people you trust. In the case of *Shampoo,* if I felt strongly about something, Hal and Warren would not proceed until they were sure they understood me completely, just because we were coworkers on the film. But until you enjoy that kind of relationship, you are likely to be working on a film where someone has come along and packaged a bunch of strangers—and it's very difficult to be intimate on short notice. There's a wonderful line from that delightful Saki story, "The Open Window"—after the young girl has woven this incredible story that takes in everyone, including the reader: "Romance at short notice was her specialty."

But intimacy at short notice is *nobody's* specialty. It's difficult. I think that a lot of young directors are very effective their first time out because they're working with old friends. Then they get a big project, and they're working with a bunch of strangers, and they feel swamped. What I am saying is applicable to *any* kind of work in which people come together to work on something with a risk factor. In movies there is a *high* risk factor. People are brought together who are highly paid, and who are really laying their asses on the line. The actor is being put in front of the camera, and he's not going to be paid his salary very often if his films do not enjoy success. That's true of everybody, so everybody's frightened. An actor's instinctive reaction to a script is, "You expect me to say this drivel? This is what I'm supposed to risk my neck for?" That's his instinctive reaction. The director, too, says, "You're gonna make me put my ass on the line for *this?*"

Filmmaking is dictated by fear. By financial pressures, temporal pressures, career pressures. You really have to be with people who are close friends, who have the proverbial grace under pressure (and it's easier with friends), and that's one reason why some movies turn out better than others. I don't know that anybody's ever bothered to investigate, but you go down and look at the number of films that have been made and pick out what you consider are the good films. I'll bet you in almost every case that the major people involved in the making of every good film—the cinematographer, the costume designer, set designer, director, actors, screenwriter—had worked together on several films and were close to each other. Strangers coming together for the first time rarely make anything good.

BRADY: A writer for *The New York Times* says, "The secret of success in this small provincial jungle is an ability to create charismatic big parts for stars." He goes on to say that only the interest of a Newman, Nicholson, Streisand or a "star" director like Coppola or Polanski "can guarantee a script's development beyond the option stage." Is that true?

TOWNE: It's too simplistic a statement to accept on face value. There are too many other variables. In other words, that writer is full of shit.

BRADY: Did you go through any culture shock coming off

scripts where you were exercising such creative powers into another adaptation for *Tarzan?*

TOWNE: No. It depends on how you view what you are doing. As for myself, I take the whole *Tarzan* thing very seriously. I see where I can make a contribution to it that has not been made, and it's extremely challenging. Consider what's been done—a bunch of Tarzan movies. I want to do something that one can enjoy, but that also has some substance to it. I have very strong feelings about the subject matter. What the story is about, when you accept it, is a feral child—a child who is raised by animals. You must be prepared to deal with that. There are certain basic questions that underlie the material, whether you express them or not: What is a man? What is the nature of man? Is a human life any more valuable than an animal's life? When you read Aquinas, there's the rock, then the animal and the human being. The whole structure of relative importance in the universe places animals on an infinitely lower scale than humans, and yet there's a question in my mind whether one form of life is inherently any more valuable than another, even if it's more sophisticated.

BRADY: Now that you've come through the tough times and are something of a celebrity, do you think you've changed any?

TOWNE: I doubt it, but there have been some shifts in attitudes toward me. If I'm in a meeting with some people, and if I say, "Look, fellas, I don't think it's gonna work this way," there is a tendency to listen to me more. Before, they tended to dismiss it a little more quickly than now. So I have to be more responsible, and I have a choice of seizing whatever power I have as an influence on other people, say, in a story meeting—or *not* taking that power. Of course, you want to exert every bit of influence you can get. It's the most useful thing you can get from success: the ability to influence your subsequent work. Professionally, there is some change.

But personally, I've just lived too long. I'm not twenty-eight or thirty years old. I've been around a long time. In some ways my professional life has been analogous to Nicholson's. He worked for fifteen years before he had any kind of recognition.

The same is true of me. So there's less of a tendency, I think, to be overwhelmed by oneself. I've worked too long, known too many people. It's just not the same as early success.

BRADY: How is it different?

TOWNE: I don't know for sure. But I remember talking with Bob Evans at four o'clock in the morning during some last-minute editing on *Chinatown*. We were both exhausted. I said, "It'll be a miracle if this is any sort of hit."

"Fuck it," he said. "I don't care if it's a hit or not. I just want it to be good." And we worked till about seven that morning and all night for the next three nights.

So it turned out all right. But if it had happened fifteen years ago I might've felt like a magician who pulled a rabbit out of a hat but wasn't quite sure how he did it. You know, magical but very uneasy about it. Well, I don't feel magical anymore, John, but at least I don't feel uneasy.

BRADY: And ultimately, how would you like to be remembered?

TOWNE: For a while . . . and nicely.

APPENDIX:
Credits Where Credits
Are Due

Though a movie doesn't get very far until a writer goes into a room, confronts blank paper, and comes out with a screenplay, the project quickly becomes a team effort involving the talents of other key participants. "Movies are a group endeavor," observed William Goldman earlier in this study. "Basically there are seven people who are essential to a film, and if the film's going to be really any good, all seven have to be at their best." These occasionally magnificent seven, according to Goldman, "in no particular order": director, producer, key players, cinematographer, production designer or art director, film editor and writer. Other possibles, depending on the nature of the film: music composer, special-effects man and makeup.

Here are the screenwriting credits for the six screenwriters featured in this book, along with the names of other key figures on the sets:

PADDY CHAYEFSKY

MARTY   **United Artists (93 mins.), 1955**
Screenplay by Paddy Chayefsky, from his teleplay
DIRECTOR: Delbert Mann

PRODUCER: Harold Hecht
DIRECTOR OF PHOTOGRAPHY: Joseph LaShelle
FILM EDITOR: Alan Crosland, Jr.
PLAYERS: Ernest Borgnine, Betsy Blair

THE BACHELOR PARTY   **United Artists (92 mins.), 1957**
Story and screenplay by Paddy Chayefsky
DIRECTOR: Delbert Mann
PRODUCER: Harold Hecht
DIRECTOR OF PHOTOGRAPHY: Joseph LaShelle
FILM EDITOR: William B. Murphy
ART DIRECTOR: Edward Haworth
PLAYERS: Don Murray, E. G. Marshall, Jack Warden

THE GODDESS   **Columbia (104 mins.), 1958**
Story and screenplay by Paddy Chayefsky
DIRECTOR: John Cromwell
PRODUCER: Milton Perlman
DIRECTOR OF PHOTOGRAPHY: Arthur J. Ornitz
FILM EDITOR: Carl Lerner
ART DIRECTOR: Edward Haworth
PLAYERS: Kim Stanley, Lloyd Bridges

MIDDLE OF THE NIGHT   **Columbia (117 mins.), 1959**
Screenplay by Paddy Chayefsky, from his play
DIRECTOR: Delbert Mann
PRODUCER: George Justin
DIRECTOR OF PHOTOGRAPHY: Joseph Brun
FILM EDITOR: Carl Lerner
ART DIRECTOR: Edward S. Haworth
PLAYERS: Kim Novak, Fredric March

THE AMERICANIZATION OF EMILY
        MGM (115 mins.), 1964
Screenplay by Paddy Chayefsky, based on the novel by William
  Bradford Huie
DIRECTOR: Arthur Hiller
PRODUCER: Martin Ransohoff

DIRECTOR OF PHOTOGRAPHY: Philip Lathrop
FILM EDITOR: Tom McAdoo
ART DIRECTORS: George W. Davis, Hans Peters, Elliot Scott
PLAYERS: James Garner, Julie Andrews, Melvyn Douglas

PAINT YOUR WAGON　　　　Paramount (166 mins.), 1969
Screenplay by Alan Jay Lerner, adaptation by Paddy
　Chayefsky, based on the stage musical with book by Alan Jay
　　Lerner
DIRECTOR: Joshua Logan
PRODUCER: Alan Jay Lerner
DIRECTOR OF PHOTOGRAPHY: William A. Fraker
FILM EDITOR: Robert Jones
PRODUCTION AND COSTUME DESIGNER: John Truscott
SPECIAL EFFECTS: Maurice Ayres, Larry Hampton
MUSIC: Frederick Loewe; additional music by André Previn
LYRICS: Alan Jay Lerner
CHOREOGRAPHY: Jack Baker
PLAYERS: Lee Marvin, Clint Eastwood, Jean Seberg

THE HOSPITAL　　　　United Artists (103 mins.), 1971
Story and screenplay by Paddy Chayefsky
DIRECTOR: Arthur Hiller
PRODUCER: Howard Gottfried
DIRECTOR OF PHOTOGRAPHY: Victor J. Kemper
FILM EDITOR: Eric Albertson
ART DIRECTOR: Gene Rudolf
PLAYERS: George C. Scott, Diana Rigg

NETWORK　　　　United Artists (121 mins.), 1976
Story and screenplay by Paddy Chayefsky
DIRECTOR: Sidney Lumet
PRODUCER: Howard Gottfried
DIRECTOR OF PHOTOGRAPHY: Owen Roizman
FILM EDITOR: Alan Heim
PRODUCTION DESIGNER: Philip Rosenberg
PLAYERS: Faye Dunaway, William Holden, Peter Finch, Robert
　Duvall

ALTERED STATES   Warner Bros. (102 mins.), 1980
Story and screenplay by Sidney Aaron (pseudonym for Paddy
  Chayefsky), based on the novel by Paddy Chayefsky
DIRECTOR: Ken Russell
PRODUCER: Howard Gottfried
DIRECTOR OF PHOTOGRAPHY: Jordan Cronenweith
FILM EDITOR: Eric Jenkins
PRODUCTION DESIGNER: Richard McDonald
SPECIAL EFFECTS: Chuck Gaspar, Bran Ferren, Robbie Blalack,
  Jamie Shourt
PLAYERS: William Hurt, Blair Brown, Bob Balaban, Charles
  Haid

WILLIAM GOLDMAN

MASQUERADE   United Artists (102 mins.), 1965
Screenplay by Michael Relph and William Goldman, based on
  the novel *Castle Minerva* by Victor Canning
DIRECTOR: Basil Dearden
PRODUCER: Michael Relph
DIRECTOR OF PHOTOGRAPHY: Otto Heller
FILM EDITOR: John Gutheridge
ART DIRECTOR: Jack Stevens
PLAYERS: Cliff Robertson, Jack Hawkins, Marisa Mell

HARPER   Warner Bros. (121 mins.), 1966
Screenplay by William Goldman, based on the novel *The
  Moving Target* by Ross Macdonald
DIRECTOR: Jack Smight
PRODUCERS: Jerry Gershwin, Elliott Kastner
DIRECTOR OF PHOTOGRAPHY: Conrad Hall
FILM EDITOR: Stefan Arnsten
ART DIRECTOR: Alfred Sweeney
MUSIC: Johnny Mandel

PLAYERS: Paul Newman, Lauren Bacall, Julie Harris, Arthur
Hill, Janet Leigh, Robert Wagner, Shelley Winters

BUTCH CASSIDY AND THE SUNDANCE KID
Twentieth Century-Fox (112 mins.), 1969
Story and screenplay by William Goldman
DIRECTOR: George Roy Hill
PRODUCER: John Foreman
DIRECTOR OF PHOTOGRAPHY: Conrad Hall
FILM EDITORS: John C. Howard, Richard C. Meyer
ART DIRECTORS: Jack Martin Smith, Philip Jefferies
MUSIC: Burt Bacharach
PLAYERS: Paul Newman, Robert Redford, Katharine Ross

THE HOT ROCK   **Twentieth Century-Fox (101 mins.), 1972**
Screenplay by William Goldman, based on the novel by Donald
E. Westlake
DIRECTOR: Peter Yates
PRODUCERS: Hal Landers, Bobby Roberts
DIRECTOR OF PHOTOGRAPHY: Ed Brown
FILM EDITORS: Frank P. Keller, Fred W. Berger
PRODUCTION DESIGNER: John Robert Lloyd
MUSIC: Quincy Jones
PLAYERS: Robert Redford, George Segal

THE STEPFORD WIVES   **Columbia (115 mins.), 1975**
Screenplay by William Goldman, based on the novel by Ira
Levin
DIRECTOR: Bryan Forbes
PRODUCER: Edgar J. Scherick
DIRECTOR OF PHOTOGRAPHY: Owen Roizman
FILM EDITOR: Timothy Gee
PRODUCTION DESIGNER: Gene Callahan
PLAYERS: Katharine Ross, Paula Prentiss, Peter Masterson

THE GREAT WALDO PEPPER   **Universal (108 mins.), 1975**
Screenplay by William Goldman, based on a story by George
Roy Hill

DIRECTOR: George Roy Hill
PRODUCER: George Roy Hill
DIRECTOR OF PHOTOGRAPHY: Robert Surtees
FILM EDITOR: William Reynolds
ART DIRECTOR: Henry Bumstead
AERIAL SUPERVISOR: Frank Tallman
MUSIC: Henry Mancini
PLAYERS: Robert Redford, Bo Svenson, Susan Sarandon

ALL THE PRESIDENT'S MEN

Warner Bros. (138 mins.), 1976

Screenplay by William Goldman, based on the book by Bob
    Woodward and Carl Bernstein
DIRECTOR: Alan J. Pakula
PRODUCERS: Robert Redford, Alan J. Pakula
DIRECTOR OF PHOTOGRAPHY: Gordon Willis
FILM EDITOR: Robert L. Wolfe
PRODUCTION DESIGNER: George Jenkins
PLAYERS: Robert Redford, Dustin Hoffman

MARATHON MAN
Paramount (120 mins.), 1976

Screenplay by William Goldman, based on his novel
DIRECTOR: John Schlesinger
PRODUCERS: Robert Evans, Sidney Beckerman
DIRECTOR OF PHOTOGRAPHY: Conrad Hall
FILM EDITOR: Jim Clark
PRODUCTION DESIGNER: Richard MacDonald
PLAYERS: Dustin Hoffman, Laurence Olivier, Roy Scheider,
    William Devane

A BRIDGE TOO FAR
United Artists (175 mins.), 1977

Screenplay by William Goldman, based on the book by
    Cornelius Ryan
DIRECTOR: Richard Attenborough
PRODUCERS: Joseph E. Levine, Richard P. Levine
DIRECTOR OF PHOTOGRAPHY: Geoffrey Unsworth
FILM EDITOR: Anthony Gibbs
PRODUCTION DESIGNER: Terry Marsh

PLAYERS: Dirk Bogarde, James Caan, Michael Caine, Sean
Connery, Edward Fox, Elliott Gould, Gene Hackman,
Anthony Hopkins, Hardy Kruger, Laurence Olivier, Ryan
O'Neal, Robert Redford, Maximilian Schell, Liv Ullmann

MAGIC　　　　　　Twentieth Century-Fox **(106 mins.), 1978**
Screenplay by William Goldman, based on his novel
DIRECTOR: Richard Attenborough
PRODUCERS: Joseph E. Levine, Richard P. Levine
DIRECTOR OF PHOTOGRAPHY: Victor J. Kemper
FILM EDITOR: John Bloom
PRODUCTION DESIGNER: Terry Marsh
PLAYERS: Anthony Hopkins, Ann-Margret, Burgess Meredith

ERNEST LEHMAN

EXECUTIVE SUITE　　　　　　MGM **(103 mins.), 1954**
Screenplay by Ernest Lehman, based on the novel by Cameron
Hawley
DIRECTOR: Robert Wise
PRODUCER: John Houseman
DIRECTOR OF PHOTOGRAPHY: George Folsey
FILM EDITOR: Ralph E. Winters
ART DIRECTORS: Cedric Gibbons, Edward Carfagno
PLAYERS: William Holden, June Allyson, Barbara Stanwyck,
Fredric March, Walter Pidgeon, Shelley Winters, Paul
Douglas, Louis Calhern, Dean Jagger, Nina Foch

SABRINA　　　　　　Paramount **(112 mins.), 1954**
Screenplay by Billy Wilder, Ernest Lehman and Samuel Taylor,
based on the play *Sabrina Fair* by Samuel Taylor
DIRECTOR: Billy Wilder

PRODUCER: Billy Wilder
DIRECTOR OF PHOTOGRAPHY: Charles Lang
FILM EDITOR: Arthur Schmidt
ART DIRECTORS: Hal Pereira, Walter Tyler
PLAYERS: Humphrey Bogart, Audrey Hepburn, William Holden

THE KING AND I   Twentieth Century-Fox (133 mins.), 1956
Screenplay by Ernest Lehman, based on the stage musical with
  book by Richard Rodgers and Oscar Hammerstein II, based
  on the book *Anna and the King of Siam* by Margaret Landon
DIRECTOR: Walter Lang
PRODUCER: Charles Brackett
DIRECTOR OF PHOTOGRAPHY: Leon Shamroy
FILM EDITOR: Robert Simpson
ART DIRECTORS: Lyle R. Wheeler, John de Cuir
MUSIC: Richard Rodgers
LYRICS: Oscar Hammerstein II
CHOREOGRAPHY: Jerome Robbins
PLAYERS: Deborah Kerr, Yul Brynner

SOMEBODY UP THERE LIKES ME   MGM (112 mins.), 1956
Screenplay by Ernest Lehman, based on the autobiography by
  Rocky Graziano, with Rowland Barber
DIRECTOR: Robert Wise
PRODUCER: Charles Schnee
DIRECTOR OF PHOTOGRAPHY: Joseph Ruttenberg
FILM EDITOR: Albert Akst
ART DIRECTORS: Cedric Gibbons, Malcolm Brown
PLAYERS: Paul Newman, Pier Angeli

SWEET SMELL OF SUCCESS   United Artists (96 mins.), 1957
Screenplay by Clifford Odets and Ernest Lehman, based on the
  novelette by Ernest Lehman
DIRECTOR: Alexander Mackendrick
PRODUCER: James Hill
DIRECTOR OF PHOTOGRAPHY: James Wong Howe
FILM EDITOR: Alan Crosland

ART DIRECTOR: Edward Carrere
PLAYERS: Burt Lancaster, Tony Curtis

NORTH BY NORTHWEST   **MGM (136 mins.), 1959**
Story and screenplay by Ernest Lehman
DIRECTOR: Alfred Hitchcock
PRODUCER: Alfred Hitchcock
DIRECTOR OF PHOTOGRAPHY: Robert Burks
FILM EDITOR: George Tomasini
PRODUCTION DESIGNER: Robert Boyle
MUSIC: Bernard Herrmann
PLAYERS: Cary Grant, Eva Marie Saint, James Mason

FROM THE TERRACE
                    Twentieth Century-Fox (144 mins.), 1960
Screenplay by Ernest Lehman, based on the novel by John
   O'Hara
DIRECTOR: Mark Robson
PRODUCER: Mark Robson
DIRECTOR OF PHOTOGRAPHY: Leo Tover
FILM EDITOR: Dorothy Spencer
ART DIRECTORS: Lyle R. Wheeler, Maurice Ransford, Howard
   Richman
PLAYERS: Paul Newman, Joanne Woodward, Myrna Loy, Ina
   Balin, Leon Ames

WEST SIDE STORY   **United Artists (153 mins.), 1961**
Screenplay by Ernest Lehman, based on the stage book by
   Arthur Laurents, from a conception by Jerome Robbins
DIRECTORS: Robert Wise, Jerome Robbins
PRODUCER: Robert Wise
DIRECTOR OF PHOTOGRAPHY: Daniel Fapp
FILM EDITOR: Thomas Stanford
PRODUCTION DESIGNER: Boris Leven
MUSIC: Leonard Bernstein
LYRICS: Stephen Sondheim
CHOREOGRAPHY: Jerome Robbins

PLAYERS: Natalie Wood, Richard Beymer, Russ Tamblyn, Rita Moreno, George Chakiris

THE PRIZE   **MGM (135 mins.), 1963**
Screenplay by Ernest Lehman, based on the novel by Irving Wallace
DIRECTOR: Mark Robson
PRODUCER: Pandro S. Berman
DIRECTOR OF PHOTOGRAPHY: William H. Daniels
FILM EDITOR: Adrienne Fazan
ART DIRECTORS: George W. Davis, Urie McCleary
PLAYERS: Paul Newman, Edward G. Robinson, Elke Sommer, Diane Baker

THE SOUND OF MUSIC
                    Twentieth Century-Fox (173 mins.), 1965
Screenplay by Ernest Lehman, based on the stage musical with book by Howard Lindsay and Russel Crouse
DIRECTOR: Robert Wise
PRODUCER: Robert Wise
DIRECTOR OF PHOTOGRAPHY: Ted McCord
FILM EDITOR: William Reynolds
PRODUCTION DESIGNER: Boris Leven
MUSIC: Richard Rodgers
LYRICS: Oscar Hammerstein II
PLAYERS: Julie Andrews, Christopher Plummer

WHO'S AFRAID OF VIRGINIA WOOLF?
                    Warner Bros. (129 mins.), 1966
Screenplay by Ernest Lehman, from the play by Edward Albee
DIRECTOR: Mike Nichols
PRODUCER: Ernest Lehman
DIRECTOR OF PHOTOGRAPHY: Haskell Wexler
FILM EDITOR: Sam O'Steen
PRODUCTION DESIGNER: Richard Sylbert
PLAYERS: Elizabeth Taylor, Richard Burton, George Segal, Sandy Dennis

HELLO, DOLLY!   Twentieth Century-Fox (118 mins.), 1969
Screenplay by Ernest Lehman, based on the stage musical with
  book by Michael Stewart, based on the stage play *The
  Matchmaker* by Thornton Wilder
DIRECTOR: Gene Kelly
PRODUCER: Ernest Lehman
DIRECTOR OF PHOTOGRAPHY: Harry Stradling
FILM EDITOR: William Reynolds
PRODUCTION DESIGNER: John de Cuir
MUSIC AND LYRICS: Jerry Herman
PLAYERS: Barbra Streisand, Walter Matthau, Michael Crawford

PORTNOY'S COMPLAINT   Warner Bros. (101 mins.), 1972
Screenplay by Ernest Lehman, based on the novel by Philip
  Roth
DIRECTOR: Ernest Lehman
PRODUCER: Ernest Lehman
DIRECTOR OF PHOTOGRAPHY: Philip Lathrop
FILM EDITORS: Sam O'Steen, Gordon Scott
PRODUCTION DESIGNER: Robert F. Boyle
PLAYERS: Richard Benjamin, Karen Black, Lee Grant

FAMILY PLOT   Universal (120 mins.), 1976
Screenplay by Ernest Lehman, based on the novel *The Rainbird
  Pattern* by Victor Canning
DIRECTOR: Alfred Hitchcock
PRODUCER: (no credit given)
DIRECTOR OF PHOTOGRAPHY: Leonard J. South
FILM EDITOR: J. Terry Williams
PRODUCTION DESIGNER: Henry Bumstead
PLAYERS: Karen Black, Bruce Dern, Barbara Harris, William
  Devane

BLACK SUNDAY   Paramount (143 mins.), 1977
Screenplay by Ernest Lehman, Kenneth Ross and Ivan Moffat,
  based on the novel by Thomas Harris
DIRECTOR: John Frankenheimer
PRODUCER: Robert Evans

DIRECTOR OF PHOTOGRAPHY: John A. Alonzo
FILM EDITOR: Tom Rolf
ART DIRECTOR: Walter Tyler
PLAYERS: Robert Shaw, Bruce Dern, Marthe Keller

PAUL SCHRADER

THE YAKUZA　　　　　　　　　**Warner Bros. (112 mins.), 1975**
Screenplay by Paul Schrader and Robert Towne, based on a
　story by Leonard Schrader
DIRECTOR: Sydney Pollack
PRODUCER: Sydney Pollack
DIRECTORS OF PHOTOGRAPHY: Okazaki Kozo, Duke Callaghan
FILM EDITORS: Fredric Steinkamp, Thomas Stanford, Don
　Guidice
PRODUCTION DESIGNER: Stephen Grimes
PLAYERS: Robert Mitchum, Takakura Ken, Brian Keith

TAXI DRIVER　　　　　　　　　**Columbia (113 mins.), 1976**
Story and screenplay by Paul Schrader
DIRECTOR: Martin Scorsese
PRODUCERS: Michael Phillips, Julia Phillips
DIRECTOR OF PHOTOGRAPHY: Michael Chapman
FILM EDITORS: Marcia Lucas, Tom Rolf, Melvin Shapiro
ART DIRECTOR: Charles Rosen
MUSIC: Bernard Herrmann
PLAYERS: Robert De Niro, Cybill Shepherd, Peter Boyle

OBSESSION　　　　　　　　　**Columbia (98 mins.), 1976**
Screenplay by Paul Schrader, based on a story by Brian De
　Palma and Paul Schrader
DIRECTOR: Brian De Palma
PRODUCERS: George Litto, Harry N. Blum

DIRECTOR OF PHOTOGRAPHY: Vilmos Zsigmond
FILM EDITOR: Paul Hirsch
ART DIRECTOR: Jack Senter
MUSIC: Bernard Herrmann
PLAYERS: Cliff Robertson, Geneviève Bujold

ROLLING THUNDER   **American International (99 mins.), 1977**
Screenplay by Paul Schrader and Heywood Gould
DIRECTOR: John Flynn
PRODUCER: Norman T. Herman
DIRECTOR OF PHOTOGRAPHY: Jordon Croneweth
FILM EDITOR: Frank P. Keller
ART DIRECTOR: Steve Berger
PLAYERS: William Devane, Tommy Lee Jones, Linda Haynes,
  Lisa Richards

BLUE COLLAR   **Universal (114 mins.), 1978**
Screenplay by Paul Schrader and Leonard Schrader, suggested
  by source material by Sydney A. Glass
DIRECTOR: Paul Schrader
PRODUCER: Don Guest
DIRECTOR OF PHOTOGRAPHY: Bobby Byrne
FILM EDITOR: Tom Rolf
PRODUCTION DESIGNER: Lawrence G. Paull
PLAYERS: Richard Pryor, Harvey Keitel, Yaphet Kotto

HARDCORE   **Columbia (105 mins.), 1979**
Story and screenplay by Paul Schrader
DIRECTOR: Paul Schrader
PRODUCER: Buzz Feitshans
DIRECTOR OF PHOTOGRAPHY: Michael Chapman
FILM EDITOR: Tom Rolf
PRODUCTION DESIGNER: Paul Sylbert
PLAYERS: George C. Scott, Peter Boyle, Season Hubley

OLD BOYFRIENDS   **Avco Embassy (103 mins.), 1979**
Screenplay by Paul Schrader and Leonard Schrader
DIRECTOR: Joan Tewkesbury

PRODUCERS: Edward R. Pressman, Michele Rappaport
DIRECTOR OF PHOTOGRAPHY: William A. Fraker
FILM EDITOR: Bill Reynolds
ART DIRECTOR: Peter Jamison
PLAYERS: Talia Shire, Richard Jordan, John Belushi, Keith
    Carradine

AMERICAN GIGOLO   **Paramount (117 mins.), 1980**
Story and screenplay by Paul Schrader
DIRECTOR: Paul Schrader
PRODUCER: Jerry Bruckheimer
DIRECTOR OF PHOTOGRAPHY: John Bailey
FILM EDITOR: Richard Halsey
VISUAL CONSULTANT: Fernando Scarfiotti
ART DIRECTOR: Ed Richardson
MUSIC: Giorgio Moroder
PLAYERS: Richard Gere, Lauren Hutton

RAGING BULL   **United Artists (130 mins.), 1980**
Screenplay by Paul Schrader and Mardik Martin, based on the
    autobiography by Jake La Motta, with Joseph Carter and
    Peter Savage
DIRECTOR: Martin Scorsese
PRODUCERS: Irwin Winkler, Robert Chartoff
DIRECTOR OF PHOTOGRAPHY: Michael Chapman
FILM EDITOR: Thelma Schoonmaker
PRODUCTION DESIGNER: Gene Rudolf
PLAYERS: Robert De Niro, Cathy Moriarty, Joe Pesci

NEIL SIMON

AFTER THE FOX   **United Artists (102 mins.), 1966**
Screenplay by Neil Simon
DIRECTOR: Vittorio De Sica

PRODUCER: John Bryan
DIRECTOR OF PHOTOGRAPHY: Leonida Barboni
FILM EDITOR: Russell Lloyd
MUSIC: Burt Bacharach
PLAYERS: Peter Sellers, Britt Ekland, Victor Mature

BAREFOOT IN THE PARK   **Paramount (104 mins.), 1967**
Screenplay by Neil Simon, from his play
DIRECTOR: Gene Saks
PRODUCER: Hal B. Wallis
DIRECTOR OF PHOTOGRAPHY: Joseph LaShelle
FILM EDITOR: William A. Lyon
MUSIC: Neal Hefti
PLAYERS: Robert Redford, Jane Fonda, Charles Boyer, Mildred
  Natwick

THE ODD COUPLE   **Paramount (105 mins.), 1968**
Screenplay by Neil Simon, from his play
DIRECTOR: Gene Saks
PRODUCER: Howard W. Koch
DIRECTOR OF PHOTOGRAPHY: Robert B. Hauser
FILM EDITOR: Frank Bracht
ART DIRECTORS: Hal Pereira, Walter Tyler
MUSIC: Neal Hefti
PLAYERS: Jack Lemmon, Walter Matthau

THE OUT-OF-TOWNERS   **Paramount (97 mins.), 1970**
Story and screenplay by Neil Simon
DIRECTOR: Arthur Hiller
PRODUCER: Paul Nathan
DIRECTOR OF PHOTOGRAPHY: Andre Laszlo
FILM EDITOR: Fred Chulack
ART DIRECTOR: Charles Bailey
PLAYERS: Jack Lemmon, Sandy Dennis

PLAZA SUITE   **Paramount (114 mins.), 1971**
Screenplay by Neil Simon, from his play
DIRECTOR: Arthur Hiller

PRODUCER: Howard W. Koch
DIRECTOR OF PHOTOGRAPHY: Jack Marta
FILM EDITOR: Frank Bracht
PRODUCTION DESIGNER: Arthur Lonergan
PLAYERS: Walter Matthau, Maureen Stapleton, Barbara Harris, Lee Grant

LAST OF THE RED HOT LOVERS
Paramount (98 mins.), 1972

Screenplay by Neil Simon, from his play
DIRECTOR: Gene Saks
PRODUCER: Howard W. Koch
DIRECTOR OF PHOTOGRAPHY: Victor J. Kemper
FILM EDITOR: Maury Winetrobe
ART DIRECTOR: Ben Edwards
PLAYERS: Alan Arkin, Sally Kellerman, Paula Prentiss, Renee Taylor

THE HEARTBREAK KID
Twentieth Century-Fox (104 mins.), 1972

Screenplay by Neil Simon, based on the story "A Change of Pace" by Bruce Jay Friedman
DIRECTOR: Elaine May
PRODUCER: Edgar J. Scherick
DIRECTOR OF PHOTOGRAPHY: Owen Roizman
FILM EDITOR: John Carter
PLAYERS: Charles Grodin, Cybill Shepherd, Jeannie Berlin, Eddie Albert, Audra Lindley

THE PRISONER OF SECOND AVENUE
Warner Bros. (98 mins.), 1975

Screenplay by Neil Simon, from his play
DIRECTOR: Melvin Frank
PRODUCER: Melvin Frank
DIRECTOR OF PHOTOGRAPHY: Philip Lathrop
FILM EDITOR: Bob Wyman
ART DIRECTOR: Preston Ames
MUSIC: Marvin Hamlisch
PLAYERS: Jack Lemmon, Anne Bancroft

THE SUNSHINE BOYS   MGM (111 mins.), 1975
Screenplay by Neil Simon, from his play
DIRECTOR: Herbert Ross
PRODUCER: Ray Stark
DIRECTOR OF PHOTOGRAPHY: David M. Walsh
FILM EDITOR: John F. Burnett
PRODUCTION DESIGNER: Albert Brenner
PLAYERS: Walter Matthau, George Burns, Richard Benjamin

MURDER BY DEATH   Columbia (94 mins.), 1976
Story and screenplay by Neil Simon
DIRECTOR: Robert Moore
PRODUCER: Ray Stark
DIRECTOR OF PHOTOGRAPHY: David M. Walsh
FILM EDITORS: Margaret Booth, John F. Burnett
PRODUCTION DESIGNER: Stephen Grimes
PLAYERS: Eileen Brennan, Truman Capote, James Coco, Peter
    Falk, Alec Guinness, Elsa Lanchester, David Niven, Peter
    Sellers, Maggie Smith, Nancy Walker

THE GOODBYE GIRL   Warner Bros. (110 mins.), 1977
Story and screenplay by Neil Simon
DIRECTOR: Herbert Ross
PRODUCER: Ray Stark
DIRECTOR OF PHOTOGRAPHY: David M. Walsh
FILM EDITORS: Margaret Booth, John F. Burnett
PRODUCTION DESIGNER: Albert Brenner
PLAYERS: Richard Dreyfuss, Marsha Mason, Quinn Cummings

THE CHEAP DETECTIVE   Columbia (92 mins.), 1978
Story and screenplay by Neil Simon
DIRECTOR: Robert Moore
PRODUCER: Ray Stark
DIRECTOR OF PHOTOGRAPHY: John A. Alonzo
FILM EDITORS: Sidney Levin, Michael A. Stevenson
PRODUCTION DESIGNER: Robert Luthardt
PLAYERS: Peter Falk, Ann-Margret, Eileen Brennan, Sid Caesar

CALIFORNIA SUITE   Columbia (103 mins.), 1978
Screenplay by Neil Simon, from his play
DIRECTOR: Herbert Ross
PRODUCER: Ray Stark
DIRECTOR OF PHOTOGRAPHY: David M. Walsh
FILM EDITOR: Michael A. Stevenson
PRODUCTION DESIGNER: Albert Brenner
PLAYERS: Alan Alda, Michael Caine, Bill Cosby, Jane Fonda,
  Walter Matthau, Elaine May, Richard Pryor, Maggie Smith

CHAPTER TWO   Columbia (124 mins.), 1979
Screenplay by Neil Simon, from his play
DIRECTOR: Robert Moore
PRODUCER: Ray Stark
DIRECTOR OF PHOTOGRAPHY: David M. Walsh
FILM EDITOR: Michael A. Stevenson
PRODUCTION DESIGNER: Gene Callahan
PLAYERS: James Caan, Marsha Mason

SEEMS LIKE OLD TIMES   Columbia (102 mins.), 1980
Story and screenplay by Neil Simon
DIRECTOR: Jay Sandrich
PRODUCER: Ray Stark
DIRECTOR OF PHOTOGRAPHY: David M. Walsh
FILM EDITOR: Michael A. Stevenson
PRODUCTION DESIGNER: Gene Callahan
MUSIC: Marvin Hamlisch
PLAYERS: Goldie Hawn, Chevy Chase, Charles Grodin

ROBERT TOWNE

THE LAST WOMAN ON EARTH   Filmgroup (71 mins.), 1960
Screenplay by Robert Towne
DIRECTOR: Roger Corman

PRODUCER: Roger Corman
DIRECTOR OF PHOTOGRAPHY: Jack Marquette
FILM EDITOR: Anthony Carras
PLAYERS: Antony Carbone, Betsy Jones-Moreland, Edward
Wain

THE TOMB OF LIGEIA American International (80 mins.), 1964
Screenplay by Robert Towne, based on a story by Edgar Allan
Poe
DIRECTOR: Roger Corman
PRODUCER: Roger Corman
DIRECTOR OF PHOTOGRAPHY: Arthur Grant
FILM EDITOR: Alfred Cox
ART DIRECTOR: Colin Southcott
PLAYERS: Vincent Price, Elizabeth Shepherd

VILLA RIDES   **Paramount (125 mins.), 1968**
Screenplay by Robert Towne and Sam Peckinpah, based on the
book *Pancho Villa* by William Douglas Lansford
DIRECTOR: Buzz Kulik
PRODUCER: Ted Richmond
DIRECTOR OF PHOTOGRAPHY: Jack Hildyard
FILM EDITOR: David Bretherton
PRODUCTION DESIGNER: Ted Haworth
PLAYERS: Yul Brynner, Robert Mitchum, Charles Bronson

THE LAST DETAIL   **Columbia (105 mins.), 1973**
Screenplay by Robert Towne, based on the novel by Darryl
Ponicsan
DIRECTOR: Hal Ashby
PRODUCER: Gerald Ayres
DIRECTOR OF PHOTOGRAPHY: Michael Chapman
FILM EDITOR: Robert C. Jones
PRODUCTION DESIGNER: Michael Haller
MUSIC: Johnny Mandel
PLAYERS: Jack Nicholson, Otis Young, Randy Quaid

CHINATOWN   **Paramount (131 mins.), 1974**
Story and screenplay by Robert Towne

DIRECTOR: Roman Polanski
PRODUCER: Robert Evans
DIRECTOR OF PHOTOGRAPHY: John A. Alonzo
FILM EDITOR: Sam O'Steen
PRODUCTION DESIGNER: Richard Sylbert
MUSIC: Jerry Goldsmith
PLAYERS: Jack Nicholson, Faye Dunaway, John Huston

THE YAKUZA   **Warner Bros. (112 mins.), 1975**
Screenplay by Paul Schrader and Robert Towne, based on a
   story by Leonard Schrader
DIRECTOR: Sydney Pollack
PRODUCER: Sydney Pollack
DIRECTORS OF PHOTOGRAPHY: Okazaki Kozo, Duke Callaghan
FILM EDITORS: Fredric Steinkamp, Thomas Stanford, Don
   Guidice
PRODUCTION DESIGNER: Stephen Grimes
PLAYERS: Robert Mitchum, Takakura Ken, Brian Keith

SHAMPOO   **Columbia (112 mins.), 1975**
Screenplay by Robert Towne and Warren Beatty
DIRECTOR: Hal Ashby
PRODUCER: Warren Beatty
DIRECTOR OF PHOTOGRAPHY: Laszlo Kovacs
FILM EDITOR: Robert Jones
PRODUCTION DESIGNER: Richard Sylbert
MUSIC: Paul Simon
PLAYERS: Warren Beatty, Julie Christie, Goldie Hawn, Lee
   Grant, Jack Warden

INDEX

ABOUT THE AUTHOR

John Brady brings unique qualifications to this study of screenwriters using the interview technique. He is author of *The Craft of Interviewing,* and many of his interviews with the world's leading writers have appeared in *Writer's Digest,* the magazine that Brady has edited since 1975. He has also been associate editor for the 13-30 Corporation (Knoxville) and assistant to the editorial director at Warner Bros. Records (Hollywood), and he has written for *New York* magazine, *New Times, Playboy,* the Sunday *New York Times* and numerous other publications. Brady lives in Cincinnati with his wife, Lilia, and their daughter, Linde.